by
w.

D1438732

910239

THE
DOUKHOBORS

THE

DOUKHOBORS

George Woodcock and Ivan Avakumovic

FABER AND FABER
24 Russell Square
London

First published in England in 1968
by Faber and Faber Limited
24 Russell Square London WC1
Printed in Great Britain by
Hazell Watson & Viney Ltd
Aylesbury, Bucks
All rights reserved

SBN 571 08927 5

277441

CONTENTS

ILLUSTRATIONS

1 The Doukhobors come to Canada, 1898. *The Public Archives of Canada.*

2 Doukhobor women ploughing, near Swan River, Saskatchewan, 1899. *Provincial Archives of Alberta.*

3 A Doukhobor village in the Thunder Hill Colony, 1902. *Provincial Archives of Manitoba.*

4 Doukhobors reaping their first harvest, Thunder Hill Colony, 1899. *Public Archives of Canada.*

5 A millenarian march, 1902. *Public Archives of Canada.*

6 The first Sons of Freedom march nude, 1903. *Provincial Archives of Alberta.*

7 Peter the Lordly Verigin, first leader of the Doukhobors in Canada. *Provincial Archives of British Columbia.*

8 Peter the Purger (Chistiakov) Verigin, second leader of the Doukhobors in Canada. *United Press International.*

9 Landseekers walking to lay claim to vacated Doukhobor homesteads, 1907. *Public Archives of Canada.*

10 Peter Chistiakov Verigin on his arrival at Brilliant from Russia in 1927. *Wide World.*

11 The meeting-house at Verigin, Saskatchewan, built in 1917. *Ingeborg Woodcock.*

12 A typical Doukhobor meeting in British Columbia during the 1950s. *Doukhobor Research Committee.*

PREFACE

By a series of historical accidents, the tiny dissenting sect of the Doukhobors was drawn out of the obscurity in which most Russian peasants lived during the nineteenth century and into the glaring light of twentieth-century North American publicity. If a dynamic young leader, Peter Vasil'evich Verigin, had not galvanized them into open defiance of the tsarist state in the 1890s, and if Tolstoy had not been there to denounce their persecution with all the weight of his world-wide reputation, they might well have been crushed out of existence as other sectarian groups had been before them. If the Russian émigré geographer and anarchist Peter Kropotkin had not travelled over the Canadian prairies in 1897, the idea of a migration to the Northwest Territories might never have occurred to their friends in western Europe. If the Doukhobors had not come to Canada, they might never have entered the kind of situation in which their bizarre behaviour—as it appeared to most North Americans—would have been opposed and stimulated for decades by conservative prejudices on the part of large sections of the population and by a government policy that was once described aptly by Elmore Philpott as fluctuating 'between long periods of ignorant indifference and short official bursts of frenzied hostility'.[1] However exotic the more violent actions of the Sons of Freedom, the zealot wing of the Doukhobors, may appear to us, it is sobering to reflect that none of these extremer types of behaviour—nudism, arson, dynamiting—was part of the Doukhobor pattern of life before the sect reached Canada. Fire-raisers and nude paraders have never represented more than a small minority of an otherwise peaceful (indeed pacifist) community, anxious only to live according to its own beliefs. Today the arsonists and the nudists may well be a minority moving towards extinction, but they are as peculiarly Canadian, as demonstrably the products of stresses generated in a society emerging from the pioneer stage, as any of their more conformist neighbours in the prairies of Saskatchewan and the mountain valleys of British Columbia.

But the story of the Doukhobors has its general as well as its national significance. It is arguable that if they had migrated anywhere else than Canada they would have encountered very similar difficulties; in vital respects their history in Canada resembles that of the early Mormons, another theocratic sect, in the United States. Since well before the Reformation, sects like the Doukhobors and the Mormons have posed the inevitable conflict of loyalties between a monolithic church or state and a minority group that seeks not merely to follow its own way of life but also to challenge external authority in the name of its own inspired system of internal customs. It has been suggested that the Doukhobors fell into conflict with Canadian society because they insisted on following a pattern of behaviour different from that approved by the modern state, a pattern based on local rather than centralized loyalties, a pattern that rejects industrialism in the name of a mystique of the soil, a pattern that has no room for any conformity but its own. Certainly, in the peculiar form it has taken during the past two generations, the Doukhobor problem reflects the history of a land where the spacious makeshift life of the pioneers, which had room for quite large pockets of eccentricity, began to disappear as soon as land grew scarce and authority moved in. The Doukhobors, as much as Louis Riel's Métis, can be seen as representatives of simple cultures caught in the trap of a closing frontier, with nowhere farther to go in their efforts to escape from the modern state.

But the situation cannot be seen entirely in simple terms of ancient versus modern, or even of the free individual versus the regimented state. The medieval church was even more ferocious than the modern state in its pursuit of theocratic heretics whose doctrines resembled those of the Doukhobors; Canada, after all, has not yet imitated the Albigensian crusade. And the Doukhobors first came into conflict with authority, not in any modern state, either democratic or totalitarian, but in autocratic, agrarian, Holy Russia, where the shadows of the Middle Ages hung more heavily than anywhere else in nineteenth-century Europe.

The history of the Doukhobors therefore alerts us to the existence of an element in common between past autocracies and modern democracies, which makes them, in some cases at least, share the same enemies. In themselves, the Doukhobors have never represented a real threat to either the Russian or the Canadian governments; the majority of Russian peasants, like the majority of Canadians, were actually hostile to the Doukhobors and unlikely to be influenced by their actions, and in both countries the members of the sect have, like radical sects elsewhere, remained a tiny minority of the population. Yet Canada and Russia, despite such widely divergent systems of government, both felt impelled to bend this small, resistant minority into the pattern of conformity. The tsarist government appeared willing, as a last resort, to destroy the Doukhobors rather than condone their dissent, and, when world publicity made that impossible, it was glad to expel them. Even the Canadian authorities have allowed themselves to be provoked into such rigorous measures as seizing the children of Doukhobor zealots in an attempt to re-educate them into conventional good citizens. This fact brings us to those profound questions about our own society that the history of such a group as the Doukhobors can hardly fail to imply. How well has a democracy succeeded when it has failed to reconcile its most extreme dissenters? How far has the majority—or those who claim to act on its behalf—the right to impose its principles and its way of life on a small and at first harmless minority? (Here we must remind ourselves that the destructiveness of the Sons of Freedom arose during a long battle with the Canadian authorities in which the errors were not all on one side.) Is uniformity in education, or the need for vital statistics, or such a formal point as demanding an oath of allegiance in exchange for a homestead, sufficient justification for penal action, which inevitably creates bitter and lasting resentment?

The fact that the story of the Doukhobors has such wider resonances should not blind us to its intrinsic significance. The Doukhobors are the most interesting of Canada's smaller minorities, and not merely because, by resisting assimilation so obstinately, they have acquired the special romantic appeal that belongs to lost causes and to forlorn hopes. They are also living examples of a type of messianic and millenarian Christianity that in western Europe was largely moribund by the end of the seventeenth century and that elsewhere has long lost its revolutionary character. And, though in the 1960s their attachment to the land is a matter of sentiment rather than of practice, they were until recently the last of our agrarian rebels. Finally—and here the Doukhobors float in one of the important streams of the North American tradition—they have a long past of practical religious communism.

The tradition of self-contained Utopian communities, which was dying in the eastern United States by the 1850s, followed the frontier into the West during the latter part of the nineteenth century and enjoyed a last flowering in western Canada during the 1890s and the early part of the twentieth century. Some of the Canadian communities, like the Finnish Utopia of Sointula on Malcolm Island off the coast of British Columbia, were founded by groups following the traditions of secular socialism, but the most interesting—and the most successful—were undoubtedly those that attempted to create a Christian communism. Among them the Christian Community of Universal Brotherhood, which the Doukhobors established in the prairies and later moved to British Columbia, was not only one of the largest ventures of its kind ever undertaken in North America, in terms both of membership and of achievements, but was also, for almost twenty years, astonishingly successful. The story of its achievements and its eventual failure is one of the most fascinating aspects of the Doukhobor record.

The failure came in part from the unrelenting hostility of Canadians devoted to free enterprise (in and out of the government) to the Doukhobor experiment in Christian communal living, but it was also precipitated by disintegrative influences within the ranks of the Doukhobors. This interplay of external pressures and internal weaknesses appears in other aspects of Doukhobor history. While it is true that the Doukhobor situation has exposed Canadian society in the undignified stance of a giant caught bullying an admittedly rather provocative pygmy, the Doukhobors' own struggle against assimilation—whether carried on desperately or in resignation—illuminates some of the difficulties that a small minority defending its position with mainly pacifist tactics is bound to encounter.

These tactics have aroused the sympathies of some intellectuals and have at times created doubts even in the minds of government administrators who were near to the situation, but there seems no reason to assume that nude parades and house burnings, the characteristic protest activities of the Sons of Freedom minority among the Doukhobors, have won from the general and uninformed public anything better than increased antagonism. On the other hand, it may also be argued that, by maintaining cohesion among the hard core of Doukhobors, such tactics have helped to preserve them as a distinctive group and have delayed assimilation as long as the powerful trends towards social uniformity (which are deeper and less visible than those towards political uniformity) will allow. Such considerations clearly have a profound bearing on the question of the effectiveness of civil disobedience, particularly if it is carried out in a provocative manner by a small minority whose way of life marks them off clearly from a hostile or indifferent majority.

One of the characteristics of the Doukhobors as a community that has aroused particular hostility is an evasiveness regarding their own affairs that is often interpreted as evidence of dishonesty. In fact, this characteristic is a heritage of the deviousness that life under the tsars made a necessary self-protective device among Russian peasants, whether they were Orthodox or sectarian.

Who is it that the Russian deceives . . . ? [wrote Alexander Herzen in 1851.] *Who, if not the landowner, the Government official, the steward, the police officer, in fact the sworn foes of the peasant, whom he looks upon as heathens, as traitors, as half-Germans? Deprived of every possible means of defence, the peasant resorts to cunning in dealing with his torturers, he deceives them, and he is perfectly right in doing so. . . . It could not be otherwise; if he spoke the truth he would by so doing be acknowledging their authority over him.*[2]

To Doukhobors the violent persecutions they underwent under the tsars were a traumatic experience remembered from generation to generation, and this memory—reinforced by their many unfortunate encounters with officials and neighbours in Canada—has tended to freeze their attitude towards those in authority, or even towards non-Doukhobors of any kind, in the pattern of distrust and deception appropriate to the Russian environment of the 1890s and doubtless also of the 1960s.

For the historian, this attitude presents difficulties that are compounded by the fact that the Doukhobors not only sprang from a predominantly illiterate peasant society, but also developed a principled objection—rather like that of the Brahmins—to the transmission of doctrine or even history by written means. The letter, they said, kills; and the principal means by which traditions and beliefs are even now preserved among them is through orally transmitted hymns and psalms, which often convey their messages with such obliquity that even Doukhobors disagree on their interpretation. Before the sect begins to figure in non-Doukhobor accounts and to draw the attention of Russian historians in the early nineteenth century, its record is nebulous; and even after 1800 many important events in Doukhobor history have come down to us only through the oral tradition. Because of their attitude towards written literature and their tardy acceptance of education, the Doukhobors themselves have produced very few scholars. Three histories of the sect written by Doukhobors exist; two have been published, but only in Russian, and one, in English, has only been produced in a mimeographed, privately circulated form.[3] All of them contain valuable information that it might have been hard for a non-Doukhobor to collect, but all of them are amateurish in presentation and apologetic in intent, designed to portray the Doukhobor movement as favourably as the facts permit.

For this approach, it can be said that it at least helps to offset the tendency of the printed literature in English to dwell on the dramatic, and even melodramatic, elements in Doukhobor history and to neglect other necessary aspects of a balanced view. Because their actions have been sensational, the Sons of Freedom, who constitute possibly an eighth of the people of Doukhobor origin now living in Canada, have in recent years received the lion's share of attention; the more numerous 'Orthodox' or Community Doukhobors, who have tried to remain peacefully self-contained, have received correspondingly less publicity, and the Independents, the most assimilated of the three Doukhobor groups, have been almost ignored by English Canadian writers. It would be unfair to class all such writers as hostile to the sect. Aylmer Maude, though disillusioned when he came to write *A Peculiar People* (1904), went out of his way to be fair and objective, and the same applies to J. F. C. Wright, whose *Slava Bohu* was a balanced even if somewhat excessively popularized presentation of Doukhobor history. But since *Slava Bohu* appeared in 1940, no book published in English has viewed dispassionately the whole scope of Doukhobor history; we have had to be content with the limited studies of sociologists, the propaganda utterances of politicians, and the reportages of journalists. No ethnic group outside the two founding races of Canada has attracted so much attention as the Doukhobors, but the attention has been so directed as to produce an effect of historical chiaroscuro, highlights set off by deep obscurities. We have tried, as far as the records allow us, to make the light even.

ACKNOW-
LEDGEMENTS

Our thanks are due to many people: to the numerous Doukhobors of various persuasions who over almost twenty years have provided information and often hospitality, and especially to Messrs William Koochin, Peter P. Legebokoff (editor of *Iskra*), Peter N. Maloff, Joseph E. Podovinikoff, Florence Podovinikoff, Eli A. Popoff, V. A. Sukhorev, Koozma J. Tarasoff, Gabriel W. Vereshchagin, John J. Verigin (Honorary Chairman of the Union of Spiritual Communities of Christ), and the late Michael (the Archangel) Verigin; to Magistrate William Evans, Mr Hugh Herbison, Professor Stuart Jamieson, Mr Stanley Orris (editor of the *Grand Forks Gazette*), Mr Sidney Simons, Professor A. W. Wainman, and others too numerous to mention who have been and are working for a solution to the Doukhobor problem and who have placed their knowledge at our disposal; to Professors M. S. Donnelly, J. A. Laponce, R. S. Milne, and W. J. Stankiewicz for assistance and encouragement; to Professor Harry B. Hawthorn, the Public Archives of Canada, the Provincial Archives of Alberta, British Columbia and Manitoba, the University of Saskatchewan Library, and Mrs Ingeborg Woodcock for permission to print photographs from their collections; to Mrs Catherine Easto for secretarial assistance and for preparing the typescript of the book; and not least to our wives for their help and their patience.

We wish also to acknowledge our debt to the institutions and libraries of whose facilities at various times we have made use, including the British Museum, the London Library, the Public Record Office, and the Library of the Society of Friends in London; the Lenin Library and the Tolstoy Museum in Moscow; the Library of the Institut d'Études Slaves in Paris; the Hoover Library at Stanford University; the University of British Columbia Library; the Library of the Spiritual Communities of Christ at Grand Forks, B.C.; and the Provincial Archives in Victoria.

We are deeply grateful to the Canada Council and the Committee on Research of the University of British Columbia for making our visits to these archives and libraries possible, and also to the Canadian Broadcasting Corporation for facilitating field research between 1962 and 1966 in the preparation of a series of television and radio documentary programs on the Doukhobors; we would also like to thank the producers of these programs, Messrs John Edwards, Harold Gray, and Alex Pratt.

1 THE PEOPLE OF GOD

The Doukhobors are a pacifist sect of Russian Christians. They have no church organization and hence no form of internal census, while centuries of strained relations with Russian and Canadian governments have bred into them a fear of giving information about themselves that makes it difficult to estimate their numbers more than roughly. In Canada a cautious guess would place the number of people of Doukhobor descent at approximately twenty thousand, though many of these have already lost such distinguishing characteristics as religious practices, Russian language, etc., and have merged into the larger Canadian society. In Russia the nature of the Communist régime adds to the difficulty of making even a roughly accurate estimate, but, remembering the great purges from which the Doukhobors, like all radical sects, suffered during the Stalinist era, it is unlikely that they exceed in number their fellow believers in Canada; in fact, a Canadian leader of the sect visiting Russia in 1966 was told that there were eleven thousand declared Doukhobors in the country. In addition, there are minute groups of Doukhobors in the United States. But in all, this sect, which circumstances have brought so luridly into the light of history, must at present number considerably less than fifty thousand adherents throughout the world. It is unlikely that at any time it was more numerous.

Today, in Russia, the Doukhobors still retain a dwindling communal identity in areas of the Don Valley, of the Caucasus, and of Siberia. In Canada many of them cultivate prairie farms in the wheatlands of Saskatchewan and Alberta; these are mostly the Independent Doukhobors, who renounced Community organization half a century ago and do not submit to the hereditary leadership vested in the Verigin family, which is accepted unquestioningly by the majority of the Orthodox Doukhobors—the members of the Union of Spiritual Communities of Christ—who live mainly in the interior of British Columbia, inhabiting the neglected orchard lands in the west Kootenays and in the Kettle Valley around Grand Forks that a generation ago their fathers cultivated as a self-sufficient community with thousands of members and millions of dollars' worth of assets. These Orthodox Doukhobors, though now they are rarely farmers in a true sense, still cling to the land, growing their own garden produce and carrying on occupations—such as logging, sawmill operating, carpentry, and fruit picking—that enable them to avoid the cities of coastal British Columbia, where until recently few Doukhobors were to be found.

The Ishmaels of the sect are the radical Sons of Freedom, who have been responsible for most of the extreme demonstrations of rebellion against the Canadian government and against the modern North American way of life. Their following has fluctuated since they came into existence in the prairies more than sixty years ago; in recent years they have numbered at most 2,500, scattered in various parts of the Kootenays, where they inhabit settlements of wooden shacks, easily burnt down and reconstructed according to the waves of fanatical enthusiasm to which they are subject. Their principal village is Krestova, situated on a barren plateau overlooking the Slocan Valley, where they live on land that once belonged to the Doukhobor community; there is a second important settlement at Gilpin in the Kettle Valley. For a brief period in the 1940s and 1950s a small schismatic group founded a millenarian community on Vancouver Island, and in 1962 a protest march through the mountains brought several hundred Sons of Freedom into Greater Vancouver and the Fraser Valley. But these westward thrusts have been exceptional. For the last fifty years the Sons of Freedom, as well as the Orthodox Doukhobors, have mostly remained and carried out their activities in the isolating shelter of the Selkirk mountains, within a triangle roughly marked by the cities of Nelson, Grand Forks, and Trail.

This geographical isolation reflects a consistent attempt by Doukhobors, as individuals and as a community, to withdraw from the religious, moral, economic, and political systems both of tsarist and communist Russia and of capitalist-democratic Canada. It is an attempt that follows quite consistently from their religious beliefs and from what we know of their early history.

The Doukhobors emerged into history around the middle of the eighteenth century. They called themselves 'People of God' or merely 'Christians', implying that adherents of other sects or churches were only false Christians. The name of 'Doukhobor', like other names treasured afterwards, was first used in anger and derision by one of their opponents, Archbishop Amvrosii Serebrennikov of Ekaterinoslav. It means 'Spirit Wrestlers', and it was intended by the archbishop, when he invented it in 1785, to suggest that they were fighting *against* the Holy Ghost; in adopting it, the Doukhobors subtly changed its connotation, claiming that they fought *with* the spirit of God, which they believed to dwell within them.

Such a belief implied, as it implies today, the complete rejection of the idea of a mediatory priesthood, and, in this and other respects, the Doukhobors stand on the extreme left of the theological spectrum. From the traditional churches they differ in having no liturgy and no ikons, no fasts and no festivals, no churches and no priests. They acknowledge no sacraments, and in denying the importance of baptism they are more radical than the Anabaptists. From the Quakers they differ in rejecting the doctrine of redemption. They believe heaven and hell to be states of the mind, and for this reason they bury their dead without ceremonial; they regard marriages as free unions between individuals, not contracts bound by laws of church and state. Finally, they are marked off among modern Christians from all but a few similarly exclusive millenarian sects by their rejection of the Bible as the ultimate source of inspiration. The only visible symbols of their faith are the loaf of bread, the cellar of salt, and the jug of water that stand on the table in the middle of their meeting-houses, symbolizing the basic elements of existence.

It is easier to say what the Doukhobors have abandoned in traditional Christianity than to create a consistent picture of what they actually believe, particularly as there appear to have been changes in belief since the sect came into existence. But there is a central, constant element in Doukhobor Christianity from which the peculiar structure and behaviour pattern of the sect naturally follow. It is the belief in the immanence of God, in the presence within each man of the Christ spirit, which not merely renders priesthood unnecessary, since each man is his own priest in direct contact with the divine, but also makes the Bible obsolete, since every man can be guided, if only he will listen to it, by the voice within.

The only real ceremonial act among Doukhobors is the deep bow by which on entering the meeting-hall each man recognizes the divine spark within his neighbours.

From this central belief that the word waits within every man until he cares to listen spring quite logically the attitudes that have brought Doukhobors into conflict with the larger societies from which, despite many efforts, they have been unable to escape. Since the direction of their behaviour must come from within, they naturally deny the right of the state or other external authority to dictate their actions. And, since all men are vessels for the divine essence, they regard it as sinful to kill other men, even in war; hence springs the pacifism that is the most durable and widespread of Doukhobor attitudes, shared even today by all who accept the name, from the virtually assimilated Independents of the rich prairie farmlands to the austere zealots of the Sons of Freedom shack villages.

At first sight there is much that seems eminently reasonable in the religious attitudes of the Doukhobors. In spite of their rejection of the Bible, they appear to be attempting to follow out literally—like other primitive Christians—the ethical teachings of the New Testament and the way of life traditionally ascribed to the first generations of early Christians. This reasonable side of Doukhoborism led Tolstoy into the error of believing that he had discovered a group of peasants who, without the advantages of book learning, had evolved a system of thought very similar to his own, and it also deceived both tsarist encyclopaedists and western theologians, like Aurelio Palmieri, into classifying the Doukhobors as one of 'the rationalistic sects'.[1]

In fact, though, what impresses anyone who has closer contact with the Doukhobors—as it eventually impressed certain of Tolstoy's disciples —is the marked dichotomy in their reasoning. A half-literate Doukhobor, educated in the endless religio-political discussions that are a feature of the idle winter months of a people until recently attracted towards seasonal employments, will often present an informed and well-argued criticism of non-Doukhobor society and then, in stating his own alternative, will break into an irrational discussion of prophecies and dreams in which he clearly believes implicitly. A respected leader has only to recount and interpret a vision according to his own fancy for action to follow. To give one recent example of this: the site of the Sons of Freedom settlement at Hilliers on Vancouver Island was chosen to accord with a dream that had visited the man who became its leader, Michael 'the Archangel' Verigin. And today, more than eighty years after her death, the orally transmitted prophecies of the nineteenth-century woman leader, Luker'ia Kalmykova, still circulate, under the name of 'The Sayings of Lushechka', among the Doukhobors in Canada.

Not merely are dreams and prophecies valued, but Doukhobors see a special merit in the irrational, spontaneous act, though their attitude differs from that of Gide and other advocates of the *acte gratuit*, since they believe that such actions, far from being unmotivated, are divinely inspired. By following that divine inner voice, the Doukhobors hope to achieve both the external and the internal kingdoms of God. For it is characteristic of them that they are not only chiliasts seeking to create a Christian realm on earth, but also mystics seeking an enlightenment in dimensions inaccessible to the senses. There is in many of them, as Hugh Herbison remarks in his excellent essay on the Doukhobor religion, 'a calm, blissful confidence, rooted in the surety of divine companionship', and this feeling, he explains, gives a flavour of mystical communion to the sobranie, the Doukhobor meeting, which, even for the outsider, can be an extremely moving experience.

The character of the sobranya is completely alien to political system, man-made legalities and democratic procedure. The underlying principle is that God is present and available; and it is His will, not rules nor order and majorities of men, which is expected to influence decision. Moreover, it is assumed that as the same God is in every heart, the desired unanimity depends upon each person's giving up his own individuality so that the God within him may merge with the God in others, and in this corporate union is found the consensus of the meeting. . . . The effectiveness of the sobranya lies not in a building, which is unnecessary; not in ritual, which is minimal; not in the preaching, which is incidental; not in personal communions and prayer, for which there is no provision; and not in the heightened sensitivity of mind and heart reaching for truth, because this is not characteristic. The sobranya is a settling-down into the past, an immersion of self into the group. The singing at a sobranya is monotonous, persistent, inescapable; it is vocal magic which takes the place of other forms and determinants of unity.[2]

Music, indeed, is one of the most significant elements in Doukhobor religion, and must have been so from an early stage in the development of the sect. It is choral, bringing together all members of the Community, men, women, and children; it is entirely vocal (musical instruments are considered sinful) and thus can be interpreted as out-flowing from the divinely inspired spirit within each of the singers. And the psalms and hymns that are set to it are the authentic expression of the Doukhobor people, of their beliefs and history, recorded mainly by anonymous folk bards and welded into tradition by the very method of oral transmission that rendered written religious literature unnecessary to a peasant people living in a rural society where literacy was rare. The corpus of psalms and hymns was called 'The Living Book', since it was constantly growing and changing according to the experiences of the sect, in contrast to the Bible, which represented, in Doukhobor eyes, the frozen wisdom of a past age. The very possession of scriptures not preserved in writing, and therefore not easily accessible to non-members of the sect, enhanced the Doukhobor feeling of being a special people, isolated by their beliefs and their experiences from the rest of Christendom. The oblique symbolism of the psalms, as well as the styles of singing, were designed to render their meanings more obscure to outsiders, and it was not until 1900, when the Russian Marxist Vladimir Bonch-Bruevich visited the Doukhobors in Canada, that a large selection of the Living Book was put into writing.[3]

In isolating them from other Christians, the Living Book, and the traditions and beliefs it recorded, gave the Doukhobors a sense of intimate unity; that unity has been personified in their leaders. To outsiders the phenomenon of leadership among the Doukhobors has always been puzzling. In theory the sect rejects all authority; it was for this reason that Tolstoy imagined its members to be Christian anarchists like himself. In practice they have submitted, at least since the last third of the eighteenth century, to the direction of spiritual-temporal rulers whose authority is almost dictatorial and has been accepted, if not by all Doukhobors, certainly by a majority. The explanation of this apparent paradox can be found in a doublethink formula rather like Orwell's 'All animals are equal, but some animals are more equal than others.' All men have a spark of the divine within them, but in some the spark is magnified so that they become manifestations of deity. According to Doukhobor thought, the historical Christ was one of a progression; there are always Christs on earth, and among them are the Doukhobor leaders. The succession is not—as among Tibetan Dalai Lamas—by reincarnation, since the new Christ is already alive on the death of the predecessor, but the charisma of the divine leader is regarded as hereditary and passes through restricted lineages. The leader is not a priest; he has no liturgical function. Rather he is a prophet whose visions and intuitions, however irrational they may seem, are regarded as more penetrating than those of other men. A favourite Doukhobor explanation of the apparent contradiction between the theoretical anarchism of the sect and its practical authoritarianism is that all Doukhobors are indeed free, and that it is their freedom that enables them to recognize the wisdom of the leader's advice and to follow it. But there have been many incidents in Doukhobor history which suggest that moral and even physical coercion rather than voluntary acceptance often characterized the relationship between the Doukhobor living Christ and his fellow believers.

How the Doukhobor religion developed and whence it came are questions that can be answered, at best, with enlightened conjecture. The peasant masses of Russia in the eighteenth century lived out their lives in the obscurity of all illiterate and ahistoric cultures, and movements that developed among them might continue long in obscurity before they attracted the attention of the literate and became matters of written record. In seeking the origins of the Doukhobors we have to rely entirely on their own oral traditions, some still handed down from mouth to mouth and others recorded fragmentarily by non-Doukhobors a considerable time after the events to which they refer took place.

Some of the origin legends that Doukhobors still pass on from father to son belong plainly to the realm of fantasy. Even today old sectarians will assure one that their people are descended from the Biblical heroes of the burning fiery furnace, Shadrach, Meshach, and Abednego, who, according to this account, would be the first Doukhobors to dabble in fire; the more sophisticated maintain that the three were merely spiritual ancestors. More than once, in Doukhobor villages in Canada, we have also encountered the romantic legend that the first of the Doukhobors was a Russian Grand Duke who travelled abroad and, under the influence of the Quakers, decided to give up his rank and fortune and live a simple Christian life among the peasants of his own country. No member of the Romanov family made any such act of renunciation, and the tale probably has its origins in the fact that at a relatively late date—in the 1890s —a man of high rank, Prince D. A. Khilkov, gave his estate to his peasants and lived for a time among the Doukhobors, whom he helped materially on their pilgrimage to Canada.

These two legends demonstrate the inherent improbability of much that is told by the Doukhobors about their own past. However, there are some more credible statements that are not only accepted in present-day Doukhobor tradition, but were also recorded by non-Doukhobor Russian scholars when many of the events to which they refer were within living memory. The pioneer in these studies was a theological student, Orest Novitskii, who in the first quarter of the nineteenth century prepared a doctoral thesis on the sect that was published in 1832, with an enlarged edition in 1882.[4] According to Novitskii and other nineteenth-century historians, the Doukhobors first emerge into clear light as peasants in southern Russia, gathering around a literate teacher who appears from outside the village and settles among them. The first such teacher on record is a nameless figure, a retired non-commissioned officer who arrived in 1717 or 1718 at the village of Okhotcheye in the Ukrainian province of Kharkov. He set himself up as a friendly adviser, arbitrating the differences between the peasants, trying to settle their problems, preaching that the church had perverted the real teachings of Christ, that all men were brothers and hence equal, and that the laws of God forbade the killing of other men. Even here the elements of improbability enter in, since one version of the story of the teacher of Okhotcheye portrays him as a Prussian influenced by Quaker doctrine. In a more likely version he is a Russian conscript who, after being punished in a disciplinary battalion for preaching the pacifist principles to which he had become converted after he became an NCO, was eventually expelled from the army and wandered like a pilgrim into the Ukraine.

This teacher was not the only one of his kind at this period. Throughout the early eighteenth century, heresies similar if not identical to those of the Doukhobors were spreading through the frontier regions of Russia, and in 1734, during the reign of the Empress Anna, a decree was issued against a sect called the Ikonobors, or 'Ikon Wrestlers', of whose doctrine it was said that 'the weed has begun to spread in not one but in many places.'[5] Doukhobor traditions accept the Ikonobors as spiritual ancestors, and it may well be that in inventing the name 'Doukhobor' in 1785 the Archbishop Amvrosii was perpetrating a scornful play upon words, since for him those who opposed ikons would also be enemies of the Holy Spirit.

It is when we try to trace Doukhobor ancestry farther back, beyond the Ikon Wrestlers and the teacher of Okhotcheye, that the trails fade out to invisibility and we are left with the conjectures of historians. Some of these trace Doukhoborism to the Great Schism—the Raskol—that divided the Russian Orthodox Church after the Patriarch Nikon had in 1654 carried out a series of liturgical reforms involving such curious questions as whether two or three fingers should be used in making the sign of the cross, and how many times Alleluia should be sung during a service. But the Raskolniks, the Old Believers who resisted Nikon's reforms, never attacked the basic doctrines of the Russian Orthodox Church; they began as defenders of an old way and often ended, paradoxically, as reformers, but they based their doctrines as firmly on the Bible as did their Orthodox persecutors, and they still believed in church organization—as did most

1 *The Doukhobors come to Canada: a scene on board the immigrant ship*
Lake Huron, *bringing the first party to leave Russia in December 1898.*

2 *For lack of horses, the Doukhobor women plough the prairies near Swan River, Saskatchewan, during their first summer in Canada—1899.*

3 *After three seasons on the prairies, the Doukhobors had built themselves villages like this in the Thunder Hill Colony. Photographed in 1902.*

4 *Working together, Doukhobors reap their first harvest with scythes brought from Russia. Thunder Hill Colony, 1899.*

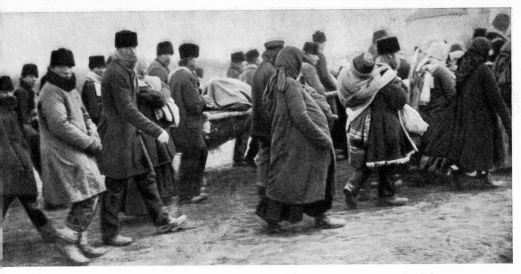

5 In the autumn of 1902 a wave of millenarian enthusiasm sweeps through the Doukhobor villages of the prairies, and hundreds of them set off on foot, carrying their sick on litters of poplar poles, to a mythical land of everlasting sunshine.

6 1903. The first Sons of Freedom march nude through the prairies in protest against what they believe to be the growth of materialism in their brethren.

7 *Peter the Lordly Verigin, first leader of the Doukhobors in Canada.*

8 *Peter the Purger (Chistiakov) Verigin, second leader of the Doukhobors in Canada.*

9 *In 1907, when the Doukhobors are dispossessed of their lands in the prairies, landseekers wait for 40 hours to lay claim to the vacated homesteads.*

10 A Doukhobor leader joins his people. Peter Chistiakov Verigin on his arrival at Brilliant from Russia in 1927. The ceremonial bread, salt and water are on the table. The leader stands with his hand on the boy's shoulder. The white-bearded man is the famous Tolstoyan, Paul Biriukov.

11 The meeting-house at Verigin, Saskatchewan. Built in 1917, it is the finest surviving example of traditional Doukhobor architecture.

12   *A typical Doukhobor meeting in British Columbia during the 1950s.*

13   *A modern Doukhobor family in British Columbia.*

14 The courtyard of a Community house in British Columbia; behind each
door, in the heyday of the Christian Community, a family would live,
sharing food with its neighbours in the communal kitchen. Now, in the
1960s, the Community houses are being abandoned for new dwellings on
the lands that the Doukhobors have bought back from the Government
of British Columbia.

15 *Annual memorial service at the tomb of Peter the Lordly and Peter Chistiakov Verigin, 1965.*

of the sects that can in various ways be regarded as offshoots of the Raskolniks. The Doukhobors, with their radical rejection of churches and priesthoods, with their denial of the uniqueness of the historical Christ, their proclamation of the immanence of the deity, and their neglect of the Bible in favour of their own body of orally transmitted doctrine, represent an attitude so completely divorced from Russian Orthodoxy in either its official or its schismatic form that it seems necessary to find their origins elsewhere.

Sergei Stepniak, the nineteenth-century Russian revolutionary who knew the Russian peasants from years of direct contact with them as a Populist agitator, remarked that the Doukhobors and the equally pacifist Molokans 'were the only sects which grew up on their own ground, independent of the Raskol.' [6] The closest resemblances to the Doukhobors in fact exist among those millenarian sects whose emergence in both western and eastern Europe predated either the Reformation or the Raskol. Such western European movements as the Brethren of the Free Spirit in the thirteenth century put forward the doctrine of the indwelling of God in man, and believed that heaven and hell were states of the mind. They and the Bohemian Adamites, who appear to have derived from them, rejected the Bible in favour of the promptings of the Spirit, while latter-day Christs were almost a commonplace in pre-Reformation heretical sects.

In Russia the doctrines of the Bogomils gained a foothold in the thirteenth and fourteenth centuries, and throughout the period up to the Great Schism sectarian groups appeared, like the fifteenth-century Judaizers, who denied the divinity of Christ and opposed the use of ikons, while during the sixteenth century, in the turbulent reign of Ivan the Terrible, appeared many heresiarchs who set themselves up as false Christs. None of these earlier groups, either in western or eastern Europe, can be regarded as providing more than parallels to the Doukhobor movement, combining an urge to simplify Christian practices with a desire to hurry on the Second Coming of the Messiah and the establishment of his millenial kingdom. Nor is there any evidence to support the suggestions of nineteenth-century Russian historians that there was any link between the early Doukhobors and the English Quakers; when Quakers did come into direct contact with the Doukhobors in the early nineteenth century it was only, as we shall see, to realize the extent of their differences.

However, there is one line of descent whose plausibility is suggested both by Doukhobor tradition and by some significant fragments of external evidence. During the seventeenth century a wanderer, said to be a deserter from the army, established himself as a hermit in a cave on the shores of the Volga. His name was Danilo Filippov. At first Danilo devoted himself to an intensive study of the Bible and the Orthodox liturgy, on which he based his teachings to the peasants who gathered around him, but in the end he decided they were useless and put them into a sack which he threw into the Volga. He declared that the truth was to be found instead in 'the golden book, *the living book* . . . the Holy Spirit',[7] and that this Spirit, which he held to be God, dwelt within every man. He further taught that Christ was born as other men were, that on the cross he died in the flesh but rose in the spirit, and that this spirit was incessantly resurrected. Danilo Filippov in fact regarded himself as one of the resurrections, a living Christ, and his disciple and successor, Ivan Suslov, who died in 1716, appointed twelve apostles and was worshipped by his followers in a deserted church in a village beside the Volga. The heresy of Danilo Filippov gave birth in the direct line of his apostolate to some of the most curious of all Russian sects, including the Khlysty, a company of dancing flagellants, and the Skoptsy, who castrated themselves to the greater glory of God.

Among the early Doukhobors there is no hint of such bizarre eccentricities. There is not even any evidence that they practised nudism before the first Sons of Freedom movement in Canada in 1902, and the arsonism that has been a feature of the radical wing of the movement for much of the past half century can be traced no farther back than to the famous burning of the arms in the villages of the Caucasus in 1895, an act that evoked such persecution from the tsarist authorities that it was branded by suffering on Doukhobor memory. Yet, though the Doukhobors could not compete in sheer oddity of behaviour with such spiritual descendants of Danilo Filippov as the Khlysty and the Skoptsy, their traditions recognize him as one of their early ancestors in dissent, and their doctrines of the indwelling of the divine spirit and of the nature and incessant rebirths of Christ bear a close resemblance to his. Even more interesting is the fact that, like Danilo, they not only use an oral scripture of their own in place of a rejected Bible, but actually call it, as he did, the Living Book. And to this day the Doukhobors sing in memory of Danilo an ancient hymn entitled 'In his youth he walked much'. It describes the prophet weeping by the riverside after he has dropped into it 'my golden book and the church keys'. But the historic Christ appears and says to him, 'Do not weep . . . the golden book I shall have rewritten . . . and upon a firm true path I shall set you.'[8] We do not know the exact nature of the link between the Doukhobors and Danilo Filippov, but that the link existed can hardly be doubted, and it seems probable that the first Doukhobor teachers were his followers.

Until the middle of the eighteenth century the Ukraine appears to have remained the centre of Doukhobor activity. The first of their leaders who is a tangible historical figure belongs to this period. Round about 1750 Silvan Kolesnikov, whose descendants are still prominent among Canadian Doukhobors, arrived as a stranger in Nikol'skoye, a village of free peasants in the province of Ekaterinoslav, and made it the centre from which he spread his teachings among the mixed population of the Ukraine and southern Russia. Whence he came is not known, but he was certainly a literate man. He claimed to be transmitting doctrines that had come to him from other teachers, and appears to have been an itinerant preacher influenced by the followers of Danilo Filippov. He found a receptive audience among the peasants of Nikol'skoye and the neighbouring villages, from which the people would flock each Sunday to listen to his preaching. He was more prosperous than his neighbours, but whether, like later Doukhobor leaders, he owed his greater wealth to contributions from his followers is not known; certainly he had the reputation of distributing generously whatever he received.

Silvan Kolesnikov died in 1775. The period of his rule at Nikol'skoye coincided with the later reign of the Tsarina Elizabeth and the early years of Catherine the Great, a time when sectarians were left relatively unmolested by the authorities, particularly if they lived in the remote parts of the Ukraine and did not attract too much attention. Kolesnikov continued at Nikol'skoye into an apparently peaceful old age, and was able to hand over the leadership to his sons Kiril and Peter. His followers went unpersecuted largely because of the touch of worldly wisdom in his makeup, which led him to teach the tactics of the soft answer; he was the master who first instructed the Doukhobors in survival by evasion, telling them that the external acts of religion were unimportant and that a Doukhobor might profess any appropriate religion—the Orthodox faith in Russia, Roman Catholicism in Poland, Islam in Turkey—provided he remained true within himself to his beliefs and lived a good and simple life. 'An apple is recognized by its taste,' he is said to have taught, 'a flower by its scent, and a Christian by the good deeds of his life.' Some of the Doukhobor ceremonial forms that survive to this day are said to have been initiated by him, including the custom of bowing to the God within every man. He differed from his successors in using the New Testament as well as oral Doukhobor teachings in his sermons, but this may have been a manifestation of his technique of evasion. The same may be said of the fact that he did not overtly proclaim himself a Christ or establish a court of apostles, though he may have done so in secret, since a later leader claimed to have derived his divine right from Kolesnikov.

The lack of dramatic militancy in the teachings and practice of Silvan Kolesnikov may explain why after his death the leadership of the Doukhobor movement passed out of the hands of his sons into those of the much more dynamic Ilarion Pobirokhin. Pobirokhin became prominent around the time of Kolesnikov's death in 1775. By then Doukhobor doctrines had spread out of the Ukraine into Great Russia, and it was at the village of Goreloye in the province of Tambov to the southeast of Moscow that Pobirokhin began to prophesy. A wool-dealer who travelled extensively between Tambov and the Ukraine, he appears to have derived his beliefs directly from those who carried on the tradition of the Ikonobors persecuted in the reign of the Empress Anne, for, unlike Kolesnikov, he openly denounced the worship of images and all the ceremonials of the Church. While Kolesnikov had used the Bible, even if only to give a covering of orthodoxy to his teachings, Pobirokhin rejected it completely, claiming that it was a source of dissension among Christians because of the varying interpretations that could be put upon its teachings. Under his guidance a great expansion of the Doukhobor oral literature of hymns and psalms took place, with a consequent defining of doctrine in more complex and extreme forms.

In particular, Doukhobor tradition credits Pobirokhin with the composition of the catechismal psalm, 'What Manner of Person Art Thou?', with its series of questions and answers defining Doukhobor beliefs. The answer to the title question, with which the psalm also begins, is 'I am a person of God.' God created man in order to give His spirit a body on earth, but man can only realize the presence of God through the possession of a clear conscience and the performance of good deeds. The Doukhobors, who are God's people, are further defined as the spiritual descendants of Abel. They are also seen as perpetual wanderers, on pilgrimage from a 'land of oppression' and 'a state of confusion' towards the promised land of enlightenment and truth, a view that Doukhobors—who see themselves as permanent exiles—have retained to this day and on more than one occasion have tried to put into practice by attempting pilgrimages to an earthly paradise. They are destined to fight by the spiritual weapon of the word of God, whose kingdom is actually within their own hearts, and who is defined in words that echo those of earlier messianic sects like the Brethren of the Free Spirits: 'God is Divine Reason; God is a spirit; God is man.'

It is when Pobirokhin's psalm defines the antagonists against whom the weapons of the spirit are to be used that we can perceive how the social discontents of the Russian peasantry in that age of serfdom and oppression became incorporated into his essentially religious radicalism. These antagonists are 'those in authority, those who live at the expense of the toil of others, those who as thieves and robbers withhold from the people the divine truth that should be freely available . . .' The struggle against them must be carried on with love for one's fellow men and without anger, for 'war and the taking of human life and all forms of hate towards our fellow men are the most impermissible deeds for a servant of God.' [9] After these anarchistic and pacifistic statements, the psalm goes on to say that the Doukhobors' temples are men's bodies and their churches are built within the hearts of men; that their only candles are faith, and their only baptism is suffering for truth; that every day is a holy day to be observed by the practice of good deeds and forgiveness; that their Holy Communion is the profession of Christ, and their commemoration of Christ consists of doing good to those who have harmed them. Pobirokhin's rejection of Kolesnikov's instructions to his followers to survive by openly professing what they do not privately believe is expressed in a question and answer that states explicitly that Doukhobors do not attend services in man-made Orthodox churches and do not pray to the ikons within them lest their hearts should become as stony as the churches and their natures as wooden as the ikons. Here, in a psalm dating from the late eighteenth century, we find expressed the basic doctrines that unite all Doukhobors even today, however they may differ in their ways of expressing them.

Two innovations of great importance took place during Pobirokhin's reign. The first was the attempt to establish a form of religious communism among the Doukhobors of Goreloye. Since the Doukhobors were living among other Russians, and not in the isolation they later enjoyed at Milky Waters and in the Caucasus, it is likely that this attempt was little more than a rationalization of customs of co-operation already embodied in the traditional Russian *mir*, the village commune. However, the fact that the experiment could take place in any form without interference shows that the villagers of Goreloye were free peasants and not serfs.

More important at the time was Pobirokhin's attempt to build on the basis of this community a theocratic despotism similar to that established in other sects deriving from the teachings of Danilo Filippov. Pobirokhin was a small man, with considerable charm and a persuasive tongue, but he suffered from the arrogance that is so often the besetting sin of the undersized. A report of the Bishop of Tambov to the Holy Synod of the Russian Orthodox Church in 1769 presents a rare and illuminating vignette of Pobirokhin in action.

> There were with . . . Ilarion Pobirokhin . . . only about eight men, and the aforementioned Pobirokhin was sitting at a table in the front part of the room, and the others were all standing and singing in front of him from the Bible, the 14th chapter of the prophet Zacharias . . . When they had finished singing these psalms, the aforementioned Pobirokhin interpreted them contrary to the Holy Church, saying that he had not found anywhere in the Scriptures that one should bow to wooden, or copper, or silver, or gold, or stone images, but that one should bow to man.[10]

This, according to Pobirokhin, was because man is created in the appearance and likeness of God.

Pobirokhin was in fact a personality ideally fitted to bring out into the open the authoritarian side of Doukhoborism, since he possessed not only the ability to convince his followers but also a lust for power and a vast sense of his own importance. When he proclaimed himself the living Christ, deriving his title by spiritual inheritance and deathbed testament from Kolesnikov (a sign that by this time he had assumed general leadership of Doukhobors in the Ukraine as well as Great Russia), his followers accepted willingly, and he proceeded to appoint twelve apostles to preach on his behalf and twelve 'death-bearing angels' who apparently had power to punish backsliders, though there is no record of the form the punishments actually took.

These developments brought dissension among the Doukhobors. At least one of the leading members of the sect, the tailor Semeon Uklein, who was Pobirokhin's son-in-law, broke with the leader over his rejection of the Bible and his self-deification and joined the Molokans or 'Milkdrinkers', the rival pacifist sect that agreed with the Doukhobors in rejecting war and wordly authority, but disagreed with them in accepting the Bible as an authoritative guide to moral and spiritual life. Uklein became a leader among the Molokans, and he took with him a number of Doukhobors discontented with Pobirokhin's rule.

This schism did not, however, materially lessen the spread of Doukhoborism during the period of Pobirokhin's rule. 'The teaching spread like a steppe fire,' remarked Orest Novitskii of this period. 'Simultaneously it caught fire in the Moscow region, in the Ukraine, among the Don Cossacks, in Transcaucasia.'[11] This success in proselytization drew down on the Doukhobors the attention of a government that, in the later days of Catherine the Great, was becoming more hostile to dissenters. Already, in 1769, Pobirokhin had fled from Goreloye, disturbed by an ecclesiastical investigation, but, not being pursued, he returned to carry on his activities. In 1779 the first major government investigation of the Doukhobors appears to have taken place. Not many years later Pobirokhin, whose activities rendered him the reverse of inconspicuous, went with his apostles into the city of Tambov, where he proclaimed that he had come to judge the world. He was brought up for trial about the end of the 1780s, and with his family and some of his apostles he was sent into Siberian exile, whence he never returned.

He was one of many Doukhobors to be treated in this way, and by the early 1790s there had already been a considerable dispersal of the sect to the various regions on the periphery of the Russian Empire that were selected as suitable to receive banished sectarians. Some went to Finland and to the neighbouring region of Kola, others to Archangel, and some of the leaders to the Solovetskiye Islands in the White Sea; there were Doukhobor exiles near the sea of Azov, on the islands off Estonia, in the Caucasus, and in Siberia. Everywhere they went they did not merely cling obstinately to their own faith, but actually made converts, particularly among the Cossacks and even to a small extent among the Finns, so that their dispersion, designed originally to break up the sect into small, isolated fragments, became a means by which their gospel was spread among the Russian peasantry. Most peasants were, indeed, hostile to the Doukhobor exiles, less from Orthodox loyalty than from local xenophobia; but there were always discontented people, longing for some escape from the intolerable conditions under which they lived, who were attracted not only by the anarchistic and chiliastic aspects of Doukhoborism, but also by the practical brotherliness expressed in the warm hospitality that Doukhobors have traditionally extended to neighbours and strangers alike.

It was not long before the tsarist authorities realized that mere exile was no cure for the Doukhobor challenge, and, urged on by the clergy of the Russian Orthodox Church, they began to apply more severe forms of punishment. By this time the Doukhobors were regarded as especially dangerous, not only because of the extent of their religious heresies, but also because the government authorities had begun to realize that underlying the Doukhobor pretensions of libertarianism was to be found a concept of authority eminently disloyal in conservative eyes; the Doukhobor leaders appeared to them not merely as false Christs but also as false tsars. Another important reason for the increasing severity of the persecution of Doukhobors in the 1790s, during the reign of the mad Tsar Paul, was that soldiers who held Doukhobor beliefs at the time of conscription or had acquired them during service began to reject military discipline. These men included both Cossacks and soldiers in infantry regiments, and some of them, who held the rank of non-commissioned officers, must have been men of long service. Such conscientious objectors were subjected to severe punishment in their regiments before being sent into exile with hard labour, but many sustained their refusal to bear arms, and in 1806 Doukhobor conscripts threw away their muskets in the battlefield.

Mass trials of Doukhobors were common during the 1790s. Novitskii records the sentencing of thirty-one Doukhobors from the Ukraine to life-long hard labour in the mines of the Ekaterinburg region in the Urals for the crime of preaching their doctrines in the streets, and the infliction on thirty-four other Doukhobors of severe floggings, followed by confisca-tion of their property and exile to Siberia; a higher court in the latter case 'reduced' the sentence to hard labour in the Ekaterinburg mines and decreed that the Doukhobor children should be taken away from their parents, to be brought up in the Orthodox faith.[12] For these examples quoted by the historian who was nearest to the events themselves, there were probably many others that escaped his notice. As conditions be-came more unsettled towards the end of Paul's reign, vindictive and bigoted local governors took authority into their own hands and inter-preted in the most severe way the various ukases that had been issued against the sect since the reign of Anne. In 1801, conducting an inquiry on behalf of Paul's successor, the Emperor Alexander I, Senator Lopukhin expressed his view that 'No sect until now has been so severely prose-cuted as the Doukhobors, though they are by no means the most harmful. Many have been tortured; and whole families have been exiled with hard labour and have been incarcerated in the cruellest of prisons. Some-times there has been no room in their cells for them to stand upright or to lie down full length. . . . They have been called up for the army out of their turn, have been subjected to abuse, and burdened with official requisitions.'[13]

It is true that Lopukhin was to make his report under the easy rule of an emperor with liberal inclinations, but even in the 1790s there were some high government officials who spoke up for the Doukhobors and stressed their virtues as well as their faults. For example, in 1792 Kokhovskii, the governor of Ekaterinoslav province, one of the areas where the sect was most numerous, spoke of the generally good behaviour of the Doukhobors, their industry, their lack of drunkenness, their concern for the welfare of their homes. They were even, he reported, very regular in their payment of taxes, carried out their social obligations to their fellow villagers, and—except for their heretical religious practices—led exemplary and moral lives.

It appears also that persecution cannot have been very searching in the Doukhobor Rome—the village of Goreloye in Tambov province—for a few years after Pobirokhin's death his successor appeared and assumed the role of the living Christ. Savelii Kapustin, who was to preside over one of the most interesting periods of Doukhobor history, was already forty-seven when he arrived in Goreloye. His place of birth is unknown. At the age of twenty he was conscripted into the army, in which he had served for twenty-five years, becoming a corporal in the Guards and acquiring an education on the way. He was remembered, not only by his followers, but also by non-Doukhobors who encountered him, as a tall, dark-complexioned, and very handsome man, with a military bearing and a long stride. He had a remarkably exact and retentive memory that enabled him to recollect almost everything he read or heard (he is said to have been able to sing two hundred Doukhobor psalms), and his mass of self-taught knowledge combined with a native eloquence to impress the Doukhobor peasants even more than the attainments of his predecessor Pobirokhin. Kapustin, who had received an honourable release from the army, arrived in Goreloye in 1790, very shortly after Pobirokhin had been sent into exile. Though he posed as a stranger to outsiders, he was immediately accepted as the heir to the leadership and married the daughter of Nikifor Kalmykov, one of the leading local Doukhobors.

Why he was so unquestioningly accepted is a matter of conjecture, though the oral traditions of the Doukhobors offer a number of possible explanations. One is that he was in fact the son of Pobirokhin, brought up in concealment to live as a non-Doukhobor until the time came for him to assume the leadership of the sect. But it is certain that in 1743, when Kapustin was born, Pobirokhin had not been recognized as the living Christ and leader of all the Doukhobors, and it seems likely that the tradition of his having been brought up under another name than his father's stems from a confusion with the fact that Kapustin himself took the precaution of discarding his wife when she became pregnant so that their child would be born in the house of his wife's father, proclaimed to be illegitimate, and brought up under the name of Kalmykov. This precaution Kapustin thought necessary, since his son, Vasilii, as the child of a soldier, would automatically be liable to conscription, whereas as Vasilii Kalmykov he could at least take his chance with the other peasant boys when lots for conscription were drawn.

Another tradition that is still current among Doukhobors in Canada states that Kapustin was Pobirokhin's 'spiritual son' and tells how, having accepted Kapustin as his disciple and successor, Pobirokhin kept in touch with him secretly and, on the eve of being sent into exile, paid a visit to him and spent a day and a night instructing him in the mission that was planned for him.[14] Again, this tale has no basis outside oral tradition, and it is possible that Kapustin was neither a physical nor a spiritual son of Pobirokhin, but merely appeared at an opportune time when a vacuum in the leadership of the sect was waiting to be filled by the first persuasive, personable, and moderately educated man who arrived, primed with a knowledge of Doukhobor doctrines and endowed with charisma.

In one important respect Kapustin appears to have resembled Silvan Kolesnikov more than he did Ilarion Pobirokhin. While assuming all Pobirokhin's pretensions to the role of the living Christ, he counselled discretion and evasion as a means of avoiding persecution, and he appears to have carried out his own recommendations with exemplary skill, so that he was able to navigate without persecution the dangerous first decade of his rule until the assassination of the Tsar Paul and the accession to the throne of the enlightened Alexander I, the only Autocrat of All the Russias who befriended the Doukhobors. To Alexander the sect was to owe not only a quarter of a century relatively free from persecution, but also an opportunity for Kapustin to bring together many of the diverse groups of free peasants and serfs, of Cossacks and soldiers, who regarded themselves as People of God, Doukhobors, and to weld them into a cohesive sect.

2 MILKY WATERS

Alexander 1 has always been remembered by the Doukhobors as their great benefactor. They think of him not only as an emperor, but as a just man who acted under the inspiration of God. And, indeed, it was to his enlightened policies that they owed a great measure of release from persecution and also an opportunity to exist and develop as a self-contained community.

Nevertheless, Alexander's actions were not motivated by any special affection for the Doukhobors. It is true that in the early years of his reign, which lasted from 1801 to 1825, he was influenced by the liberal teachings of the Enlightenment, which had been transmitted to Russia by French tutors to the aristocracy and by the less reactionary émigrés from Revolutionary France who inhabited Alexander's court and served in his armies. These teachings suggested to him that persecution was neither a humane nor an effective way of dealing with religious dissent. But, while he introduced a wide degree of tolerance for religious minorities, he still had in mind the interests of the Russian Orthodox Church that even this liberal tsar recognized as one of the most important buttresses of his authority, and for this reason he wished to isolate the Doukhobors from the rest of the population so that they would have less opportunity to proselytize.

These reasons for transplanting the Doukhobors into a region of the Empire where they could be left to flourish in their own eccentric beliefs without infecting the rest of the Russian population were mingled with more mundane considerations of imperial policy. When Senator Lopukhin and his colleague Neledinskii-Meletskii were sent to the Ukraine in 1801, it was to investigate what had until recently been a frontier region, with a view to integrating it more closely with Russia proper, and in such an investigation the groups of sectarians who were scattered all over this area naturally came in for attention. The more solidly Orthodox the region became, the more easily it might be assimilated into the increasingly centralized Russian state. On the other hand, there were uses for the dissenters farther away on the new frontiers that were being established at this time, and particularly in the region north of the Crimea that had only recently been wrested from the nomadic Tartars. The area had already been used as a place of exile during the 1790s, and the Mennonites had been allowed to establish a colony there even before Alexander came to the throne. When the tsar received Lopukhin's report of the harsh and foolish treatment local governors had meted out to the Doukhobors during the chaotic years of the preceding reign, accompanied by a plea from the Doukhobors of Ekaterinoslav province to be allowed to live together on their own, he took the opportunity to combine policy and principle and granted their request.

The area chosen for the Doukhobor settlement was in Taurida, along the Molochnaya River, which in English is generally described as the Milky Waters. It was a region of fertile virgin soil with a magnificent climate, which a few decades later was to make the nearby seacoast one of Russia's leading resort areas. At the beginning of the nineteenth century it was a wild and empty country, where the Tartars still roamed and where the only settled neighbours of the Doukhobors were the Mennonites who preceded them and the Molokans who came shortly afterwards. Since no differences are so sharply marked as those between rival groups of dissenters, the relationship between these three sects on the shores of the Milky River was peaceful but suspicious; in later years none of them spoke well of each other.

On 25 January 1802, Alexander issued an edict that for a quarter of a century was to be the charter of the Doukhobors. He ordered the appointment of a 'trustworthy and humane' person to supervise the emigration of the Doukhobors to Milky Waters. Representatives of the Doukhobors were to proceed to the area of future settlement in the company of suitable officials in order to select the sites for villages. The arrangements were generous. Each migrant was to be given approximately forty acres of land, and in addition each family was to receive an interest-free loan of a hundred roubles (a considerable sum in 1802), to be repaid after ten years at the rate of five roubles a year. For five years the Doukhobors were to be free of taxes. Finally, though it is not mentioned in the decree, there appears to have been at least a tacit understanding that Doukhobors would not be pressed too strongly to take part in military service.

Almost immediately the first contingent of Ukrainian Doukhobors proceeded to Milky Waters under the leadership of Kiril Kolesnikov. There were thirty families in all, totalling 296 'souls' (males). They founded the village of Bogdanovka—Gift of God—and the experiment proved so successful, both agriculturally and as a community, that the authorities considered it worth further development, and when the Doukhobors from Tambov and Voronezh provinces petitioned the tsar in 1804 for permission to settle beside the Milky Waters and around the salt lagoon known as Milky Lake at the mouth of the river, this was immediately granted. Some 494 'souls' reached the Milky Waters as a result of this second migration, which was led by Savelii Kapustin, who, as the acknowledged prophet of the sect, automatically became the leader of the whole Milky Waters settlement and established his headquarters at the new village of Terpeniye or Patience which the Tambov Doukhobors founded. In the years that followed many people who had held secret Doukhobor beliefs proclaimed themselves and asked permission to join the Milky Waters settlement, and at the same time there were others who pretended to be Doukhobors in order to get free land and to escape from the oppressions of landlords and bureaucrats in the more settled regions. Generally speaking, serfs were not allowed to go, though some did so clandestinely, as did some deserters from the army. Some exiles from Siberia and Finland reached the Milky Waters, but others were not allowed to leave their places of exile. As a result, in Siberia particularly, some Doukhobor villages grew up and continued on their independent way outside the close community of the faithful governed by Kapustin and his successors. Kropotkin found these Siberian Doukhobors in the 1860s, living under a 'semi-communistic brotherly organization', and there is little evidence that they maintained any close contact with their brethren who emigrated to Milky Waters.

But large and small groups continued to reach Taurida during the two decades after the establishment of the colony. In 1816, 228 Cossacks came from the Caucasus and ninety families from Finland, including some Finns and Swedes who had married into the sect. It was not until

1821 that the authorities finally decided to disallow migrations; a group of Cossacks in fact arrived as late as 1824. In 1827 there were 3,985 Doukhobors in eight hundred households settled along the Milky Waters; they lived in nine villages—five beside the Molochnaya River and four around the Milky Lake.

Those who reached Milky Waters were only a portion, and perhaps even a minority, of the Russian peasants who actually professed Doukhobor beliefs. The most striking piece of evidence bearing on this point is provided by a petition presented in 1811 by two leading Doukhobors named Loponosov and Surkov who asked that four thousand members of the sect in various Great Russian provinces be allowed to settle in the Balkan frontier area of southern Bessarabia. The minister of police asked the local governors to carry out an investigation. They discovered that the groups covered by the petition consisted of 3,186 men and women, 'of sober life', plus children. The largest group, some 1,660 men and 1,063 women, were concentrated in Saratov, a province that hitherto had not been known as a Doukhobor stronghold, and there were also appreciable groups in Tambov and Orenburg. The petition was rejected on the grounds that conditions in southern Bessarabia were not peaceful enough to allow settlement, since the Russian armies were still fighting in the Danubian principalities in the south, and the area was subject to Turkish raids. It seems likely that most of the four thousand Doukhobors covered by this petition had to remain at home, since if they had all reached Milky Waters the population of that settlement would have been much greater than it was in 1827.[1]

In fact, there was no consistent official policy towards Doukhobors who wished to go to Milky Waters. Alexander I, at least in the early part of his reign, would doubtless have liked to see them all gathered together and out of harm's way, but the local governors were not always co-operative, and in this they were encouraged by the bishops of the Russian Orthodox Church, whose vindictiveness towards the sectarians was boundless. The French invasion of 1812 was used in a number of cases as an excuse to refuse permission to emigrate and, as his reign went on, Alexander tended to oppose less strongly those advisers who favoured a hard policy towards sectarians.

What happened to the Doukhobors who did not reach Milky Waters is not known, except for those in Eastern Siberia whom Kropotkin and others encountered later in the century. The likelihood is that, deprived of leadership, most of them eventually lapsed into the Orthodox church or at best lived, according to Silvan Kolesnikov's advice, as concealed

Doukhobors. History, certainly, tells little more of them, and concentrates on the members of the Milky Waters settlement, who with their descendants and those of the settlers in Siberia (who in 1833 numbered about a hundred exiles plus a few converts) form the Doukhobor movement that has survived into the mid-twentieth century and with which we are from this point concerned.

Yet the emigrants who gathered at Milky Waters during the early years of the nineteenth century were certainly representative of the sect as a whole. In background and tradition they were less divided than their widespread places of immediate origin—Finland, the Ukraine, the Caucasus, and the regions to the east of Moscow—might suggest. Those from Finland and the Caucasus were mostly exiles from either the Ukraine or Great Russia, and those from the Ukraine appear to have been the descendants of Great Russian serfs who fled to the region during the seventeenth century when it was still a place of refuge where the Zaporozh'ye Cossacks, themselves originally fugitives from Muscovite power, maintained a precarious autonomy as guardians of the marches that shielded Russia proper from the perils of Tartar raids. The Doukhobors have never considered themselves Ukrainians as distinct from Russians, and they speak not Ukrainian but a Russian dialect that, like their songs and folk customs, is slightly modified by the fact that many of them lived for generations in the Ukraine. Moreover, the fact that they already saw themselves as pilgrims suggests a past of wandering in search of freedom even before they set out with their wagons and herds on the great trek to the Milky Waters.

That social discontent and religious fervour were mingled in the motives that made people Doukhobors, and brought them eventually to Milky Waters, is shown by the fact that the emigrants were in class terms remarkably homogeneous. The great majority of them were free peasants, though the tsarist authorities were certainly justified in their suspicions that fugitive serfs were being welcomed into the settlements; it was doubtless for reasons of concealment that a number of families were given new names by Kapustin shortly after they reached Milky Waters. There were also many soldiers, some of them legally discharged, others freed from Siberian exile, and, again, a proportion of deserters whose presence the rest of the colonists concealed by silence and evasive answers. Most of those ex-soldiers were peasant conscripts who rarely held a higher rank than that of corporal, but a number of Cossacks arrived, and among them a few junior officers. There were also a few village artisans and some rural traders of Pobirokhin's type. No member of the noble landowning classes appears to have joined the Doukhobors at this time, though at least one renegade Orthodox priest, Father Basilevskii, lived for a period at Milky Waters. According to Doukhobor traditions, he had a great deal to do with the establishment of the older types of singing that were used by the sect until, in the late 1920s, more complex chants were developed in Canada by Gabriel Vereshchagin, under the encouragement of the reigning leader, Peter Petrovich Verigin.

It was the non-believers, coming in desperate search for a refuge from autocratic authority, who formed an abrasive element within the colony. Some of them were members of rival sects, like the Molokans, and these eventually found a place in the colonies of their own religionists who were later settled at Milky Waters. Greater problems were created by non-Doukhobor deserters from the army, and by men exiled for crimes other than religious dissent who, when they saw the real Doukhobors departing for Milky Waters, claimed to be of their faith and actually obtained permission to join the colony. Their arrival aroused immediate disagreement in the Community, and Kapustin is said to have defended them, urging his followers to accept them as brothers and to reform them by example.

The colonists at Milky Waters accepted certain obligations in return for their free land and their period of relief from taxation. They made roads and cut down timber for the use of the army. In other respects, however, their physical isolation preserved them at first from undue interference on the part of the authorities. Tilling the rich soil north of the Crimea, they became prosperous; they extended their cultivation far beyond the limits of their original land grants, so that government investigators in 1822 found that they were cultivating an average of a hundred acres per 'soul' instead of the forty acres that had been allotted to them under the decree of 1802. They impressed officials and passing visitors as industrious and restrained in behaviour almost to the point of austerity. In 1807 a report made by the local authorities to St Petersburg described them as good farmers who were sober in habits, prompt in paying taxes, and in general obedient. Orest Novitskii, who was by no means an apologist for the Doukhobors but who had gathered his information conscientiously at the time of the Milky Waters settlement, summed up his impressions with this remark : 'To the credit of the Doukhobors one must say that they are sober, laborious, and frugal, that in their houses and clothing they are careful to be clean and tidy; that they are attentive to their agriculture and cattle-breeding, occupations which have been and still are their chief employment.'[2]

The success of the Doukhobors as farmers at Milky Waters was due not merely to the fact that they had more and better land than before. They were in fact such keen farmers that their land never seemed enough, and they eagerly bought more from non-Doukhobors in the Milky Waters region until the authorities put a stop to their expansion. Undoubtedly their tendency not to drink as heavily as ordinary Russian peasants at this period was also an important element in their success, while the fact that they were not forced to serve in the army at a time of almost un-interrupted warfare against the French, the Turks, and the Persians meant that they had enough able-bodied young men who knew that they would be able to reap the fruits of their labour. They were also fortunate in having as neighbours the Mennonites, whose reliance on the Bible they did not share, but whose agricultural efficiency they praised by imitation. Not only did they learn new farming methods from the Mennonites; they also borrowed the design of their wooden houses and, in the case of the men at least, even their form of dress.

The Doukhobors stayed at Milky Waters for forty years. In community affairs and also in terms of relations with the tsarist authorities, these decades can be divided into two roughly equal periods, with the dividing point between 1818 and 1820. During the earlier period the colony was run as an experiment in communism, well administered and reasonably united; relations with the central authorities, represented by Alexander I and his immediate advisers, remained good almost to the end of this period, though from 1815 onwards there was increasing friction with local officials. The second period, marked by the death of Kapustin and later of Alexander, was a time of the abandonment of communism, of the decay of internal administration, and of disunity within the sect; relations with the central authority, dominated by the conservative Tsar Nicholas I and his reactionary advisers, deteriorated and the Doukhobors became once again a persecuted minority.

From the time Kapustin arrived at Milky Waters in 1805 his authority was not only supreme, but also remarkably well concealed. He developed to the highest degree that self-protective division between pretence and practice that later deceived Tolstoy and many other superficial observers of the Doukhobors. To outsiders who questioned them on their leaders, Kapustin's followers were instructed to say, 'Among us, no one is greater than another'; the identical answer is still given by Doukhobors in Canada. The effectiveness of this pretence is shown by the fact that Tolstoy was by no means the first to be deceived by it. Novitskii in his narrative of the Doukhobors makes use of an account of 'the origin of the

Doukhobors and their doctrine' that was written in 1805, with some knowledge of the progress of the Milky Waters colony in its early years, and used extensively in the 1890s by Vladimir Chertkov and other Tolstoyans as part of their propaganda in favour of the Doukhobors, then undergoing great persecutions in the Caucasus; the author is not known, but he may have been the freemason N. I. Novikov who was interested in Doukhobor affairs during Kapustin's rule. On the organization of the Doukhobors, this account tells us:

In their Society there are no elders who rule or administrate, but rule and administration are by all and each. Written regulations they also have none, and one might suppose that there ought to be disagreement and disorder amongst them. Yet no such disorder has ever been noticed. In the Milky Waters, three, and even five families live peacefully together in one large cottage.

As to the management of the families separately, the weakness and dependence of the female sex, the inexperience of youth, and the education of the system naturally require another system. In every family there must of necessity be an elder one, and the father in the flesh is this elder one. His duty is to care for the needs of his family, to watch the conduct of the children, correct their faults, and teach them the law of God. When the father dies his place is taken by the elder of the brothers, and in the case of incapacity of the latter, his place is taken by the one most capable.[3]

This rather idyllic account mingles truth with error; the Doukhobor family did have an authoritarian structure, to such an extent that right up to the time of the emigration to Canada at the end of the nineteenth century, marriages were arranged by parents in patriarchal style, so that often the bride and bridegroom did not see each other until the day of the wedding. But the authoritarian family did not complement a libertarian structure within the Community as a whole. On the contrary, paternalism reigned throughout, with the Christ-leader as the universal father. The Community 'of needs required outstanding leadership to have unity and orderliness. Kapustin very ably filled this role and the common folk got to worship him as a nearly-God deity.'[4] The words are not those of a hostile critic, but of a modern Doukhobor, Eli Popoff, recording the traditions of his own people.

Yet it would be a gross over-simplification to suggest that Kapustin ruled merely as an autocrat, a petty tsar justified by divine right. Among a sect as governed by obscure and irrational collective impulses as the

Doukhobors, there has always been a relationship between the people and the leader that is understood intuitively rather than codified. The collective will expressed by the people in the sobranie, the meeting of the village or even the whole sect, emanates from the same inner spirit as the will of the inspired living Christ, and the times of harmony and even material prosperity among the Doukhobors have been those in which the leaders, like Kapustin and, in later years, Luker'ia Kalmykova and Peter Vasil'evich Verigin at his best, followed policies that found a ready response in the hearts of their followers.

It was Kapustin who established a kind of constitution, unwritten like that of the United Kingdom, that gave expression to this peculiar relationship, and for this reason the Doukhobors still speak of him as their 'Moses' or their 'lawgiver'. He, rather than Pobirokhin, appears to have established the principle of hereditary leadership; from his time, even if the leaders were not in the direct line of descent, they all belonged to the same ruling lineage. To assist him, Kapustin appointed a council of twenty-four elders. Their role was to carry out the business of the Community, including relations with the tsarist authorities and with non-Doukhobor merchants, and to implement the broad decisions on policy that emanated from Kapustin and were often expressed in the form of psalms. Disobedience to the will of the leader or of the council of elders was, in Kapustin's time, punished by eviction from the Community, and the same punishment was inflicted for crimes such as theft; Kapustin also established the principle, from which Doukhobors have only rarely departed in later generations, that members of the sect should not have recourse to courts of law, since this would imply a recognition of human as distinct from divine government.

Parallel to the institution of leadership supported by the oligarchic council of elders, there was the sobranie, in which the women as well as the men took part. The sobranie appears to have served three purposes, as it does among Doukhobors to this day. First it was a religious meeting, beginning with the chanting of hymns and psalms around the table carrying the symbolic bread and salt. Then, when a level of common feeling had been established by this kind of spiritual participation, the meeting would turn to discussing the everyday business of the community. Everybody, from the leader downwards, had the right to speak and the goal aimed at was unanimity, which was necessary before any decision could be implemented. Because the Doukhobors retained their distrust of the authorities, the gatherings of the elders and of the sobranie were concealed from outsiders, and it is difficult to establish more than a general idea of how their business was conducted. The evidence we have regarding the procedure followed at Milky Waters is based on oral traditions collected by outsiders like Bonch-Bruevich at the end of the nineteenth century, when there can have been no surviving Doukhobors who were adults in the early years of Milky Waters. Bonch-Bruevich talks of compulsory voting,[5] but it is at least possible that a sense of the meeting was felt—as among the Quakers—and that a consensus rather than a vote was the actual means of arriving at a decision. This brings us to the final function of the sobranie. It gave the leader a means of ascertaining the feeling of the group on particular issues before he reached his own decisions, and it also gave him a means of influencing their attitude in the receptive atmosphere created by the musical evocation of common traditions and common longings, an atmosphere in which the prophetic tone would be heard and understood.

Parallel to this threefold political structure of the Doukhobor sect, which with little variation has survived down to the present day, stood the less durable economic organization of the Milky Waters Community. Kapustin brought with him the system of primitive communism that he had already developed in a rudimentary way at Goreloye in Tambov province, and for more than a decade, from the time of his arrival in 1805, a serious attempt was made to create a Christian Utopia at Milky Waters. There were common herds of cattle and sheep. The land was tilled in common, and in the villages there were common granaries and mills and also communal baking ovens, which supplied to the various households all the bread they needed. The members of the Community were encouraged to make farming their principal occupation, though, apart from the crafts necessary to self-sufficiency, such as metal-working and weaving, there were also a few cottage industries, such as the manufacture of linen and of gaily coloured woollen sashes and caps for sale outside the Community. Individuals were discouraged from trading. This was done by the elders on behalf of the Community as a whole.

The metropolis of Milky Waters was Kapustin's village of Terpeniye, and the centre of the metropolis was a peculiar institution called Sirotskii Dom, or Orphan's Home, a large two-storied wooden building in a great orchard made beautiful with gardens, fountains, and even wooden statues. The name, which conveys anything but the real nature of the institution, appears to have been borrowed, with so much else, from the neighbouring Mennonites, who ran a Waisenamt or Orphan's Office, which looked after orphans and any other Mennonites who, through misfortune, were unable to provide for themselves. Among the Doukhobors there was no need for such an institution, since it was considered an elementary religious duty for the relatives or neighbours of an orphan or a person incapacitated from work by age or illness to support him.

The Orphan's Home, endowed with lands and herds, in fact fulfilled a number of quite different functions, some of which are suggested by the fact that among themselves the Doukhobors called it 'Zion'. It was the palace of the leader, and provided him with an official role *vis-à-vis* the tsarist authorities, that of manager of the Orphan's Home. It served as a hostel where visiting strangers could be entertained. It contained the treasury of the Community, and taxes were paid to the government not by individual Doukhobors, but by the Sirotskii Dom on their behalf. Finally, it was a kind of college of vestals, since a choir of virgins were among its inhabitants; they were taught the words and music of the Living Book, so that it might be preserved and passed on intact and uncorrupted to later generations.

The Orphan's Home was to continue as the financial and governmental centre of the Doukhobors, and as the repository of cultural traditions, until the end of the nineteenth century. By 1816 it was already the only surviving institution of Kapustin's communist experiment. In the summer of that year the first Western visitor found his way to Milky Waters. He was Robert Pinkerton, an English colporteur of the Bible Society. Remarking on the fact that when they came to Milky Waters the Doukhobors had everything in common, Pinkerton recorded that 'now every family has its own private property, cattle, fields, etc. Still they have fields of corn, gardens and flocks which belong to the whole community, and the revenues of which are applied for the common benefit of the society.'[6] By this he meant the lands belonging to what he called 'the Chancery', i.e. the Orphan's Home.

When Kapustin sanctioned the abandonment of communism and conducted a sharing out of the Doukhobor lands, he destroyed the egalitarian basis of the Milky Waters colony by allotting larger shares to his own relatives than to the ordinary settlers, and an economic stratification of the community quickly took shape. Kapustin and the Kalmykov clan, together with the families of the elders, formed an oligarchy that not only controlled the government of the Community and the property vested in the Orphan's Home, but also held most of the best land. The less affluent peasants, with little land or even, in some cases, none at all, inevitably became dependent on their richer brethren. Nobody went in deep need; Doukhobor rules of mutual aid prevented that. But there is no doubt that the poorer members of the Community were exploited, and as early as

1818 the richer Doukhobors were even employing labourers from neighbouring Russian Orthodox villages. In a few years all pretence at communism had vanished and the Doukhobors became, and remained for many years, more individualist in their economy than the ordinary Russian villagers who maintained the communal traditions of the *mir*.

The visitors who came to Milky Waters from abroad were mainly evangelical Christians who expected to find fellow spirits among the Doukhobors; they were disappointed to discover how different the Doukhobors were from the radical nonconformists of the West. Pinkerton, with his cargo of Bibles, was probably the most disillusioned of all, having travelled so far to find people who, when he offered copies of the scriptures, 'refused to accept any copies, remarking, "That what was in the Bible was in them also." '[7] He had one moment of hope, when an old shepherd told him, 'Yes, I can read the Word of Life'; it turned out that the old man was illiterate but knew by heart the Living Book of the Doukhobors.

Pinkerton found a better welcome among the Bible-using Mennonites of the Milky Waters, and what they had to tell him about their neighbours anticipates the complaints that have been made over the last hundred and fifty years by non-Doukhobors about Doukhobors, and in Canada as often as in Russia.

Their neighbours, the Mennonites and other German Colonists, speak well of their morals; but all complain of the reserve and shyness of their characters . . . Their neighbours seem to know little of their religious tenets. The Mennonites say they are a peaceable and industrious people, but accuse them of hypocrisy; hence, say they, when some of the members were convicted of drunkenness, they denied the fact, and maintained that their members were all holy. . . . Their whole aspect and manner of intercourse with strangers, indicates a degree of shyness and distrust which is quite extraordinary; hence also, their evasive answers to all direct enquiries respecting their sect . . .[8]

What Pinkerton did not take sufficiently into account was the intensity of persecution that had made the Doukhobors evolve evasion as a means of dealing with the authorities or with passing strangers.

Pinkerton was somewhat consoled later in 1816 when he went to visit a famous waterfall in Finland, some forty miles north of Vyborg, and there encountered the ninety exiled Doukhobors who later found their way to Milky Waters. They were a melancholy group, nostalgic for the south. Their children had been taken away but now, thanks to the benevo-

lence of the tsar, the families were reunited again. Pinkerton found that
only 'one or two' could read, and they had no books at all, yet one among
them, an illiterate man, had 'a more intimate acquaintance with the Scriptures than many I have met with' and 'explained some texts to us in a
manner which would have done honour to an Oxford or Cambridge
divine.'[9] The difference in the impressions Pinkerton gained from the
Doukhobors at Milky Waters and those in Finland is perhaps due to the
fact that the former were now living in a completely Doukhobor setting
under the magnetic influence of Kapustin and the exclusivist doctrines
embodied in his psalms, whereas the exiles in Finland did not possess the
developed version of the Living Book and still maintained the earlier Doukhobor tendency to follow the Bible as well as their own oral traditions.

The first of the long series of encounters between the Quakers and the
Doukhobors also resulted in the revelation of deep doctrinal differences,
in spite of the fact that the two sects shared an uncompromising pacifism.
William Allen, an English Quaker, and Stephen Grellet from Pennsylvania
were encouraged by Alexander I to pay a visit to the Milky Waters settlement, which they reached on 29 May 1819. Both kept journals and recorded their impressions. They arrived in the evening, spent the night at
the Mennonite settlement of Altona, and returned the next day for a
second visit to the Doukhobors.

Allen records mainly his disappointment with the elders, whom he
found 'well dressed according to the custom of the country but with
something in their countenances which I did not quite like.' It was when,
after expressing sympathy for the Doukhobors in their past sufferings, the
two Quakers began to question them on their religious beliefs, that
Allen became discouraged.

*It soon appeared that they have no fixed principles; there was a studied
evasion in their answers and though they readily quoted texts, it is plain
they do not acknowledge the authority of Scripture, and have some very
erroneous notions. I was anxious to ascertain their belief respecting our
Saviour, but could learn nothing satisfactory . . . My spirit was greatly
affected and I came away from them much depressed.*[10]

Grellet was just as distressed by his encounter with the Doukhobors,
but he was a man with a more concrete mind, and he mingled his views
on the religious failings of his hosts with the first surviving description by
a western observer of Doukhobor religious practices. He tells how, as
soon as he and Allen arrived at Terpeniye, they were introduced to the
chief elder, 'ninety years old . . . nearly blind, but very active in body and

mind.' Fourteen other elders were also present, but it was the old man who answered most of the Quakers' questions. Grellet too found the Doukhobors evasive, but on some points they made no attempt to conceal views that scandalized the Quakers.

They . . . stated unequivocally that they do not believe in the authority of the Scriptures. They look upon Jesus Christ in no other light than that of a good man. They therefore have no confidence in Him as a Saviour from sin. They say that they believe there is a spirit in man to teach and lead him in the right way, and in support of this they were fluent in the quotation of Scripture texts, which they teach to their children; but they will not allow any of their people to have a Bible among them. . . . Respecting their manner of solemnizing their marriages, they declined giving an answer; but a very favourite reply to some of our questions was, 'The letter killeth, but the Spirit giveth life.' [11]

Leaving with a heavy heart for Altona, Grellet found himself unable to sleep, 'my mind being under great weight of exercise for the Duhobortski. I felt much for these people, thus darkened by their leaders, and I did not apprehend that I should stand acquitted in the Divine sight, without seeking for an opportunity to expostulate with them and to proclaim that salvation which comes by Jesus Christ.' It was this feeling that led him and Allen to ride out again to Terpeniye, arriving at ten o'clock in the morning when the Doukhobors were just about to begin one of their religious meetings.

They all stood, forming a large circle; all the men on the left hand of the old man, and the women on his right; the children of both sexes formed the opposite side of the circle; they were all cleanly dressed; an old woman was next to the old man; she began by singing what they call a psalm; the other women joined in it; then the man next to the old man, taking him by the hand, stepped in front of him, each bowed down very low to one another three times, and then twice to the women, who returned the salute; that man resuming his place, the one next to him performed the same ceremony to the old man, and to the women; then, by turns, all the others, even the boys, came and kissed three times the one in the circle above him, instead of bowing. When the men and boys had accomplished this, the women did the same to each other; then the girls; the singing continued the whole time. It took them nearly an hour to perform this round of bowing and kissing; then the old woman, in a fluent manner, uttered what they called a prayer, and their worship concluded;

but no seriousness appeared over them at any time. Oh, how my soul
bowed before the Lord, earnestly craving that he would touch their hearts
by his power and love. I felt also much towards the young people. I em-
braced the opportunity to preach the Lord Jesus Christ, and that salvation
which is through faith in Him . . .[12]

If Quakers, who in their time had been one of the most radical sects of
the Reformation in England, were shocked by Doukhobor beliefs and by
Doukhobor religious observances, which Allen found 'painful to witness',
it is not surprising that Orthodox Russian Christians should maintain their
hostility to the sect. By the time of Pinkerton's visit in 1816, there had
already been a perceptible shift in official attitudes towards the Doukhobors; it began on a local level and only afterwards became a matter of
national policy. The trouble appears to have been instigated by local
Orthodox churchmen and by renegade Doukhobors, including the turn-
frock priest Basilevskii; they found a willing accomplice in the military
governor of Kherson, a French émigré named Langeron, who was himself
a Roman Catholic.

The Doukhobors were accused of attempts to proselytize among the
Orthodox Russians who were now beginning to appear in the neighbourhood of Milky Waters. Sixteen of them were arrested, including Kiril
Kolesnikov, who was kept in prison for two years and then released because no substantial evidence had been obtained against him. In February
1816 the church appointed an investigator, Father Nalimskii, whose mission to Milky Waters reached the level of high farce; on the night of his
arrival he got drunk and made his way into the house of Nikolai Zak-
harov, where he started a fight with several of the Doukhobors. The
church authorities unhappily sentenced this exemplar of Russian Orthodox living to four months' confinement in a monastery, but they did not
cease their efforts to harass the colonists at Milky Waters. On 19 July,
Kapustin was arrested at their insistence, and, though he was in poor
health and seventy-three years of age, he was kept in prison under harsh
conditions and subjected to interrogations that sometimes lasted for a
whole day; he admitted none of the charges laid against him of perverting
the faith of Orthodox Russians, and eventually he was released.

The Doukhobors now approached Langeron, who visited the Milky
Waters at this time, with a plea for redress. He drove them out of his
presence with threats and abuse, shouting: 'You know neither God nor
Emperor: if I were Emperor I would shoot you all down!'[13] He also proposed in public that the Milky Waters settlement should be dispersed and

its members sent to live among people like the Turks, who were neither Christians nor Russians. When Alexander heard of Langeron's statement, through a petition submitted by two of the Doukhobor elders, he naturally disapproved of the resistance on the part of a local official to his own liberal policies; he pointed out that the persecutions of the Doukhobors for the three decades up to 1801 had succeeded merely in increasing their numbers, and that Langeron's attempt to revive such practices 'will not reform the Doukhobors, but will further incense them.' [14] By a decree dated 9 December 1816, Alexander actually improved the status of the Doukhobors by changing their category from that of a heretical sect under the minister of police to that of colonists under the minister of the interior, a liberal freemason named Kozodavlev. At the same time Lavinskii, the civil governor of Taurida, was instructed to carry out an investigation into the charges of immoral living and of giving refuge to fugitives that were brought against the Doukhobors. He reported that he had found nothing amiss at Milky Waters, and recommended that no change should be made in the treatment of the Doukhobors. The Doukhobors now became the centre of a feud between the military and civil officers of the region, since Langeron refused to accept Lavinskii's findings and angrily reported to Alexander that the Doukhobors were not Christians, but complete unbelievers. He also demanded satisfaction for what he claimed was the false accusation that he had expressed a wish to shoot the Doukhobors down. Alexander's opinion on this question is doubtless implied in his ironic answer to the irascible military governor. 'In accordance with the rules of the Christian religion, we must forgive our neighbours all injuries.' [15]

Langeron was unwilling to accept a rebuke even from the highest authority and, with the support of the archbishop of Ekaterinoslav, agitated for a further investigation. Lavinskii once again sent his officials to Milky Waters, where they arrested forty recent arrivals from Finland on suspicion of being deserters, but almost immediately released them; they could find no evidence of other irregularities.

Finally, on 2 January 1818 Lavinskii went personally to the settlement and delivered a report that completely exonerated the Doukhobors from the charges laid against them. He found them a quiet-living people who had no record of stealing from their neighbours, and who were severe with drunkards. They were industrious, had cultivated their lands extensively, and had good cattle herds and stud farms; as well as providing their own food, they made their own clothes out of linen and wool they themselves produced. All those suspected of being deserters or fugitives had

been able to furnish proof that they were covered by the decrees allowing exiled Doukhobors to settle in Milky Waters. As for the accusations
that the Doukhobors were attempting to proselytize, Lavinskii discovered
that the Doukhobors were hiring sixty Orthodox peasants as farm-
workers, but none of these had become Doukhobors, nor had any of the
inhabitants of the nearby Orthodox village of Novo-Aleksandrovsk,
whose people were in regular contact with the Doukhobors. Finally, the
report placed the blame for the unjust accusations on the ex-priest Basilevskii and on another former Doukhobor, Baev, who had been expelled
from the colony for hoarding grain.

Langeron again protested, declaring that Doukhobor heresies were
more dangerous than any others to the Christian faith and to Russian
morality, but the minister of the interior disagreed with him. The temporary rehabilitation of the sect in official eyes was consummated in May
1818, when Alexander, on a tour through Russia in the company of his
minister, Arakcheev, visited Milky Waters and stayed overnight in the
Orphan's Home. He attended a religious service and was impressed by the
appearance of order and efficiency in the colony. In his turn he accepted
a petition from the Doukhobors on behalf of some members of the sect
who had been flogged and sent to Siberia merely on religious grounds,
with the eventual result that these victims of persecution were allowed to
return from exile and join the colony at Milky Waters. From that time
onwards Alexander had a special place in the affections of Doukhobors,
and in later years he was even incorporated into the mythology of the
sect. A legend is still occasionally heard among Canadian Doukhobors
that in 1825 he did not really die in Taganrog, as was generally believed,
but secretly renounced earthly power, became a pilgrim, and eventually
arrived at Milky Waters, where he lived for a time in humble anonymity
among the Doukhobors whom he had once rescued from persecution.

The Doukhobors had been saved from the plots of Governor Langeron
and the archbishop of Ekaterinoslav by a fortunate combination of circumstances. As a group they still retained the strength they had acquired
through their reunion at Milky Waters. Throughout the inquiries they
were able to maintain a close-lipped unity, so that the two informers
against them found no support within the Community. If there were
army deserters living in the colony, their presence was well concealed.
The other main accusation against them, that of proselytization, appears
to have been exaggerated. Finally, they benefited from the liberalism that
persisted in certain St Petersburg circles right to the end of Alexander's
reign, so that the minister of the interior and other high officials were

ready to take up their cause in opposition to the reactionaries in the church and the military services.

But this happy situation depended really on two individuals, Alexander, the liberal tsar, and Kapustin, the dynamic leader. Alexander became steadily more conservative in the few years that were left to him after his visit to Milky Waters, and Kapustin disappeared under very curious circumstances. During November 1817 the elders of the village of Goreloye reported that their leader had died on 7 November and been buried on the following day. For some unknown reason, the local authorities became suspicious and ordered that his grave be opened. It contained the body of a man with red hair and whiskers; Kapustin's formerly black hair had on his last appearance been almost white, and he was clean-shaven. Ignoring this embarrassing discrepancy between the corpse and the living man, the Doukhobors persisted in their story of Kapustin's death; but the authorities retained their suspicions that he was still alive, and they were correct. Even some Doukhobor writers now admit that Kapustin, having recovered from his illness, decided to go into hiding to avoid further trouble. When August von Haxthausen visited Milky Waters in 1843 in connection with an investigation of Russian land tenure, the Mennonites showed him the cave where Kapustin had lived out his last years, withdrawn from all but his trusted intimates and protected by the habit of evasive answers that he had taught his followers. A fissure in the river bank, hidden by brushwood, led by a zigzag passage into a rock chamber in which there still stood a bed and a rusting stove; light and air were provided by a wooden tube that went up to the surface of the ground and was also concealed by bushes. From this retreat Kapustin, the invisible presence, guided the Doukhobors until his death in 1820.

After Kapustin's death the system of hereditary leadership that he had imposed upon the Doukhobors began to show its weaknesses. Kolesnikov and Kapustin had both been able men who, in different ways, understood the kind of diplomacy a radical sect must employ in order to survive relatively untroubled in the conditions of tsarist Russia; even Pobirokhin, despite his unfortunate visions of grandeur, had been a brilliant and forceful man, capable of inspiring and uniting his followers. Vasilii Kalmykov, Kapustin's twenty-eight-year-old son, who now succeeded to the leadership, was lacking in all the necessary qualities of intelligence, character, and charismatic attraction. He was a drunkard, concerned only with his own pleasures, who neglected Doukhobor affairs to such a degree that power shifted out of his hands into those of the oligarchy of elders. In the remaining years at Milky Waters the Doukhobor sect held together more by the strength of its institutions and its beliefs, and by the shared memories of persecution, than by the quality of its leadership, which reached its lowest level during the extremely difficult years between 1820 and 1840.

The death of Alexander I in 1825 meant the final end of the interlude of relative tolerance that Russian sectarians of all kinds had enjoyed during the first two decades of the nineteenth century. It is possible that even had he lived, the trend of events would not have been very much different. In the last years of his reign the liberals and freemasons who had shared in shaping his early policies were already losing their influence; conservatives like the sinister Count Arakcheev and the fanatical Filaret, archbishop of Moscow, were taking their place in the emperor's councils. Some years before the emperor's death, the policy adopted towards the Doukhobors by the central government was obviously wavering between the earlier liberalism and a stricter administrative attitude, reflecting the differences of opinion among the tsar's advisers.

As early as 1817, for example, an announcement was made in the council of ministers that the emperor had decided not to allow any more Doukhobors to join the settlement at Milky Waters, but this decision was only partially put into practice, since the emperor often proved accommodating when he received an actual petition from a group of Doukhobors who wished to join their fellows. Later, in 1820, a curiously ambiguous government ruling declared that Doukhobors could not be exempted from civil duties but at the same time could not be forced to carry them out. In 1821 a decree was issued forbidding any further migrations to Milky Waters, though, as we have seen, a few Doukhobors did reach the colony until as late as 1824, after which the trickle of new arrivals was finally halted. In 1822 it was ordered that Doukhobor land holdings, which had grown considerably and without official sanction, should be reduced to the forty acres per soul allowed under the edict of 1802, and in the same year it was decreed that no Doukhobor should hold public office as a village headman or in any other capacity outside the Milky Waters colony. In 1824 the State Council decided that if Doukhobors did not carry out their duties, they should be taken to court and the judges should rule on their responsibilities. Only later, after the death of Alexander I, did the Russian authorities resort to autocratic administrative action.

The lingering doubts concerning future government policy towards the Doukhobors were quickly removed on the accession in 1825 of Alexander's soldier brother, Nicholas I. Nicholas was an absolutist by conviction, convinced that the maintenance of the Russian state depended on the very institutions the Doukhobors most fervently opposed, the army and the Russian Orthodox Church. In his autocratic code it seemed appalling that such acts as the refusal of military service should be condoned, and so, from the beginning of his reign, he opposed leniency towards pacifist sectarians. His attitude was hardened by events that seemed to threaten his rule, such as the Decembrist uprising of liberal army officers in 1825 and the nationalist insurrection of the Poles in 1830. These were the acts of political rebels, while the Doukhobors were religious dissenters, but this difference did not seem important to Nicholas, who recognized the opposition to his own absolutist rule implicit in the Doukhobor rejection of the claims of human government. A further special reason for his antagonism was that the Doukhobors were making converts among the Cossacks. The loyalty of the Cossacks was important to the imperial government because they were used not only to defend the southern and eastern border regions threatened by half-civilized tribes, but also internally to deal with civil disturbances where the ordinary conscript army could not be trusted; any weakening of the Cossack military tradition was a danger to the state that could not be tolerated.

The autocratic attitude of Nicholas was undoubtedly more popular among local officials than Alexander's liberalism, and it was inevitable that from 1825 onwards the pressure on the Doukhobors should increase. Almost immediately after his accession Nicholas began to turn his attention towards the problem, and on 6 February 1826 he issued his first decree relating to the sect.

It was directed partly at the Doukhobors already at Milky Waters and partly at those who were still scattered outside the colonies. The latter were the most harshly treated. Serfs who succumbed to the Doukhobor heresy were to be sent for military service or, if unfit, to be exiled to Siberia; fugitive serfs who had made their way to Transcaucasia were rounded up and conscripted. On the other hand, Don Cossacks who became converted to Doukhobor beliefs (as some did during the 1820s) were to be sent to the Caucasus, where it was thought they would have to defend their lives and property, arms in hand, against the mountain tribes and thus be weaned of their pacifistic inclinations. Doukhobor religious services and the teaching of Doukhobor doctrines in public were to be forbidden. The decree even contemplated dealing with free Doukhobors by scattering them so that each family would live in a different Russian Orthodox village and by parting children from their parents; by this method it was thought that they would be more susceptible to the influence of the local priests who sought their reconversion. As for the Doukhobors at Milky Waters, they were left relatively undisturbed, and Nicholas actually rejected a proposal of his advisers that they should be transported to Siberia and there broken up into small settlements placed well apart from each other; for the time being they were merely to be deprived of passports so that they could not travel or earn money away from their own villages, and every effort was to be made to render contact with the Orthodox population as difficult as possible.

But neither harsher measures against the Doukhobors scattered over the empire nor the attempt to isolate the Milky Waters settlement were enough to remove the dangers Nicholas saw in the continued existence of such a sect, and soon an attempt was made to reimpose military service on the Milky Waters Doukhobors. Though the right to hire substitutes was recognized generally in Russia, as far as the Doukhobors were concerned it was steadily more restricted; while in 1834 they were allowed to find substitutes among the local Moslem Tartars, in 1839 they were restricted to finding them either in their own sect or among the pacifistic Molokans who were their neighbours. To deal with those soldiers who became converted to Doukhoborism while in the army, a more savage policy than mere imprisonment and exile was adopted. In peacetime they were flogged through the ranks, and a number of them died in the process, while during the Russo-Turkish war of 1828–9 Nicholas ordered that those who refused to bear arms should be placed in forward positions where they were certain to be killed.

Savagery might solve the problem of Doukhoborism within the armed forces, but the Milky Waters settlement presented a different and more complex problem. When Alexander allowed the colony to be founded in 1801, the province of Taurida was still an unopened frontier, and the dissenting sects were its pioneers. By the 1830s the region was becoming settled, and this meant that the Doukhobors were slowly being surrounded by Orthodox Russians who, even if they were not swayed by the doctrines of the sect, looked at its prosperity and wondered at the rewards of dissent. Thirty years earlier the Doukhobors had been an asset to a liberal administration; now they were an embarrassment to an autocracy, and the government began to look for an excuse to end the Milky Waters experiment and give away the rich lands to the Orthodox farmers who envied the Doukhobors.

A sombre and obscure series of events within the Community provided Nicholas with his excuse and his opportunity. Vasilii Kalmykov's drunken reign came to an end with his death in 1832, and he was succeeded by his son Ilarion, a weak and degenerate youth of sixteen who quickly followed his father's example of drunkenness and became a mere puppet of the council of elders. What happened then is obscured by a tangle of rumours and accusations emanating partly from the Mennonites, who never approved of the Doukhobors, and partly from the tsarist authorities, and complicated by the imaginativeness—or perhaps the credulity—of an account that Baron von Haxthausen wrote as a result of his visit to Milky Waters in 1843, after the majority of the Doukhobors had left.

Even in Kapustin's day tales had spread among the Mennonites of drunken orgies in the Orphan's Home, and when Vasilii Kalmykov became leader it was said that the girls who sang in the Orphan's Home were virgins only in name and that the elders and the living Christ joined them in elaborate sexual orgies. Later, on the accession of Ilarion Kalmykov, the elders allegedly provided him with a succession of six virgins to ensure the maintenance of a hereditary succession. The Orphan's Home became a den of crime, according to Orest Novitskii, and though all the Doukhobors at Milky Waters knew what was happening, none of them dared to reveal it.[16]

It is impossible to pass definitive judgement on any of these stories, since they are not supported by the evidence of actual witnesses. It is true that in some millenial sects the elect have been regarded as above sin and sexual activity has been elevated to a manifestation of spirituality; this was certainly the case among the Brethren of the Free Spirit and the Bohemian Adamites in western Europe. But nothing in the early doctrines of the Doukhobors has been revealed, even by their enemies, that suggests they had reached such conclusions and put them into practice. Accusations of sexual excesses were accepted ammunition in religious disputes up to the end of the nineteenth century, and these particular allegations against the Doukhobors at Milky Waters must be treated with the skepticism one normally accords sixteenth-century Protestant stories of mass fornications in nunneries. Significantly, the tsarist authorities, who made use of every plausible accusation against the Doukhobors on expelling them from Milky Waters, had nothing to say about sexual misdemeanours.

But such tales—whether true or not—are merely the light relief to the graver accusations levelled at the Doukhobors during the 1830s, when the allegations of immorality were deepened into charges of mass murder. Sinister rumours began to spread among the neighbours of the Doukhobors; their substance is contained in Haxthausen's account :

The Council of Elders constituted itself a terrible inquisitional tribunal. The principle, 'Whoso denies his God shall perish by the sword,' was interpreted according to their caprice; the house of justice was called Rai i muka, *paradise and torture; the place of execution was on the island at the mouth of the Malotchnaya. A mere suspicion of treachery, or of an intention to go over to the Russian Church, was punished with torture and death. Within a few years about two hundred people disappeared, leaving scarcely a trace behind.*[17]

The above quotation is from the English edition of Haxthausen's account, which appeared in 1856. In the French edition, published in 1847, nine years nearer the events of which he talks, Haxthausen's allegations are even more astonishing. 'Dans le courant de deux années, près de 400 individus disparurent à jamais, sans laisser presque de traces.'[18]

The stories of death and torture in the idyllic setting of the Orphan's Home were not unwelcome to the tsarist authorities, who carried out judicial investigations which lasted for five years, from 1834 to 1839. According to Novitskii, in spite of the evasive and unco-operative attitude that the Doukhobors all adopted, twenty-two bodies of murdered people were exhumed; some of them had been buried alive and others beheaded and mutilated.

This is the substance of the indictment as far as it can be presented nearly 130 years afterwards. The lacunae and the inconsistencies are obvious. Haxthausen, by tampering with his own figures, shows the unreliability of his second-hand information. His first figure of four hundred dead, almost one tenth of the whole population of the colony, is clearly absurd, since terror on such a scale would have led to mass escapes from Milky Waters and there is no suggestion that any such escapes did take place, nor did any Milky Waters Doukhobor at the time of the alleged massacres make any statement about them. A total conspiracy of silence over such a horrifying series of events seems beyond the possibility of belief.

If we reject Haxthausen as irresponsible and unreliable—as obviously we must—there remain the findings of the government investigation. The report of this investigation has never been published as a whole or read by a single scholar, and whether it exists today no one knows. Some facts from it were released, and there is no reason to doubt the discovery of twenty-two corpses by the investigators. But we do not know how the mode of death was determined. We do know, on the other hand, that Langeron, the Doukhobors' old enemy of twenty-three years before, took part in the inquiry, and Aylmer Maude repeats the ugly rumours that circulated at the time that 'the whole of the property of the Orphan's Home . . mysteriously disappeared after it had been taken charge of by the officials.' [19] The one document stating clearly the government's case is the proclamation issued by Prince Vorontsov, governor-general of New Russia and Bessarabia, on 26 January 1841, giving the reasons for the tsar's decision to expel the Doukhobors from the Milky Waters colony. The preamble is quoted at length because it shows so admirably the clash of two systems of divine right, that of the tsars and that of the Doukhobors, and because it puts forward the overt reasons for the departure by Nicholas 1 from the policy of his predecessor; Alexander's liberalism is condemned by implication.

 . . . *You, the Doukhobors, have denied the dogmas adopted centuries ago by the state church, and, as much by ignorance as by error, you have formulated and accepted peculiar beliefs which are incompatible with the inner peace of the Church. Not content with placing yourselves in opposition to religion, you have, by your conduct and your acts, disturbed the public peace. As stubborn law-breakers, resisting orders from above, you have already long merited severe punishment: but the Emperor Alexander, trusting in God, hoped that by kindness and forgiveness you might be led to the path of duty and truth. In fatherly forbearance and indulgence, he agreed not only to forget all your faults and to turn away from your guilty heads the punishment you deserved, but he also commanded that instead of your being, as in the past, scattered in many places and living— so to speak—in hiding, you should be brought together in a single community by assigning to you broad lands with all the uses and privileges attached thereto. For all these favours and benefits he demanded of you only that you should respect the laws, live in peace and refrain from disturbing the public peace. In what way have you shown your appreciation of all these indulgences? Hardly were you installed on your new property than in the name of your beliefs and at the orders of your religious leaders, you committed atrocious acts; you tortured and persecuted men whom afterwards you put to death; you gave asylum to malefactors and criminals who had escaped from the hands of justice; you screened and hid from the knowledge of authority the crimes and misdeeds of your brothers, and not for a single instant did you cease to be rebels, insubmissive to government. It is for these acts, contrary to all divine and human laws, that many of you have been thrown into prison and will receive a deserved punishment.*

All your crimes have been discovered, and the innocent blood which you have shed calls down upon your guilty heads the rigours of the law. By your actions you have rendered youselves unworthy of the indulgence and pardon which were granted to you by His Majesty, and you have exhausted the patience of the authorities, who in the end are convinced that the public peace demands that you should be transferred into distant regions where you will no longer be injurious to your fellow men. Informed of all your misdeeds, His Imperial Majesty has ordered that all individuals belonging to the harmful sect of the Doukhobors shall be colonised in the Transcaucasian provinces.[20]

At this distance in time, with no access to the report of the judicial commission and no contemporary statements by the condemned sectarians, it is difficult to pass more than a tentative judgement on the case against the Doukhobors. However, it seems unlikely that, even in the days of Nicholas I, the findings of an investigation that lasted five years could be wholly fabricated. Unfortunately, the cruelties of religious fanatics are more clearly and commonly established in history than the sexual promiscuity of minority sects, and it is not impossible that at one moment in their history the Doukhobors, isolated at Milky Waters like the Anabaptists in Münster, should have found the sense of their divine mission becoming so demanding that destruction did not seem too bad a fate for the heretical. Pobirokhin appointed his 'death-bearing angels', and while they may originally have dispensed the spiritual death of excommunication, the temptation to reinforce such a punishment with a physical death is one from which many Christian sects have suffered, the established churches most of all.

We are inclined to believe that, though Haxthausen's allegations must be dismissed as exaggerated, a few murders were in fact committed within the Milky Waters colony in the early 1830s, and that certain of the elders must have been responsible. In this connection Aylmer Maude, who claims to have heard Doukhobors in Canada admitting that misdeeds among their ancestors led to the expulsion from Milky Waters, makes a shrewd point:

It should . . . be noticed that whereas the Doukhobors have at other times stood up to the Russian Government with great courage and tenacity, they, on this occasion, submitted in a way suggesting that they had lost confidence in themselves and in their Leader.[21]

The Doukhobor historians have been noticeably reticent with regard to the deaths at Milky Waters; at most they are inclined to suggest, as

Koozma Tarasoff does, that the case is not proven. But Tarasoff does make one telling point, when he asks: 'Even when certain criminals are found within the Doukhobor community, was it justifiable to condemn the whole group?' [22]

This question immediately casts suspicion on the motives underlying the actions of the tsarist authorities, for clearly the only crime of which the majority of the Doukhobors could be condemned was their obstinacy in refusing to submit to the Orthodox church and in refusing to give information to the civil authorities. Prince Vorontsov in his proclamation asserted that 'many' Doukhobors had been thrown in prison in connection with the murders and would receive their due punishment. (There is no actual record of the trial or sentencing of the culprits in these cases, and even Doukhobor traditions are silent about them.) In view of this statement it is difficult to see why the Doukhobors as a whole should also have been punished by losing their homes and going into exile in Transcaucasia. The real reasons for their expulsion are to be sought outside the context of the crimes committed at Milky Waters, which merely provided a convenient excuse for the drastic policy that was already in the minds of Nicholas and his advisers. Settled safely on the far side of the Caucasus, the Doukhobors would have little contact with members of the Russian Orthodox Church; their neighbours would be mainly Moslems, and it was hoped that the need to defend themselves from these marauding tribesmen would be a means of weaning the Doukhobors from their pacifism. Finally, Transcaucasia was, as Taurida had been forty years before, the new frontier, and the Doukhobors could once again serve by acting as pioneers the very state against which they rebelled; they were later to do the same on the Canadian prairies and in British Columbia.

With an air of great benevolence, the tsarist authorities made certain concessions to the emigrating Doukhobors. They were allowed to take their moveable belongings, while for their buildings they would be compensated by the government in accordance with the findings of a special commission. Those who had acquired real property (and this very clause shows that some of the Doukhobors had become individually wealthy) were allowed to sell it, or to cede it to the crown in return for compensation, by 15 May 1841. Those who decided to return to the Orthodox Church were exempted from the requirement to emigrate, were allowed to keep all their property, and were promised the tsar's protection and special favour.

The emigration began as soon as the roads into the Caucasus were passable in the spring of 1841. During that year eight hundred Doukhobors left Milky Waters. They included all those whom the tsarist authorities regarded as influential members of the sect, and they were led by Ilarion Kalmykov. In 1842 another eight hundred started out on the long road into exile, mounted in their covered wagons and singing their mournful psalms; nine hundred followed in 1843 and as many in 1844. By the time the few remaining emigrants left in 1845, more than four thousand had abandoned the rich, sunny lands north of the Crimea. The years of labour they had put into breaking the land and building the villages were lost to them, and those who had to sell their property or accept the compensation offered by the government received a derisory sum, while the funds and the properties of the Orphan's Home were lost to the Community.

Yet the feelings of the Doukhobors as they left the villages along the Milky Waters were not entirely sorrowful. They were leaving a place that, in their own barely admitted thoughts, was associated with a disturbing corruption of their ideals. They were going to a place where, as in the early days in Crimea, they would be out of sight of their enemies and able to run their lives in peace as they wished. Finally, they were fulfilling the role in which they have always seen themselves, the role of pilgrims destined to be wanderers on the face of the earth until the millenarian future promised in Kapustin's hymns.

Few preferred to make their peace with the tsar as the price for staying at Milky Waters. According to Novitskii, only twenty-seven families remained at first and accepted the Orthodox faith. These were rich Doukhobors, and they became richer by acquiring cheaply the properties left behind by their less materially minded brethren. Later on others returned, when they found that their faith was not sufficiently warming to counteract the cold of the Caucasus. According to the Soviet historian N. M. Nikol'skii, the community of lapsed Doukhobors at Milky Waters finally numbered a thousand.[23] A church was built for their special use, and they prospered as merchants, cattle dealers, and farmers; these were the members of the sect whose rebellion had been based originally on economic frustration. Now that their desire for material prosperity had been satisfied, they were quite content to return to orthodox society. It was the religious zealots and the poor, those whose varied hungers had not been satisfied, who went to the Caucasus. They formed the great majority of the sect. In all, no more than a quarter of the Doukhobors at Milky Waters elected to remain or returned afterwards; the rest refused to make their peace with Church and tsar, retained their ideals of pacifism and of Christianity outside the Church, and set off for the Caucasus with the comforting feeling that their very sufferings marked them as the elect.

3 CAUCASIAN EXILE

The Caucasian uplands to which long convoys of Doukhobors found their way each summer from 1841 to 1845 lay on those southern slopes of the great mountain range that had been won from the Turks little more than a decade before. It was classic frontier territory, in the sense that the tsar's peace ran only in the towns and the military settlements, and the mountainous regions were still for the most part unpacified. The people among whom the Doukhobors had been sent to live were tribes of warlike traditions who still carried arms and rarely hesitated to use them in personal feuds, tribal combats, or marauding raids on those who intruded into the fastnesses that they regarded as their own.

If man in the Caucasus was dangerous and unpredictable, nature was predictably harsh, and the Doukhobors, accustomed for more than a generation to the bland seacoast climate and the fertile soil of Milky Waters, must have sung their psalms in an even more mournful tone when they realized the conditions that now faced them. The first contingent settled in the province of Tiflis, five thousand feet up in the Mokryje Gory (Wet Mountains), where they founded nine settlements and established in their third village of Goreloye a new Orphan's Home. They had to find their way through roadless passes into a region as uncultivated as

Milky Waters had been in 1802, but far more forbidding. The landscape was so bare that one group of twelve trees that stood in strange isolation was credited by the Doukhobors with a miraculous origin; they believed the trees had been planted by early Christians to celebrate the twelve apostles and were self-renewing, dying to the roots and then springing up again fresh and green like the true Christian faith. Only the flowers in spring and summer softened the bleakness of the region; they were so brilliant and so abundant that the only memory of the Caucasus many old Doukhobors in Canada still retain is that of playing in childhood through the meadows enamelled with blossoms like a *millefiore* tapestry.

But the spring came late and the winter early in the Wet Mountains; the snow was deep and the frosts severe. Even on the southern slopes wheat ripened just once in three years; oats and barley were the most reliable grain crops, and they sometimes failed. The soil was poor even for vegetable growing, and only the grass grew thick and green.

In this new, hard, and in some ways terrifying environment the Doukhobors had at first little to rely on but their own steadfastness, since they now had almost no leadership. Ilarion Kalmykov, never much more than a puppet leader, died a few months after reaching the Caucasus and left two young sons, Vasilii and Peter. The weakness of the Kalmykovs emerged in Vasilii. 'Vasilii Larionovich's oddity', according to the Doukhobor historian Peter Maloff, 'consisted of usually wearing women's clothes and being usually in the company of girls while avoiding boys. It was said of him that he was physically abnormal from birth, i.e. half-man, half-woman. This, however, none knew exactly.' [1]

The more vigorous brother, Peter, was soon chosen as the future leader. But in 1841 he was still a child, and an elder named Levushka ruled temporarily in his place. For some reason that has not been remembered, Levushka offended the tsarist authorities and was sent to Siberia. In his place, the council of elders assumed regency and ruled the colony until, around 1856, Peter Kalmykov was regarded as possessed of the spirit of God and took over the dual roles of leader and living Christ.

In these circumstances the peasant vigour and independent resourcefulness of the Doukhobors showed itself to best advantage. Soon a second region of settlement, about a hundred and fifty miles away from the Wet Mountains in the province of Yelizavetpol, was opened to them; this had a more temperate climate, in which grain would ripen, and there they set up four more villages. They were joined by the Cossack Doukhobors who had been exiled earlier to the Caucasus, and, though there are no clear records, it seems likely that other members of the sect arrived who had not been part of the Milky Waters colony, for the growth in numbers was too great to be attributed to natural increase. Four thousand Doukhobors left Milky Waters in the early 1840s, but within half a century they had multiplied fivefold: Doukhobor estimates of their own population in the Caucasus about 1890 place it at approximately twenty thousand.[2]

Taking advantage of the great pastures in the Wet Mountains, the Doukhobors in this region abandoned their traditional agricultural pattern for an almost entirely pastoral economy, based on large herds of horses and cattle and on flocks of sheep. Since they were not yet vegetarians, these animals provided much of their food; and they imitated their mountaineer neighbours by adopting a winter garb of sheepskin coats, with the fur worn inside, and sheepskin caps. A regular exchange of cattle for grain and fruit went on between the Wet Mountains and the Yelizavetpol colonies, and eventually the Doukhobors built up a considerable trade in their cattle and horses with outside communities and with the military authorities of the Caucasus. In fact, by hard work and adaptability they overcame the disadvantages of their new situation to such an extent that the period from about 1850 to 1890 was perhaps the most prosperous in Doukhobor history.

It was a prosperity that smiled on some more than on others. No attempt was made in the Caucasus until the 1890s to re-establish the complete communism of the early years at Milky Waters. The pastures and the meadows for growing hay were held in common, but the herds were owned individually and the soil was tilled in individual plots; these were in the possession of large joint families not unlike those that survive in modern India, in which the sons, even after marriage, continued to work under the supervision of the father, and the eldest of them took over the patriarchal role on the father's death. There also appear to have been a few artels or co-operative workshops run by Doukhobor craftsmen.

Though public opinion demanded that no one in the Community should actually want, and the prosperous could usually be shamed into providing for the poor, a class system soon began to appear, as at Milky Waters, and there were rich peasants who employed their less fortunate neighbours. In fact something very near to a Doukhobor aristocracy arose among families like the Verigins, the Kotel'nikovs, the Vereshchagins, the Podovinnikovs, the Kolesnikovs, and the Gubanovs, all of whom were in some way connected with the ruling Kalmykov dynasty and for this reason considered themselves superior to the ordinary Doukhobor peasant. Their pretensions revealed themselves not only in larger herds and more splendid clothes, but also in their houses built of wood, a material so expensive and difficult to get in the treeless Wet Mountains that most of the people lived in adobe houses with sod roofs.

The leaders continued to govern from the Orphan's Home, which in the 1860s was reconstructed on an elaborate scale. It consisted of two buildings, a brick-built hall for the people to gather in their sobraniia and a two-storey wooden building that became the residence of the leader and his favourites and assistants. One of the latter was the ataman, who acted as a kind of steward and was responsible for collecting reports on the crops and herds and the general condition of the Doukhobor villages. In each village a portion of land was set aside as an endowment for the Orphan's Home, and this was worked communally by the local people, who also cared for the herds and flocks belonging to the Orphan's Home. In addition, individual farmers were expected to make contributions to the Orphan's Home, and these may well have been in the form of a tithe based on production. Out of such diverse assets the Orphan's Home built up a communal fund; its exact amount was never divulged by any leader and is still a matter of conjecture among students of Doukhobor history; estimates vary between 500,000 and 2,000,000 roubles, of which some was deposited in a bank in Tiflis, while the greater portion was kept in gold and silver in the coffers of the Orphan's Home itself.

These funds were used to maintain the leader and his associates; there appears to have been no thought in the minds of pious Doukhobors of questioning in any way the expenditure or style of life of the living Christ. Indeed, when prosperity came to the Transcaucasian settlements, the ordinary people seem to have gained a vicarious satisfaction from the splendour which their leaders, imitating the Moslem chieftains of the region, began to affect. Yet it would be unjust to suggest that all the wealth accruing to the Orphan's Home was consumed by the leaders; the common granaries of the Orphan's Home were available to all Doukhobors in times of poor harvests, and the funds were used to succour distress on those admittedly not very frequent occasions when an old person or an orphan or even a hopelessly alcoholic peasant had no one who would assume responsibility for his welfare. Contributions to the Orphan's Home also formed a kind of primitive insurance, since if a Doukhobor family were impoverished by a fire or by the theft of its herds by marauding Moslem tribesmen, it would be helped by the Orphan's Home. In addition, the leaders and their atamans continued to pay the taxes for the community as a whole from the funds collected by the Orphan's Home. Perhaps it would be inaccurate to call the Orphan's Home a communistic institution; rather, it combined in miniature the functions of a palace, a Vatican, a treasury, and a welfare centre.

The prosperity of the Doukhobors came largely from their ability to adapt themselves to the harsh mountain climate and from the vigour with which they set about transforming their tracts of roadless wilderness into civilized settlements dotted with villages. But they were also assisted by the unexpected benevolence of external human circumstances. Having expelled the Doukhobors from Milky Waters, the tsarist authorities, who were troubled with other internal problems and with the international tensions leading up to the Crimean war, appear to have left them comparatively unmolested, doubtless at first in the hope that their new environment would be sufficient to break down their obstinacy. For almost fifty years the banishment of Doukhobors to Siberia was extremely rare, while the Orthodox Church wielded little power in this frontier region and was certainly in no position to harry the sectarians of various beliefs who were settled in pockets through the mountains. Military service was no longer a problem, since the Doukhobors were doubly protected from it: their settlements were technically, according to the terms of their exile, penal colonies, and therefore exempt from conscription, which was not in any case introduced into the Caucasus until 1874.

Moreover, with the death of the martinet Tsar Nicholas I in 1855 and the accession of Alexander II, the liberator of the Russian serfs, the spirit of the first Alexander's early days was reborn, and the local representatives of the tsarist government, who were not without admiration for the Doukhobor achievements in the Caucasus, began to look on them with a certain benevolence. There was also a general renewal of interest in the pioneering of marginal areas, particularly as farmers and herders like the Doukhobors helped to feed the army units that guarded the frontiers and so reduced the difficulties and expenses of extended supply lines. For this reason, not only were the Doukhobors in the Caucasus handled generously during the reign of Alexander II, but when Russia gained control of the Amur region in the 1850s, their brethren who had remained in Siberia at the time of the Milky Waters settlement were encouraged to establish pioneer villages along the banks of the Amur river.

If the authorities became in practice more benevolent than they appeared at the time when the Doukhobors were sent into exile, the native tribes of the mountains did not prove the kind of menace that everyone had anticipated. The legendary and often accepted reason for this was given by Aylmer Maude in the brief account he wrote of the Doukhobors during the 1890s.

The wild hill tribes were favourably impressed by their non-resistant neighbours, who, when molested, neither retaliated nor sought police protection; and on coming to know the Doukhobors, the Mohammedan tribes in their vicinity decided that they were a worthy people deserving protection, and that they were certainly not Christians. 'We know the Christians,' said they; 'the Christians always fight.' These new-comers evidently belonged to a better religion, for they tried to return good for evil. So the Mohammedans concluded that this sober, God-fearing, industrious folk were inheritors of the True Faith, which they—the ignorant Mohammedan natives of the district—had forgotten or neglected.

Later, in 1904, Maude amended his opinion in a significant footnote in which he cast doubt on the authenticity of this story. 'It was current among those who sympathized with the Doukhobor migration, but I am afraid it hardly tallies with what little is authentically known of the relation of the Doukhobors to other sects and tribes.' [3]

The evidence indeed seems to support Maude in his second version and to suggest that the Doukhobors owed their immunity from major interference on the part of the native tribes to circumstances other than their meekness of behaviour. First of all, they were a cohesive and numerous group; and individually most of them were physically superior to their hillmen neighbours. Then, they impressed the native peoples by their industry and by their great herds, from which a few cows and horses might occasionally be discreetly rustled to feed the Moslem villages; moreover, they pleased them by their dedication to the virtue of hospitality, which is traditionally valued among Moslems : many a wild village chief was inhibited from plundering a Doukhobor herd because he had broken bread with its owner. Something of the relationship between the local peoples and the leading Doukhobor families can be appreciated from the account given by the Doukhobor Vasilii Nikolaevich Pozdniakov, who was born in the Caucasus in 1869, of the Verigin family of Slavyanka in the Yelizavetpol settlement, later to provide a Doukhobor ruling dynasty that has not yet come to an end.

Being rich the Verigins could not find their equals among the simply living Doukhobors and had to look for friends elsewhere. The country near Slavanka is inhabited by many Tartars, Mohammedans, known as desperadoes and robbers. Many of them are polygamists and particularly the nobility. Much of the land belongs to their petty Princes, and the peasants are generally very dependent from the landlords and sharply treated by them. The Verigins were on best terms with the Tartar Princes;

they visited frequently each other and this acquaintance was not without influence on them.

The four elder sons of Verigin were also illiterate and were spending most of their time in the mountains, looking after the cattle. There they made themselves famous by their intrepidity and even the Tartars feared them.[4]

This passage suggests that the leading Doukhobors competed with the Tartars in both hospitality and at least the threat of violence, and there is evidence that in fact Doukhobors during this period did occasionally shoot cattle rustlers and robbers who attacked their farms. Certainly, when the arms of the Doukhobors were burnt in 1895 in a mass return to pacifism, the piles of richly ornamented muskets and pistols rose remarkably high, and were set off with thunderous salvoes from many barrels of gunpowder. Some of these weapons were used by the bodyguards that the Doukhobor leaders of the Transcaucasian period employed to escort them on their journeys from village to village and between the widely scattered settlements; two of them are portrayed in a surviving photograph, armed *cap-à-pie* with swords, long ornamented daggers, Colt revolvers, and bandoliers stuffed with rifle cartridges. There is no record of the bodyguards' ever having been involved in battle, but their very existence indicates that at this period the Doukhobors lost their faith in the power of non-violence to such an extent that they were willing to exploit the deterrent possibilities of a show of armed might to impress their fiercer neighbours. Their mild neighbours, such as the Armenians, often entered the employment of the richer Doukhobors as shepherds and manual labourers, and in time they formed a kind of marginal proletariat, largely dependent on the Community without sharing its religious faith.

Information on the Doukhobors in the Caucasian period is more copious and varied than it is for any previous phase, mainly because in the 1890s the sect attracted the attention of Tolstoy and his disciples, and a little later, on moving to Canada, came into contact with other literate and literary people who recorded whatever the Doukhobors might be disposed to reveal of their recollections. All this evidence points to the fact that, as the preceding pages will already have suggested, the Doukhobors of the 1860s and 1870s were very different in their way of life, if not in the beliefs they expressed, from the mixture of poor peasants, discharged soldiers, fugitive serfs, and army deserters with changed names who came together at Milky Waters two generations before. They had become welded into a Community that, in abandoning equality, had—to all appearances—loosened its hold on those ideals of the simple and peaceful life with which Doukhoborism began. Perhaps such a development became inevitable as soon as the first breach in equality came with the acceptance of the divinely inspired leader and his oligarchy of elders; certainly it was encouraged by the personalities of the two leaders who governed the fate of the Doukhobors from the middle of the 1850s to the middle of the 1880s.

Peter Kalmykov grew up to have a more dynamic personality than any of the dull and shadowy predecessors who bore his family name. The strength of will that had characterized Kapustin was born again in him, and for the first time in a quarter of a century the elders found their power curbed by an imperious hand. But if Peter Kalmykov possessed the force of character of his ancestor in leadership, he did not share his spiritual interests. The whole Kalmykov period, in fact, is characterized by the lack of the new psalms and hymns that have always signified a time of religious activity among the Doukhobors; from the death of Kapustin in 1820 to the emergence of the Verigin dynasty in 1887, the Living Book almost ceased to grow, and material achievements took its place. Peter Kalmykov typified this development. He took part in the religious life of the Community in an almost purely formal way; his real passion was hunting. This lean, tense man enjoyed nothing so much as to rove the valleys and mountains of his domain in search of game. He liked also, when he rested from hunting, to refresh himself with vodka, and in his cups he was liable to displays of bad temper in which he would beat and insult his followers. This behaviour had at least the advantage of scaring the Doukhobors into obedience, and, despite his love of drinking, Peter Kalmykov appears to have been a fairly shrewd manager who had an uncanny knack of detecting dishonesty in his elders. He was also the first of the Doukhobor leaders to proclaim the doctrine of 'Do as I say, not as I do', supporting his conduct by the rather ingenious explanation that he was the Christ whose fate and duty it was to sin and behave outrageously so that, by offering his people the temptation of his example, he might test their steadfastness in maintaining the Doukhobor doctrine.

But Peter Kalmykov's greatest contribution to Doukhobor history was his marriage, in 1856 at the age of 20, to a grey-eyed girl of sixteen, Luker'ia Vasil'evna Gubanova. Luker'ia was a girl with a strength of will equal to that of her husband, and an intelligence and a truth of character far surpassing his. He tried to break her will in the early years of their marriage and failed; Luker'ia took seriously the equality of women that is at least theoretically acknowledged in Doukhobor doctrine (women as well as men are vessels of the divine spark), and in the end her husband, who despised those who gave in to his tantrums, cherished her as a personality just as much as in the beginning he had admired the prettiness of her face and the grace of her movements. How much he appreciated her his last act showed. In 1864, when he was about 28, Peter Kalmykov was stricken by an intestinal sickness while hunting, and within three days he was dead. His marriage had produced no children, and as the faithful gathered around his deathbed, the feeling uppermost in almost every mind was not so much grief for the departing leader as anxiety as to who would follow him. At last one of the elders plucked up his courage enough to ask the dying man to name his successor. Peter roused himself and pointed to Luker'ia. 'I am leaving you to my little cuckoo.'

As Russians, the Doukhobors were not unaccustomed to the rule of women, for during the eighteenth century there had been four reigning tsarinas. Luker'ia was the first and only woman leader among the Doukhobors, but it was accepted without opposition that the Holy Spirit had entered into her, and her accession went unopposed. The trust that the Doukhobors placed in this vigorous young woman was not misplaced. 'She was clever and had a certain kind of good nature, for which she was beloved by everyone who knew her,' recalled Vasilii Pozdniakov, twenty years after her death. 'Her management was so intelligent and peaceful that the Doukhobors remember her until now with best feeling.'[5] And in terms of material happiness, the twenty-two years of Luker'ia's reign were the golden age of Doukhobor history.

Luker'ia was a woman of few pretensions. 'I am only a woman' was a phrase often on her lips, and, if she did not choose to offend her followers by anything so radical as a denial of the doctrine of divine leadership, her rule was distinguished by an absence of undue grandeur and by a strict practicality. In her brother Michael Gubanov, in the ataman of the Orphan's Home, Ivan Baturin, and in Alesha Zubkov, the *starosta* or chief elder of the village of Goreloye, she found a group of men who could be trusted with the day-to-day administration of the Community's affairs, particularly in the Wet Mountains colony, which remained the centre of Doukhobor administration in the Caucasus, though the establishment of villages in the Yelizavetpol district, a hundred and fifty miles away, and later in other scattered parts of Transcaucasia, inevitably involved a certain decentralization of administration and the rise of local ruling cliques, like the Verigins in Yelizavetpol. It also involved differing local interests that were later to help in producing rifts within the Doukhobor Community.

But in Luker'ia's reign those rifts were mere threats in the future, un-observed by most of the Doukhobors, and she herself created a certain unity among the scattered villages by refusing to allow the local officials to be more than administrators. She decided on the general policies of the Doukhobor Community, and in particular she kept in her own hands the vital matter of relations with the non-Doukhobor world. She was always on the road, travelling between the settlements and the villages, attended by her bodyguard in case of attack by the Moslem tribesmen. Her arrival in a village would mean a gala day of rejoicing; beginning with the wel-come of the villagers, ranged in a great V on the village green, the white-shawled women on the right and the men on the left of the table sym-bolically laid with its great peasant loaf of rye bread and its dish of salt; continuing in psalm singing and feasting; and ending in a kind of durbar at which Luker'ia, always approachable, would listen to the complaints and requests of her followers.

Often she acted as judge and the punishments she decreed were rough-and-ready, but usually effective, since, although illiterate, she had a native shrewdness of judgement. Thanks to the examples of the various Kalmy-kov leaders from Vasilii down to Peter, drunkenness had become wide-spread among the formerly sober Doukhobors, and while Luker'ia did not choose to do anything so drastic as forbidding the use or manufacture of vodka, she did attempt to stem its abuse by sending for known drunkards, calling on them to repent, and if they relapsed ordering a public whipping with twigs. To make an offender look and feel foolish was Luker'ia's favourite method of punishment. She was particularly anxious to stamp out wife-beating, from which she herself had suffered before she learnt to retaliate in kind, and her favourite punishment for husbands who offended in this way was to have them locked up in a chicken coop for the night. By the time a man had lived down the laughter of his neigh-bours after such an episode, he was usually willing to abandon the whip as an argument in domestic disputes.

Yet Luker'ia was far from being a severe ruler, and there was little of the puritan ascetic in her character. During her reign people lived as abundantly as they chose, and the tithes of the Orphan's Home were never so great as to be an excessive burden on the faithful. If communism had vanished, sharing where it was needed had not ceased. The man who had suffered a bad harvest was not allowed to go short; the small peasant who had lost his only cow would be supplied from the herds of the Or-phan's Home or from those of a richer peasant who had received an admonition from the leader. At the same time, Luker'ia made no attempt to curb the gaining of wealth by the richer families who were her friends or relatives, and who quickly surrendered to the example of conspicuous spending that was provided by neighbouring Moslem chieftains.

The weddings of the richer Doukhobors, in particular, became affairs of great ostentation. In theory, Doukhobor marriage is a simple and mutually revocable contract between two people who express their willingness to live together. No further ceremony is needed, though it is customary for the occasion to be marked by the singing of psalms. Under Luker'ia, however, extravagant and expensive wedding feasts, sometimes costing several hundred roubles, became customary among those who could afford them. Yet the Doukhobors never departed so far from their native simplicity as to resume the custom of the dowry. A girl who could work hard in the house and the farm brought her own contribution to the household into which she was received, and it was for her personal qualities that a family would seek a wife for its son. For this reason Doukhobor brides in the Caucasus were usually eighteen or nineteen, since by this time they had proved themselves as potential housewives, whereas their husbands were often two or three years younger; the usual age at which boys married in this period was sixteen.

There was another consideration: the Doukhobor ideal of feminine beauty was and remains the steatopygous earth-mother figure, well nurtured with starchy or creamy foods such as *bliny* (pancakes), *kasha* (millet gruel), *pirogy* (fruit or cheese puffs), and *borshch* (cream-laced cabbage and beetroot soup), the staple dishes of Doukhobor cooking, and buxom girls had a better chance of being well married than their slender sisters.

As we have already said, marriages at this period were often arranged with little regard for the feelings or wishes of the wedded couple, and the bride would have to live in a joint household under the vigilant eye of a formidable mother-in-law. Yet Doukhobors whose parents were married in this way in the Caucasus insist that such unions were often very successful and that divorces—which consisted in those days of a mere disavowal of the marriage partner—were much less common than they are today among Doukhobors who have become assimilated to Canadian mores and who marry according to the demands of romantic love.[6] Since Hindu marriages started in the same way are often extremely harmonious, it is quite possible that these claims are justified.

Luker'ia's period, even more than the early days at Milky Waters, represents the high point of good relations with the tsarist authorities, largely because, unlike Kapustin, Luker'ia made no attempt to conceal her position of authority in the Community and was willing to co-operate wherever she could with the local officials. At the Orphan's Home lavish hospitality awaited the civil servants and army officers who travelled through the Wet Mountains. When visitors were distinguished, Luker'ia would provide a feast for them, with excellent wines from the secret cellar of the Orphan's Home, and she is said to have astonished her guests by taking glass for glass of champagne with the hard-drinking officers. The local Armenians, who were less prosperous than the Doukhobors, enviously attributed the good treatment the latter received during Alexander II's reign to the more intimate favours that—they asserted—Luker'ia conferred upon the various governors-general of the Caucasus. There is no real evidence, however, that these officials esteemed her for anything more than her generous personality and her willingness to make their tasks easier by adopting a co-operative attitude.

No one esteemed her more than the Grand Duke Michael, the tsar's brother, who was appointed governor-general of Caucasia during the 1870s, and, with General Loris-Melikov in charge of the armed forces, conducted the campaigns against the Turks in this mountain region during the war of 1877–8. The grand duke had visited Goroloye on several occasions and it is possible that, knowing the pretensions of the Doukhobor leaders, he found a certain piquancy in enjoying the hospitality of a woman theocrat who treated him as an equal, addressing him by his Christian name and patronymic instead of using his honorific title, and who, at least in theory, set herself up as a rival to his brother's autocracy. But there was also a solid business-like aspect to their relationship. The Doukhobor farms provided food for the Russian forces fighting on the Turkish border, while the Doukhobor herds provided excellent remounts for the cavalry.

But this, in the end, was not enough. In order to bring the siege of the Turkish city of Kars to a successful conclusion before the winter of 1877 set in and the roads of the Caucasus became impassable, the grand duke needed to expand his transport services so as to keep the besieging forces well supplied with ammunition. The only people in a position to help him were the Doukhobors, who owned wagons and teams in plenty, and he accordingly set off over the mountain roads to Luker'ia's headquarters in Goreloye.

His proposition was a simple matter of political blackmail. The Doukhobors were threatened from two sides. If the siege of Kars failed it was conceivable that the Turks would invade Russian Transcaucasia, and in that event the farms and villages the Doukhobors had worked so hard to create would be pillaged and they themselves would be subjected to the whims of barbarous occupiers. On the other side, conscription had been introduced into the Caucasus in 1874, and by a mere stroke of the pen the grand duke could declare that the Doukhobor settlements were no longer penal colonies, in which case their young men would be liable to callup for active service in the firing line. But the tsar did not wish to force Luker'ia's followers to fight against their religion, and he would be content if the Doukhobors provided the men, the horses, and the wagons to form a transport column. He guaranteed that they would not be asked to take up arms and that they would always remain behind the firing line. And he promised good payment for their services.

Luker'ia was placed in a painful dilemma. If she agreed, it would mean that, even if indirectly, the Doukhobors would be going against their religion and supporting if not taking part in war. If she refused, she would commit her people to a campaign of passive resistance to oppression that she felt incapable of leading and that she suspected the Doukhobors themselves, softened by prosperity, might be unable to sustain. Her brother Michael and Zubkov, who over the years had become her right-hand business adviser, advised her to accept the grand duke's demand. She called the elders of the Wet Mountains villages together in an emergency meeting —there was no time to consult the villages of Yelizavetpol—and explained the situation. She was only a woman, she told them, and perhaps she would not have the strength to lead them in the trials that might come from refusal. But they must remember that this was only a temporary concession, just as the present was only a passing phase during which the Doukhobors were resting from their spiritual labours. Later a time would come when others would lead them again in the struggle for the kingdom of God. Sensing her dilemma and their own, they agreed; and within two weeks a great caravan of four hundred covered wagons from the villages of Yelizavetpol and the Wet Mountains camped in the meadows of Goreloye. Luker'ia gathered her people in a great sobranie and addressed the men who would be going on the only military campaign in Doukhobor history. If they should be given arms in bad faith, they must fire above the heads of the Turks; they must refrain from looting and succour the wounded of both sides. The assembled Doukhobors sang a parting psalm and the long trains of wagons began to trail down through the passes towards the front.

The Grand Duke Michael kept his word. No Doukhobor was forced to bear arms, and, except for a few men who were wounded slightly by shells that fell behind the lines, they all returned safely to their villages. The material rewards for the venture were great. According to one account the Doukhobors made a million and a half roubles out of providing transport.[7] In addition, they were offered a tract of fertile land in the mild climate of Kars, which had been captured from the Turks, and there Luker'ia moved five thousand of her poorer followers, who founded six new villages. At the same time a smaller additional tract was handed over to the sect in the province of Tiflis, where eight hundred people were settled in three villages. This was the peak of Doukhobor settlement in the Caucasus.

The late 1870s were in every way a time of increasing material prosperity. But they were also a time of growing moral crisis. Few people in the Doukhobor Community, and least of all their leader, were happy about the compromise with their principles that had earned them wealth and land and had bought immunity from persecution. It is notable that from this time Luker'ia Kalmykova became more puritanical in her behaviour. She began to forbid her followers to frequent the drinking houses run by the Armenians, and to regulate the consumption of vodka at weddings, which had become great occasions for drunkenness. Nevertheless, she felt herself incapable of resisting when the authorities began to drive deeper the wedge between Doukhobor principles and practice that the Grand Duke Michael had so adroitly inserted in 1877. During the following winter, soldiers were billeted in the Doukhobor villages. Then, in 1881, the Tsar Alexander II was assassinated by members of the People's Will Party, and this blow in the long battle between Russia's autocratic rulers and its revolutionary parties had its effect on the fate of the Doukhobors.

Embittered by the murder of his father and encouraged by his evil genius Pobedonostsev, Procurator of the Holy Synod, Alexander III turned back into the reactionary path of his grandfather Nicholas, and began an immediate policy of deliberalization. Alexander II's more enlightened advisers were dismissed, rigorous repression was applied not only to the violent activists who had been responsible for the death of Alexander II, but also to the mildest of reformers, and on the waves of the mounting government terror the influence of the Russian Orthodox Church and of the army once again became dominant in the councils of the tsar. The bishops advised a renewed repression of the sectarian minorities; the generals advised harsh measures against pacifists. From that time onwards there was talk of extending conscription to include the Doukhobors, and Luker'ia Kalmykova, who foresaw clearly enough what was likely to happen, is said to have advised her followers to submit until the coming of a leader who, she prophesied, would return to them the spiritual glories of the past and make them pilgrims once again. Some accounts tell that the conscription actually began during her life, but the decree making military service universal in the Caucasus and bringing the Doukhobors within its scope was not in fact issued until 1887, a few months after her death.

The surrender of 1877 had evidently put into Luker'ia's mind not only the thought that as a woman she did not have the strength to lead the Doukhobors in their traditional way, but also the desire to leave her growing realm in the hands of a successor who would regenerate the sect, and in 1882 she took under her tutelage the young man, Peter Vasil'evich Verigin, who was to become the most celebrated of all the Doukhobor leaders.

Peter Verigin's origin was to become a matter of mystery once he was taken into the Orphan's Home, but when he was a boy no one doubted that he was the son of Vasilii Verigin, one of the rich peasants of the Yelizavetpol village of Slavyanka. Vasilii was a member of the new aristocracy that had developed under Luker'ia's rule in the villages of the Caucasus, and at least one other Doukhobor, Vasilii Pozdniakov, remembered him with distaste.

He was totally illiterate—as almost all the Doukhobors were—and a man of harsh temper. Being once elected Elder of his village, he showed himself a real despot. He used to walk about in the village with a whip and to give lashes for the least disorder or disrespect. His fellow-countrymen were often sorry for having elected for themselves such a severe commander, and they were glad when . . . his term of service ended.[8]

Peter was the sixth of Vasilii Verigin's seven sons. He was born in 1859, on Peter's Day, the 29th of June, one of the few festivals the Doukhobors celebrated. Unlike his four eldest brothers, he was literate; Vasilii Verigin hired a tutor to educate his three youngest sons, Peter, Gregory, and Vasilii, and when they had gained a bare ability to read and write he set up a store for them to run in Slavyanka, an unusual enterprise among the Doukhobors, who—in spite of their acceptance of individual farming—were still inclined to disapprove of individual trading, which they left mostly to the Armenians.

As tall and robust as the rest of his family, Peter Verigin differed from his illiterate and extroverted elder brothers in exhibiting a withdrawn moodiness. He immersed himself in Doukhobor traditions and learnt by heart a great proportion of the Living Book, but his education also gave him a view wider than that of most sectarians, and as a youth he was already studying the Bible.

Peter Verigin attracted the attention of Luker'ia Kalmykova while he was still a boy; he was not only handsome and intelligent, but he was also of noble blood in Doukhobor terms, since his mother, Anastasia Verigina, was the granddaughter of Savelii Kapustin, and it was therefore conceivable that the Holy Spirit might inspire him to leadership. Luker'ia's interest expressed itself in a dramatic manner when at the age of twenty Peter married Evdokiia Grigor'evna Kotel'nikova, the daughter of the other leading family of Slavyanka. As soon as Luker'ia heard of the wedding, she set off in haste and anger from the Wet Mountains to the Yelizavetpol settlement. Since she could not now forbid the marriage, she ordered that it be dissolved. According to one of Peter's brothers, she told Anastasia Verigina that she had already selected Peter for a special purpose which must not be revealed, but which meant abandoning even his parents and dedicating himself to the service of God. She ordered peremptorily that the couple should be parted, and when the Kotel'nikov family refused to submit she insisted, contrary to all Doukhobor traditions, that the separation should be made official. The case was taken to the district court, where eventually the marriage was annulled; the Kotel'nikovs and their relatives became henceforward Peter's dedicated enemies. Evdokiia herself was pregnant when Peter finally left her and set off to join Luker'ia in the Orphan's Home at Goreloye, and shortly after his departure she gave birth to the child who was eventually to rule the Doukhobors in Canada as Peter the Purger.

Meanwhile Peter Vasil'evich Verigin became the pupil of Luker'ia Kalmykova; for many hours they would withdraw together to a rococo wooden tower she had specially built outside the Orphan's Home and that was forbidden to all others. Rumours flourished, particularly among non-Doukhobors, about their relationship. Was Peter the lover of Luker'ia? Or her son? Or perhaps both? Almost certainly he was neither, and the true explanation seems to be that which Prince Shervashidze, the governor of Tiflis, gave in a confidential report to the tsar some years after Lukeri'a Kalmykova's death.

Luker'ia . . . kept him in attendance, not as a courtier, but as an heir, preparing him, by frequent conversations and directions, for the exalted position due to his race, to the joy and happiness of all true-hearted Doukhobors; who, as a result of their education and the traditions of their sect, could not conceive of the possibility of doing without someone to replace Luker'ia and without having a God-Man at the head of the sect . . .[9]

This conclusion is supported by the hostility Peter's presence in the Orphan's Home immediately aroused among those who had formerly been closest to Luker'ia Kalmykova, her brother Michael Gubanov and Zubkov, her assistant in dealing with the business of the sect. Verigin interfered little with the running of the Orphan's Home, where he held no official position; he occasionally ran messages for Luker'ia to the outlying villages or took down from her dictation letters to government officials, but most of the time he spent with her appears to have been occupied with his training in the Doukhobor traditions and with his readings from the New Testament, which Luker'ia would interpret according to Doukhobor doctrines. It was this role as the pupil that angered Luker'ia's friends, who had always hoped that on her death the control of the Community would fall into their hands, with Gubanov exploiting his relationship to become leader and Zubkov, the more intelligent and capable of the two, retaining control of the treasury and guiding policy so as to continue a profitable co-operation with the tsarist authorities. Peter Verigin was proud and unpredictable; the one thing of which his enemies were sure was that he would not be easy to manipulate.

Even before Luker'ia Kalmykova's death the struggle between Verigin and his rivals appears to have passed beyond the confines of the Orphan's Home. Gubanov, Zubkov, and their group of supporters, centred on the village of Goreloye, developed into a rudimentary bureaucratic party and reaped the kind of unpopularity that comes quickly to all such groups; they were supported only by the richer Doukhobor peasants, particularly in the Wet Mountains colony. On the other hand, as it became evident that Peter Verigin was being groomed by Luker'ia Kalmykova for the sectarian leadership and that he was in conflict with Gubanov and Zubkov, he became without any great effort the unproclaimed crown prince of all those who were in opposition to the existing order. The young supported him because they were tired of the long rule of old men. (Zubkov had ruled over Goreloye with a hard hand for more than a quarter of a century.) The poor and those who were pioneering in the remoter settlements saw him as their champion against the rich and the settled. But, like many other leaders whose appeal has a radical populist character, he also enjoyed the loyalty of the fundamentalist devout, of all those old people who still carried in their minds the teachings of Pobirokhin and

Kapustin and who believed that the purity of Doukhobor acts and doctrines had been sullied by the years of prosperity.

The struggle came into the open with the death of Luker'ia in 1886.
During that summer she became too ill to rely any longer on the wise
women who cured Doukhobor sicknesses with herbs and spells, and went
down to consult the doctors in Tiflis while Peter went to Slavyanka,
where he is said to have seen his former wife Evdokiia. Luker'ia appears
to have made other visits to Tiflis, and on the last of these, according to
the account—quoted by Aylmer Maude [10]—of an exile from another sect
who happened to be living with the Doukhobors at this time, Peter accompanied her and telegraphed to Evdokiia to meet him in Tiflis. She
joined him, but Luker'ia learned of her presence and, after an angry outburst, fell down in some kind of a fit; she was taken back immediately to
Goreloye and died two days afterwards, having refused to see Peter again
or to recognize him as her successor. A different account of Luker'ia's last
days tells of her making a deathbed statement that she was leaving the
Doukhobors in Peter Verigin's charge and exhorting Gubanov and Zubkov
not to hinder his succession. Since the question of the leadership became
a bitterly fought issue immediately after her death, both versions must be
regarded with caution. All one can say with any certainty is that Luker'ia
Kalmykova never made a public avowal that Peter Verigin was to succeed
her; if she had done so it would have been impossible for his accession to
be disputed.

During the three days while Luker'ia's body lay in state, the two parties began their manoeuvres. Zubkov, Gubanov, and Ivan Baturin, the
manager of the Orphan's Home, told the mourning Doukhobors who
came from the outlying villages to pay their last respects to the dead
leader that no heir had been named, and that therefore the succession,
together with the managership of the Orphan's Home, fell to Gubanov as
her brother. It was at best a dubious argument, since the Doukhobor
leadership was and is regarded as hereditary, and Peter Verigin could
trace his descent from Kapustin, while Gubanov could not. But it was
convincing enough to win over the elders of Goreloye and a fairly strong
group of the more substantial peasants from other villages. Assured of
their support, Zubkov took the first step by telling Peter Verigin that he
must now leave the Orphan's Home, where the Gubanovs would hence-
forth rule. Verigin did not commit himself. 'I shall go if I must,' he said,
but he also insisted that he would be directed by the divine guidance and
would wait until the ceremony that is always held at the graveside six

weeks after a Doukhobor's death to celebrate the liberation of the soul from earthly ties and its entry into eternal bliss.

Verigin's actions during the intervening period were nicely calculated to appeal to his most likely followers, the poor and the pious. When he was asked about the leadership he would adopt an air of mystery, and instead of answering directly would put on a prophetic air and announce that the second coming of Christ was at hand. Vasilii Pozdniakov was then seventeen, and the strange events of that time remained vividly in his mind when he came to write of them many years later.

Verigin's words were spreading rapidly and interpreted differently. Very soon a party of his friends was formed around him and they suggested to the people that he himself is the Christ. Some of them were saying, they had been told by the late woman-manager [Luker'ia] that Verigin shall judge all the universe; others had seen him doing miracles; and an old man was relating that the night of Verigin's birth he had seen a star falling on the house of the Verigins and dispersing; he knew that Christ had been born, but ought to be silent; but now it is time to reveal it.[11]

The atmosphere of dark religious emotions, of prophetic hysteria, which had been lost to the sect since the days of Kapustin, began to hang over the settlements. The people were stirred; a perilous vision of their destiny had been born again, and the man who evoked it projected the charismatic appeal of the past leaders whom now even the oldest Doukhobors could hardly remember. Very soon Verigin had his ardent propagandists, prominent among them an old ex-sailor, Ivan Makhortov, who had been conscripted into the Black Sea fleet in the reign of Nicholas I and whose support carried weight because he had been one of Peter Kalmykov's intimate friends. Then, in the Wet Mountains village of Bogdanovka, a few miles from Goreloye, the first mass recognition of Peter Verigin as the divinely inspired leader took place during the New Year festivals. This was Vasilii Pozdniakov's native village.

. . . Verigin approached a very religious old man and inquired of him loudly; how would he act if he had to demolish an old house; would he begin from the roof or the walls. The old man got troubled wih this unexpected question and, falling at Verigin's feet, begged him to explain it. This was the first bow to the ground to Verigin. He did not answer the old man's question, but raised him; and the old man, while rising, kissed Verigin's hand.

After that Verigin continued to be so mysterious all the day long, and everybody whom he was addressing was kissing his hand. He had much success with us, and departed the next day. Our villagers were very satisfied that they were the first to recognize Christ, and the rumour about this event spread rapidly in all the villages.[12]

By this time, two to three weeks after Luker'ia's death, the division in the Doukhobor Community had become clearly defined. The drift of opinion within the sect was so obvious that Verigin's supporters were already known as the Large Party, while the Small Party to which Pozdniakov refers, centred on Gubanov and Zubkov, began to realize that in any contest over the leadership they would certainly be defeated. They were left with two alternatives, one immeasurably more attractive than the other. The first was to submit to Verigin; Zubkov knew very well that this would mean the end of his own power, since Peter Verigin was hardly the man to forget or to forgive the rivalries of the past. The second was to exploit the credit they had already established by their policy of co-operation and to make use of the government to protect what seemed to Gubanov and Zubkov most important, their control over the Orphan's Home.

To this end they departed in two ways from the Doukhobor traditions as established by Kapustin in the early days at Milky Waters. They brought an action in the district court, claiming that as the Orphan's Home was vested in Luker'ia Kalmykova's name, it was her property and therefore should descend to her brother, Michael Gubanov. This unprecedented appeal for 'Governmental participation in their Communal affairs', as Prince Shervashidze remarked, 'caused great surprise'[13] among the officials. But Zubkov was adroit enough to realize that to ask intervention in a dispute among Doukhobors was a risky gamble unless special inducements were offered to make sure of a favourable verdict. Accordingly, he broke the unspoken rule that forbade Doukhobors to denounce even their enemies within the sect, and informed the governor-general, Zumbatov, that Verigin was proclaiming himself a prophet, a false Christ, and a false tsar, which led the governor-general to fear an upsurge of religious zealotry that would once again turn the Doukhobors into an intransigent minority.

A third party was thus introduced into the situation as vigilant police officers began to converge in the Wet Mountains settlements. The Doukhobors in Canada have always claimed that Zubkov also promised and eventually paid large bribes to the tsarist officials, and some non-Doukhobors like Bonch-Bruevich repeated these allegations. Such accusations are supported by no tangible evidence, but at least it can be said that, taken in the context of Russian practices during the nineteenth century, when so many Russian civil servants accepted bribes, they are not incredible.

Meanwhile, in the village of Slavyanka an extraordinary incident took place that had a profound effect on the competition for leadership. The precise details of what happened are not very clear. Prince Shervashidze's report alleges that:

> *Here, in solemn gathering, before all the people, his mother, Anastasia, submissively announced that her son Peter was begotten not by her husband Vasilii Verigin, but by Peter Kalmykov, who, to the great joy of all her family, had honoured her by his holy attentions at the time of his last visit to the village of Slavianka; and that this great secret was well known to Luker'ia Kalmykova, who had only awaited Peter's coming of age in order, during her own lifetime, to hand over to him the inheritance of his ancestors.* [A Doukhobor leader theoretically came of age at 30, when the Holy Spirit was held to enter into him.] *After these words, both she and her husband fell at Peter's feet, and when they had done so all the people imitated them.*[14]

That Anastasia Verigina did make a sensational statement at Slavyanka is likely. But was it exactly the statement Prince Shervashidze reported, which smells somewhat of the older accusations of promiscuity brought against the Doukhobor leaders? No Doukhobor account confirms it, but one Doukhobor historian, V. A. Sukhorev, remarks that many of his fellow sectarians believe that it was Luker'ia Kalmykova, and not Anastasia Verigina, who gave birth to Peter Verigin (really Peter Kalmykov II) in the house of the Verigins on 29 June 1859.[15] This may have been the announcement that Anastasia really made. Whether it was the truth or not would in the circumstances be irrelevant; the statement that Peter Verigin was the son of Peter Kalmykov would be enough to assure his election, even though he looked little like the wiry former leader and much like the tall robust Vasilii Verigin.

The Doukhobors gathered in their thousands by the grave of Luker'ia on the day in January 1887 when the six weeks of mourning were ended and the liberation of the dead woman's soul allowed her successor to be hailed. The Small Party and the Large Party gathered and mingled there, and the police watched as together they sang their psalms and bowed down to the snowy earth in oriental fashion to commemorate their departed leader. The feast that is usual among Doukhobors on such occasions followed, and still the tense truce between the two parties was maintained. Finally, when the meal was ended, there came the time when the people gathered in sobranie would customarily name the leader by a collective act of homage. Ivan Makhortov stepped forward from the ranks and called upon them to acknowledge Peter Verigin 'our leader in the spirit of Christ'. He then bowed low before Verigin, touching his brow to the ground. Standing in their great ceremonial V, the Doukhobors wavered. Seven out of every ten followed Makhortov's example. The rest remained standing, a substantial and stubborn minority. The Doukhobor sect was irrevocably split, and the split was never to be healed. From this point, until Verigin's followers finally departed from Russia, settlements and villages and families were to be divided within themselves as the two factions of the sect followed their different ways.

But on that dramatic day beside the grave that represented the good but departed days of Luker'ia's reign, it was not only their own divisions that showed the Doukhobors that a new and difficult era had dawned for them. No sooner had Peter Verigin been acclaimed than the attendant police stepped forward and arrested him; his followers watched in perplexity as they saw him being thrust into the coach that took him down to the local government headquarters at the city of Akhalkalaki. The times of persecution were coming back, they realized, riding sadly towards their villages. They must prepare to meet them.

4 THE BURNING OF WEAPONS

After the arrest of Peter Verigin, the Doukhobors who had acknowledged him were carefully watched by the tsarist police and subjected to discriminative proceedings that were doubtless intended to hasten their submission to authority, but which had the double effect of making them more rebellious and of deepening the division between them and their former brethren who followed Gubanov and Zubkov into collaboration with the authorities.

First, the disputed ownership of the Orphan's Home came up for judgement. After lengthy litigation, which profited only the lawyers and those officials who accepted bribes, the decision was given in favour of Gubanov, in spite of the fact that even non-Doukhobors living in the locality of Goreloye testified that it was generally known that the Orphan's Home was the property of all Doukhobors and was customarily vested in whatever leader the Community as a whole accepted.

In justice to Gubanov and his associates it must be recorded that when the case was decided in their favour they did not treat the assets of the Orphan's Home as their personal property, but administered them for the benefit of the portion of the Community who followed their lead. Until long after the Revolution of 1917 the building itself continued to stand as a symbolic centre for the Doukhobors who did not leave Russia; it was demolished some time between the two World Wars.

For the majority of the sect, however, the benefits of the Orphan's Home were lost. There was no longer any insurance against bad crops or loss by fire and robbery, no longer any communal fund for cushioning the effects of personal misfortune, and since the Large Party contained most of the poor Doukhobors and also many of the old people (who in Doukhobor history have always been inclined to join with the young in supporting a new prophet), such a misfortune could only add to their grievances against their former brothers. Not only were the members of the Small Party heretics who had denied the true leader. They were also rich men who had robbed the poor; and the Living Book had a great deal to say in condemnation of such people. To resentment therefore was added, among Verigin's followers, a sense of martyred virtue. The schism between the two groups became so wide and so bitter that they would not share the same pastures or even the same villages, and migrations took place until certain places were entirely Small Party and other places entirely Large Party.

The loss of the Orphan's Home was only one of the misfortunes that struck the Large Party. Before the year was ended their new leader had been removed into exile, and conscription was reimposed on them.

After his first arrest, Verigin had been closely questioned by the local officials in Akhalkalaki and had shown great virtuosity in avoiding any statement that might incriminate him. He was, he declared truthfully, a victim of the intrigues of the Gubanov faction. Less truthfully, he posed as one of the brothers in Christ, with no ambitions to raise himself up as a leader among his equals. His slightly arrogant blandness proved impenetrable, and, though he was sent on to the provincial capital of Yelizavetpol to be questioned by Governor Nakashidze, he retained his sang-froid so completely that he was finally allowed to go back to his village of Slavyanka.

By this time the authorities were enforcing conscription, and the young Doukhobors had to make a painful choice which had not been imposed on members of their sect for almost half a century. Most of them, remembering the compromises of Luker'ia's time, unwillingly submitted; but some individuals resisted, and Verigin was suspected not only of encouraging them, but also of preaching secretly a return to the more rigorous Doukhoborism of the past, with its rejection of worldly wealth and its implied negation of all authority but that of the acknowledged theocrat.

During the summer of 1887 he was taken back to Yelizavetpol, where he lived under police supervision in the house of an Armenian merchant. Then, for a period, he was allowed to return to Slavyanka. In mid-August he was finally arrested as a disturber of the peace and taken first to Yeliza-vetpol and then to the prison in Tiflis. As a political prisoner, he did not pass through an ordinary court. Instead, like other opponents of tsarism, he was sentenced by administrative order to five years' exile in Shen-kursk, in the far northern province of Archangel. After a journey of fif-teen hundred miles by coach and railway and—for the last two hundred and fifty miles—by sleigh, he reached Shenkursk in October, when the hard northern winter had already begun. He was accompanied by a cousin, Ivan Verigin, and in the spring he was joined by two of his closest followers, Vasilii Ob'edkov and Dmitrii Lezhebokov.

His exile was not especially rigorous. Shenkursk was a small town, and Verigin had been well supplied with funds by his followers before he left Tiflis. He rented a house, and as soon as the good weather came he and his companions found occupation in cultivating a garden and tending a horse and two cows they had bought. Verigin was forbidden to go beyond the city boundaries and to proselytize for his religion. Otherwise he and his followers enjoyed, at least in the beginning, a fair degree of freedom, and they were able to mix with the many religious and political exiles who lived in Shenkursk.

Exile became Verigin's university. Through the long winter evenings of the north he talked to sectarians of other faiths, and he came into contact with opponents of the existing order whose objections were political as well as moral and religious. For the first time he met the disciples of Tol-stoy and learnt of their teacher's philosophy, so close to that of the early Doukhobors in its advocacy of peasant communism, its pacifism, and its opposition to governments, yet so distant in its rejection of mystical and prophetic religion and in its denial of the principle of theocratic author-ity. He even encountered political revolutionaries, but their ideas were too distant from his own to make an immediate impression on him, and it was some time before he assimilated even the philosophy of Tolstoy.

Among these exiles Verigin was a rich man. Over the difficult roads from the Caucasus his followers found their way, evading the police and sometimes travelling under false passports, carrying reports from the Cau-casus and fresh supplies of money. The money he dispensed generously. He gave to all the beggars of Shenkursk, provided dinners for the poor that were sometimes attended by as many as 120 men, entertained with presents and stories the schoolchildren who came to see him, and kept open house in the evenings for his fellow exiles, with whom his detractors accused him of playing cards. In fact, he practised Doukhobor hospitality so lavishly that he aroused the suspicions of the local governor, an arch-conservative who could not imagine any other motive in the Doukhobor leader's actions than that of corrupting the minds of the people of Shen-kursk. When Verigin disobeyed the governor's orders to curb his hos-pitality he was expelled in the summer of 1890 and sent several hundred miles farther north to Kola, an Arctic port in the province of Murmansk, which lies adjacent to Lapland.

Climatically Kola was rigorous, facing a frozen winter sea over which the dawn barely broke for months on end. But in other respects Verigin was even better treated than in Shenkursk. His relatives and close friends were now being sent into exile, and his brother Vasilii, his sister Varvara and her husband, Ivan Konkin, were allowed to join him in Kola; Ivan Konkin was a Doukhobor poet and singer, and already one of Verigin's most trusted associates. Apart from the companionship of his own people, Verigin enjoyed the friendship of the local police chief, who remembered nostalgically the hospitality he had received from Luker'ia Kalmykova as a young officer in the Caucasus and was therefore well disposed towards the Doukhobors. He took Verigin under his protection, reproached him fraternally for allowing himself to be cheated by beggars, and gave him manure for the garden the Doukhobors cultivated to while away the short Arctic summer. As Verigin himself recollected, 'I was in no way op-pressed.' He was still in Kola when the term of his exile came to an end in 1892, but instead of being allowed to return to the Caucasus he found that another five years had been arbitrarily added to his sentence, and he was ordered to return to Shenkursk, where he was joined by further exiles, including his brother Gregory and old Ivan Makhortov. They lived in a small community of about a dozen people, including Nicholas Voronen, the first of those vaguely idealistic political exiles who during the 1890s began to gravitate towards the Doukhobors because of im-agined affinities which often were non-existent.

Official concern over the situation among the Doukhobors in the Cauca-sus was the main reason for the continuation of Peter Verigin's exile. The tsarist officials had hoped that, by separating the Large Party from its leader, they would deprive its members of any inspiration to further resistance and that gradually the members would fall under the influ-ence of Gubanov and the Small Party, who co-operated with the authori-ties even to the extent of acting as informers. In this calculation they showed an understandable ignorance of Doukhobor psychology. As at the time of expulsion from Milky Waters, the sect had once again divided between the rich and lax on the one hand and the poor and zealous on the other. The former—the Small Party—based their attitude largely on an alleged deathbed prophecy of Peter Kalmykov that after the death of Luker'ia they would have no living Christs among them; they were already—like later schismatic groups—advancing towards a more rationalistic form of Doukhorborism deprived of belief in the divine leader and the millenarian fate of the sect. The latter—the Large Party—like the pilgrims who had left the Milky Waters for the Caucasus fifty years before, were confirmed by the loss of their leader, the loss of their communal funds, and the loss of their exemption from military service, in their hopes of a millenarian destiny; the restless conviction stirred among them that they had only to endure this period of martyrdom to its bitter end for the prophecy embedded in one of Kapustin's psalms to be fulfilled:

The virtues of the community shall overcome the kingdom of this world, which is drawing near to its end. Then shall the Doukhobors be known to all mankind, and Christ Himself shall reign as king. Around Him shall gather all the nations. Only after they have passed through great tribulation shall this honour be done to the Doukhobors. There shall be a great struggle but the truth shall conquer, and the kingdom of God shall come on earth.[1]

Instead of yielding to the continual pressure of the authorities, Verigin's followers turned inward upon their will to suffering and their hope for an apocalyptic victory. The open dealing with the world that had characterized the reign of Luker'ia Kalmykova came to an end. Once again the Doukhobors—or at least those of the Large Party—turned towards people outside their faith a curtain of evasions and silences. The only voice from outside to which they listened was that of Peter Verigin far away in the North.

Up to the early months of 1893 this secretive turning inward of the sect was the only sign that any radical change in their way of life might be impending. With rare exceptions the young men went into the army when they were called, carrying in their minds the exhortations of their elders not to kill if ever they found themselves involved in battle. Taxes were still paid. The antagonism between the Large and the Small parties grew in intensity, but the only violence it caused was the driving away with sticks and stones of cattle belonging to rival factions.

All this time, in Verigin's mind, as in the minds of his followers, there lurked the prophecy of Luker'ia Kalmykova that after her would come a leader to guide the Doukhobors back into righteousness, and his restiveness was increased by his discussions with the political exiles and his study of the doctrines of Tolstoy. The stages by which Verigin came into contact with Tolstoy's thought are still difficult to determine. In 1896, carrying Doukhobor caution to an absurd extreme, he pretended to a correspondent that he had not read Tolstoy and asked to be enlightened about his writings; yet in the same year he sent the Doukhobors a letter in which he reproduced verbatim but without acknowledgement a long passage from *The Kingdom of God Is Within You*. It included Tolstoy's translation of a passage from William Lloyd Garrison's *Declarations of Sentiments*, proposed to a Boston Peace Convention in 1838, and eventually metamorphosed into a psalm still sung by the Doukhobors in Canada. The evidence of exiles who knew him at the time leaves no doubt that by the end of 1894 the moral tracts of Tolstoy and the populist poems of Nekrasov were among his favourite reading, next only to the New Testament. And since the basic ideas of Tolstoy's philosophy had certainly been communicated to him in conversation before 1890, it seems unlikely that he waited even as late as 1894 to read them for himself. If he pretended not to be influenced by his rival teacher, we can doubtless attribute this vanity to a conviction that a living Christ's statements must always appear to be *sui generis*, welling directly out of a mystical contact with the divine.

The interplay of Tolstoyan theories and of long-abandoned Doukhobor precepts in Verigin's mind led to the elaboration during 1893 and 1894 of a series of directives which were to change entirely the lives of the majority of Doukhobors in the Caucasus (their brethren in the Amur were exempted by distance from these perturbations). They were in fact to precipitate an open war between the Large Party and the authorities, fought on one side with the weapons of civil disobedience and on the other with all the means of physical coercion that the autocratic state could call to its assistance.

Following a practice generally adopted by Doukhobor leaders, Verigin couched his directives in the form of oral messages in which he would speculate on the true Christian way of life and advise his followers on the proper way to act; whether they should accept his advice was theoretically optional, but those who failed to do so were liable to be ostracized by the zealot majority, so that the only real alternative was either to accept the leader's views or to desert the Large Party. The first such message was brought from Shenkursk in the autumn of 1893 by his trusted lieutenants, Ivan Konkin and Vasilii Ob'edkov. It called on his followers to return to the ancient Doukhobor traditions of Christian communism. They should forgive all debts within the Community and pay off all their debts to outsiders; then they should redistribute their property so that all things would be held in common.

The directive was couched in such vague terms that there was scope for varied interpretations in the sobraniia of the different villages. Divergences of practice that were to become extremely important in a later Canadian setting were already evident in this Transcaucasian attempt to revive communist institutions. Vasilii Pozdniakov's village of Bogdanovka, which claimed the honour of having first publicly recognized the indwelling Christ of Peter Verigin, carried out a fairly thorough communalization, cancelling debts, distributing money, cattle, and even clothing and then establishing common institutions—blacksmiths' and carpenters' shops where the artisans worked for no wages but took whatever they needed from the common stores. The boundaries between holdings were disregarded. All herds were tended and all lands were ploughed and harvested by the villagers working together; each family took what it needed from the crop, and the rest was sold for the benefit of the communal fund. The villagers began to feel that their lives were becoming happier and easier now that they had freed themselves from the toils of private property. Then, seeing the money growing in their common coffers, they became uneasy that as a group they were so much better off than their neighbours. Accordingly, 'since much property hampers one's progress', they decided to give away their surplus money, clothing, and cattle to other villages and even to the poor Tartars and Armenians who lived near them. Other villages interpreted the advice of Peter Verigin less rigorously. In Orlovka, for example, the peasants pooled half their actual cash and used this as a communal fund to relieve distress; in addition the richer peasants from Orlovka made gifts to their poor brethren of livestock and implements, but there was no common working of the lands, no pooling of herds, and in general only a slight degree of communism. Even within the villages there were disagreements, and a number of the weaker brethren deserted to the ranks of the Small Party.

A consequence of this move towards religious communism was the first outbreak of open resistance to the tsarist government. The members of the Large Party began to withhold taxes. They also refused to participate in the government scheme for Village Prudential Funds, which was intended to establish reserves for use in time of scarcity, on the grounds that if their own mutual aid institution, the Orphan's Home, were returned to them, there would be no need for such funds.

Meanwhile, in Shenkursk Peter Verigin was not only theorizing about reforms in the Doukhobor way of life, but also putting them into practice within his own small Community. He and his companions had shared their goods since his return to Shenkursk in 1892, and he had also instituted twice-weekly dinners for the poor children of the town, a practice that got him into trouble with the local Russian Orthodox priests, who claimed that he was using his charity to subvert the minds of the young. Soon the free dinners and the meals on Verigin's own table began to change in character, and the vegetables he was proudly growing in his hotbeds on the edge of the Arctic Circle played a much greater part in the menu. He and his immediate followers had turned vegetarian, deciding that it was wrong not only to kill men, but also to harm any living being. In adopting this belief they were introducing into the Doukhobor tradition a new element derived from Verigin's reading of Tolstoy. At the same time Verigin reintroduced the old Doukhobor ban on drinking, and for good measure added smoking to the index.

In due course the advice to refrain from drinking, smoking, and meat-eating was dispatched by messenger to the Caucasus. The date 4 November 1894—the festival of Michael the Archangel—was fixed as the day on which this further step towards the achievement of spiritual purity should take place. Giving up smoking and alcohol were comparatively easy for most members of the sect, since these practices had already fallen under Luker'ia Kalmykova's disapproval during the last years of her reign and had been largely abandoned at that time. Liquor was poured away and tobacco was burnt in little ritual bonfires in all the villages of the Large Party.

The ban on meat-eating, on the other hand, encountered strong opposition. Like any other pastoral people living in a cold mountain climate where grain grows reluctantly, the Doukhobors in the Wet Mountains were in the habit of eating large quantities of meat. At least three hundred families broke away over this issue to form a middle group; while the hard core of Verigin's followers became known as the Fasters, these meat-eating dissidents were called the Butchers. Unlike the original Small Party, who were motivated partly by family enmity towards Verigin and partly by concern for their own wealth, the Butchers included many Doukhobors who had supported Verigin because they regarded him as Luker'ia's chosen heir and also because they disapproved of the way in which Gubanov and his followers had allied themselves to the tsarist authorities in order to gain control of the Orphan's Home. Among them were some of the most able men of the sect, including Alesha

Vorob'ev, who had acted as Verigin's representative for a while when he was first in prison; they refused to compromise their basic Doukhobor principles by co-operating with the authorities or by carrying tales to them about the plans of their Fasting brethren. Nevertheless, when later questioned by the tsarist officials, Vorob'ev made a very illuminating comment about the variety of Doukhobor attitudes towards Peter Verigin —a variety that goes far to explain the complicated fissions within the sect at this period.

Some looked on him as the Apostles looked on Christ, and considered him a Saviour, or the 'Door to the Kingdom of Heaven'; others considered him as a God-Man or earthly Deity; others only considered him a prophet; and there were also sensible men who simply looked on him as on an ordinary man. What was most important was his influence among us as a public Leader.[2]

Such men as Vorob'ev were prepared to support Verigin as long as he continued in the traditions laid down by Kapustin, but were unwilling to accept innovations like vegetarianism that must eventually destroy the pastoral economy of the villages in the Wet Mountains. Verigin's next quasi-Tolstoyan directive was hardly calculated to placate them. He advised his people to abstain from sexual intercourse 'during the time of our tribulation'. Even the Fasters found difficulty in accepting this decree; the women healers carried on a brisk trade in abortions among wives who conceived after the arrival of Verigin's message, and, according to Pozdniakov, there were even cases of infanticide. However, as he remarked, 'the young people were containing themselves and not marrying, and ready to meet Christ, according to Verigin's saying.'[3]

Whether or not Verigin intended it, all these reforms in the Doukhobor pattern of living acted as means of sorting out those whose zealotry made them accept unquestioningly the new pattern into which he was remoulding the sect. By this time, thanks to his association with socialist exiles and his reading of Tolstoy, he was combining the religious messianism of Pobirokhin and Kapustin with a distinctly political radicalism. Without in any way abandoning his own theocratic control over the faction that remained loyal to him, he began to preach in almost anarchistic terms the evils of governments and the necessity to replace their rule by a Christian communist utopia. He was also inspired by the example of the followers of Tolstoy who at this time were courting suffering, imprisonment, and exile for their pacifist principles, and he now evolved a strategy of civil disobedience that went far beyond mere passive resistance. The Doukhobors, he decided, must shortly manifest in a spectacular manner their repudiation of the compromises made during the war of 1877–8, and their condemnation of physical violence and of the autocratic state that was founded on brute force.

Once again, in calling his people to resistance Verigin was only asking them to carry out on a large scale acts he had already carried out individually and for which he was to suffer in his own way, though not so drastically as many of his followers. In 1894 Tsar Alexander III died and was succeeded by his ill-fated son, Nicholas II, an unintelligent autocrat who throughout his reign remained the tool of reactionary counsellors and died a martyr to his own limitations. One of Nicholas's first acts was to demand an oath of allegiance from all his subjects; those who refused to take it would be subject to punishment. There is no reason to suppose that this ukase was followed out consistently in every remote village of the Russian countryside or every deep slum of its cities, but the oath was certainly exacted of all who took any part in public life, and it was used as a kind of test on exiles, like Verigin, who were not subjected to the most rigorous conditions of banishment.

Verigin refused to take the oath. Oaths, he maintained, were wrong in themselves; moreover, his allegiance was to God alone. He was threatened with flogging, but still he refused, and in the end the authorities in Shenkursk decided to leave him alone and await instructions from St Petersburg. They were unwilling to take the responsibility for what might happen in the Caucasus if it were heard that the living Christ of the Doukhobors had been forced to endure the first stage of the sufferings inflicted on the historic Christ of Judaea. At the same time, they recommended that he be sent into some remoter exile beyond the Urals, and it was obvious that his relative accessibility to his followers would soon come to an end. Accordingly, he sent Vasilii Ob'edkov to the Caucasus with instructions to return immediately with two responsible delegates to whom he would deliver the most important of all his messages. On the way they were to make inquiries in Moscow in case he was already on his way to Siberia.

His brother Vasilii, who had returned from Kola to the Caucasus, and Vasilii Vereshchagin, a member of one of the prominent Doukhobor families, accompanied Ob'edkov on his return journey. In Moscow they discovered no trace of Verigin, so they went on to Shenkursk, where they found him still awaiting orders to depart. Immediately he sat down to instil his oral instructions firmly into the minds of his visitors. Christ had forbidden oaths; therefore no Doukhobor should swear allegiance to the tsar. It was wrong to kill any of God's creatures; therefore no Doukhobor should either directly or indirectly take any part in war. Military service must be rejected, and those already in the army must return their arms and uniforms to their officers and refuse henceforward to take any part in violence. Last of all came the order that the messengers were to deliver to selected elders who would keep it secret until immediately before the event. On St Peter's day, 1895—29 June, which was also Peter Verigin's name day—the Fasting Doukhobors were to collect all the weapons they had acquired for keeping off robbers or for hunting or for mere vanity and destroy them in great bonfires that would symbolize their complete break with all the compromises that had marred the purity of the Doukhobor faith.

A few days later, on 4 November 1894, Verigin set out for his Siberian exile, accompanied by Ob'edkov. His brother Vasilii and Vereshchagin went with him as far as Moscow, whence they would continue southward to the Caucasus. As a moneyed exile, Verigin was offered the right to travel by sleigh at his own expense; instead, he bought clothes for the poor people he had so often feasted in Shenkursk and insisted on walking with the poor prisoners of the convict chain, staying at night in the cold and crowded roadside prisons, and at the end limping into the railhead town of Vologda on blistered and frostbitten feet.

In Moscow, Verigin and the other prisoners were put into the verminous cells of the notorious Butyrskaia prison, and a meeting took place that was to affect profoundly the later destiny of the Doukhobors. Tolstoy was in the city at the time. As a result of his interest in peasant movements, he had already heard of the Doukhobors as a sect of primitive pacifist Christians, though he had no knowledge that Verigin was a close reader of his tracts and that his teachings were being incorporated without acknowledgement into the ever-changing texture of the Living Book. When he heard that a leading Doukhobor was imprisoned in the city on his way to Siberia, he immediately sought permission to see the man. The authorities had no intention of allowing such a potentially dangerous encounter to take place; but they feared Tolstoy's powers as a publicist, and for that reason they did nothing to prevent his meeting the three lesser Doukhobors, Vasilii Verigin, Vereshchagin, and Ob'edkov, who were free men. These replied to his questions with the caution they would have used in talking to any other aristocrat. Verigin's role in the sect was never mentioned, and by the time Tolstoy had finished talking to the sectarians, he had acquired a sense of revelation, a feeling that at last he had met the natural peasant anarchists of whom he had always dreamed. As his critical former disciple Aylmer Maude pointed out, his error was completely understandable.

> Knowing nothing of all this [Verigin's role] and meeting men who externally appeared to meet the requirements of his teaching, he could hardly avoid falling into the error of regarding them as examples of true Christianity in practical life.
>
> They worked with their hands, yet were dignified and full of confidence in themselves and their group. They produced more than they consumed; rejected the Church and State; acknowleged (apparently) no human authority, yet lived together and co-operated in a closely knit community. They professed the very principles of Christian anarchy dear to Tolstoy; and (apparently) put these into actual practice without that disintegrating result so painfully evident in the failure of the Tolstoyan colonies, and which, through all history, has accompanied attempts to carry on work collectively without recognizing ourselves as part of a social organism we cannot suddenly reshape when and how we will.
>
> No wonder Tolstoy (with his impatient desire for quick results) wrote that what was occurring among the Doukhobors was 'the germinating of that seed sown by Christ eighteen hundred years ago: the resurrection of Christ himself,' and added that the main condition for the realization of Christian life 'is the existence and gathering together of people who even now realize that towards which we are all striving. And behold, these people exist!' [4]

His appetite whetted by what he had heard, Tolstoy, who sensed that Verigin was at least a revered teacher among the Doukhobors, became so impatient to meet him that he nagged the police officials into giving him a promise that he would be allowed to speak to Verigin at the station before the prisoners left for the east. Again, however, he was disappointed, for Verigin was concealed until Tolstoy had finally lost patience and gone away, and then he was hurried on to the train which immediately departed. Perhaps it was fortunate for the Doukhobors that the meeting did not take place; when Tolstoy finally did meet Verigin more than seven years later, on his way to Canada, he was sufficiently unimpressed to describe him as 'a man not yet born in the spirit.'

The Trans-Siberian Railway was still almost a decade from completion, and after Verigin and Ob'edkov reached the railhead beyond the Urals they had to travel on by horse-sleigh to Tobol'sk, which they reached in February, and then to their final destination of Obdorsk by reindeersleigh. By this time they had been four months on the road and had travelled more than three thousand miles. Once again they were on the Arctic Sea; Obdorsk was a dismal, frozen village on the mouth of the northward flowing river Ob, a remote outpost concerned in the winter with trapping and in the summer with fishing, and endowed with the customary Siberian complement of political exiles.

Verigin now decided to live alone and sent Ob'edkov back to the Caucasus; he moved into a small shack on the edge of the settlement, where he once again began to cultivate vegetables and to assist the poor, not only with money, but also with manual work. His actions went parallel to his thoughts, for he was developing a theory of education by labour that would fit into Doukhobor traditions and that many years later was to have a profound effect on the outlook of his followers in Canada. As at Shenkursk, he spent his evenings in discussion with the political refugees, and one of them remarked that 'he completely rejected education and earning one's living by using the mind. He prefers physical labour, and goes so far as to condemn even literacy. In debating he shows a lively brain, and might have been an excellent lawyer. He is good at defending his own arguments, though he is constantly elaborating them until— apparently unaware of the fact—he carries them to absurdity.' [5]

However much Verigin may have argued against literacy, he continued to read and to work what he learnt into the fabric of the new Doukhoborism that he was still elaborating. As he was setting his sect upon a militant and unfamiliar course, he decided in 1896 to give it not only a new policy but also a new name, suggested by one of his links with the literate world. John C. Kenworthy, the leader of a group of English radically minded Christians, who collaborated with anarchists in London and knew the well-known Russian exile Peter Kropotkin, had written to the Doukhobor leader. The name of Kenworthy's group struck Verigin's imagination; it was called the Brotherhood Church. Immediately, by one of the messengers who still went through extraordinary hardships to maintain secret communication between their leader and his adherents in the distant Caucasus, Verigin sent a letter of advice to his followers:

Dear brothers and sisters, I offer for your consideration that we should in future call ourselves 'The Christian Community of Universal Brotherhood.' The name 'Doukhobor' is not understood by outsiders; and though we shall in future still invoke the Spirit of the Lord, to strive against the weakness of the flesh and against sin, yet the name 'Christian Community of Universal Brotherhood' will tell more clearly that we look on all men as our brothers, according to the command of the Lord Jesus Christ. From this time we will, to the praise of the Lord, take the name of 'Christian Community of Universal Brotherhood.' Inform all the brothers and sisters.[6]

Though Verigin did not emphasize the fact, the new name also gave his followers a resounding title by which to distinguish themselves from the heretics of Gubanov's Small Party. Moreover, it suggested the stress on social and economic factors in Verigin's new Doukhoborism; the sect was to be a community not merely in spiritual but also in material terms, and Verigin was to stress even more than Kapustin the intimate connection between these two levels of living. In a letter he wrote to Kenworthy at the same time he significantly remarked that 'recently among us a movement has arisen making for the perfecting of actual life.'[7]

Like a true Doukhobor leader, Verigin put so many masks between himself and the world of non-believers, even in his letters, that it is now impossible to be sure whether he believed that his actions at this time were bringing the Doukhobor millenium closer to fulfilment. But his concern for the image that his sect should present to the world suggests that he at least realized that under his leadership they had reached the historic point of transition where, through suffering, they would emerge from the obscurity of sectarian Russia into an international fame which, in one way or another, they would henceforward tenaciously retain.

In fact, by the time Verigin's letter renaming the sect reached the Caucasus, the world outside Russia had already heard of the extraordinary heroism his followers had generated in the face of a persecution unparalleled in their history, a persecution whose aim was either to force them into conformity with the will of the tsar or to exterminate them physically. Whatever Verigin may have suffered in exile or in following his weary convict journeys was little to what his followers now began to endure for following his 'advice'.

On Easter Day, 1895, the Doukhobors who had been enrolled in the army began to follow out Verigin's instructions to refuse military service. Eleven of them were serving in a reserve batallion at Yelizavetpol. Matvei Lebedev had actually shown himself willing and efficient enough to become a corporal, but the very qualities that in other circumstances might have turned him into a good soldier now turned him into a leader in resistance and martyrdom. On Easter morning he told the ten Doukhobor privates that they must begin their rejection of war by refusing to go on church parade. The inevitable sequence of events followed. Sought out by the sergeant-major, Lebedev handed back his rifle and declared that the government and its actions were against the teaching of Christ; arrested, he tore the epaulettes from his uniform. He was confined in a dark underground cell and fed on bread and water. Afterwards the process was repeated with all his ten companions.

They were brought into court almost two months later, where Lebedev declared that the only ruler under whom he would serve was the Tsar of Heaven and he would sooner endure any suffering, even that of the firing squad, than kill another man either in war or in peace. He was sentenced to three years of confinement in the penal battalion at Ekaterinograd, and his companions to two years each. Their example was soon followed by Doukhobor conscripts in Kars, Akhalkalaki, and other garrison towns of the Caucasus. There were at that time, according to Vasilii Pozdniakov, only about sixty Doukhobors in active service, and all of them gave up their arms.

The punishments they endured in the penal battalion were medieval and unremitting. They are described at length in the various books and pamphlets in which Tolstoy's disciple, Vladimir Chertkov, later gathered the letters and accounts of the men who had suffered in the penal battalions, but they are summed up concisely in a single paragraph by Pozdniakov, who later lived in exile with some of these first resisters to military service. The curious English of his unknown translator simply adds to the stark vividness of his account.

From the very first day the bloody chastisement commenced. They were flogged with thorny rods, whose thorns were remaining in the flesh, and thrown in a cold and dark cell afterwards. After few days they were requested again to do the service, and for the refusal flogged again. And so it was going on and no end was seen. Besides they were always hungry, because they were eating no meat and were given too little bread. They were physically exhausted; many were sick; but the doctor was refusing to admit them in the hospital, unless they would agree to eat meat. The chaplain was requiring the performance of the Orthodox rites, and they were driven to the church by fists and musket's butt-ends. Their position was unbearable; so that those few of them which were acting not by their own conviction, but only by Verigin's advice, gave it up, but the majority was convinced and held out.[8]

At least one of the original eleven resisters, a Doukhobor named Sherbinin, died at Ekaterinograd as a result of beatings with the rods, which were actually bundles of thorny acacia branches.

At other places the tsarist officers tried to break the will of the Doukhobors by the macabre procedure that had been inflicted on the well-known novelist Dostoevsky nearly fifty years before, when he was convicted of belonging to a subversive organization during the reign of Nicholas I. Like Dostoevsky, five of the disobedient Doukhobor soldiers were led into the barracks yard at Akhalkalaki, where they were lined up before a troop of Cossacks who were ordered to dismount and load their rifles. The Doukhobors prayed and calmly awaited their death. But the retreat was then sounded, the Cossacks lowered their guns, and the Doukhobors were again asked to take back their arms. They refused, and now the Cossacks rode among them brandishing their swords; still the disobedient conscripts remained firm. Finally, they were beaten and sent back to their cells. An even more bizarre story reached the English newspapers; it told of gibbets being erected and the Doukhobor soldiers being led up to them and clothed in white shrouds in an ineffectual attempt to frighten them into submission. After serving part of their sentence in the penal batallion, those of the Doukhobor soldiers who neither died nor submitted were exiled to Yakutsk in Siberia.

While the Doukhobors in the army were going through the first stages of their difficult resistance to authority, their brethren in the Caucasus were drawing near the moment of their great manifestation of defiance against the prevalence of violence and the power of the state. Verigin's instructions regarding the ceremonial burning of the arms had been transmitted by Vasilii Vereshchagin and Vasilii Verigin to two or three trusted elders in each of the three main Doukhobor colonies, who in turn decided to hold a separate burning for each settlement: in the Wet Mountains near the village of Orlovka, in Yelizavetpol near the Verigin family stronghold of Slavyanka, and in Kars near the village of Spasskoye. There were secret meetings in all the villages, but how many people were told about the plans, and how much they were told, is uncertain. Some accounts suggest that the whole secret was kept until the very eve of St Peter's day and that then the arrangements were hurriedly completed. This however does not seem to accord with what actually happened. Some days before 29 June there were signs of great activity in all the villages dominated by the Large Party. Firewood and kerosene were being collected, and Verigin's followers were seen gathering arms by their enemies of the Small Party, who were still Doukhobors enough to sense the peculiar exaltation building among their former brethren. They knew something was afoot, and they had time to inform the authorities. The Kotel'nikov clan in Slavyanka, the family of Verigin's former wife, reported the activities in the Yelizavetpol district out of sheer malice; Gubanov and

Zubkov reported them because—or so they asserted—they feared that the Large Party was mobilizing to march on Goreloye and repossess the Orphan's Home by force.

Nakashidze, the governor of Tiflis, issued immediate orders for three companies of infantry and three hundred mounted Cossacks to be sent to guard Goreloye, and set off in person to supervise operations. In the Yelizavetpol region the authorities did not take the matter quite so seriously, and Colonel Seratov and the district attorney, Strelkov, led a troop of Cossacks to Slavyanka. In Kars, where almost all the Doukhobors were in favour of Verigin, there was no tale-bearing, and the officials were either ignorant of what was afoot or did not consider it important enough to warrant their interference.

The consequences of the burning of the arms varied considerably in the different settlements. At Spasskoye, in the province of Kars, the arms were placed on a hilltop in a pyre that contained fifteen wagon loads of firewood. They were doused with many gallons of kerosene and at midnight the elder Ivan Osachov put the torch to the fire. From all the villages the faithful came walking and riding at the signal of the leaping flames to gather in their great V fifty yards away from the fire and chant their psalms through the night until the following noon. The singing and the rattle of musketry as the loaded guns went off in the fire awakened the local Moslems and Armenians, who gathered in astonishment at this strange act of their unpredictable neighbours. At dawn the police came, but all they did was take away some of the molten metal as evidence. The Doukhobors were so disappointed by this anti-climax that they decided their young men who had not been called up should hand in their military reserve papers to the official in charge of the district, a Tartar named Birakov. This they did, expecting immediate punishment. But Birakov was not without sympathy for the Doukhobors. When the young men insisted on giving up their papers, he accepted them reluctantly and promised to forward them to the higher authorities; then he sent the men home unpunished. The governor of Kars was less lenient and ordered the arrest of fifteen Doukhobors who were regarded as ringleaders in the night's events.

At Slavyanka there was a little more excitement, for Colonel Seratov's Cossacks, arriving after the fire had been lit, attempted to stop the people of the other villages from reaching it. The Doukhobors continued on their way, ignoring commands and even whiplashes, until they were able to form up around the fire and chant their psalms. Then the young men came up to hand in their reserve papers, which annoyed District Attorney

Strelkov so much that he started beating them with his fists and ordering their arrest. Eighty Doukhobors were taken at Slavyanka before the meeting finally dispersed, and the prisoners were escorted to Yelizavetpol.

In the Wet Mountains the mood of Verigin's followers was more militant, partly because this was also the stronghold of their rivals of the Small Party. At the same time the forces of the state were more numerous and more prepared for trouble. Here the symbolic fire was built on the top of a low, flat-topped hill about two miles from Orlovka; it consisted largely of dung-cakes, since wood was hard to get in the Wet Mountains, and seventy gallons of kerosene were needed to get the blaze going. Governor Nakashidze with his small army was at Goreloye, waiting to intervene in case the Large Party attacked the Orphan's Home. As soon as they saw what was happening at Orlovka, the Small Party realized their mistake and went to the governor to tell him that, though the followers of Verigin had intended to attack them, now, seeing so many soldiers, they had decided to burn their arms out of malice. They did not make clear against whom such a roundabout form of malice might be directed, but it was evident to Nakashidze that something unusual and puzzling was taking place and that he must find out the cause of it.

Up to this point Nakashidze may only have intended an investigation, followed by a few arrests to satisfy his desire for law and order. He decided to call the heads of all Doukhobor households to a meeting at Bogdanovka, and early the following morning he sent a few Cossacks out as messengers to transmit his orders. The villages were deserted, for their inhabitants had gone back to the scene of the fire to hold another service, and here the Cossacks came upon them, two thousand strong, chanting their psalms around the smoking embers. The sergeant in charge of the Cossacks delivered the governor's command. 'We are busy praying,' replied the elders. 'If the governor wishes to speak to us, let him come here. He is only one man, and there are many of us.' Nakashidze sent another messenger. This time the reply was almost patronizing. 'We must finish our prayers, and after that, if the governor still wishes to see us, we shall go to him.'

It is easy to imagine the fury such an answer aroused in a high official of an autocratic state, accustomed to having every order obeyed without question. The governor turned to Captain Praga, the commander of the Cossacks, and ordered him to drive the Doukhobors to Bogdanovka. At Orlovka, without warning, Praga ordered his men to ride upon the Doukhobors and flog them into submission. Instinctively the Doukhobors tightened their ranks as the horsemen galloped upon them, swinging their lead-tipped whips and lashing out at men and women indiscriminately. After three such charges the retreat was sounded, and the bruised and bleeding sectarians were herded into marching formation and they set off, chanting mournfully, towards Bogdanovka. Meanwhile Nakashidze and his entourage had started out from Bogdanovka; they halted by the roadside as the column came in sight. As the governor got out of his carriage, Praga ordered the Doukhobors to bare their heads. Those whose caps had not already been whipped away refused. 'If the governor greets us,' one of them explained, 'then we will greet him in our own Christian manner.' Praga again ordered the Cossacks to charge, and this they did even more vigorously than before, so that one elder was trampled to death under the feet of the horses and one man's eye was torn from its socket by the metal tip of a whip. The Doukhobors resisted passively, drawing their injured comrades within the circle, huddling together and offering their own bodies to the whips, so that all should share in the torment.

Nakashidze ordered the beatings to stop and the Doukhobors to go on to Bogdanovka, where he stood on the steps of his carriage and began to make a speech, expressing the hope that they had learnt their lesson and that in future they would be willing to obey. They could only obey, one of the elders explained, if the orders of the government were not opposed to their conscience. Then the young men began to come forward and throw their military reserve papers at the governor's feet. Nakashidze lost all sense of proportion or legality and ordered the Cossacks to prepare to shoot into the crowd. At this point a member of Nakashidze's entourage, generally said to have been Count Kropinskii who had come recently from St Petersburg, intervened dramatically, drawing his sabre and shouting to the governor, 'If you give the order to fire, I shall split your head in two!' Jolted back to reason, Nakashidze ordered the Cossacks to sheathe their carbines and escort the Doukhobors back to their villages.

This grisly incident might conceivably be explained, even if it could not be excused, as a result of the clash between the governor's imperiousness and the Doukhobors' obstinacy. Both the governor and Captain Praga, it might be suggested, lost their heads in the heat of the moment when faced by what seemed to them the extreme impudence of the Doukhobors in refusing to interrupt their prayers to suit the convenience of tsarist officials and to bare their heads before authority in the way expected of peasants in autocratic Russia. But even such tenuous justifications cannot be brought forward to mitigate the calculated atrocities that followed. For months, which eventually stretched into years, the tsarist authorities attempted to break the spirit of the Doukhobors by a deliberate policy of terror and repression.

It began on the very day of the beatings at Orlovka and Bogdanovka. Praga and his Cossacks were billeted on the Doukhobors. 'They quartered in our villages over a fortnight,' Vasilii Pozdniakov remembered, 'and were riding about the villages, plundering everywhere and beating everybody who fell into their hands. In one night, by permission of their commander, they violated several women, among whom was a girl of sixteen.' [9]

Pozdniakov himself was a conscript who had ended his term of service before Peter Verigin's message of resistance had reached the Doukhobors, and he was picked on, as a reserve corporal, for special punishment by the Cossacks. In all, he was given three hundred lashes and kept imprisoned for two weeks in a corn loft on bread and water.

Today, more than seventy years after the event, Captain Praga still performs a kind of demoniac role in Doukhobor traditions, and his actions are narrated in at least one of their often-sung historical psalms. His victims are also celebrated, their sufferings and courage woven into the Doukhobor consciousness. Almost every sobranie held in Canada still opens with the hymn to their memory, 'Sleep on, you brave fighting eagles', which has inspired many a latter-day Doukhobor to choose a path of rebellion and imprisonment, The sufferings of the Doukhobors in the Wet Mountains lasted long after Captain Praga had departed, for the whole circumstances of the burning of the arms were reported to St Petersburg. A special inquiry was immediately ordered, and General Surovzev was sent to Tiflis to investigate. He called the Doukhobor elders before him and tried to reason with them. Like many modern generals, he even pretended that he too would like to see the day when there was no more war. But the time for that had not yet come. 'The time may not yet have come for you,' said the spokesman of the Doukhobors, 'but it has come for us.' When General Surovzev accused them of not being prepared to lay down their lives for the tsar, they answered: 'You say wrong. We are ready to lay down our life for every man, as well as the Tsar; if we saw him being tortured, we would lay our life down for his sake as well as for any other man, but we cannot murder for any man, because it is forbidden by God.' [10]

There is no evidence that as a result of the inquiry Governor Nakashidze and Captain Praga were punished or even reproved for their excesses. On the other hand the officials in St Petersburg decided, even before the inquiry was completed, that Verigin's supporters in the Wet

Mountains should be treated with the utmost severity. They were regarded as the most stubborn of the Doukhobors and it was hoped that
the example of their punishment would not be lost on their brethren in
the Kars and Yelizavetpol settlements. This harsh policy may in part
have been due to the fact that at this time some Russian Orthodox soldiers followed the example of the Doukhobors in refusing to bear arms.

The destined victims of autocracy were divided into a number of
groups according to the enormity their offences assumed in official eyes.
Men who had served in the army, like Pozdniakov, were called up for a
month's training, and on their refusal were sentenced to two years in
prison and eighteen years' exile. Those who had not yet served but who
had handed in their reserve papers were also imprisoned, and some of
these were later sent to Siberia. There were about three hundred in all
who underwent some kind of imprisonment at this time, including a
number of the men who had been arrested in Kars and Yelizavetpol at
the time of the burning of arms.

For the remaining 4,300 Veriginites in the Wet Mountains another mass
exile was planned, far more rigorous than those their forefathers had
undergone. They were ordered to leave the homes and the farms they
had built up with so much labour and to trek under armed escort to the
malarial valleys in the region of Batum. On 8 July the first party of 35
families set off with 52 wagons, and during the next fortnight another
439 families left the Wet Mountains. What they could not take in their
wagons they were forced to sell or leave behind. Once again it was a case
of the wealthy Doukhobors benefiting at the expense of the poor, for the
members of the Small Party were the principal buyers. Livestock was sold
off at a third or even a fifth of its value; ploughs and other farm equipment went for next to nothing. Even at these prices the exiled families
could not sell all their possessions. One farmer, Nikolai Zibarov, left
3 1/2 tons of wheat behind him, to be plundered afterwards by the
soldiers and by his neighbours. And as the convoys began to move down
towards the hot valleys, the exiles rode past the fields where the crops
they had planted that spring still stood unharvested; they were to be
reaped by Gubanov's followers, whose loyalty the government bought by
allowing them to profit as much as possible by the misfortunes of their
brethren.

Four Georgian valleys were picked to receive the Doukhobors. The
exiles were split up, three or four or five families in each village of
strangers, and they were forbidden to maintain communication with their

brothers in Yelizavetpol and Kars. They were given no land and were allowed to buy none, yet they were also forbidden to leave their assigned villages in search of work. Some of the Georgians took pity on them and secretly allowed them small pieces of land to cultivate gardens or employed them as labourers, but there were also many who exploited their misery to pay them derisory wages. They would hardly have kept going at all if the Kars and Yelizavetpol Doukhobors had not risked punishment by bringing food to them secretly.

As the exiles were beginning this new existence, Michael Androsov set out to carry the news to Peter Verigin at Obdorsk. His journey was a minor odyssey, as he travelled by ship and train, by troika and sleigh, into the far north, meeting strange people on his way, constantly evading the police, and finally being arrested as he entered Verigin's house in Siberia. The police magistrate at Obdorsk was fortunately a reasonable and sympathetic man, who took it upon himself to let Androsov out of his cell for long enough to dine with Verigin. Verigin questioned the messenger about all that had happened, and then hurriedly exchanged boots with him before the police arrived to start Androsov on his return journey by reindeer-sleigh. Verigin's boots contained his message to the Doukhobors, which was spread among his followers as soon as the messenger returned, via several local prisons, to the Caucasus. It was necessary, went the message, to suffer with Christ. Though the body might be harmed, the spirit was invulnerable. Therefore, at all costs the faithful must remain steadfast in refusing to obey the government.

The message was hardly necessary. Not a single Doukhobor going into exile had accepted the official offer that he would be allowed to stay in the Wet Mountains if only he would give his allegiance to the tsar. And the tribulations the Doukhobors now underwent did not lessen their resolve to live out their faith. Even on the journey into exile some died— from sickness, from exhaustion; one of them, Kiril Konkin, from flogging. Once they reached the low valleys they began to contract malaria and dysentery, and malnutrition, with its attendant diseases, took an inevitable toll. In just over a year there were more than 350 deaths, or about 80 per thousand, a rate several times the normal even in Russia at that period, and as time went on the proportion increased. Living mainly on bread, and usually little of that, the Doukhobors stubbornly continued their passive resistance.

'The policy of the officials', said Aylmer Maude, 'was to cut them off from communication with the outside world as completely as possible, and to oblige them to abandon their principles, by the practical threat of slowly exterminating them should they refuse to submit.'[11] But tsarist Russia, for all its despotic methods, could not in the long run keep the Doukhobors hermetically sealed from the outside world, and, in the end, it was help from outside that saved them from what at first seemed the certainty of extermination.

5 FAILURE ON CYPRUS

Modern totalitarian dictators are single-minded about the terrors they create; terror is the climate in which they thrive. Older tyrannies, like that of tsarist Russia, tended to be more ambivalent about the kind of power they wielded. During the reign of Nicholas II the imperial government was in fact wielding a legal terror to counteract the illegal terror of its extreme opponents. But in theory the Russian autocracy was a patriarchal and benevolent system in which the tsar ruled as the father of his people; even the peasants shared this belief, and during the nineteenth century there were rural risings whose participants believed that by trying to depose unjust local officials they were carrying out the real will of the tsar. This conception created an inevitable dichotomy in the actions of tsarist officials. They would suppress an armed rebellion with an act of horrifying public terror; the violence of others gave them an excuse they gladly accepted. But in other cases, where violence did not arise, they would often act furtively, as if they were half-ashamed of their own deeds, and sometimes they cowered before the possible verdict of public opinion and did not act at all. This was why Tolstoy, one of their most outspoken critics, was never touched. And this was why they sought to keep the persecution of the Doukhobors secret by suppressing communication with the outside world and censoring press reports within Russia. They hoped to starve them into submission without public discredit.

But Russia was changing rapidly. The railway and the telegraph provided rapid links between even the remote Caucasus and the cities where liberal and radical views were sustained in spite of the autocracy. More important for the fate of the Doukhobors, they provided a link with the village of Yasnaya Polyana, where Tolstoy unhappily sought to combine the roles of a country squire and a Christian anarchist and, above all, to act as the conscience of a Russia entering upon its great era of revolutionary change.

The man who made the link active was Prince D. A. Khilkov. He had served as an officer in a regiment of Hussar Guards that was quartered in the Doukhobor villages at the end of the Russo-Turkish war of 1877–8. He was impressed by what he saw of Doukhobor life and convinced by their arguments against the forms of Russian Orthodox religion, and he accepted the criticism of his own aristocratic existence that was implicit in their teachings. During the war he had killed a Turk in battle, and now the memory of his act began to haunt him. He resigned from the army and settled down to cultivate his estate, but, although he was an excellent practical farm manager, he found that he was still not at peace with his wealth : he divided his lands among the peasants, attempting to live like one of them. Eventually he was exiled to the Caucasus, where he frequently visited the Doukhobors. He was aware of the burning of the arms and of the persecutions that followed immediately afterwards, and on 14 July, six days after the first exiles set off for the Georgian valleys, he intervened in the best way he could think of by writing to Tolstoy, with whom he had been in contact since 1887. He urged Tolstoy to give publicity to the situation in Russian as well as in foreign papers.

Tolstoy, who had been so much impressed by the Doukhobors he met the previous year, was anxious to help them. They had, after all, two great claims on his attention. They were victims of the evil system of tsarism; they were also peasants who—he believed—were practising the religious anarchism that he himself had failed to sustain. His first thought was to bring their plight to the attention of his friends abroad, and he wrote immediately to John Kenworthy of the Brotherhood Church. Then, to gain fuller knowledge of the actual situation, he sent a number of his followers on investigatory trips into the Caucasus. The first to go was I. M. Tregubov; later he was followed by Paul Biriukov, a former naval officer turned pacifist, and by A. M. Bodianskii, a nobleman who, like Khilkov, had distributed his lands to his peasants and become a practising Tolstoyan. All of them sent harrowing reports of sickness and starvation among the Doukhobors in the valleys of Georgia, and of the maltreatment of the conscientious objectors in the disciplinary battalions. Bodianskii, writing to Tolstoy in mid-September, appears to have been the first person to realize that there was little prospect of the Doukhobors receiving any better treatment while they remained in Russia. They should emigrate, he suggested, to some country where they would be allowed to live in accordance with their beliefs.

Such a view was, for the present at least, repugnant to Tolstoy, who believed that the non-violent struggle against the evils of tsarism must be carried out within Russia, and that suffering was a long-term weapon in that struggle. But world public opinion was another weapon; having failed to persuade Russian editors to incure official displeasure by attempting to publish material on the Doukhobors, Tolstoy turned to the press of England. Recruiting Kenworthy as an intermediary and a translator, on 10 September 1895 he wrote a letter to English editors appealing for publicity to be given to the persecution of the Doukhobors and enclosed Biriukov's report, 'Persecution of Christians in Russia'. The letter and the report appeared in *The Times* on 23 October 1895, and Tolstoy followed them up with an article which appeared the following month in the *Contemporary Review*.

These documents carried the vast international prestige of Tolstoy's name and were read by many educated people in Russia as well as in Western Europe. But they were not the first report of the persecution of Doukhobors to reach the English public. As early as September 1894 the *Daily Chronicle* had commented on the punishment of Doukhobor soldiers who gave up their arms in the Kars region. Moreover, the English Quakers, who had worked with the Tolstoyans in providing relief during the 1891–2 famine in Russia, became interested in the situation of the Doukhobors, perhaps through Kenworthy, even before Tolstoy's appeal appeared. In November 1895 the Quaker Meeting of Sufferings discussed the situation and wrote to the exiled Doukhobors, criticizing them for the imprudence that had brought on their tribulations. Their letter was probably carried to Russia by Kenworthy, who visited Moscow in December, and a reply reached the Quakers in the spring of 1896. It was signed by three of the Doukhobors, Ob'edkov, Zibarov, and Ponomarev, but also by the Tolstoyan Bodianskii, who for some years was to play a controversial role in Doukhobor affairs. In part the letter told with moving simplicity of the Doukhobor predicament. 'We have no land and receive no pecuniary relief . . . They do not allow us to bury our deceased brethren freely, but demand four or five roubles for a small piece of land for a grave.' But in defining their attitudes towards authority the writers displayed a sophistication in argument that suggests that Bodianskii's part in composing the reply had been considerable. They defined two kinds of power, founded on evil and good respectively. 'The power of love is an inward and spiritual one and comes from the spirit of God. The power of violence is outward, of the flesh, founded on force, arising from lusts and fears.' The power of the state, including the power of the law and the power of wealth, is derived from violence. But evil, which comes from the lack of good will, can be conquered only by good, meaning in practice the virtues of humility, patience, self-denial, and forgiveness. Therefore the Doukhobors find it impossible to use violence in their resistance to the Russian state.[1]

Tolstoy had found it relatively easy to draw attention to the plight of the Doukhobors, but the police watched the exiles in Georgia so closely that it was difficult to provide practical relief of any kind, though occasionally the Tolstoyans did contrive to get relatively small sums of money to the exiles. On the other hand Tolstoy and his disciples did not relax their efforts to stir the consciences of the tsarist authorities. On 31 October 1896, for example, Tolstoy wrote to Lt-Col. Morgunov, commander of the Ekaterinograd penal battalion, asking for lenient treatment for the Doukhobors under his control.

The military authorities, who have condemned them, and you, who are executing on them the sentence of the Court, evidently regard the conduct of these men as harmful, and believe in the efficacy of these severe measures which are directed against them. But there are people, and many (to whose number I also belong), who regard the conduct of the Doukhobors as great heroism, most useful to humanity. In this light, such conduct was regarded by the ancient Christians, and similarly it is, and will be, regarded by the Christians of the new time.

Thus the views concerning the conduct of the Doukhobors may be entirely opposite. In one point only all are agreed, both those who regard this conduct as good and useful, and those who believe it to be harmful —on this point, namely, that men who refuse military service from religious conviction, and are ready to endure for this every kind of suffering and even death, are not vicious, but highly moral men who, owing merely to a misunderstanding of the authorities (a misunderstanding which will probably soon be corrected), are placed in the same position as the most criminal soldiers.[2]

Tolstoy indicated to Morgunov the courses that lay before him; he could either treat his prisoners compassionately and refrain from making demands on them that would only lead to disobedience and further punishment, or he could 'torture them to death'. In the latter event, Tolstoy assured him sternly, 'you will bring upon yourself an invisible but most heavy calamity in the consciousness of the evident transgression of the will of God, as known to you; the consciousness of an irreparable, cruel, evil deed.'

It is said that on receiving this letter, Morgunov was so disturbed that his conduct towards the Doukhobors became less harsh, but it may in fact have been St Petersburg that was disturbed by Tolstoy's public revelations. At about this time it was decreed that religious objectors should no longer be sent to the penal battalions. As a result some of the men in Ekaterinograd were actually dispatched to Siberia before their sentences were completed.

Meanwhile the Tolstoyans decided to circumvent the silence of the Russian newspapers by issuing a pamphlet on the Doukhobor question. V. G. Chertkov, Tregubov, and Biriukov prepared the text of an 'Appeal for Help'. With a preface by Tolstoy, it was circulated as a pamphlet on 12 December 1896. It began in resounding, accusatory tones:

A terrible cruelty is now being perpetrated in the Caucasus. More than four hundred people are suffering and dying from hunger, disease, ex-haustion, blows, tortures and other persecutions at the hands of the Russian authorities.[3]

It carried on to present the grim effects of a year's homeless and land-less exile in the Georgian valleys:

In one place of exile situated in the Signak district, 106 deaths occurred among 100 families (about 1,000 people) settled there. In the Gory district, 147 deaths occurred among 190 families. In the Tionet district, 83 deaths occurred among 100 families. In the Dushet district, 20 deaths occurred among 72 families. Almost all are suffering from diseases and disease and mortality are constantly increasing.[4]

Tolstoy, in his preface, sought to reinforce the horror of the facts themselves with an idealistic assessment of the Doukhobors. They were not merely human beings subjected to unjust and insufferable persecu-tions; they were also exemplars of the 'awakening of the Christian spirit' which in his view was 'now appearing in all corners of the earth'. 'Christ's disciples', he insisted, 'were just such insignificant, unrefined, unknown people, and other than such the followers of Christ cannot be.' Among them was taking place 'the true resurrection of Christ', the maturing of the teaching he had spread eighteen centuries ago. The ferocity the Russian government directed against them in 'a persecution like those of pagan times', and 'the wonderful meekness and firmness' with which the Doukhobors endured these tribulations, were alike signs that the accomplishment of God's purpose on earth was near. That purpose, of course, was a Tolstoyan society, in which men and women irradiated by inner peace would establish the external kingdom of God. The particular significance that Tolstoy attached to the Doukhobors in this connection tells us less about the sect than about his own desperate eagerness to interpret events in accordance with his own hopes. It was this chiliastic view of the role of the Doukhobors that caused him, in letters to Verigin, Ob'edkov, and other members of the sect, to encourage them in their resistance, and later made him reluctant to accept the idea of emigration, which seemed a kind of surrender.

Inevitably, the 'Appeal for Help' created annoyance in official and ecclesiastical circles in St Petersburg, and, in January 1897, when Chertkov, Tregubov, and Biriukov attempted to present a memorandum in the same lines to the tsar, they were arrested, though Tolstoy, as always, was left untouched. Biriukov and Tregubov were exiled to Estonia, as was Prince Khilkov, whose continued presence in the Caucasus was considered undesirable. Chertkov, who had influence at court, was allowed to leave the country, and travelled to England—in the 1890s a favourite refuge for anti-tsarist expatriates. There, at Purleigh in Essex, he set up a Tolstoyan colony. As a communitarian experiment it was not very successful, for Chertkov was a notoriously quarrelsome pacifist. But he was also an energetic propagandist, and his appearance in England marked a major turning-point in the destiny of the Doukhobors.

Very shortly after his arrival, he collected the 'Appeal for Help' of the previous year and other documentary material on the sufferings of the Doukhobors and published them in a volume entitled *Christian Martyrdom in Russia*, which made a great impression among pacifists, radical Christians, and the English political Left, as well as among the considerable community of Russian refugees. The book sold widely and resulted in a flow of donations. At the same time, the Society of Friends officially took up the Doukhobor cause and set up its own assistance fund.

The immediate problem was one of communication. How could the money that had been raised be transmitted to the Doukhobors? All mail entering Russia was censored, and any attempt by Chertkov or the other Russian Tolstoyans in England to reach the Caucasus would have led to an uncomfortable exile in Siberia. Eventually an Englishman, Arthur St John, a former captain in the Royal Inniskilling Fusiliers, was chosen for the task. He had the confidence of Tolstoy, who had been in correspondence with him since his conversion to pacifism some years before, and on his arrival at Yasnaya Polyana he was given a letter of introduction to the Doukhobors. 'He will tell his friends about you,' said Tolstoy, who could not resist adding a little homily on the need for international Christian brotherhood.

St John reached the Caucasus at the end of December 1897 and travelled for a fortnight among the exiles, towards whom his reaction was nothing short of rhapsodical.

As for the impression they made on me, I wish I could in some way describe it. The brotherly way of them—Freemasonry is nothing to it. The interest they took in one. The intense feeling of a mutual tie. There is a sureness, a safety about them of something human realised, something of which we have dreamed. They move and have their being in an air of human brotherhood. It is evident what is their 'God', their main principle of life. Their life is a song of days to come. But the theme of it—surely it is not new, surely we have heard it long ago, for it tells of 'Peace on earth; good-will towards men.' [5]

An unnamed Russian Tolstoyan accompanied him from Moscow and sent Chertkov a report of the visit which gives a vivid impression of the condition of the exiled Doukhobors. The two men found them almost completely penniless. Some were even talking of fasting to death in the district police chief's courtyard. On 1 January 1898 the representatives of the exiles from all the Georgian valleys gathered to welcome St John and his companion, and to receive the several thousand roubles that the former had brought from England.

All those who had come over for the meeting assembled in one hut; altogether there were about 150. It was so crowded that all had to stand. The door was open and the passage was also crowded. St John and myself and a friend from Tiflis were seated round the table. Notwithstanding the crowd there reigned complete silence....

First of all I gave them the greetings of all their friends—Russian as well as foreign, also from Leo Tolstoy. I told them I had to hand over some money and letters. . . . In a few words I related how and where the money was collected; then it was counted and handed over. One of the Doukhobors then said that all who were present wished to express their thanks in their own way, and the whole crowd began to move and made a low—a very low—bow. A general sigh stifled with emotion was uttered, and one could hear sobbing. Seeing before me the backs and the heads of the bowing people—people whom I respect so highly, and who have suffered so much for the truth—expressing this murmur of gratitude, and seeing also their deeply moved faces, I was touched to the soul.[6]

St John found that even these followers of Verigin who had not been sent to the lower Georgian valleys were under very close supervision. In both the Kars and Yelizavetpol provinces they were forbidden to go from one village to another, though they did so in secret to arrange what help they could for their exiled brethren. Those in most distress were two hundred or more young men who had handed in their military reserve papers and, after a period of imprisonment, had been exiled in June 1897 to extremely isolated Moslem villages in the provinces of Baku, Erivan, and Yelizavetpol.

They are in a specially trying position, as they are settled separately, in places which can only be reached by narrow wild foot-paths; they suffer much from fever, and are often unable to work, even when work is to be had. In some of these Mohammedan villages the priest bids the inhabitants take care of the exile, calling him a guest sent to them by God. They collect half bushels of wheat for him from each household and surround him with care and affection, notwithstanding the fact that the Russian official who brought him to the village first of all told them what a dreadful criminal this man was. However, it is far from being so everywhere.[7]

Later St John was arrested and expelled to Turkey, while his Russian companion was sent to Siberia. The money St John had brought provided temporary relief from the immediate peril of starvation, but it was obvious that with the ever-intensifying vigilance of the tsarist authorities the refugees could not be regularly supplied, and the relief that did reach them would only postpone a conclusion that seemed inevitable. In a letter to the foreign press in March 1898, Tolstoy pessimistically prophesied that if the present persecution continued, in three or four years there would be no Doukhobors left.

Yet it was only a few weeks after St John's expulsion that the first rays of light began to break into the darkness of their situation. And here it is possible that their leader, Peter Verigin, played a part. Verigin has often been criticized for living relatively comfortably in his sub-Arctic exile while his followers were suffering at home. Short of performing some deliberate criminal act that would have led him to the salt mines, it is hard to see what more he could do, far away in Obdorsk, than to continue cultivating his garden and doing odd jobs for his neighbours. It is true that through those messengers who occasionally reached him he encouraged his brethren to continue in their defiance of authority regardless of the consequences, and it is easy to liken him to the generals and politicians who send other men to die. Yet if Verigin had done anything else he would have violated not only his own convictions but also those of his followers, who felt that in their sufferings they were in truth bringing back to the Doukhobor religion the will to spiritual struggle that it had lost during the lax dynasty of the Kalmykovs. Verigin had his faults: he was vain, autocratic, and often devious. But he was not a coward, either physically or morally; had he been so, he could have made his peace immediately with the tsarist authorities on the condition of withdrawing his 'advice' to the Doukhobors and leading them into the co-operative attitudes from which Gubanov and the Small Party were at this time drawing so many benefits. He did not choose to do so. On the other hand, with some courage, he did what little he could to ease the lot of his followers by appealing on 1 November 1896 to the Empress Alexandra. The letter, with its peculiar form of address—that of a ruler speaking to his equal—is so characteristic of the man and his preoccupations that it is worth reproducing at length.

May the Lord God preserve thy soul in this life, as well as in the future age, Sister Alexandra.

I, a servant of the Lord Jesus Christ, am living in the testimony and glad tidings of his truth. I am in exile since the year 1886 from the Doukhobor's Community of Trans-Caucasia. The word 'Doukhobor' should be understood thus: that we in the spirit and with our souls profess God (see the Gospel: the meeting of Christ with the Samaritan woman at the well.)

I implore thee, sister in Christ the Lord, Alexandra, pray thy husband Nicholas to spare the Doukhobors in the Caucasus from persecution. It is to thee that I address myself, because I think thy heart is more turned towards the Lord God. And there are at this moment more women and children suffering; hundreds of husbands and parents are confined in prisons, and thousands of families are dispersed in the native villages, where the authorities incite the population to behave coarsely with them. This falls specially heavily upon the Christian women! Lately they have been putting women and children into prisons.

The fault on our part is that we, as far as is possible to us, endeavour to become Christians. In regard to some of our actions, our understanding may not be sufficiently enlightened.

Thou art probably acquainted with the teaching of vegetarianism; we are sharers in these humanitarian views. Lately we have ceased to use flesh as food, and to drink wine, and have forsaken much of that which leads to a dissipated life, and darkens the light of the human soul. Refusing to kill animals, we in no case regard it as possible to deprive men of life. If we were to kill an ordinary man or even a robber, it would seem to us that we had decided to kill Christ.

The State demands that our brethren should learn the use of the gun, in order to know well how to kill. The Christians do not agree to this; they are put into prisons, beaten and starved; the sisters and mothers are coarsely defiled as women, very often with railing exclamations, 'Where is your God?' 'Why does he not help you?' (Our God is in heaven and on earth and fulfils all His will.)

This is sad especially because it is all taking place in a Christian country. Our community in the Caucasus consists of about twenty thousand. Is it possible that such a small number could injure the organism of the State, if soldiers were not recruited from among them? At the present moment they are recruited, but uselessly; thirty men are in the Ekaterinograd penal battalion; where the authorities are only tormenting themselves by torturing them. Man we regard as the temple of the living God, and we can in no case prepare ourselves to kill him, though for this we were threatened by death.

The most convenient manner of dealing with us would be to establish us in one place where we might live and labour in peace. All state obligations in the form of taxes we would pay, only we cannot be soldiers.

If the Government were to find it impossible to consent to this, then let it give us the right of emigration into one of the foreign countries. We would willingly go to England or (which is most convenient) to America, where we have a great number of brothers in the Lord Jesus Christ.

From the fullness of my soul I pray the Lord for the welfare of thy family.

The servant of Christ, PETER.

(Living in exile in the Government of Tololsk)[8]

In this letter there are inexactitudes (e.g. Verigin did not go into exile until 1887) and exaggerations (he implies that all the twenty thousand Doukhobors in the Caucasus are his followers and are being persecuted), while he glosses over the fact that the Christian Community of Universal Brotherhood, as his disciples had now become, accepted vegetarianism as a result of his 'advice'. But he does play eloquently on the chords that might appeal to the empress: the puritanical distaste then current in the imperial household for the 'dissipated life', and the suffering of women and children.

What effect Verigin's letter had at the time is not recorded. It was followed in 1897 by a petition from the Society of Friends in London to the tsar himself, while the Doukhobors continued to concentrate their appeals on the women of the imperial family. In the spring of 1897 a Tolstoyan, Paul Boulanger (who was later exiled for his work in favour of the Doukhobors), managed to break the press boycott by persuading a Russian paper to publish an article on the situation in the Caucasus, and this, according to Tolstoy, was read by a highly placed and pious civil servant, K. K. Grot, who was close to the Dowager Empress Maria. It is possible that he drew it to her attention, for when the dowager empress visited the Caucasus at the end of the year she accepted, probably from Ivan Abrosimov, one of Verigin's couriers, a petition requesting that the Doukhobors be exempted from military service or allowed to emigrate. She transmitted the petition to the senate, which acted as an ultimate court of appeal (subject of course to the personal will of the tsar), and the senate in turn sent it to Prince Golitsyn who was the governor-general of the Caucasus, with the instruction that the second request of the Doukhobors should be granted, but only with strict qualifications. Golitsyn, who had shown himself extremely unsympathetic to the Doukhobors, had no alternative but to implement the senate's decision, and late in February an order was issued, stating that exemption from military service could not be granted, but that 'all Doukhobor vegetarians, except those of military age and those who have not completed their military service' would be allowed to leave Russia provided they obtained passports, paid the costs of their emigration, and signed an undertaking that they would never return to the Russian Empire, under pain of being 'straightway exiled to the farthermost corners of the Empire'.[9]

All this would have been no more than empty words if it had not been for Tolstoy and the Doukhobors' sympathizers in England. The sectarians themselves had no idea where they might go, and those who were in exile in Georgia had no money with which to finance their departure. At the same time, the local authorities, having made their gesture in deference to the dowager empress, continued to persecute the followers of Verigin. When the Doukhobors approached Prince Golitsyn with an appeal for relief, he answered that they could not be helped because they did not wish to obey the authorities; the Doukhobors replied that they would pay taxes and in every other way obey the authorities, except on the one issue of refusing to kill. This enraged Golitsyn, who threatened to wipe them from the face of the earth and, when they approached him a second time, stormed at them: 'You will have no mercy! I thought you were going to become men, but I see you are the same lunatics as before.' [10] He even continued to obstruct those who might help the Doukhobors out of their predicament, and Tolstoy complained of 'the excessive zeal of the Caucasian authorities' in 'not admitting any communication whatever with the Doukhobors.' [11]

Tolstoy himself was unenthusiastic about emigration, as, curiously, was Peter Verigin once it became a definite possibility; as late as August 1898 he wrote to Tolstoy that he was 'almost positively' opposed to emigration, remarking shrewdly that wherever they went the Doukhobors would carry their peculiarities and would meet the same kind of people. He was even skeptical whether there was much more freedom abroad than in Russia. But neither Verigin nor Tolstoy opposed emigration when it became evident that the Doukhobors actually wanted it, and Tolstoy immediately threw himself into the task of collecting the considerable funds that would be needed. He wrote to rich men in Moscow and St Petersburg asking for donations, and, while some of them refused, others did respond, and one gave as much as five thousand roubles.

But it was in England, with its lack of any kind of restrictions, that the work of raising funds went ahead most vigorously. Chertkov had now been joined by Tolstoy's friend and translator Aylmer Maude, who after many years in Russia as a carpet merchant had returned to England in September 1897. The news that permission to leave had been granted the Doukhobors reached England in March, and at the end of that month Chertkov issued his first appeal, which circulated mainly among Russian exiles and among those interested in the problems of Russia. Interest in the fate of the Doukhobors grew appreciably after the *Daily Chronicle*, on 29 April, published an appeal from Tolstoy. At the same time the Society of Friends set up a special committee of four to administer its Doukhobor Fund and work in co-operation with Chertkov's Tolstoyan Committee.

Money began to flow in, slowly but steadily, and as the weeks went by the attitude of the authorities in the Caucasus became somewhat less obstructionist, doubtless because of pressure from St Petersburg, where the departure of the Doukhobors was now considered desirable; it had proved impossible to break their will to resist military service, and the adverse publicity the scandal created in foreign countries was evident even to the most obtusely reactionary official in the capital. Accordingly, there was less hindrance of communication with the Doukhobors, and it became evident that as soon as a destination had been found for them, the authorities would not impede their departure, even if they would not assist it.

The selection of a suitable place for settlement was difficult and urgent. The authorities had granted permission to leave more rapidly than had been expected, and the Doukhobors were very eager to go. At the same time, a place had to be found where there was plenty of land on which they could live as a group, in relative isolation and preferably under a government less concerned with religious and political orthodoxy than that of tsarist Russia.

As soon as Tolstoy received news of the permission to emigrate he began to discuss with his friends and followers various regions that might have these qualifications, and on 13 March he wrote to the Doukhobors, through an intermediary, mentioning four places that had already been suggested. These were Texas, Chinese Turkestan (the present province of Sinkiang), Chinese Manchuria, and Cyprus.

The idea of a migration to Manchuria had been suggested by a newspaper editor, E. E. Ukhtomskii, and Tolstoy thought it an excellent one. The Russian railway through Manchuria was in the course of construction, and Tolstoy suggested that to send the Doukhobors there would not only get the Russian government out of what was becoming an internationally embarrassing situation, but would also provide an excellent labour force for the completion of the railway. The Russian government evidently did not agree, for when Ukhtomskii put the plan to Count Murav'ev, the minister for foreign affairs, it was received coldly, and after that quietly vanished from consideration.

Tolstoy's attention then shifted to Texas, which had been suggested to him by C. F. Willard, a member of the 'Christian Community' in Georgia. Texas had been the site of communitarian settlements in the past, when followers of the socialist Fourier from France, and later from Russia, went there in an unsuccessful attempt to set up phalansterian colonies. The memory of these attempts lingered; there were characters in Dostoevsky's novels who had been through such experiences, and to many Russian radicals the name of Texas still rang the appealing bell of a lost cause. Tolstoy may have been influenced by these memories, and by the thought that Doukhobor farmers might be successful where socialist intellectuals had failed, for he wrote urgently to his American disciple Ernest Crosby, asking him for information about the price of land in Texas and the cost of transport there, and urging him to raise funds in the United States. It was not the American soldiers fighting against Spain at that time who were the real heroes of the age, he assured Crosby, but the Doukhobors who were 'being martyred alone, without witnesses', yet who were holding to their convictions and covering their tyrants with shame. 'Yet nobody knows these heroes or takes an interest in them.' [12]

The hope of finding a home for the Doukhobors in some part of the United States continued throughout 1898, and towards the end of the year Tolstoy was extremely encouraged by a meeting with the commissioner for immigration of Hawaii, which had just been annexed formally by the Americans. The islands were still underpopulated, and the commissioner, full of the zeal of newly acquired office, talked to Tolstoy in enthusiastic tones. He was interested in taking at least three thousand Doukhobors to work at guaranteed wages in the Hawaiian sugar-cane plantations; the American government might even pay half their fares. Tolstoy was taken up in the euphoria of the occasion and decided that Hawaii was undoubtedly the best place of all for Doukhobor settlement, though, as he wrote shortly afterwards to Verigin, he also considered that 'what is important is not where we live, but the conditions that surround us and our own internal spiritual state.' [13]

All these schemes for emigration to the United States, to the Far East, to Brazil, to Central Asia, faded away one after another. In the end, just as England was the most hospitable place for Russian political exiles, so the British Empire turned out to be more ready than other parts of the world to receive the Doukhobors. The first place where they actually found a refuge outside Russia was that which Tolstoy had least favoured: the Mediterranean island of Cyprus, which had been under British rule since 1878.

Emigration to Cyprus was strongly supported by the Quakers, whose views carried a great deal of weight among the Doukhobors' foreign sympathizers, partly because the Society of Friends had much experience of relief work and partly because of its powers of fund-raising. At first sight, there was much to be said for their choice. Cyprus was relatively close to Batum, the port from which the Doukhobors would have to sail, and the cost of transportation would be comparatively small. Land was available on the island, and the climate was not extreme. Finally, it was a British territory, and in those days before 1914 the very thought of compulsory military service was repugnant to most Englishmen, so that there seemed no prospect of the Doukhobors' being expected to violate their religious principles.

It was Arthur St John who initiated the negotiations regarding settlement on Cyprus. On 17 May he wrote to the chief secretary of the government of Cyprus inquiring on behalf of the committee in England whether the immigration of up to 3,200 Doukhobors would meet with the approval of the government, and where on the island they might settle. His letter was accompanied by an introductory note from Edmund Brookes, secretary of the Quaker committee, in which he described the Doukhobors as 'exemplary in their lives as citizens, being of exceptional sobriety, uprightness and industry'.[14]

Almost immediately afterwards St John made his way to Cyprus to investigate the situation personally. From Larnaka, on 1 June, he forwarded to the chief secretary a letter from Chertkov, 'one of the chief actors in the matter',[15] that throws much light on the emergency plans that were evolving at this time. Chertkov estimated that eight thousand of the Large Party of the Doukhobors would certainly wish to leave Russia, and that the three thousand members of the Middle Party (or the 'Butchers') would probably follow them.

What we want now is to find in Cyprus a kind of pied à terre *where we could bring over without further delay as many as our means will at present allow which will not at all events be a great number . . . The number of emigrants in the first instance will at best be counted by the hundreds, not by the thousands . . . If sufficient land were ultimately not available in Cyprus, why we should then turn our eyes to another country and establish them in parties of a few hundreds or thousands in different places.*[16]

The British government, stimulated by the growing publicity given to the Doukhobor issue in England, was already closely watching the situation in Russia. Quite independently of St John's efforts, the British consul in Batum reported on 27 May that the Doukhobors were now interested in going either to the United States or to England. He spoke highly of them and slightingly of their oppressors.

The sectarians since their establishment in Trans-Caucasia have by their good behaviour, diligence, sobriety and hard-working qualities, brought nothing but prosperity to the barren localities in which they were originally settled.

The authorities he blamed for 'drastic measures which at one time threatened to lead to something equivalent to open revolt'.[17]

It was therefore presumably with some knowledge of the situation that Joseph Chamberlain, the colonial secretary, received the letter that the high commissioner of Cyprus, Sir W. F. Haynes Smith, sent to Whitehall on 5 June, after St John had discussed the situation with him. While the high commissioner believed the Quakers had so far raised only enough money to pay the cost of settling on Cyprus 'some hundreds' out of the thousands of Doukhobors who wished to leave Russia, he was not opposed to the sectarians' settling on the island, 'provided they do not become paupers'. In fact he thought they 'might be of advantage to the island.' He suggested that they should be settled in one village, and should be as far as possible self-sufficient. Then he touched, unwittingly, what was later to become one of the rawest nerves in Doukhobor relationships with outsiders. 'The second essential is in my view that a proper school should be established and the children taught to learn and speak English.'[18]

It was the political aspect of the proposal on which the high commissioner asked advice of the Colonial Office, and this created a brief flurry of anxiety in Whitehall, where some of the officials feared that a Doukhobor settlement on Cyprus might be a haven for agitators against Russia or even for Russian spies. Eventually the question was referred to the highest level, where Lord Salisbury, prime minister and foreign secretary, finally gave his approval.

But this policy decision was perhaps the simplest of the problems connected with the Doukhobor immigration to Cyprus. Suitable land had to be found, funds had to be raised for transportation and for the expenses of settlement, and the unexpectedly stringent requirements that the Colonial Office eventually decided to impose had to be met. Finally, the Doukhobors themselves had to be given some opportunity to know what they could expect, and at the end of June the first group of Doukhobors was allowed out of Russia, with the stern warning from the tsarist authorities that they would not be allowed to return. The group consisted of Ivan Ivin and Peter Makhortov with their families, and they were accompanied by Prince Khilkov. They arrived in London on 2 July, where they told the aid committee that their brethren wished to be removed from Russia immediately, 'no matter where'. They did not even ask for land, so long as they could have useful work, and if all else failed they would take 'their children in their arms and start walking on foot.'[19] Yet when the two Doukhobors and Khilkov went almost immediately to Cyprus, they returned disappointed, complaining of the climate, which was too hot, and of the soil, which was too sandy. They felt that at best it would serve as a temporary refuge, and in the event they were right.

By now, however, it was already too late to make another choice. The departure of Ivin and Makhortov had been regarded as a signal by their brethren that it was time to leave the valleys of Georgia, and they began to sell to their Moslem neighbours what wretched belongings they still possessed and to drift down toward Batum, where their delegates waited anxiously on the British consul to find out when they could leave for Cyprus.

Meanwhile in England the Society of Friends now took the main initiative, inviting the leading Tolstoyans, Chertkov and Biriukov—who had just reached England—to join in their meetings. They printed an appeal that was sent to eight thousand individual Quakers, reminding them that their own predecessors had endured persecutions similar to those inflicted on the Doukhobors for opposing war, and called upon the Mennonites to follow suit. The fund rose quickly. By 9 August £10,475 had already been guaranteed, largely from the wealthier Quakers; one contributor pledged £2,000 and eight guaranteed £1,000 each. Among the latter were Edmund Brookes and the two chocolate magnates, J. S. Fry and George Cadbury.

At the same time the Quakers continued negotiations with Joseph Chamberlain on permission for the Doukhobors to enter Cyprus. They assured him that the industrious Doukhobors 'could not fail to be of help to the Cypriots',[20] that their presence would result in 'a distinct accession to the prosperity of the colony', and that there would be 'no pauperism' among them.[21]

Negotiations also began with the Cyprus Company regarding the acquisition of land on the island. The company's representative gave the Quakers an enthusiastic reception, and one of the directors, Alexander Dunlop, even suggested going to Cyprus to organize the landing of 3,500 Doukhobors at Larnaka, whence they would go to the estates that would be opened to them. For their land the Cyprus Company wanted a rent of £200, and they were willing to sell it eventually at £2,000; there is no record of the extent of land involved, but for an area where it was thought several thousand people might settle, the price was undoubtedly cheap—so cheap, indeed, that one is surprised the Quakers did not suspect that it might have disadvantages.

The arrangements with the Colonial Office were much more complicated than those with the Cyprus Company. The high commissioner had voiced his approval of the Doukhobor immigration immediately after meeting St John, when he was still under the influence of the ex-officer's urgent appeal, but soon he began to have second thoughts, to complain about the lack of proper arrangements for receiving the Doukhobors and to worry about local reactions. 'The Cypriot is extremely jealous of outsiders,' he remarked, and he reiterated his warning that, since work was scarce on the island, the Community must be self-sufficient from the start. He reminded Chamberlain that the same requirement had been made in the case of the Armenian refugees admitted to Cyprus, who had the advantage over the Doukhobors of speaking one of the island's languages, Turkish.[22]

These and other doubts were expressed by the Colonial Office on 29 July, when the under-secretary wrote on Joseph Chamberlain's behalf to John Bellows, the secretary of the Quaker relief committee for the Doukhobors. Chamberlain granted that he had 'no reason to doubt the statements made as to the good character and industry of the proposed settlers.' What he did doubt was the adequacy of the funds collected by the Quakers to fulfil the conditions the government felt obliged to impose: there must be enough land, adequate buildings and implements, sufficient seed, and a reserve fund that would pay for the Doukhobors to leave the island in the event that their settlement proved a failure.[23]

By this time over £20,000 had been accumulated in various funds for the Doukhobors. The Quaker guarantees amounted to £11,895, of which £4,605 was in hand; in addition the Tolstoyans had collected approximately £5,000, while the Doukhobors themselves had pooled their scanty individual reserves of money and made up a fund of £4,700, which would almost all be spent in paying for passports and chartering a ship. This left approximately £17,000 in the hands of the English committees for all the other expenses and for the reserve fund that the British government demanded.

Such a sum was still quite obviously insufficient, as the Colonial Office pointed out, to guarantee all the three thousand Wet Mountains Doukhobors who wished to leave Russia and to finance them until their first harvest on Cyprus. Chamberlain therefore expressed his trust 'that only such a number of immigrants may be sent to Cyprus as it is possible for your Committee to guarantee provision to the extent required.' [24]

The reserve fund was the main obstacle to concluding the arrangements. The high commissioner thought that twenty pounds per Doukhobor should be demanded. He also suggested that some of the public lands could be made available for settlement by a group of at least four or five hundred Doukhobors under government supervision. Chamberlain was even more cautious, and on 5 August surprised the Quaker committee by demanding not less than twenty-five pounds for each immigrant. The Quakers bargained hard, and at last, on 12 August, the Colonial Office agreed to fifteen pounds for each immigrant; moreover, it would not expect actual cash to be deposited but would accept a guarantee from the Society of Friends, to remain in force up to the end of 1900, after which it was felt the experiment would either have failed or be well on the way to success.

This decision meant that the first stage of the emigration could go ahead, and the consul in Batum was instructed to tell the delegates of the Doukhobors that they could now charter their ship, while Paul Biriukov and the Quaker Wilson Sturge were sent to Cyprus at the expense of George Cadbury to supervise the landing on behalf of the Tolstoyans in England and the Society of Friends.

In Batum the eleven hundred Doukhobors of the first party had already been waiting anxiously since the beginning of August, owing to Chertkov's having prematurely informed them that arrangements were complete. The Russian authorities, as the British consul reported later, 'acting upon instructions received from a higher quarter, would render no assistance whatsoever to the Doukhobors',[25] but a German naphtha manufacturer named Richter allowed nine hundred of them to sleep on the floor of a great iron shed in his disused factory, while the contractor for the new fire hall accommodated the rest in the uncompleted building. In Batum it was easier to get work than it had been in the Georgian valleys, and many of the Doukhobors, both men and women, were able to earn seventy or eighty kopeks a day, most of which they saved, living on a diet of tea, bread, and a few potatoes. A decrepit French freighter, the *Durau*, was chartered, and a few days were spent fitting it out with improvised bunks. Finally, on 18 August, the ship sailed, with 1,126 Doukhobor men, women, and children on board. The British consul stood on the dockside to watch their departure, and then went back to his office to warn the other two parties into which the Wet Mountains Doukhobors had been divided not to move down into Batum until they had heard from their brethren about conditions in Cyprus and the availability of land there. It was a wise warning, for no more Doukhobors actually went to Cyprus.

At first, when they landed at Larnaka on 26 August 1898, everything seemed very promising. Arthur St John was there to welcome them; on the same day he wrote to the committee in London : 'I have revived hopes of their staying in Cyprus for good, and being a blessing to the island and an instrument of the manifestation of good-will, God's Kingdom on Earth, here in the Old World between Europe and Asia.'[26] Wilson Sturge and Biriukov arrived three days later, having made a roundabout journey via

Alexandria and Beirut. The high commissioner promised to be helpful, the English newspapers on the island welcomed them, and the Turks were friendly because they found that the Doukhobors were iconoclasts and did not eat pork. Only the Greek newspapers, perhaps because of the influence of Greek Orthodox priests, were critical; they disapproved of the Doukhobor opposition to the tsarist government, and they feared that the presence of these immigrants would cheapen labour and raise the cost of food.

The land that had been acquired for the Doukhobors lay in two localities, at Athalassa and at Pergamo. They spent some days in quarantine quarters on the swampy ground near Larnaka, where the English doctor was impressed by their fine physique and 'meekness, composure and reasonableness', and then moved on to their destinations. Paul Biriukov accompanied one convoy on its way to Athalassa; and he wrote a vivid description to John Bellows in England:

We marched the whole night with a caravan of wagons stretching several versts. It was a spendid moonlight night: warm, quiet. I rode up and down the caravan accompanied by a mounted policeman whom the Governor gave me, and kept things in order. The journey was quite a fairy dream. Amid the wild barren scenery of Cyprus in a moonlight night are advancing wagons harnessed with bullocks and mules, laden with the Doukobors' baggage, women and children. The men and strong women are advancing in small groups between the wagons; some singing hymns. We meet on the way caravans of camels with bells, and Arabs swaying on the top . . .

So we march on one hour—another—and a third. Midway we make a halt of three hours, and the bullocks are fed . . . Then we gradually crawl on further . . . We get to a turn off the high road, go along it, and see in the moonlight in the distance an oasis—the tops of palms and shining white walls of buildings. This is Athalassa. The nearer we approach, the thicker and more varied becomes the vegetation; we see cotton plantations, groups of olive trees, bullrushes, etc., and the palms become grander and finer. I perceive bunches of dates upon them which I long to eat; but they are not yet ripe; and they are too high. At last we ride up to the house itself; we ascend a little hillock and hear the trickling of a stream. The wagons drive up one at a time; and by nine in the morning on the banks of the stream were already planted twenty-five tents, and the people actively moving about among them.

The place is beautiful, and I hope the Doukhobors will settle in it permanently.[27]

It was 'the land where the lemon tree blooms', the Mediterranean vision of north European romantics taking shape and form. And if it filled the intellectual Biriukov with literary visions, it may well have reminded the oldest Doukhobors of the lushness of Milky Waters remembered from their childhood. They were pleased with what they saw. The land looked fertile, and there were no Cossacks. At first sight the only disadvantage was the lack of buildings, and this applied as well to the other site at Pergamo. The houses there were completely decrepit, but the wells and the cisterns were in good repair.

The Doukhobors set to work with a will, turning the soil and sowing vegetable seeds, and they also started to build houses of mud bricks, like those in the Wet Mountains. Men and women worked together, and one English lady who had gone out to see the latest novelty on the island looked on with astonishment.

At Pergamo the 500 Russians settled there were building their mud-brick houses, and swarming at the work like boys playing football. And for force and strength, and regularity like a steam engine, I never saw anything to equal a middle-aged woman who, with garments kilted up to her thighs, was kneading the earth for brick-making by treading it. Such mighty limbs were a revelation to me.[28]

When the walls were completed, roofs were made of poles and reeds and covered with earth to keep out the heat.

Yet as summer continued and autumn came on, it became clear that the settlement was not working out by any means as well as the Quakers had hoped. The Doukhobors were willing and co-operative with those who tried to help them. But their work seemed disorganized for lack of effective leadership. They indulged in endless debates, and the time that should have been spent in working tended to be consumed seeking unanimity about tasks on which no individual would take the responsibility of making a decision. Some wanted to work on their own and took jobs on neighbouring farms, while others tried to maintain the pattern of communitarian work that Verigin had reintroduced among them. Undoubtedly the unfamiliarity of the soil and the climate contributed to the bewilderment of peasants who had been used to the cold-weather agriculture of the Wet Mountains. The Russian Tolstoyans who joined them seem to have done very little more than spread discontent among the settlers by complaining about the conditions on the island, while St John, of whom so much was expected, was accused by the Quaker secretary, John Bellows, of having 'lost his head in the disorganization all around him.'[29]

As a consequence neither housing nor farming went ahead as quickly as they should have done. Many people stayed for a long time in tents pitched in marshy spots infested with mosquitoes, and as late as December a report appeared in the British Quaker periodical *The Friend* to the effect that the houses that had been built were six times more crowded than prison cells in Britain. Some of the settlers lived in undrained dugouts, and even the adobe houses were badly ventilated. The latrines were never adequate.

Unsanitary housing and the impure water of the locality would have spread sickness even among healthy people, and the Doukhobors had come to Cyprus weakened by malnutrition and in many cases already suffering from malaria and other sicknesses. The doctor who was attached to them worked as hard as he could in the circumstances and reported spending forty pounds in a single month on drugs, but he complained of the poor diet that the situation and Doukhobor principles combined to force upon the sectarians. They would not eat meat or even drink Bovril. There were none of the fresh dairy products to which they had been accustomed in the Wet Mountains, for only condensed milk was available, and it was not until December that they were reported to have vegetable crops ready for consumption.

Only two months after their arrival the first deaths were reported, and as the weeks went on more and more of the Doukhobors were afflicted with malaria and dysentery. The mortality rate rose steeply, particularly among the women.

Those who survived, weakened by poor food and sickness, found the climate almost unendurable. The hopes with which they had come were slowly dissipated, and their discouragement with Cyprus was increased by the urgings of their Russian sympathizers who, having in the first place hastened their departure from Batum, now pressed on them the need to leave Cyprus as the only hope of evading extermination. Finally the news reached them that a new refuge had been found in Canada, and that their brethren were already preparing to go there. Any will they had ever felt to succeed on Cyprus was now finally dissipated, and they had no other thought than to join the emigration to the New World. They wrote to the Doukhobor Committee of the Society of Friends, thanking them for their 'brotherly care', but pointing out that they would like to settle with their brethren and that 'this is impossible here, as there is little convenient and cheap land to be got . . .

Even if it were possible for all our brethren to settle down here, even then we dread the extremely hot climate here, which resembles that from

*which we suffered in exile, where, out of 4,000 of our people, about 1,000
have already died.*

*We fervently appeal to you not to enter into great expense in establish-
ing us here, but in as much as will be possible to transport us into a place
more suitable for us to live in. From what we hear, Canada is such a place,
and we will patiently and in obedience to God's will, await our turn when,
with the assistance of our friends, it will be possible for us to join our
brethren. We are well aware that a great number of our brothers have yet
remained in the Caucasus, amid great oppressions and without any means
of subsistence, and we beg you first to think of them. And we hope that
our friends will also not forget about us here either, and will relieve our
position.*[30]

At last, on 27 April 1899, they boarded the *Lake Superior*, the third of
the four great parties of Doukhobors to cross the Atlantic. Many of their
companions lay in the dry soil of the island. No record of the exact number of deaths has survived, but Bonch-Bruevich claimed that 108 had died
in less than eight months. This does not seem an exaggerated figure: 1,126
Doukhobors sailed from Batum to Cyprus, but only 1,010 joined the *Lake
Superior* to make the voyage to Canada. For this group, ironically, freedom
on Cyprus with an annual death rate of about 150 per thousand had proved
even more lethal than persecution in the Georgian valleys, where, according to the most extreme estimates, 1,000 out of 4,300 Doukhobors died in
over three years (an annual death rate of about 80 per thousand). In either
case, the Doukhobors who followed Verigin believed that they would have
been doomed to vanish in a few years if Canada had not agreed to admit
them. This consideration—that emigration to Canada meant survival—has
to be borne in mind as the basic fact underlying all we shall recount of
their life in that country.

6 CANADIAN EXODUS

Even before the first and only contingent of Doukhobors arrived in Cyprus it seemed certain that the island would not be able to take all the eight thousand members of the sect who were anxious to leave Russia. The report on the island by Khilkov, Ivin, and Makhortov had left doubts, particularly in the minds of Chertkov and the other Tolstoyans, on the permanence of the settlement even for the eleven hundred exiles already there, and their Committee did not wait until the news of sickness and deaths arrived in October before considering alternative places of immigration for the Doukhobors. The Quakers thought that here again the Tolstoyans were being excessively hasty, but—as we have seen—events on Cyprus soon demonstrated that they were merely showing necessary foresight.

Ivin and Makhortov insisted that the Doukhobors wished to settle in either England or America. The lack of cheap land made England impossible, and the Committee does not appear to have thought it worth approaching the Home Office for permission to import such a large body of refugees. Like Tolstoy, his followers considered Texas and Hawaii, and even Brazil and Argentina. But, although the Dominion government was at this time engaged in publicizing the uninhabited West in Britain and on the continent, no one appears to have thought of Canada as a possible refuge for the Doukhobors until, by chance, a member of the Committee read an article by the anarchist, Prince Peter Kropotkin, that recounted, among other things, his impressions of the colonies of Mennonites he had seen on the prairies.

Kropotkin had gone to Canada in 1897 to attend a meeting of the British Association in Toronto, and afterwards travelled through the west as far as Victoria. In March 1898 he wrote of his experiences in *The Nineteenth Century* and described the favourable conditions the Mennonites had obtained for settlement on the prairies; they had received their land in large blocks, instead of in quarter sections of 160 acres as happened to individual farmers under the Dominion Lands Act, and had been allowed to settle in villages instead of being required to reside each on his own homestead. This enabled them to maintain their own form of communal organization.

Kropotkin, who more than thirty years earlier had visited the newly founded settlements of Doukhobors on the Amur River and had admired their spirit of mutual aid, was anxious to help their Caucasian brethren. As soon as Chertkov approached him he went to Purleigh and convinced the Tolstoyan Committee that Canada was in fact the best of all the possible places for the Doukhobors to settle. It was immediately decided that the two delegates, Ivin and Makhortov, should go to Canada to assess the situation, and in the meantime Kropotkin and Chertkov each wrote to James Mavor, professor of political economy at the University of Toronto, an expert on the prairies and immigration and a friend and admirer of both Kropotkin and Tolstoy. Kropotkin, in his letter of 31 August 1898, stressed the three points on which the Doukhobors would expect assurance: no obligation of military service; no interference in the internal organization of the sect; and block land grants, since the Doukhobors 'cannot live in isolated farms.'

Kropotkin's letter stimulated an already existing interest on Mavor's part. Mavor had suggested independently to the minister of the interior, Clifford Sifton, that the Doukhobors might fit admirably into his plans for the accelerated settlement of those prairie regions that were soon to become the provinces of Saskatchewan and Alberta. At the same time he had written in July to Tolstoy, who assured him that the Doukhobors were excellent farmers and, on a specific question that Mavor raised about education, expressed the opinion that the Doukhobors would send their children to school, provided 'the children would not be obliged to receive religious training.' [1]

With Kropotkin's and Tolstoy's letters in hand, Mavor intensified his negotiations with Sifton and on 8 September told him specifically that the Doukhobors would expect not only exemption from military service, but also an assurance that they could hold their land in solid blocks or reserves, and that they would 'wish to be consulted' with regard to the form of education that might be expected of their children. In view of later developments, it is important to stress that the Canadian government was aware of these expectations even before the Doukhobor delegates landed in Canada.

Ivin and Makhortov had sailed from Liverpool on the *S.S. Vancouver* on 1 September, before Kropotkin or Chertkov received replies to their letters to Mavor. They were accompanied by Khilkov and Aylmer Maude. The fares of the two Doukhobors were provided by Arnold Eiloart, whom Maude described as 'an eccentric member of a queer colony that had a brief existence in Purleigh';[2] they were accompanied by their wives and children, so that the Canadians could see samples of well-behaved Doukhobor families. Khilkov and Maude paid their own fares; Khilkov, who could ill afford even such Spartan accommodation, travelled steerage with the Doukhobors, while Maude, who was wealthy and 'a bad sailor', travelled first-class, 'feeling much ashamed of myself for such un-Tolstoyan self-indulgence'.[3]

The *Vancouver* docked at Quebec on 10 September, and the party went on immediately to Montreal. There Maude's connections in the carpet industry led him to James Morgan, a merchant in the same field, who introduced him to R. B. Angus, a banker and a director of the Canadian Pacific Railway. Angus in turn arranged a meeting with Thomas Shaughnessy, the vice-president of the CPR. The proprietors of the railway were as anxious as the Dominion government to populate the unopened regions of the northwest with European immigrants, and Shaughnessy immediately struck a bargain with Maude by which the railway would transport the Doukhobors from the port where they landed to the point on the railway nearest to their site of settlement for the extremely low price of six dollars a head.

Equipped with passes to travel wherever they wished in their search for land, the party set off for Ottawa, where they met Clifford Sifton and his deputy minister, J. A. Smart. In the discussions at that time, and later on in October, the attitude of the Canadian authorities was made quite clear; and it was communicated by Maude in a letter written on 17 September to the Tolstoyan committee in England. Marriages must be registered, but Doukhobors would be given the advantage of the clause in the Militia Act that exempted from service 'Quakers, Mennonites, or Tunkers, and every inhabitant of Canada of any religious denomination, otherwise subject to military service, who from the doctrine of his religion, is averse to bearing arms . . .' Education lay in the domain of the provincial governments, but it was not compulsory in the outlying areas, and in any case religious instruction was forced on no one in Canada. 'The case seems to be', he concluded, 'that Canada is as free as any country in the world.' [4]

Certain practical gestures had also been made by the ministry of the interior. Free shelter would be provided in the immigration halls until the Doukhobors were settled in their own villages, and a bonus per head of five dollars, normally granted to agents who signed up immigrants abroad, would be placed in a special fund to be utilized for the benefit of the Doukhobors when they reached Canada. As for the land, every endeavour would be made to allocate this in one place, but the Doukhobors would each have to make entry, individually, according to Canadian law, for the 160-acre homestead allotted to him. However, 'they were not required to perform, on each separate homestead, the work legally necessary before a homestead can become individual property, but were allowed to do an equivalent quantity of work on any part of the "township" they took up, thus facilitating their communal arrangements.' [5]

This, it should be emphasized, was not a special concession to the Doukhobors, but accorded with modifications of the Dominion Land Act made before the emigration of the sect to Canada had even been envisaged. In the late 1870s the act had been amended by the addition of the Hamlet Clause to facilitate the settlement of Mennonites. The clause read as follows:

If a number of homestead settlers, embracing at least twenty families, with a view to greater convenience in the establishment of schools and churches, and to the attainment of social advantages of like character, ask to be allowed to settle together in a hamlet or village, the Minister may, in his discretion, vary or dispense with the foregoing requirements as to residence, but not as to cultivation of each separate quarter-section entered as a homestead.

In May 1898, at least two months before James Mavor made his first approach to Sifton, the act was further amended to allow, in the case of co-operative farming associations, for improvements to be carried out in proportion to the total grant rather than in proportion to the individual quarter section. In other words, the Doukhobors would be completely within their legal rights if they ignored the residence clauses of the act by living in villages instead of on individual homesteads, and if they cultivated their land communally according to their own convenience rather than breaking and tilling the specified acreages on each quarter section.

One final point about the negotiations of 1898 should be mentioned. There remains, between Doukhobors and Canadian officials, a dispute as to whether it was made clear in 1898 that eventually, in order to obtain full title for their land, the Doukhobors would individually have to take oaths of allegiance to the Crown. Such a requirement does indeed exist in the act, but how clearly this was pointed out to Maude or Khilkov or the Doukhobor delegates is not evident from the documents that are available. One can dismiss the legend later put out by Peter Verigin, and to this day believed by many Doukhobors, that Queen Victoria personally declared that the Doukhobors were to live in Canada for ninety-nine years free from all earthly laws. The queen is not on record as having expressed any opinion about the Doukhobors, and even a democratic country like Canada could hardly countenance an island of theocratic autonomy in the midst of its territory. Maude says clearly that he informed Ivin and Makhortov, and also the committee in England, that the immigrants would be required to live according to 'the laws of Canada'. But he does not mention at any point that he specifically warned them—or was himself warned by Sifton or Smart—that an oath of allegiance would be required at some time in the future. The oath of allegiance had of course been one of the principal grounds of contention between the tsarist authorities and the Doukhobors; and if such a warning had in fact been given in 1898, it would certainly have aroused protests from the Doukho-bors and misgivings among their supporters, especially Tolstoy and the Tolstoyans. Yet at no point in the correspondence relating to the negotiations of 1898, or in the accounts of those who made the arrangements for the immigration of the Doukhobors, have we found a specific reference of any kind to the oath of allegiance. It thus seems probable that nobody at the time even thought of mentioning what was later to become one of the most important causes of controversy between Doukhobors and other Canadians.

After the first discussions in Ottawa the party set off for the prairies, where W. F. McCreary, the commissioner for immigration in Winnipeg, provided them with information and arranged for guides. By this time the Canadian Pacific Railway had been completed for twelve years and enough immigrants had flowed into the prairies to fill most of the good land to the south of its line. In order to find blocks large enough to fulfil Doukhobor specifications, the delegation had to search in the regions north of the railway that had not yet been opened up and about which the ordinary settlers were still doubtful because of the shortness of summer and the severity of winter.

The first area they visited was in the Edmonton district. Near Beaver Lake they discovered an area of twelve townships—472 square miles in all—that would have provided ample good land for all the Doukhobors to settle in one colony. It seemed to offer the ideal solution, and Maude and his companions hurried back to Ottawa to make the final arrangements. Here, however, they found themselves in the eye of a storm aroused by the Conservative opposition. For some years Ukrainian immigrants—or Galicians as they were called at the time—had been settling on the prairies, and the Conservative opposition, seeking any stick to beat Sifton's immigration policies, put about the report that they were 'a very rough and troublesome folk'. The religious unorthodoxy of the Doukhobors and their record of resistance to governments made them appear equally undesirable to the anti-government newspapers.

As a result [says Maude] *an opposition to the location of the Doukhobors in the Edmonton district sprang up; pressure was brought to bear on the Government, and when we thought all had been favourably settled, we learnt that we could not have the land we had selected. The search had to recommence, in other, less tempting parts of the country.*[6]

The search was not made any easier for Maude and Khilkov by the attitude of their companions. Without any reason, Ivin and Makhortov suspected the two non-Doukhobors, as Maude says, of 'making money out of the Canadian Government at the expense of the Doukhobors';[7] later on Makhortov attacked Khilkov openly, and Tolstoy soothed his friend's hurt feelings by remarking: 'What you wrote about Ivin and Makhortov . . . did not embitter me. All descriptions of Doukhobors . . . are so idealistic, that they become unbelievable, and therefore such incidents only lend reality to the picture.'[8] Even more frustrating was the fact that the two Doukhobors, brought up in a highly group-conscious society under a theocratic leader, showed themselves devoid of initiative or decisiveness.

Everything in Canada was new and strange to them; they of course spoke only Russian; and they were reluctant to take on themselves the responsibility for any decision. Their usual reply, when a prompt decision on any point was urgently necessary, was to say: 'We cannot decide; we are not empowered. Wait until all the brothers are here and then the matter can be discussed.'[9]

Meanwhile Maude and Khilkov were receiving urgent messages from the Doukhobors in the Caucasus, whose only wish was for arrangements to be made so that they could leave Russia quickly.

The Canadian Government, on its side, naturally wanted some responsible person to treat with; and thus the curious result was arrived at; that Hilkoff and I had, unwillingly, to accept the role and responsibility of plenipotentiaries for people whom I, at least, knew little of, and whose delegates more or less distrusted us both.[10]

Khilkov returned to the prairies with the two Doukhobors, while Maude remained in Ottawa to repair as best he could the damage caused by adverse publicity. Maude then set off on a brisk trip through the United States to generate support for the Doukhobor immigration. He met Jane Addams, the pioneer Chicago social worker, William Dean Howells, the novelist, and Tolstoy's disciple, Ernest Crosby; but perhaps the most fruitful contact he made, so far as the future of the Doukhobors was concerned, was with Joseph Elkinton, the Philadelphia Quaker who was to be instrumental in stimulating American interest in the Doukhobors and their problems.

Meanwhile, in his search for the second-best areas of settlement, Khilkov had been unable to find another single block with enough satisfactory land for the Doukhobors to settle as a united colony. Eventually, with the lukewarm assent of Ivin and Makhortov, who suspected that this was a device intended to split up the sect, he decided to accept land in three areas. What later became known as the North Colony was situated seventy miles north of Yorkton in the territory of Assiniboia; here six townships, totalling 216 square miles, were reserved for the Doukhobors. For the South Colony, thirty miles north of Yorkton, fifteen townships, totalling 540 square miles, were reserved. The third reserve was established in Saskatchewan Territory, near Prince Albert. It consisted of twenty townships, but only even-numbered mile-square sections were reserved for Doukhobors, so that in this area their settlement would be mingled with that of non-Doukhobors. Altogether the reserves totalled about three-quarters of a million acres, but official records of 1906 show only about half of this, a little over 400,000 acres, as having been in the possession of Doukhobors in 1906. The discrepancy can be explained by the fact that the larger blocks of land included considerable areas of swamp and other uncultivable territory to which the Doukhobors never in practice laid any kind of claim.

Finally, on 5 October, a formal agreement was approved by the minister of the interior. Curiously, it made no specific reference to the areas of land involved. It merely confirmed the bonus of $5, plus an additional $1.50 towards transportation, for each Doukhobor, and the arrangement regarding the immigration halls. Subsequently, in December, an Order in Council extended to the Doukhobors the military exemption already granted to other pacifist sects. The only reference to the lands in any document passing between Maude and the authorities appears in a letter from Deputy Minister Smart, dated 1 December, in which, confirming the arrangements made on 5 October, he mentions that he is arranging with the railway companies for them to hand over certain sections held by them in the Doukhobor reserves. The Liberal government and the railway companies appear in fact to have been so eager to recruit the Doukhobors in their recurrent role of frontier pioneers that they chose to waive formalities in the interests of haste. This lack of detailed written agreements between the principal parties involved in the arrangement was eventually productive of great misunderstanding, since it enabled the Doukhobors to claim rights they did not legally possess and Sifton's successors to act in ways not in the spirit of the understanding reached in 1898.

As soon as substantial accord was reached on 5 October, Maude and Khilkov cabled to Chertkov that arrangements could begin for bringing the immigrants from Russia. About 2,100 of the exiles from the Wet Mountains were left in the valleys near Batum, and these would have to leave first. In addition, more than four thousand members of the Large Party in Kars and Yelizavetpol provinces wished to emigrate. Verigin, his six brothers, and about four hundred of his followers were in or on their way to Siberia and were not covered by the order granting permission to leave. On the other hand, the settlers in Cyprus were as eager to depart as their brethren in the Caucasus. Altogether this meant that nearly 7,500 Doukhobors would be ready to leave as soon as the appropriate arrangements could be made, and that eventually, on their release from Siberia, another five hundred would wish to follow them.

Two immediate problems had to be considered. The first was that of regulating the entry of Doukhobors into Canada, since the Canadian government did not wish more than four thousand to arrive in the prairies during the winter months for fear the immigration halls would be overcrowded. The Doukhobors, on the other hand, were eager to leave immediately. A group of delegates who claimed that they represented three thousand Doukhobors had already approached the British consul in Batum on 2 October with a request for permission to go to the areas in

Canada that they understood had already been chosen for them; they were under the impression that if they did not leave Russia by the end of the year it would be too late. The consul telegraphed London, stressing that in his view the Doukhobors were 'most desirable colonists'.[11] On 3 October the Foreign Office replied that 'Doukhobors should not start for Canada or make arrangements with that object in mind till you hear further.'[12] Not until 27 October does the Canadian government itself appear to have been sufficiently satisfied for the governor-general to wire that no objection would be raised to the arrival of the Doukhobors.

The first to leave were the remnant of the Wet Mountaineers in Georgia. They were in the greatest distress and the most financial need. The responsibility for raising the money to transport the first party of approximately 2,100 exiles devolved mainly on the Tolstoyans. The Quakers had already tapped their richest sources in financing the Cyprus migration, and still felt that the Canadian venture was premature; however, they agreed to guarantee £2,500, or approximately $12,000.

They were not called upon to provide the full amount of the guarantee. The total cost of transporting the Wet Mountaineers from the valleys of their exile to the prairies of Canada amounted to approximately $40,000. Of this, $15,000 was spent on chartering the freighter *Lake Huron* from Liverpool, $14,000 was to be paid on the arrival of the ship at Batum, and $1,000 on the safe delivery of the immigrants in Canada. The cost of bringing the Doukhobors to Batum by railway would amount to $500 and a similar amount would be spent on lumber to fit out the holds of the *Lake Huron* with berths. The remaining $9,000 would pay the rail fares in Canada, allowing for reductions for the children.

Out of their scanty remaining property, the two thousand Doukhobors managed to raise $16,500. The Tolstoyans at Purleigh had about $5,000 in hand after they had made their contribution to the Cyprus immigration. Only $1,400 of the Quaker guarantee was needed. The largest single sum, approximately $17,000, came from Tolstoy. He had collected it mainly among wealthy Russians. His own contribution, his last novel *Resurrection*, which he had brought out of a drawer to revise and complete for the benefit of the Doukhobors, would not be ready for publication until the end of 1899. Then it was to provide funds over several years to help the Doukhobors after their settlement in Canada; altogether it yielded about $17,000. It is an interesting index to the puritanism of English nineteenth-century Quakers that the Society of Friends refused to handle funds coming from the sale of *Resurrection* because, while they appreciated Tolstoy's 'motives in writing the book', they considered it 'unsuitable for general reading'! [13]

Leopold Sulerzhitskii, a young aristocrat who was later to become an active associate of Stanislavskii in the Moscow Arts Theatre, made the arrangements in Batum for the departure of the first shipload of Doukhobors on board the *Lake Huron*. A renowned lady-killer, but also a sincere anarchist-pacifist who had served his own term in prison for refusing to take the oath, Sulerzhitskii approached his task with great responsibility, assuming full charge of the operation to the extent of becoming nominal owner of the *Lake Huron* in order to exonerate the real owners for any mishap to the passengers on the high seas. He was accompanied by Tolstoy's son Sergei, who had been in England consulting with the committee at Purleigh. On 6 and 7 December the Wet Mountains Doukhobors abandoned their huts in the valleys of exile, leaving symbolic bread and water on the tables, and travelled by train into Batum. There Richter's warehouse was available to them, and they camped among their chests and bundles in the cold, echoing shed. Once again, they had come too soon; they had to wait through ten days of fog and rain before the *Lake Huron* steamed into the harbour. Three children died. A family was isolated with scarlet fever. A child was born, its parents ashamed of having broken Verigin's 'advice' to avoid sexual intercourse.

As his followers were waiting, dejected and fearful of the unknown, yet anxious to leave what they did know, Verigin himself was still in Siberia. Even he was stirred by the thought of the great journey and the new home in a free land where, God willing, he would eventually be able to join his followers. Before the frosts of autumn clamped the north in their grip, and while the talk of Canada was still new in the ears of the Caucasian exiles, Vasilii Pozdniakov was chosen as a messenger to make the two months' journey, by rail and steamer and on foot, to Obdorsk. Verigin was now being carefully watched in the hope of keeping messengers away from him, but Pozdniakov posed as a fish peddler and met Verigin after dark in a field on the edge of the village. They spent the night in talk, and Verigin revealed his plans for the future of the Doukhobors in Canada.

'I want the Doukhobors to live in communities [he told Pozdniakov] *but they ought to be based on a free principle. Each family should have a separate house, a pair of horses, and a cow at their disposal. The increase of the cattle should join the common herd and be common. All the work in the fields should be done together. Each family should get its allow-*

ance in corn for itself and the forage for the cattle. The remaining revenue should be common and be kept in the cash office of the community.' And he said to me afterwards: 'Transmit my words to the Doukhobors—let them arrange themselves in that manner.' [14]

It was a vision that looked back to the past community created by Kapustin in the early days at Milky Waters, but it also anticipated, with variations, the kind of Doukhobor society for which Verigin himself would work, once he reached Canada, for the rest of his life. Pozdniakov by now was somewhat disillusioned with Peter Vasil'evich and sharply critical of the callousness with which—it seemed to him—the leader regarded the sufferings of his followers. 'But nevertheless, the image of the coming life in Canada, which he represented, was so attractive, that I left him filled with hope in the radiant future of the Doukhobors.' [15]

That vision, which Pozdniakov obediently transmitted to his brethren before he was sent off into Siberian exile for his refusal of military duties, consoled the Doukhobors during their dreary days of expectation until the *Lake Huron* arrived and Sulerzhitskii and Captain Evans set the men to work building berths in the holds and coaling the ship. On 21 December the *Lake Huron* sailed with 2,134 Doukhobors on board; only the Razanov family, infected with scarlet fever, was left behind. On the first smooth lap of the journey through the Black Sea, Sulerzhitskii was assisted by two English doctors, one of whom, Dr Mercer, became very popular among the exiles because of his efforts to learn Russian. At Constantinople they were joined by a Russian doctor, Aleksei Ilich Bakunin, nephew of the great anarchist Michael Bakunin and an admirer of the Doukhobors, and by a Russian nurse, Sasha Satz.

The journey through the Mediterranean was deceptively smooth, and the Doukhobors enjoyed the sunlight and the unaccustomed freedom from anxiety. As they had arranged themselves in the holds according to their villages, life on shipboard was well organized and not intimidatingly strange; while the women washed clothes and prepared food, the men went about the various tasks apportioned to them. Since the ship was short-handed in order to save expenses, ninety-four of them, including some who had formerly been sailors, were recruited as a supplementary crew, while the boys were put to work chipping away rust.

Beyond the Pillars of Hercules the weather changed, and in mid-Atlantic the ship rode through an eight-day storm. Many of the Doukhobors were incapacitated by seasickness, and terrified by this strange new illness. Despite the exhortations of old Ivan Makhortov, who let no one forget that he had once served in the tsar's navy, many firmly believed they would never reach land. Moreover, the graver sicknesses of their exile followed them across the Atlantic. By the time the *Lake Huron* came in sight of Halifax on 24 January, after a slow voyage of more than a month, ten of those who hoped to find a new and happier life in Canada had been sung with psalms to rest in the sea. Yet when the calm weather came, three days off land, the men cleaned down the ship with such zest that the Canadian quarantine officers reported they had never seen so well kept a ship come into Halifax harbour.

It was the tug carrying the quarantine officers and other visitors that gave the chanting Doukhobors their first view of Canadians, against the background of dark conifers and snowy earth that was the land itself. James Smart, the deputy minister of the interior, was there in person, with Khilkov and the two original Doukhobor delegates. Joseph Elkinton and another Quaker from the United States had come, together with reporters from newspapers in the Maritimes and Montreal, and J.T. Bulmer, a delegate from an unnamed labour organization. The Quakers prayed, the Doukhobors bowed, the newspapermen noted the exotic dress of the new-comers and questioned Captain Evans about them, and Bulmer made a speech. He praised their courage and their pacifism. He declared that they belonged to 'the races we want in this country—the great northern races of Europe', and he ended in a peroration which, if they made much of Khilkov's translation of it, must have seemed strange to these Russian peasants who guided their lives not by the printed word but by the un-written Living Book.

I do not know the name of your emperor, but the name of your patron and friend, Count Tolstoy, is as well known in Canada as in Russia, and I hope that one of the boys now listening to me, fifty years hence, will fill like him, with honour to his country, the literary throne of the world. On behalf of the working-men of this country, I welcome you to Canada and bid you God-speed.[16]

The Doukhobors bowed again, this time with their brows to the deck, and Vasilii Popov, their spokesman, explained to the gaping onlookers that he and his brethren were bowing to the Spirit of God in their hearts which had made them welcome the exiles as brothers into their own land.

On the whole the impression the Doukhobors made was excellent. The health officer, Dr Montizambert, remarked on their excellent physique. The reporters were intrigued with their clothes and their music, 'like that of a mighty choir chanting a solemn *Te Deum'*, as the *Halifax Morning Chronicle* described it the next day. And after all the attacks in the Conservative press, Deputy Minister Smart was pleased with the dignity and the fine bearing of the Doukhobors and the disciplined quietness of their children. Canada seemed to be getting an excellent bargain.

From Halifax the *Lake Huron* sailed on to Saint John, where the onlookers cheered as the first Doukhobors stepped on land and clubwomen from Montreal welcomed the unsmiling children with gifts of candy. Five trains of colonist cars were waiting to carry the immigrants on their long journey into the prairies. If the Doukhobors made a good impression on the first Canadians who saw them, the new land on which they now disembarked impressed them in turn. They liked the cleanliness and comfort and warmth of the colonist cars with their great coal-burning stoves. They liked the bread, milk, and cheese that were provided for them, and the excellent meals in the immigration halls on their way; the more naïve among them imagined that all this was provided freely, not realizing that it came out of the government bonus which, after some discussion, was being administered by the immigration service on their behalf. The democratic behaviour of Canadian officials and politicians was surprising to peasants accustomed to tsarist bureaucrats; in Quebec they were astonished at the zeal with which the chief of the immigration office worked, from nine in the morning until eleven at night, and pleased when the Speaker of the provincial legislature came to welcome them. Perhaps most of all they were impressed at the absence of Cossacks and the scarcity of policemen. Many of them decided that Canada must be a good and peaceful country, but there were others, swayed by the suspicion that is natural to the Russian peasant and intensified among the Doukhobors by long persecution, who decided that only experience would tell.

As the Doukhobors moved westward their impressions of Canada deepened, and during the months of winter, before they were able to take possession of their lands, their characteristic attitudes towards Canadians—and the attitudes of Canadians towards them—began to take shape. Until they reached Winnipeg on 28 January, they were merely objects of passing curiosity; the people in the Maritimes and in Quebec who welcomed them never expected to see them again. Into the prairies, however, they came as future residents. Those who lived there already were critically inquisitive about these strange sectarians who would become their neighbours. And the Doukhobors in turn watched, with a certain apprehension, the habits and attitudes of the people among whom they would have to settle. For, as they had learnt from experience, however isolated their villages might for the time being remain, complete isolation was impossible. The outside world would always make its demands upon them.

On the prairies the society in which the Doukhobors would have to find their place was in the process of solidification. The old North-West, where every community was a law unto itself, had died with Louis Riel, the leader of the doomed Métis rebellion of 1886. Along the line of the CPR and to the south, the best land was already settled; towns and even one city—Winnipeg—were taking shape as the centres of farming areas that were beginning to prosper. To the north settlers were only just starting to penetrate. Many of them, like the Doukhobors themselves, were from the great empires—German, Austrian, and Russian—of pre-1914 Europe, and a certain tension already existed between these and the immigrants from the British Isles, who often felt that they had a better right to advantageous treatment.

In many ways the West hovered in an interregnum between a society of pioneers and a society of established farmers. The fierce competition for land that was a feature of the next decade had not yet begun. The customs of mutual aid that characterized the pioneer movement in North America were still to an extent perpetuated. The Doukhobors, for example, were astonished to discover that it was the accepted custom for a hungry traveller to take anything he might need from the caches of food that they saw stacked beside the prairie roads. At the same time, the manners of the prairies still followed the boisterous, rough-and-ready code of the frontier, though the Canadian west had never—apart from the two Métis rebellions—known the kind of violence that had been customary on the frontier south of the American border. Before the settlers arrived the Indians had been pacified with less bloody methods than those used in the United States, and the North West Mounted Police had established the skeleton of an administrative system that even in the 1890s was still tenuous and incomplete. Outside the towns schools hardly existed, and over great areas of the prairies the only roads were tracks worn by the pioneer carts traversing the plains where buffalo grass pushed up among the scattered bones of the exterminated bison. The reserves that had been chosen for the Doukhobors were in regions still loosely governed as territories dependent on the federal government. Not until 1905 would the provinces of Alberta and Saskatchewan be carved out of the Northwest Territories, and several years were to pass before government authority would be sufficiently consolidated to pose a threat to any community's self-sufficiency.

Their first weeks in the west the Doukhobors spent in various immigration halls: at Winnipeg, Selkirk, Brandon, and Dauphin in Manitoba and at Yorkton and Prince Albert in Assiniboia. To the people of Winnipeg, where they occupied two halls, they were objects of great curiosity. Every day visitors would come asking questions about their religion and their life in Russia. The Canadians were impressed to learn that the Doukhobors made their own clothes, and even more impressed by the skill of the old men who carved wooden spoons which they would give away as souvenirs. The Doukhobors, on the other hand, were disgusted by the fact that some of their visitors chewed gum and tobacco, and in this and other respects they found little difference between the Germans and the English. They showed little interest in the tracts that evangelists tried to give them. To deal with the idle sightseers who behaved uncouthly, the Doukhobors developed a non-violent technique of mimicry that in most cases was successful in conveying its message over the barriers of linguistic incomprehension.

In Winnipeg the Doukhobors were under the leadership of Vasa Popov, a dedicated disciple of Peter Verigin who had given all his money and property into the common fund and was deeply shocked to find that some of his brethren had kept money to themselves and had been seen in the town trying to change roubles into dollars. Thanks to Popov's good organization and his co-operation with the local immigration authorities, the Doukhobors in Winnipeg were well fed and their health improved rapidly. In Brandon, where Nikolai Zibarov was in charge of three hundred emigrants, a more Spartan attitude prevailed and the food was scanty; there were only two meals a day—a breakfast of tea and bread and a lunch of cabbage and kasha (gruel)—and only on Sundays were small quantities of Canadian cheese provided. This diet was in part due to a fanatical dedication to the ideal of a simple life on Zibarov's part that was later to have more dramatic manifestations.

The cost of feeding the Doukhobors in the immigration halls and their initial expenses on the prairies were paid out of the fund created from the bonus of five dollars allowed for each settler on arrival at Winnipeg. This was now administered by a small committee consisting of the commissioner of immigration, William F. McCreary, a Winnipeg merchant named Thomas McCaffrey, and Prince Khilkov. Later a young Christian anarchist, Herbert P. Archer, who had arrived in Canada to work among the Doukhobors, was added. At its peak the fund amounted to $36,000, to which the government added a further grant of $20,000, which the Doukhobors partly repaid; it is worth noting that the Doukhobors enjoyed no favours that would not have been given in the normal course of procedure by a government of an empty land anxious to secure a considerable group of promising immigrants.

As mainly illiterate farmers, the Doukhobors during these first weeks in the west were restless without manual work and anxious to add to their funds by their own efforts. The men went out to shovel snow and cut firewood for the local householders, and in Brandon the women took in washing. It was this industriousness that led them innocently into their earliest conflicts with Canadians. It taught them, among other things, that here also the churches they opposed were still powerful. The clergy objected because they worked on Sundays and reported them to the local magistrates; fortunately, the magistrates were too sensible to proceed beyond a warning.

More serious was the fact that at Brandon many of the local residents set out quite cynically to exploit the Doukhobors. Some, it is true, would pay them a dollar or more a day; but there were others who found that the simple peasants, who had yet little sense of the Canadian monetary system and who were living communally in the immigration halls, would accept as little as fifty cents or even thirty cents a day. All at once Doukhobor labour became popular, and the general level of wages in Brandon began to fall. The situation quickly boiled up and the English-speaking labourers called a meeting in which they drafted a protest to the government, which was accused of subsidizing Doukhobors to starve the families of Canadian working men. 'Protect yourselves against the new Chinese,' shouted one orator: 'Down with the Doukhobors' read the placards that were put up after the meeting.

The Doukhobors came from a rural society where labour agitation was unknown, and during the three miserable years of their Georgian exile they had become so accustomed to working for any pittance their Moslem neighbours chose to give them that they were at first astonished that anyone should object to their doing the same thing in Canada. Fortunately Sulerzhitskii was present to explain the workers' objections. The Doukhobors, who had not the least intent of harming anybody else, immediately agreed to accept nothing less than the customary rate of wages, and the antagonism against them quickly subsided.

Even in the sub-zero winter, work would have to be started early on the reserves if all the Doukhobors arriving in 1899 were to be settled on their lands by the following autumn, and the young men of the first shipload became pioneers to establish the temporary encampments from which the settlers might afterwards spread out to their villages. A site for a reception centre was chosen in each of the North and South colonies, and Canadian carpenters were sent ahead to build log houses in both places to accommodate the Doukhobor working parties. Then, in mid-February, the first group of a hundred young Doukhobors set off by train from Winnipeg to Yorkton in the Assiniboine Territory. Thence they travelled by horse-sleigh for thirty miles to the site of the South Colony, where most of them stayed while a small group under Zibarov went on forty miles to the banks of the Swan River in the North Colony. The task of these pioneer groups was to build barn-like structures of poplar logs to accommodate the old men, women, and children who had been left behind in the immigration halls, and eventually all the later contingents from Russia. Later in February Sulerzhitskii set off for the North Colony with a second party of fifty men; travelling by train to Cowan in Manitoba, they took with them a large quantity of provisions bought out of the bonus fund. At Cowan, Zibarov met them with ten horses and six oxen, the first livestock of their new farming life, which drew the provisions by sleigh through the meagre forests to the five sheds by the riverside that marked the site of the first Doukhobor village in Canada, Mikhailovka. The weather was clear and crisp; the worst of the prairie winter was over, but the snow still lay thick and drifted in powdery swathes across the path. To the Doukhobors, accustomed to the hard winters of the Wet Mountains, it was a welcome change from the torrid Georgian valleys of their exile, and the thought of setting to work once again on their own land gave an added exhilaration to these first pioneer weeks before the mass of their brethren began to crowd into the settlements.

While these preparations were going on, the remaining Veriginite Doukhobors outside Siberia were already making their way to Canada. The 1,600 villagers from Yelizavetpol and the 3,000 from Kars did not have to depend on the help of outsiders to leave Russia. Though under police supervision, they had been allowed to stay on their farms in the Caucasus; and it is a measure of their devotion to Verigin's reformed Doukhoborism that they were willing to abandon their land voluntarily, to sell their possessions at a loss to the Small Party and to their Moslem and Armenian neighbours, and to set off in the old Doukhobor manner as pilgrims to the uncertain lands of the New World. At the same time, they had an initial advantage over their impoverished brethren from the Wet Mountains. When everything was sold there was enough money to pay the fares from their villages to the Canadian prairies and even to provide a reserve fund for use when they reached their new homes. According to the Doukhobor historian V. A. Sukhorev, the Kars Doukhobors had £20,000 (at the exchange rate of that period, $100,000) and the Yelizavetpol Doukhobors £10,000 (or $50,000).[17] Other estimates are somewhat lower.

To complete the transfer to Canada as quickly as possible, the *Lake Huron*'s sister freighter, the *Lake Superior*, was hired. Under the charge of Sergei Tolstoy, the whole of the Yelizavetpol Doukhobors and some seven hundred of their brethren from Kars sailed on this ship, which left Batum on 29 December. Six people died on the voyage, one of them of smallpox, with the result that, though the ship reached St John on 27 January, it was only late in February that its passengers were released from quarantine to join their brethren in the immigration halls of the prairies.

With their arrival, the Canadian government's limit of four thousand immigrants for the first winter had already been exceeded, and, as we have seen, it was not until the end of April that the *Lake Superior* put into the harbour of Larnaka in Cyprus to take off the survivors of that ill-fated experiment. Sulerzhitskii had gone back to Europe to supervise the migration. Arthur St John also accompanied the party across the Atlantic, together with William Bellows, son of the Quaker John Bellows, Nurse A. D. Rabetz, and Anna de Carousa, an admirer of Tolstoy. A ruthless natural selection seems to have weeded out all the weak from this contingent during their winter of sickness and death on Cyprus; by the time the ship reached Quebec on 21 May there had only been one death, and this was complemented by a birth.

Finally, at the beginning of May 1899, the *Lake Huron* left Batum carrying the largest of all the groups of Doukhobor settlers, some 2,318 sectarians from the Kars settlements. On this voyage came the only member of the Doukhobor ruling dynasty to accompany the mass emigration of the sect, Peter Verigin's aged mother, Anastasia Verigina, who was, as Maude put it, 'a sort of queen among them', and whom many regarded as the 'Mother of God'; Verigin's father had died shortly beforehand. A further group of anti-tsarist Russians accompanied this party, including Dr Vera M. Velichkina; Nurse Khir'iakova; A. K. Konshin, the Tolstoyan son of a wealthy Moscow merchant; and the young Russian Marxist, Vladimir Bonch-Bruevich, then masquerading under the pseudonym of V. Ol'khovskii but later, under his real name, to become closely associated with Lenin during the Russian civil war. To Bonch-Bruevich and his patient recording of traditions among the sectarians shortly after their arrival in the prairies, later scholars owe a great deal of their knowledge of Doukhobor culture before it became seriously influenced by the North American environment.

When the *Lake Huron* reached Canada on 5 June there were thirteen cases of smallpox, and the passengers were held in quarantine on Grosse Island in the Gulf of St Lawrence for twenty-seven days. The Kars Doukhobors, ignorant of the nature of infectious diseases, were disturbed at the thought of the patients being isolated from their families; it was only the presence and persuasions of Anastasia Verigina that prevented a difficult situation in which the Canadian authorities might have felt justified in using force and the Doukhobors might have developed a feeling of persecution right at the beginning of their life in Canada.

The total number of Doukhobors who reached Canada on these four ships has not been satisfactorily established. Bonch-Bruevich gives a figure of 7,160, Maude gives 7,363, and the reports of the Department of the Interior Land Patent Board give 7,427. Since Maude was more closely involved in the actual arrangements than Bonch-Bruevich, we can accept his statement as nearer the truth and take 7,400 as a working guess. Owing to the fact that many young men had been left in Russia because of their liability to military service, the proportion of men of working age was relatively small—approximately one fifth—and this was to have a considerable effect on the kind of life that the Doukhobors developed in their prairie settlements.

Another important factor was the way in which the settlers arranged themselves in the various reserves as they moved out from the temporary shelter of the immigration halls. The North Colony in Assiniboia was entirely settled by Wet Mountaineers who had been exiled in Georgia and had sailed on the first voyage of the *Lake Huron*. The South Colony, which was the largest in area, was the most mixed in origin. It included the whole of the people from the Yelizavetpol villages, together with those of the Kars Doukhobors who had travelled on the first voyage of the *Lake Superior* and the contingent from Cyprus, former Wet Mountaineers who were the poorest of all the immigrants. Finally, the greater part of the Kars Doukhobors who came as the last contingent on the *Lake Huron* in June 1899 were sent on to the third reserve, three hundred miles west in the Saskatchewan Territory near Prince Albert, not far from the region of Louis Riel's last rebellion. Among the immigrants these were the most prosperous, if such a term can be used to convey gradations of poverty; they had some money, and they had brought with them some saleable goods, such as oriental carpets. These differences, slight as they may have been in absolute terms, were to create relatively important economic divergences between the various colonies in the years immediately after arrival in Canada and to breed differences of outlook that had a considerable effect on future relationships, not merely among Doukhobors, but also between Doukhobors and Canadians.

While 7,400 Doukhobors reached Canada in 1899, more than 12,000 were left behind in Russia. Through its various schisms over meat-eating, sexual intercourse, and other puritanical restrictions, Verigin's Large Party had in the end become a minority movement. Although it had once been thought that the Middle Party would join the emigration, its members decided to remain in the Caucasus, and only a very few individuals from this group or from Gubanov's Small Party ever reached Canada; similarly, there was no inclination to join the exodus among the small Doukhobor settlements along the Amur River, which had not been touched by the schisms among their Caucasian brethren. Indeed, apart from Verigin himself, whose exile had been extended for a third five years, to end in 1902, the only Doukhobors remaining in the Russian Empire who were still anxious to reach Canada were the exiles in the Northern Siberian province of Yakutsk. Since the special attitudes that this group evolved before it eventually reached Canada were later to accentuate the differences of outlook among Verigin's followers, it is worth considering their experiences before passing on to the general picture of Doukhobor life as it evolved on the Canadian prairies.

The nucleus of this group consisted of about a hundred and fifty men who were exiled for various offences against military law. Later, when the main body of the Large Party went to Canada, the wives and families of the exiles were to join them in Yakutsk, and a number of prominent Doukhobors, including Verigin's six brothers and his brother-in-law, Ivan Konkin, were sent to the same area. Altogether the group seems at its largest to have consisted of between three and four hundred people.

The journey to Yakutsk was one of extraordinary hardship, as was the life that the exiles had to live there, particularly in the first two years. It took the first party of thirty men a year, from the autumn of 1896 to September 1897, to reach their destination. They went part of the way by rail, but great distances on foot, marching from 3 a.m. until dusk, with a brief halt at midday, along mere tracks over the tundras where they often had to drag the wagons carrying their supplies and possessions because the terrain was too difficult for the horses. At night, in the bleak convict shelters, their boots would freeze. The kindness of some of the officers who were in charge of the convict train, and of the merchants in the town of Yakutsk, who sold them goods at half price out of sympathy, were compensations for their sufferings, and they kept their courage alive by singing psalms as they marched.

A remote and almost uninhabited forest region called Ust Notora was their eventual destination. They had to travel the last lap of their journey by raft, down the river Aldan until they reached its confluence with the river Notora. This was their place of exile. There was no Russian habitation for sixty miles, and the nearest settlements of the semi-nomadic Yakuts and Tunguses who were native to the region were almost twenty miles away. The only building on the spot was a deserted Yakut hut. Here the exiles were told they must live; they were not allowed to absent themselves from the spot without special permission, which could only be obtained from the governor in Yakutsk, a month's journey away.

The hut was a rough structure of wood, with an earthen floor; in the winter slabs of ice were set in the window openings to keep out the cold and provide a glimmering of light. It became so cold that, in spite of heating, ice formed on the inside of the walls. The Doukhobors had not been able to afford enough warm clothes in Yakutsk, and so they had to sleep in turn, some men walking up and down in the hut while the others lay under their shared clothes. They had no oil for lighting, and the long winter nights were passed in a darkness relieved only by the flickering of the fire. There was no means of earning money, and they were unable to go away to look for work, since every month a policeman came to check up on their presence.

Eventually, however, their supplies of food ran out, and in desperation the strongest of them travelled the sixty miles through the roadless forest to the nearest Russian village. There they were lucky enough to find work, and thus help their brethren at Ust Notora. Shortly afterwards the governor gave them official permission to work in the village, and from this time their situation improved. The government made them a small allowance of ten kopecks (about twenty cents) a day each, and they bought some horses and cows out of their earnings. They began to build a large new house, and as soon as the ground thawed out they ploughed it for spring sowing. Later they set up a blacksmith's shop and a horse-operated mill.

Even so, their life was still hard. Their employers were almost all Skoptsy, and the fact that these were sectarians spiritually descended from the same prophet—Danilo Filippov—as the Doukhobors did not make them easier taskmasters. Vasilii Pozdniakov, himself one of the exiles, complained of the 'avidity' and 'eagerness for riches' of these pious castrati, and the hardness with which they forced the Doukhobors to work.

The work was lasting about sixteen hours a day, both summer and winter, with only short intervals for lunch and dinner. The most tiresome work was the threshing on the ice-floor in the winter. . . . This work, in semi-obscurity and at hard frost—was lasting all the winter long, and many were ill from it.[18]

Yet the Doukhobors could not do without this work, since the cleared land at Ust Notora was insufficient to grow food for them all when the hundred and fifty exiles and their families were assembled, while it was difficult to clear the forest because the frost lay in the ground almost the whole year round. Nevertheless the spirit in the settlement was good.

All the community was composed of equal men; they were taking themselves for brethren and nobody was striving to dominate the others.[19]

And, though the Doukhobors suffered at the hands of the Skoptsy, they made good friends with the Yakuts and Tunguses, offering them hospitality, so that first the men and afterwards the women and children would come to visit them regularly.

The serpent of dissension entered into this icy little paradise with the arrival of Verigin's brothers and Ivan Konkin a year or so later. The exiles were not prepared to transfer to his relatives the reverence they still accorded to Peter Verigin, and when an attempt was made to subject the little colony to an oligarchy of the leader's clansmen, the original members refused to accept it. Eventually almost all of them broke away, forming other small settlements, until at Ust Notora, 'a few families remained only, and Basil Verigin became absolute master then.'[20]

From 1899 onwards the Yakutsk exiles kept petitioning for permission to leave Russia. A few individuals did succeed in leaving. Gregory Verigin escaped; Ivan Konkin left by a special dispensation. But for the group as a whole permission to leave was regularly refused in spite of supporting petitions from the Society of Friends until, in the brief political thaw that followed the Russian Revolution of 1905, they were finally released from exile and allowed to join their brethren in Canada. As Pozdniakov remarked, 'an individual life in a remote country made them far more liberal and independent' than the Doukhobors who had preceded them in leaving Russia. With their arrival the emigration virtually came to an end, and since 1905 only scattered individual Doukhobors, mostly members of the Verigin dynasty, have reached Canada.

7 PIONEERS AND PILGRIMS

As the snows melted on the prairies and the wild crocus thrust through the yellow beaten-down grass, the Doukhobors began to move out from the immigration halls to join the pioneer groups on the land reserves.

They were accompanied by the volunteers who had chosen to remain with them. Khilkov, who by this time was disillusioned with the people he had once viewed so idealistically, returned to England, but Sulerzhitskii stayed, and so did Bonch-Bruevich and Doctor Velichkina, who eventually became his wife. She and the three Russian nurses travelled from village to village, and in general this small group of dedicated Russians smoothed the travails of resettlement until eventually they were relieved by other Russians or by the American and English volunteers who came shortly afterwards.

Of the whole group, Bonch-Bruevich viewed the situation with the most detachment. He was not a Tolstoyan and did not idealize the Doukhobors; instead, like a good Bolshevik, he hoped at least to begin their conversion to a revolutionary, rather than a religious, view of society. When the Doukhobors showed themselves ungrateful or suspicious he did not, like his companions, feel hurt or disappointed. He accepted it as the behaviour under stress of a group that he was trying to observe objectively, and he did not allow such experiences to deter him from his aim of learning as much as he could about the Doukhobor way of life in a new situation where issues remained confused until the arrival of Peter Verigin in 1902.

The confusion sprang from a series of problems that even a more sophisticated social group than the Doukhobors might have found hard to solve immediately. There were, to begin, problems of leadership. Verigin was now almost half a world away from them, and in the rare communications he was able to send he could do little more than suggest general lines of policy; the details of administration had to be worked out by the immigrants themselves. However, among them there was no single man strong enough or presumptuous enough to take the decisive position that belonged to the divinely inspired prophet; the most respected elders enjoyed the support of their own fellow villagers or at most of a group of villages, but never of the settlers as a whole. Had Maude and Khilkov been successful in obtaining land in one block that could have been farmed and administered as a single unit, there might have been a real incentive towards unity, as there was at Milky Waters. But in Canada the geographical divisions that had existed in the Caucasus were largely reproduced.

In his exhortations from a distance, Peter Verigin had by 1893 already laid down the general pattern of life that would distinguish the Christian Community of Universal Brotherhood from those Doukhobors who did not choose to accept his lead. It would be puritanical in morals and manners, pacifist in its behaviour to the outside world and the animal kingdom, and communistic in its economic organization, with, of course, the unwritten understanding that the traditional symbiosis of theocrat and sobranie would shape its political functioning. To emphasize his earlier 'advice' and to apply it more clearly to the new country—which he knew as little of as his followers—Verigin took the opportunity, in a letter to his parents written in January 1899, to express his 'opinion' on what 'the brothers and sisters' should do when they arrived in the country that had given them asylum.

Canada, he assured them, 'is a good place, but of course, it is necessary to get accustomed gradually to living conditions in a new country.' He had heard that in North America education was compulsory. 'This', he remarked, 'is all to the good, since simple literacy is a necessary aid in life, though it does not enlighten a man in a positive way. Nevertheless, a man who reads books can acquire information, and his thoughts will also develop in a general way. On the whole, I think that if God should grant to our people to settle in America, then learning to read and write is necessary.'

But education, Verigin knew as well as his followers, was not the most urgent task that awaited them in their new home. They must first decide how to make use of the land that had been granted to them and how to organize their social life in accordance with their ideals. Even more pressing, they must find the physical means of survival, as individuals and as a community.

Verigin's advice on organization followed the same lines as the statements he had issued from Shenkursk at the beginning of the 1890s. All the 'absolute necessities', such as cattle and ploughs, should be owned in common; the villages should equip themselves with communally owned granaries, storehouses, flour and oil mills, smithies, and joiners' shops. As for the pattern of settlement, decentralization was to be the keynote. The villages should be built on the plan that had traditionally been followed by Doukhobors at Milky Waters and in the Caucasus. They should consist of no more than fifty houses, each sheltering a family of several generations in the old Doukhobor manner. The streets should be wide and tree-lined; where the villages were not in forest areas, windbreaks should be planted, and fruit-trees wherever the climate would permit.

This ideal of a decentralized society of religious communists was pressed upon the Doukhobors not only by their own revered leader, but also by Tolstoy in correspondence and by his followers actually working among them. From a different point of view, Bonch-Bruevich was inclined to encourage them in the same direction. As a Marxist, he deceived himself into regarding the Doukhobor rejection of capitalist society as an important first step towards acceptance of a revolutionary socialist outlook. In the future, the majority of the Doukhobors in Canada were to achieve, at least for brief periods, a fair approximation of the vision that Verigin painted in the letter he sent to them on the eve of their departure. And even in the beginning the effort to create at least a partially communistic organization was forced upon them by their immediate circumstances.

In part these circumstances were shared by other settlers in the prairies at the turn of the century, though the Doukhobors had the advantage of a tradition of pioneering. Like their forbears sixty years before in the Caucasus and a hundred years before at Milky Waters, they were coming into a wilderness where only primitive or semi-civilized people—the Indians and the Métis—had lived before. There were no roads, no ferries or bridges over the wide rivers, and the dense mat of herbage that covered the rich prairie soil had never been cut with the plough.

But if the Doukhobors had pioneering traditions and a knowledge of farming that many of their fellow settlers lacked, they were hampered by poverty. The Wet Mountains villagers, whether they came from Cyprus or Batum, had spent all their funds on getting to Canada, and even the means that the Yelizavetpol and Kars Doukhobors possessed were scanty in view of their needs before the first crop would be ready. The special bonus fund of $35,000 set up by the Canadian authorities had been diminished during the winter months in feeding the first four thousand immigrants. By the time a few horses and oxen had been bought, together with the provisions that were sent ahead to the colonies, this source was greatly depleted. It is true that money still continued for years, though in diminishing quantities, to come from England and Russia, and that a new source was opened up through the interest of the American Quakers. Nevertheless, if the Doukhobors had not helped themselves by their frugality, resourcefulness, and industry, such assistance would have been wasted.

It was their extreme poverty that made inevitable in practice, during that first summer of settlement, the communal organization the Doukhobors upheld in theory. Until the first family houses were built, every detail of life was lived on a communal basis. James Mavor was sent out by Clifford Sifton in April to report on the progress of the settlement, and he and Khilkov lived for three weeks in one of the temporary villages the pioneer groups had built during the winter.

These villages were composed of a few large houses in each of which several families were accommodated. The houses were built of logs luted with clay. In the centre of the floor a large plain stove supplied heat. On two sides of a single room of which each house consisted there were two tiers of bunks, each bunk being about seven feet long and five feet wide. A bunk was provided for each family. There were in it fourteen bunks.[1]

During this first stage of settlement meals were prepared and eaten in common.

The first task of all was to locate the sites of the villages which, following Verigin's advice, it was decided to scatter broadly over the reserves. Altogether some fifty-seven villages were established during 1899; most of them were named after Doukhobor villages at Milky Waters and in the Caucasus. During the spring thirteen were established in the North Colony and thirty-four in the South Colony; later, in July, when the Kars settlers arrived in the Saskatchewan colony near Prince Albert, they founded a further ten villages. In size these settlements kept well within Verigin's optimum. Their average population was about a hundred and thirty and, when they were completed, they rarely consisted of more than twenty houses, though in the Prince Albert colony they were somewhat larger than elsewhere, averaging a population of more than two hundred.

As the Doukhobors moved out to these villages they first erected make-shift shelters, either of poplar poles or turf; sometimes, where there was a hillside, they lived the summer through in a dugout, and there were also a number of tents. Outdoor ovens were built for baking bread, and the blacksmiths set up their forges and made charcoal out of the available timber. Like most communities that have traditionally been self-con-tained, the Doukhobors found little difficulty in going immediately into operation in a strange environment, for they had among them men who knew all the necessary crafts. Among the first things they obtained through the bonus fund was a quantity of iron bars and leather, and with these they immediately set about making harness, spades, and tires for their wagons.

This self-sufficiency, which was carried into many fields of activity, un-doubtedly helped the Doukhobors to survive with very little money dur-ing the first years on the prairies. One of the first gifts of the American Quakers was three hundred spinning-wheels, and with these the Douk-hobor women span the woollen and linen thread they later wove on home-made looms into homespun cloth. Furniture was made out of hand-hewn wood, and utensils, such as spoons, were carved out of the same material. Some of these crafts continued to be practised for decades; as late as 1950 one of the writers saw hand-hewn furniture being made with the adze in a British Columbia Doukhobor village.

The first cultivation of the land was started almost immediately after the thaw of 1899. In the South Colony, a sobranie at which Mavor and Khilkov were present on 20 April decided to start ploughing. On the next day the few ploughs that the settlers had been able to buy began to cut the first Doukhobor furrows into the prairie, and elsewhere the men dug the heavy sod by hand with the spades their own blacksmiths had made. Potatoes were planted immediately, and shortly afterwards barley and oats were sown. The seed had been provided by the government's experimental farms, which advised the settlers to leave the sowing of wheat until a later season.

From the beginning the question of what form ownership should take was the subject of urgent discussion. There were special circum-

stances that made at least a degree of communal organization impera-
tive. The donations of the Society of Friends and of the Tolstoyans were
made to the Doukhobors as a group and not as individuals. Even more
important, farming equipment was so scanty that it had to be shared and,
as Aylmer Maude remarked, 'individualism was out of the question.' [2]
Bonch-Bruevich went on 24 August 1899 to the North Colony, where
there were thirteen villages inhabited by 1,395 people, all former Wet
Mountaineers who had lived as exiles in Georgia. He found that they had
thirteen ploughs—one to each village—twenty horses, twenty-one oxen,
and four cows. But even they had one plough to every 107 people. The
Cyprus exiles in the South Colony had only one plough to every 130
people.[3] In such circumstances even to think of sharing the plough among
individual farmers working in rotation was impossible; common tillage
of the soil was essential, and common ownership of whatever means of
production existed was a necessary safeguard.

It was therefore not surprising that in July 1899 an assembly of delegates from South Colony villages approved—though even at this time
there was some opposition from the richer peasants—a resolution that all
the Doukhobors should have a single common treasury, together with
common warehouses, stores, etc., in the various colonies and where necessary in the villages. The North Colony was invited to participate, and
immediately afterwards its members met to discuss the suggestion. Sulerzhitskii, who had already been present at the South Colony meeting, acted
as secretary. The North colonists opted for local autonomy modified by
fraternal relationships with their brethren forty miles away. All thirteen
villages of the North Colony would live communally and they would
have a single common treasury, but owing to the distance from the South
Colony and the difficulty of consultation, they would do it separately. At
the same time, they promised to give the South Colony whatever assistance might be asked 'if they have anything they can give'. 'All the money
earned in future', they decided, 'is to go to a cashier chosen by the
society, and to be spent only by common consent.' [4]

In the event, it was the North Colony that kept most closely to its communal intentions. In the South Colony the villages tended to go their own
way, and after the early months of adjustment it became evident that
varying compromises between communism and individualism were being
worked out. In the third colony, near Prince Albert, the trend towards
individualism was evident from the beginning. The background to these
differing situations lay in the varying origins of the colonists and in the
different degrees of wealth, the latter shown in the numbers of livestock

and of ploughs that the different villages could afford. The following chart, derived from information collected by Bonch-Bruevich at the end of 1899, shows the situation in terms of numbers of Doukhobors to each implement or animal.[5]

	Southern Colony, Cyprus exiles	Northern Colony, Georgian exiles	Northern Colony, Kars and Yelizavetpol	Prince Albert, Kars
1 horse per	67.7	27.9	22.6	14.6
1 ox per	58.4	51.7	66.1	23.4
1 cow per	73.6	58.1	47.8	20.4
1 plough per	130.2	107.3	61.7	36.1

In terms of livestock and implements, it will be seen that the Kars Doukhobors who settled near Prince Albert were more than three times as well off as their brethren from Cyprus and almost three times as well off as those from Georgia. They had arrived in Winnipeg with $35,000, which enabled them to establish themselves on a better level than the Doukhobors in the colonies of Assiniboia; but even this does not give the complete picture of their greater prosperity, for they had also been able to bring good supplies of clothes and many tools, which most of their brethren lacked. In general it was these more prosperous Doukhobors from Kars and—to a lesser extent—from Yelizavetpol who were the most inclined, even from the beginning, to lapse from the religious communism enjoined by Verigin. Even here, however, one cannot generalize. Not all Kars Doukhobors were either well off or inclined to favour private property. Two of the most idealistically communistic villages in the South Colony, Terpeniye and Verovka, were inhabited by colonists from Kars. Terpeniye was a relatively prosperous group that not only carried out successful farming and industrial activities, but also gained a great reputation for its hospitality to travellers, whether Doukhobors or strangers. Verovka, on the other hand, was rare among Kars villages in that its people were as poor as the Cyprus exiles; they arrived in Canada with only thirty dollars, but prospered in the end by an efficient communal organization. In both these villages the elders, Paul Planidin of Terpeniye and Nikolai Fofanov of Verovka, were good organizers who inspired their brethren, and it can perhaps be said that the quality of leadership was another factor that helped to determine the success or failure of co-operative or communal organization among the Doukhobors in this early decentralized phase of their life on the prairies.

By January 1900, after less than a year of settlement, there was already a pronounced shift towards individualism. According to Bonch-Bruevich, by January 1900 no fewer than 2,215 Doukhobors (or almost a third of them) had abandoned the communistic form of organization entirely and were farming as individuals and even, in some rare cases, employing their brethren as they had done in the Caucasus until Verigin introduced his reforms. The individualists were almost entirely from Yelizavetpol and Kars. About 1,600 Doukhobors—mainly in the North Colony with a few villages in the South Colony—formed 'permanent communes'. Even among these there were variations. In some cases it was merely production that was communal, the harvest being divided among the various families; but in others everything was stored in common warehouses and handed out according to need, while communal meals were favoured. Such villages tended to be puritanical and self-righteous in their attitude towards other Doukhobors who were more permissive in their arrangements. Finally, there were thirty villages, with more than 3,500 inhabitants, which Bonch-Bruevich described as 'temporary communes', practising a degree of common ownership and co-operative work but without the kind of group conviction that suggested the experiment would last for long.

Apart from the economic disparities between the various groups of Doukhobors, there are other reasons for this rapid shifting of the basis of Doukhobor life during the three years between the arrival of the mass of the Doukhobors in 1899 and that of Peter Verigin in 1902. It was only a few years since religious communism had been re-established among them in a situation of great stress, where they were inclined to react to persecution by an extreme assertion of their ideals. That situation had come to an end. They were now unpersecuted. They were, moreover, far away from Peter Verigin, whom most of them had last seen when he left for exile in 1887, and in recent months they had been mingling far more than in the past with non-Doukhobors, both Russians and Canadians. In these circumstances it was not surprising that there should be signs of the same kind of development as led to the secession of the Middle Party in Russia. A new 'independent' type of Doukhobor began to appear on the Canadian prairies.

Already, towards the end of 1889 [says Bonch-Bruevich], *I made acquaintance with some Doukhobors who, having thought deeply and having observed the lives of other people, both while in exile and afterwards in Canada, and having read a little, had come to the conclusion that all rites are useless, including even the Doukhobor rites; and that it is useless to go to Sunday meetings, for these also are a ceremony. They had also become convinced that all men are made alike and born equals; that there are no 'chosen people', such as they had esteemed their own sect to be, and that Doukhoborism is far from being 'freedom' but represents shackles rather, and that a far freer life is possible. The proselytes of this new movement were noted, and were subjected to the persecution of public opinion . . .*[6]

Yet, though the faithful majority of Veriginites might reject such openly heretical attitudes, circumstances forced almost all the Doukhobor men into contact with a way of life very different from their own. By early summer it was evident that, despite help from outside, they did not have enough resources even to feed themselves properly. Dr William Saunders, a representative of the Department of Agriculture, toured the villages at this time and reported that the Doukhobors

. . . were subsisting chiefly on dry bread made with a low grade of flour, with soup made by boiling a mixture of flour and water with vegetables such as cabbages, onions and beets, and in some instances, potatoes, of which they are very fond.[7]

The customary Doukhobor vegetarian diet is rich in cheese, butter, cream, milk, and eggs, but these were at first impossible to obtain because there were few cows and chickens. To a great extent the Doukhobors at this period actually lived off the land. They put grass into their soups and later in the season sent the children out to scour the woods for berries and mushrooms. In the North Colony, where the Swan River and the adjacent sloughs abounded with fish, they interpreted Verigin's prohibition on meat-eating rather liberally, and when Sulerzhitskii visited this area in June he found long lines of fish hanging out in the villages to dry in the sun. But even these expedients were inadequate, and the Doukhobors were forced to earn money outside the community.

This was already an accepted practice among other poor homesteaders, who would go out to earn their capital during most of their first two summers and leave the farms for their wives and children to tend as best they could. There was plenty of casual work available on farms, in sawmills, and on the Canadian Northern Railway, which was extending westward out of Manitoba towards the Rockies.

With some opposition from religious purists who distrusted the modern world and from the richer immigrants who argued that they had come to Canada to farm and not to build railways, the Doukhobors accepted this necessity. In June 1899, with Sulerzhitskii acting as their intermediary, they contracted with the construction engineer of the Canadian Northern to provide labour preparing the roadbed for the extension of the railway westward from Cowan. They were to receive fourteen cents a cubic yard of earth shifted, their pay to go to the central treasury to supply the needs of all the villages.

From the North Colony a hundred and fifty young Doukhobors set off for the railway, and for a short time everything appeared to go well. Then the Doukhobors began to leave the work, complaining that they were able to earn only a few cents a day. Sulerzhitskii, whose patience in these difficult months one can only admire, set out to investigate the situation. He found it was indeed true that the Doukhobors had been given bad stretches of line to excavate, but some good ones as well, and that on the average they had been paid about fifty-six cents a day. He also found that individual Doukhobors had been buying goods and provisions, and that these had been charged against the credit of the colony, so that the total earnings appeared much less than they should have done. It seemed as though an epidemic of selfishness had broken out among the Doukhobors, but later Sulerzhitskii discovered that the real explanation was the strength of small-group against large-group loyalty; Doukhobors in one village resented earning money that would be spent equally by another village which did not contribute so much to the work on the railways. The contract was revised to provide for payments to be made to individual villages, and the pay for swampy sections of the line was raised by two cents a yard. Immediately those who had gone on strike returned to work, and in a very few days there were twice as many at work on the grade as had been there at the beginning of the contract. With the knowledge that they were now working for their families and their friends, they laboured energetically, and the average daily wages rose steadily to eighty cents and even a dollar a day.

In addition to the railway contract, many Doukhobors went to work for individual farmers during the harvest season, and in the Prince Albert region women as well as men found employment in the local Mennonite colonies. From July to November there were hardly any able-bodied men or youths in the villages. Women, children, and old men were left to build the permanent houses and to get as much land as possible broken and cultivated by the autumn.

Under the direction of the old men, the women felled timber and cut osiers and transported them to the villages, dragging their home-made carts because the few horses were needed to transport stores on the long and muddy trail from Yorkton. In the North Colony, on the edge of the wooded zone, they made the houses of logs, luted with clay; in the South Colony, where the willows in the river valleys were almost the only trees, they used a form of building similar to English daub-and-wattle, interweaving the branches and applying inside and out a smooth coating of clay. The roofs were usually made of turf, and so, in the Prince Albert district, were many of the houses until they could later be replaced by frame structures. Within each house was built a clay oven in the Russian manner, on top of which the children and old people could lie in the cold weather. Most of the houses consisted of a single large all-purpose room, which those who could afford it would divide with curtains to give privacy in sleeping; later on bedrooms were often added. The houses were built in a double row, with a wide street in between, and behind them were built barns, granaries, stables, outdoor baking ovens, and those essential adjuncts to the Doukhobor way of life, the bathhouses, in which the people would gather, without too much fastidiousness about the segregation of sexes, to sweat themselves clean in the steam generated by throwing water upon heated stones.

None of these Doukhobor villages has survived as it was originally built, and today the places where many of them stood have been so ploughed over that the very site is hard to determine. But surviving travellers' accounts describe their charm after the mud walls had been whitewashed, neat fences had been built enclosing the meticulously planned gardens which Doukhobors love, and trees had been planted along the sides of the streets. All this took years to complete, but the essential work in creating the villages was done by the women during that first summer and autumn season of 1899.

In the traditions of the sect, however, that first generation of Doukhobor women in Canada are remembered, not as builders of houses, but as breakers of land. In the Caucasus during times of epidemic an old magic custom, derived from Russian folklore, was often practised by the girls of a village to save their community from affliction. At midnight twenty-four virgins would hitch themselves to a plough and cut a single furrow around the village to keep the evil away. Now the evil was hunger, and with the horses in use on the trail to Yorkton, the women of the North Colony attached towlines to their ploughs, tied sticks at intervals to the lines, and in teams of twenty-four, two to each stick, dragged the ploughs, guided by old men, through the thick prairie sod. All through the summer days, working by relays from dawn to dusk, they would trudge over the prairie, inspired by the eerie harmonies of their own singing. To Sulerzhitskii as he watched them, they seemed to symbolize the burdened fate of humanity chanting its protest under the innocent indifference of the sky, and Canadian and American feminists were shocked by exaggerated newspaper accounts that suggested that the Doukhobors were virtually enslaving their womenfolk. But to Doukhobors this memory stands as an important symbolic event in their history; it is woven into their mystique of 'Peace and useful toil', and to this day they often refer to it. Certainly, the women who pulled the ploughs did not see themselves submitting to servitude; at the time they probably thought of their act as a mere necessity, but later they saw it as an assertion of faith, and today Doukhobor women will still sometimes bring up this incident to confound their menfolk when the discussion in a sobranie takes a stormy turn.

On the whole, the Doukhobors had made as much progress as could be expected by the time the winter of 1899–1900 set in. Their villages were established and their houses built; their first land had been broken and their first crops—admittedly small ones—had been garnered; they had been able to afford a few more livestock, a few more implements. At the new town of Swan River, which had sprung up at the end of that season's stretch of railway building, they had built a communal barn and a warehouse and had opened the first Doukhobor co-operative store, run by Nikolai Zibarov. It survived only a few months because the brethren could not agree on the morality of engaging in trade.

But no people can rise from destitution to real prosperity in a few months, and enormous problems still remained. The frosts had come early, and food was scarce. Scurvy was occurring in some of the villages. Doukhobor complaints of the shortness of food led to disputes with the Immigration Department, who distributed some supplies but denied that there was any real lack. The commissioner in Winnipeg wrote defensively to Deputy Minister Smart; he had inspected fifteen or twenty children and had decided that they 'compare favourably with the same number of children at this end of the city or in any city of Canada'.[8] The American Quakers took a much graver view of the situation; inspired by Joseph Elkinton, their Meeting of Sufferings put out a special appeal, to which the members of the Society of Friends (who contributed $30,000) and other groups, such as the Canadian Council of Women, responded handsomely. The Quakers provided food in bulk : carloads of sugar, corn meal, rolled oats, potatoes, and onions, dried fruit donated by sympathizers in California, tea and linseed oil, wool, leather, and garden seeds. In addition they augmented the Doukhobor herds with forty-nine cattle and twenty oxen and provided a whole carload of supplies for sick people and young children. The Canadian Council of Women sent spinning-wheels and looms, stoves, tools, and cloth. The prompt help of the Quakers, whose food supplies arrived in November, undoubtedly made the difference that enabled the Doukhobors to weather the winter reasonably well. In addition to their gifts, they loaned the Doukhobors more than two thousand dollars to buy flour, which the latter repaid during 1900.

Meanwhile, relations between the Doukhobors and the immigration authorities were becoming exacerbated, and the high hopes the officials had first shown in the new settlers were beginning to dwindle. The commissioner in Winnipeg had been trying to get winter employment for five hundred of the Doukhobors.

I had secured an agreement to that effect [he wrote to the English Quaker, John Bellows] *but the Doukhobors were so dilatory and raised so many objections that I was only able to get some sixty-one. They have not given entire satisfaction, have been complaining of the price charged for board, and that they had not clothing, and so forth, and the contractor has now said . . . that he will not take any more of them at present. . . . However, it is only one more of the discouragements that we have had.*[9]

The fact was that now, after the bloom of unfamiliarity on both sides had worn off, the Doukhobors and the Canadians were beginning to find each other, as Aylmer Maude said of Ivin and Makhortov at the end of his association with them, 'men with human limitations and deficiencies, and not the plaster saints I had supposed . . .'[10] The Doukhobors were realizing that a society without tsars and Cossacks could still have its imperfections, and the Canadians were beginning to suspect that a group of millenarian Russian peasants conditioned by generations of persecution might not easily be assimilated into the kind of society that was being created in the opening west.

As their first year drew towards its end the Doukhobors in fact became the objects of resentment in many sections of Canadian society. The ranchers, who had free run of the prairies for grazing their cattle, hated them as they hated all cultivators and found every excuse to slander them. Rival land-seekers were jealous because large areas of fairly good land had been reserved for the Doukhobors. Labour leaders feared that the low rates paid to Doukhobors on the railway contracts might undermine the whole wage structure of the west. Local merchants, who at first had been favourably impressed by the honesty of the Doukhobors, became less friendly when they realized that the co-operative organization of the sect favoured wholesale buying in centres like Winnipeg. Conservatives and imperialists of Anglo-Saxon stock continued to raise objections to the exemptions from military service granted to the Doukhobors, even though the Militia Act had long remained uninvoked. And officials, like McCreary, began to weary of the inexplicable difficulties that arose out of their contact with a people whose motivations they did not understand and whose intercourse with them was hampered by linguistic incomprehension. Many of the misunderstandings that arose at this period between officials and sectarians were due partly to the use of interpreters with Ukrainian and Jewish backgrounds who neither understood nor sympathized with the Doukhobors and whom the Doukhobors in their turn disliked.

It is true that the sectarians found their defenders, both among their neighbours on the prairies and in the press and parliament. Prominent among them was Clifford Sifton, who was also defending his own good judgement; he denied particularly the suggestion that because they were conscientious objectors the Doukhobors had no courage.

Sir, there is many a man who is ready to fight, and who has no courage at all; he has nothing in the sense of true courage . . . I doubt if there are five men in this House who would show the moral courage, who would show the tenacity, who would show the fortitude which these people have shown for the purpose of preserving the faith which they believe to be the true faith.[11]

The Doukhobors were largely unaware of these public debates, conducted in a language they did not understand. The hostility they mainly encountered, often in malicious forms, was direct and personal. Fellow workers on the railway jobs would insult and annoy them in the hope of breaking down their pacifism, spitting into their food or stopping them from sleeping. Farmers with whom they worked would deliberately put meat into their soup. Neighbouring settlers would show their hostility in harsh ways, sometimes driving Doukhobors away at gunpoint. Ranchers would drive cattle into their lands. For the most part the Doukhobors endured behaviour of this kind with exemplary patience, retaliating only by verbal reproaches. The most striking instance of their forbearance occurred when an Irish settler kicked a Doukhobor boy to death for some imagined injury to one of his own children. The dead boy's relatives persuaded Arthur St John to write to the North West Mounted Police on the man's behalf. They believed the Irishman would be punished by his own conscience and that to take another life in addition to the one that had been lost would be terrible.

But if the Doukhobors did not retaliate, many of them resented the petty persecutions they had to endure and began to form an unfavourable mental picture of Canadians. When Mounted Police officers in their military-looking uniforms began to appear in the villages and explain to them the regulations relating to registration of vital statistics and other subjects, when a tactless board of school trustees seized a Doukhobor horse in lieu of taxes, and when immigration and land officers began to insist that Doukhobor males above eighteen sign individually for the quarter sections that Arthur St John and Herbert Archer were surveying, those who had been most offended by the thoughtless and brutal behaviour of individual Canadians were inclined to link the phenomena together. The conclusion they reached was that Canadians—collectively and individually—wished to attack Doukhobor principles, to mock and destroy their pacifism, their vegetarianism, their preference for a communal way of life. Who was to guarantee that ultimately they would not be forced to bear arms? Those who have endured long persecutions are naturally suspicious, and it can safely be assumed that, even though Maude had carefully explained the Canadian government's demands, the majority of the Doukhobors had no clear understanding of either the extent or the limitations of the conditions under which they had come to Canada. The Canadian government, in their eyes, was still—as a government—a manifestation of negative power, and for this very reason suspect.

In Doukhobor history zeal and rebelliousness have always gone hand in hand with poverty. As at Milky Waters and in the Caucasus, it was the richer Doukhobors who were inclined to accept the situation they found in Canada and the inhabitants of the poorer villages who began to show various degrees of discontent. At this point, in the early months of 1900, Tolstoy and his followers intervened in ways that, not always wittingly, aggravated the situation.

Tolstoy, who had been receiving reports from his followers of the differences among the Doukhobors regarding private and communal property, took it upon himself to express his disappointment. On 27 February he wrote to the Doukhobors in Canada a long letter that began with the ominous words,

All of us who profess, and wish our lives to accord with, the Christian teaching, ought to help one another. And the most needful help is—to

*point out one to another the sins and temptations into which we fall
unawares.*

He went on to tell how, after their great example of defying persecution in Russia, he had been saddened to hear that in Canada some of the
Doukhobors had begun to show an addiction to owning property. After
allowing sympathetically that they might have difficulties, he went on to
demonstrate that private property and the violence that the Doukhobors
abhorred were inextricably mingled.

*In reality, property means—that which I consider mine. I not only will
not give it to whoever wishes to take it, but will defend it from him. And
to defend from another what I consider mine is only possible by violence;
that is (in case of need) by a struggle, a fight or even by murder. Were it
not for this violence, and these murders, no one would be able to hold
property.*

*If we do retain property without using violence, this is only possible
because our property is defended by the threat of violence, and by actual
violence and murder, perpetrated upon those around us.*

*Therefore, to acknowledge property is to acknowledge violence and
murder, and if you acknowledge property, which is only maintainable by
soldiers and police, there was no need for you to refuse military or police
service. Those who perform military and police service and make use of
property, act better than those who refuse to be soldiers or policemen,
but yet wish to enjoy property. Such men wish, without serving, to make
use of the service of others for their own advantage. The Christian teaching cannot be taken piecemeal: it is all or nothing. It is inseparably united
into one whole. If a man acknowledges himself to be a son of God, from
that acknowledgment flows the love of his neighbour; and from love of
his neighbour flow, equally, the repudiation of violence, of oaths, of state
service, and of property.*

Tolstoy devoted the rest of his letter to elaborating with relentless logic
on this theme and to drawing out the contrast between the worldly and
selfish life, by which the kingdom of Heaven is lost, and the life lived to
fulfil God's will, of which the Doukhobors had 'made the trial'. He
acknowledged that he was in no position to advise them on 'the detailed
arrangements of your communal life', but he ended by stressing the principle that 'to collect property separately for one's self and to withhold it
from others—is to act contrary to the will of God and to his command-
ments.' [12]

In another context one might be justified in speculating on Tolstoy's inner motives in writing this letter. Was it merely a gesture of disillusionment that yet another group in which he had trusted for the revivification of Christianity appeared to be failing him? Was it a desperate attempt to grasp at another fading dream as men proved all too human? Or was it perhaps an expression of guilt at his own failure to live the Christian life, projected on to the Doukhobors with whom he had, over recent months, so closely identified himself?

Whatever may be said on this question, the effect of the letter on many of the Doukhobors was drastic. Tolstoy, because of his efforts on their behalf and the closeness of his teachings to many of their own, was—and still is—respected among them more than any other non-Doukhobor. Some of them were also aware of a link, which they could not exactly explain, between Verigin and Tolstoy; not realizing that their leader had taken as his own the teachings of the great novelist, they argued from similarity of doctrines that in this letter Tolstoy was merely acting as the mouthpiece of Verigin. It was, in other words, a message from the living Christ. In general, attitudes towards the letter were drawn along lines of prosperity. Those who were comparatively well off tended to ignore it; this was particularly so among members of the Prince Albert Colony, many of whom intended to take up their quarter sections and farm like other homesteaders. Those who were poor took Tolstoy's message to heart and regarded their independent brethren as bad Doukhobors.

The agitation produced by the arrival of Tolstoy's letter was kept alive by the presence of A. M. Bodianskii, one of his most assiduous followers. Bodianskii, after visiting the Doukhobors in the Caucasus on Tolstoy's behalf during 1896, had found his way to England and lived for a while in the colony at Purleigh, but his eccentricities proved unendurable even to his fellow Tolstoyans. He was quietly expelled and went on to Canada, where he arrived among the Doukhobors at the beginning of 1900.

While his fellow Tolstoyans were working hard to make the conditions of the Doukhobors on the prairies as endurable as possible, Bodianskii went among them like a Pied Piper, irresponsibly offering them the fulfilment of all their dreams. He began, in the midst of the hard prairie winter, by talking of a warm idyllic land to the south, called California, where the snow never fell, where fruits of all kinds—the true food of vegetarian Doukhobors—grew abundantly, and where the wages were twice those of Canada. The myth of the sunny abundant land to the south caught the Doukhobor imagination and was to continue a subterranean existence over two generations, surfacing on occasion with dramatic effect. Bodianskii proposed that the Doukhobors immediately migrate to California, and early in the year he and two members of the sect went there and signed an agreement with a lumber company to employ the Doukhobors at two dollars a day and sell them land on reasonable terms. The Canadian authorities were not at all pleased at the prospect of losing to the United States the immigrants over whom they had taken so much trouble. In March Deputy Minister Smart went so far as to appeal to the Quakers in London to use their influence to halt the California project, and shortly afterwards he tried and failed to stop a small group of Doukhobors, accompanied by Bodianskii and some of his non-Doukhobor Russian disciples, who crossed the border in Manitoba on their way to California. Altogether over one hundred Doukhobors went there and stayed the summer of 1900, earning an average of two hundred dollars for six months' work; most of them were dissatisfied and returned to Canada by the autumn, when the California craze died down. A handful remained and formed the nucleus of a small colony of independent Doukhobors.

Meanwhile Bodianskii returned to Assiniboia, and during the summer of 1900 he helped notably to crystallize Doukhobor discontent and give it articulate form. Working with a number of the extreme zealots of the sect, mainly from among the Wet Mountains Doukhobors, he drew up between June 1900 and the early months of 1901 a whole series of statements, some addressed to the government of Canada, others to 'All People', and one at least to the Sultan of Turkey, expressing total disapproval of Canadian laws and the Canadian government. Always these addresses bore Doukhobor signatures, but neither Bonch-Bruevich nor Aylmer Maude nor Biriukov nor any other of the writers close to the Doukhobors at the period doubted the authorship of the documents, which Bodianskii made no effort to conceal. Typical was the petition addressed to the Canadian government 'In the name of the Lord God and his Truth' by 'The Society of Universal Brotherhood near Yorkton, Sask.' and signed by twenty-two Doukhobors claiming to be the delegates of their communities. Thanking the government for its willingness to receive them and its interest in their welfare, the petitioners go on to declare that the Doukhobors consider their beliefs to be the 'laws of God' and therefore 'we ask you not to enforce against us such of your laws as contradict our beliefs, and thus to give us the possibility of living in your country without breaking openly or tacitly, directly or indirectly, our conception of the Truth.' Specifically the petition raises three issues. The first refers to the provisions of the Homestead Act.

The laws of your country require that every male immigrant, 18 years of age, who wants to settle on vacant government land, has to record it in his name, and, after a certain term, such land becomes his property. But we cannot record homesteads in our individual names, cannot make them our private property, for we believe that in so doing we should directly break God's Truth.

They ask that their land be granted 'upon the conditions given to your Indians—that is, the land to be held by the community . . .'

The other issues raised are those of marriage ('. . . we cannot recognize as correct and cannot accept any human laws as to the marriage union, being sure that all pertaining to it is in the province of God's will and human conscience') and giving information on births and deaths ('If anybody wants to know it, let him ask, but we will not, of ourselves, report it to anybody.')[13]

Bodianskii committed many foolish acts, among them the dispatch of such addresses to newspapers abroad, with the result that in foreign countries there arose a quite erroneous belief that the hard-working and conscientious Canadian officials were actually persecuting the Doukhobors: even the supporters of the Romanov autocracy at home gained some ill-concealed pleasure from these revelations. At the same time, he appears to have believed sincerely that he was helping the Doukhobors to sustain that defiance of the powerful of this world that he and many others had admired in them, and in documents like the petition just described he expressed accurately the beliefs of a large proportion of the sect. Underlying all their hesitations and disagreements at this period there appear to have been two motives that almost all of them shared: they were waiting until Peter Verigin arrived among them or sent some clear directive of future action (they would have liked to postpone all important decisions until he came); at the same time they retained their old desire to live sufficient unto themselves, an autonomous island of faith in a sea of unbelievers. As Bonch-Bruevich said of the rash of petitions that emanated from Bodianskii and his Doukhobor associates:

If we look for the political meaning of all this protest, we shall reach the conclusion that in general the protesting Doukhobors, under a Christian phraseology, cleverly hid their real, secret wish—to form a completely independent State, paying 'tribute' to the suzerain power, but having their own laws, their own customs, and governed by their own leader. The 'Law of God' to which they so often appealed in their proclamations, bade them to do what they wished to do.[14]

In retrospect the petition Bodianskii edited in 1900 can be seen as the first clear statement of Doukhobor principles to be made in Canada. Had the government heeded it, much trouble could have been avoided. Three possible courses were open to the authorities at this time. They could, first, have acted promptly and firmly, insisting that all regulations must be immediately complied with, without regard to conscientious objections. This would have brought down upon them the anger of all the friends of the Doukhobors, in Canada and abroad. Alternatively, they could have considered whether the laws should not perhaps have been amended or loosened in interpretation to accommodate the Doukhobor requests. After all, in 1959 a compromise on the marriage question acceptable to the Doukhobors was worked out, and this could have been done as easily in 1900; as for the clause demanding individual entry for quarter sections, this was surely an anomalous provision in a Land Act that provided both for settlement in villages and for the allotment of land in blocks to 'farming associations'. But any concessions of this kind would have aroused all those groups already opposed to Doukhobor settlement. While Clifford Sifton remained at the Ministry of the Interior, the government took the third and middle course of avoiding in practice any irrevocably decisive action in either direction regarding the conflicting demands of the Doukhobors and the state.

This policy, though ultimately unsuccessful, cannot be dismissed—as Sifton's critics attempted to do—as one of weakness. From the beginning of 1901 the commissioner of Crown Lands raised the question of individual entry with the Doukhobors in communications of increasing severity, and notices were posted threatening that any lands not entered by 1 May 1902 would be thrown open for general homestead entry to any settler who wished to occupy them. The Prince Albert colonists prepared to obey, those of the South Colony were divided, and those of the North Colony, led by Nikolai Zibarov, were almost unanimously recalcitrant. During December 1901 there were stormy meetings in the villages of the North Colony, followed by a gathering of delegates at Voznesenie that was attended by immigration agent Harley from Swan River. The Doukhobors asked whether they could not just pay the ten-dollar registration fee demanded by the government, without having to go through the formalities of entry. Here is their version of what followed:

'No, land is not granted on such terms,' replied he. 'You must have entries in due form. From the land that is cultivated, we all, from the Prime Minister to the last policemen, have to live.'

'We have long been persecuted,' said we, 'for not wishing to obey human laws and institutions.'

Then the official became so angry that he trembled all over, bounced on his chair, and began to say: 'Have you come here to alter the laws of Canada?'

'If you,' said we, 'cannot alter selfish, human laws, it is many times harder and more terrible for us to alter the law of God.'

The official thought a while and again became angry, and so we went on for fully five hours.

'We see,' said we to him, 'that you are exposing us to persecution and suffering. We see that there is no freedom here in Canada as you used to assure us; it is all a pretence.'

'This is your last chance!' shouted the official . . .[15]

The dialogue at cross-purposes went on, and even if this account of it is not exact, it at least conveys faithfully the atmosphere of mutual incomprehension that has given so many encounters between Doukhobors and Canadians a flavour of Gogolian comedy.

Anxious to save an experiment for which he had been largely responsible, Clifford Sifton intervened personally. In February 1902 he wrote the Doukhobors a long, reasonable, and friendly letter, in which he argued that under the law as it stood each individual must enter for the piece of land held in his name 'so that no stranger may take it from him'. He did not, however, make it clear why a similar safeguard could not be applied to land acquired in the name of a group. He reiterated in unambiguous terms the government's undertaking that, provided entries were made according to law, no interference would be made in the way the Doukhobors chose to cultivate the land.

I have decided that those who will take their homesteads and accept of free land from the Government may live together in one or more villages and instead of being compelled to cultivate each quarter-section held by each Doukhobor, that the land around the village itself may be cultivated and the work which otherwise would be required on each individual homestead may be done altogether around the village.

However, he also insisted that 'those who do not take up a homestead will not be protected by the Government after the first of May of this year [and] will simply have to leave the villages to those who take up the homesteads and buy land elsewhere from some other person.' [16]

Far from mollifying the Doukhobors, this letter merely inflamed their apprehensions. They began to talk, as they had done in the Caucasus, of leaving everything and wandering off wherever the inspiration of God might lead them. By midsummer, while the Prince Albert colonists had for the most part complied with the regulation and entered individually for their lands, only a few dozen had done so in the North and South colonies, and these were ostracized by their brethren. In fact, the government had not in May fulfilled its threat of withdrawing the lands from non-registrants, partly because such unanimity of resistance in the North and South colonies had not been envisaged and nobody had made plans to deal with the confusion that would arise if some four thousand settlers were all at once rendered homeless in the prairies. Furthermore, in other directions the Doukhobor colonies had made satisfactory progress, and Sifton was not the man to insist absolutely on regulations when the pioneering energy of the Doukhobors might still help to bring the west under cultivation and to build its railroads.

Certainly by 1902 the Doukhobors were no longer the ill-nourished, impoverished peasants who had landed in Canada three years before. Their economic progress had been steady. The comparative figures prepared by the assiduous Bonch-Bruevich for 1899 and 1900 show a striking difference already. The number of horses rose in one year from 240 to 592, of oxen from 143 to 401, and of cows from 144 to 865 (which meant that a reasonable supply of milk was now assured). Where there had been no sheep in 1899, in 1900 there were more than 400, and also more than 3,000 chickens. Equipment had multiplied in roughly the same proportions: wagons from 105 to 292 and ploughs from 93 to 199, while during 1900 the first 48 mowing machines were introduced, together with 22 horse-drawn hay-rakes and 29 disc harrows. In the various villages some 31 smithies were in regular use.[17] John Ashworth, a visiting Quaker, found that the cattle sheds in the villages were in excellent condition. Bridges had been built over the smaller rivers, and elsewhere the Doukhobors had established ferries which they operated free of charge for the benefit of all travellers. After the failure of the Swan River co-operative another had been opened in Yorkton, and at the end of 1900 Herbert Archer reported that it was 'in flourishing condition'.[18]

It is true that the harvest of 1900 had not been good, but with more land cultivated there was enough for most of the settlements, and in January 1901 thirteen villages from the South Colony informed the Society of Friends that they were no longer in need. The harvest of 1901 was so good that nobody could remember having seen such crops of grain and hay in the Caucasus, and the more materially minded members of the sect began to think that if they stayed in Canada they would soon become rich. Those who went out to work on outside farms in 1901 were making between forty and fifty dollars a month, and all that summer twenty men from each village were hired to do construction work by the CPR. By the time that year's crops were in, all the colonies were in a position to do without material aid from outside.

Meanwhile the original Russian and English helpers began to depart. Their tasks had not been easy, and most of them, in some degree at least, shared the disillusionment that Khilkov had felt. They wrote to Tolstoy as to a father confessor. Konshin had found the Doukhobors illogical and leader-ridden, 'They have a high opinion of themselves and think they know everything and can do better than anyone else.' [19] Dr Velichkina blamed the Doukhobors for accepting low wages and then working sluggishly. She claimed that many drunken Doukhobors had been picked up on the streets of Winnipeg, and Bonch-Bruevich remarked that after their prolonged privations there had been a reaction at the end of 1899, leading in many cases to smoking, drinking, and even eating meat, particularly when engaged on work away from the villages.[20] Herbert Archer remained longest of all with the Doukhobors; he actually died among them when many years later his shack on the prairies burnt down over his head. But even he wrote bitterly to Aylmer Maude in 1903: 'We have been thinking of the Doukhobors as a religious people. Really, as always, there are religious Doukhobors, but not a religious Doukhobor sect. The sect, because it is a sect, is self-centred, self-righteous, and intolerant.' [21] Only Arthur St John, good-natured and idealistic to the end, was still willing to stand up unreservedly for the Doukhobors. He found reasons and excuses even for the sensational events that dominated the autumn of 1902 and provided a quasi-apocalyptic prelude to the coming of Peter Verigin.

These events had their origin in the curious ferment of ideas that swept the North and South colonies during the preceding summer. It was a ferment to which many circumstances in addition to the land-entry dispute contributed. There was conflict between those who wished to have strict communism and those who did not. There was conflict between the older Doukhobors and the young men who came back from work on the railroads wearing English clothes and defying the authority of the elders: 'We are not in Russia here; we are all free.' This rebellion against traditional Doukhobor attitudes, like that of the property-conscious Doukhobors in the Prince Albert settlement, merely entrenched the true zealots in their stand against any concessions to the Canadian authorities that might imply a dilution of Doukhobor principles as laid down by Peter Verigin, and this was perhaps the main reason for the mass refusal in most villages of the North and South colonies to enter their lands.

The situation at this time was further modified by the fact that by mid-summer both the Doukhobors and the Canadian authorities were speculating on the possibility that Peter Verigin might be allowed to leave Russia when his third term of exile drew to an end in 1902. The more zealous Doukhobors believed that when Verigin came he would be pleased that they had interpreted to the letter his teaching about the common ownership of property. The Canadians, who by now were beginning to realize the dominant position he held within the sect, hoped that he would wield a moderating influence.

In fact, in the few letters that he had sent to his followers Verigin had been circumspect and noncommittal about controversial matters. Perhaps he feared prejudicing his chances of leaving Russia and entering Canada. Perhaps he merely wished to wait until he had seen the actual situation in Canada before he advocated any specific course of action; then, if his power over his followers remained, he would merely have to speak for the Doukhobors to obey. That his power did remain, manifested in bizarre forms, was shown by an extraordinary proclamation that fourteen Doukhobor women issued in July 1901.

Cease to pride yourselves on your rights and authorities and to exalt yourselves! Who is higher than the King of Heaven and than God? . . .

'Great is the Lord above all nations, for his goodness and mercy endureth for ever.' And His goodness is that He has been born by the Spirit of the Most Holy Virgin Mother of God the Queen of Heaven, of the blessed race of Luker'ia Kalmykova.

This Lord is our Leader, Peter Vasil'evitch Verigin. His beauty is in his wisdom; in flesh he is pure.

We strive towards him, esteem him God and Tsar, and with full desire yield ourselves to his power.[22]

Should the reader think this document incredible, let him remember the day in 1658 when the English Quaker James Naylor rode into Bristol with the people casting down their clothes in his path, hailing him as 'the son of Mary', 'the only Son of God', and chanting Hosannas as they entered the city in a pelting rainstorm!

Though Verigin himself showed no inclination at this time to wield his enormous moral power over the Doukhobors, in an unwitting and roundabout way his words were largely responsible for the events of the autumn of 1902. In comparison with the caution he showed in writing to his followers, he had been much more venturesome in the letters he wrote to friends among the political exiles and also to Tolstoy and his followers. The members of the Purleigh Community conceived what turned out to be an explosive plan; Bonch-Bruevich collected as many of these letters as possible, and in 1901, with a Tolstoyan disregard of copyright, Chertkov published them in Russian with his own introduction. By the summer of 1902 copies had reached the prairies, and the few literates in the various villages were reading the letters aloud to their brethren.

The letters reveal Verigin as an intelligent and somewhat fanciful man, afflicted with those two faults that so often trouble the autodidact: prolixity and a delight in the absurd extremities of logic. Out of them emerges a vision that—even if Verigin was unaware of it—is almost identical with the antique notion of the Golden Age.

He poses the image of a paradise where, if they are pious and abstemious, men need no longer work and yet will be sufficiently fed.

Plenty of corn exists, if only avarice were diminished. The earth freed from the violence of human hands, would begin to abound with all that is ordained for it. I do not even imagine that mankind would suffer want were it to submit to such a theory, for, feeding moderately, the eatables now in existence would suffice mankind for a hundred years, and within a hundred years the earth would have time to clothe itself completely and return to its primitive conditions. And humanity, together with the spiritual stature lost by Adam and Eve, would regain an earthly paradise.

In such a paradise, should man keep cattle? Verigin doubts it. Knives and needles, and all metal things, too, must be rejected, because in the mines 'people are tortured to obtain ore'. Money should be returned to 'Caesar's organisation ... because these tokens were devised by them'. 'If any wish to labour, let them do so; but our duty is to labour only in Christ's service.' Let the people only trust one another, let them 'carry out the saying, "If one smites thee on the cheek, turn to him the other",' and every governmental structure will fall in ruin. 'Ultimately, of course, the completest unification of the nations would result.'

And where shall this terrestrial paradise come into being? Obviously as 'near the sun' as possible, so that the brain of man can be beneficially influenced by that source of light.

Man employing food raised by an abundance of solar heat, such as, for instance, raspberries, strawberries, and in general, so to speak, tender fruits, his organism will be formed, as it were, of energy itself, because tender fruits, I suppose, contain in themselves very much, as it were, of compressed solar ether, that is to say, warmth-energy ... Feeding on food that grows, and, as far as possible, on fruits, I see to be advantageous already in this respect, that I shall consume into myself more solar heat which is energy. And in consequence of that I hope to be wiser.[23]

How far, at the time, Verigin seriously thought all this and how far he was indulging in speculative play one cannot tell. But his words, reaching the Doukhobors after they had been starved so long of the prophetic statements of leaders, made intoxicating reading for people who already felt themselves threatened with new persecutions and who had lived through the rigours of three prairie winters. How were their leader's letters to be interpreted? Even the richer farmers in the Prince Albert colony were somewhat shaken in their individualistic complacency, and the zealots had no doubt that, whoever may have been the nominal recipients of the letters, the message they contained was directed by Peter Verigin at his faithful followers. Two of his most trusted adherents in Russia, Vasilii Ob'edkov and Ivan Ponomarev, appointed themselves apostles to spread the teaching in the villages of the North and South colonies. Among the poorer villages their success was immediate, and the movement was given an enormous impetus when Nikolai Zibarov, the influential elder of the North Colony, joined the 'Sons of God', as they began to call themselves, and behaved with a zeal that outdid that of the original preachers, walking barefoot because he would not wear shoes made with the skins of Brother Ox and Sister Cow.

Not long after midsummer the most fanatical of the Sons of God began to renounce the use of animals for labour. Teams of ten or a dozen men and women would hitch themselves to wagons when they went into the nearest towns to get supplies or to sell their produce, and the animal brethren were driven into the woods where the Mounted Police rounded them up. The police sold by auction some 285 cattle, 120 horses, and 95 sheep. They were mostly bought by the unconverted Doukhobors, and the fifteen thousand dollars that they fetched was added to the trust fund the government held. The same thing happened when the Sons of God took their money, which was both Caesar's property and accursed metal, and handed it to the nearest officials they could find.

As the movement attained further heights of exaltation, everything made of leather or animal skins was burnt in ritual fires in the villages, with sheepskin coats, harnesses, boots and shoes going the same way as firearms had gone years before in the Caucasus. Metal objects were discarded. Everything that might interfere with spiritual well-being was thrown away.

But this was still only a beginning. Verigin had talked of lands near the sun, and as early as July the Doukhobors started to ask the land authorities to transfer them to British Columbia or to the fruit-growing districts of southern Ontario. Not unnaturally, the bewildered officials seem to have pigeon-holed these requests, and, once the harvest was in and the idler days of autumn had brought—as they have traditionally done for Doukhobors—a time to talk and to plan, the Sons of God decided to take matters into their own hands. By tradition they were pilgrims, and now they would go on a real pilgrimage and find the promised land where, under the beneficent sun, they would live upon fruit and meet their Messiah.

Suddenly, in mid-October, the zealous began to circulate from village to village, holding meetings and trying to convert their brethren. The Mounted Police in Yorkton reported their movements with a touch of anxiety at the 'extreme and somewhat dangerous views' they preached, and Helen Morland, a Quaker girl sent out as a teacher by the Society of Friends earlier in the summer, watched their progress with astonishment.

We had 2 or 3 hundred of the 'crazy' Doukhobors come through these villages hoping to make converts. We all tried to talk to them and find out why they had left their homes and were walking about. The idea is to go to a warmer climate, but northwards is hardly the way! What they insist on is the voice of God in their hearts which tells them each day what to do and which they say they are obeying. It is hopeless to talk to them of cold and hunger. They answer God will not [let] them suffer while they obey him and if He does let them suffer they are willing to do His will. It does seem awfully sad, particularly when there are children among them. They seem quite prepared for miracles.[24]

Whole villages were deserted as the movement grew with the kind of millenarian enthusiasm that had characterized the popular crusades of the Middle Ages. Eventually, with Zibarov and Ponomarev at their head (Ob'edkov had already retired—appalled by its excesses—from the movement), they turned southward. On 26 October, eleven hundred strong, they passed through Fort Pelly. They went on to the village of Poterpevshee, where Anastasia Verigina, the mother of their leader, was living. By now there were seventeen hundred of them. Gregory Verigin, who had escaped from Siberia and come to Canada via England, went out with his fellow villagers to meet them.

Greeting us, they wished us peace. They then invited any of us who might wish to, to 'come with us to the wedding feast.' Another said: 'We are going to meet the Bridegroom'; a third said: 'We go to preach the Gospel'; and a fourth said: 'Let us go to the Promised Land.' [25]

Gregory Verigin talked to them for two hours, trying to dissuade them. They listened quietly, but were not convinced; after all, they had the word of the leader. They asked to see 'The Grandmother', and when Anastasia Verigina came out and smiled silently upon them they departed, heading towards Yorkton.

A photograph survives that shows them on the march, a dense column receding into the distance over the dry prairie, men, women, and children mingled in its ranks. The greyish image conveys nothing more than the impression of a drab, trudging army of refugees, and it was left for the special correspondent of the *Manitoba Free Press*, who accompanied the zealots on their wanderings, to evoke, in the lush language of Edwardian journalism, the spirit of the pilgrimage after several days of progress towards the Promised Land.

They are showing signs that hunger, fatigue and emaciation have weakened their stalwart frames. Every man's face is an index, silent and eloquent, of what he has been, and is, enduring . . . A drizzling rain is falling to add to the self-inflicted miseries of these martyrs to mistaken ideals of right. Ever and anon will arise their plaintive psalm, its weird minor cadences rising and falling with varying strength, now swelling higher on the breeze like martial music, and again sinking into a mournful dirge of sorrow. Nearly all are barefooted and hatless. All their outer clothing, their heavy felted cloaks and overcoats, have been thrown away. . . .

The trail over which these thousand feet have travelled is worn level as the floor of a dancing pavilion. Their tired feet are cut and bruised, some of them bleeding. Whenever the way lies near a ploughed field the weary concourse walk across it to ease their tired feet, and the path they have travelled looks as if it had been pressed by a gigantic roller. . . . All who have seen it say it is like a dreadful dream, that it is incredible, unrealizable—hundreds of men, with the light of insanity in their eyes, roaming whither and for what they know not, and animated by a belief that brings the dark ages into the dawning twentieth century. [26]

Mennonites and other farmers along the way gave bread to the marchers, and they supplemented it by gleaning 'dried rosebuds, herbs, leaves, grasses, in fact, almost anything vegetable in its origin.' The sick and the old were borne on litters made of poplar branches and grey blankets; the blind were led by the hand. The column contained 1,060 women and children. One child was born on the way, but its mother insisted on being carried on to take part in the entry into the earthly paradise.

On 28 October, after a frosty night without shelter, the marchers tramped into Yorkton. There the immigration officials Speers and Crerar tried to persuade them to return to their homes. When the marchers refused to listen to their pleas, they enlisted the aid of the police and of local residents and herded the women, the children, and the sick, protesting but non-resistant, into the immigration hall and other government buildings. A few Doukhobors who had not been swept into the movement argued with the women, trying to persuade them to return to their villages, but without avail.

The men spent the night on the prairie to the east of the town, praying and singing until the morning. Then, at midday on 29 October, having failed to gain the release of their women and children, they marched south, six hundred strong. The authorities tried to bar their way with carts, but in vain. 'We are powerless to hold them,' reported the Mounted Police, and the pilgrims tramped on, scattering their possessions by the roadside so that the police collected two wagonloads of rubber shoes, socks, and shirts. For another week they continued, followed by the police and begging food by the way. A few stragglers broke away, but the majority went on across the Manitoba border, where the weather changed and snow began to sweep across the plains on a northeasterly wind, so that at night they slept huddled together, as one pilgrim put it, 'like wild geese'. On 6 November they reached Minnedosa, where they accepted shelter in the local skating rink. They were now exhausted and had no more spirit to continue in the bitter weather, but it was three days before, after long conferences with the immigration officials, they were loaded on to a special train, some of them actually carried by the police because they would not go voluntarily, and taken back to Assiniboia. The last of them left Minnedosa as late as 12 November. By this time the women and children, after staging a brief hunger strike at Yorkton, had already returned to their villages. The expenses of sending them home were deducted from the fund raised by selling stray animals.

The exclamations and explanations inevitably followed. The Conservative press delightedly used the incident to attack Sifton and his immigration policies. The Liberal papers, led by the *Toronto Globe*, pointed out that fanaticism was nothing new, and that this had been a singularly harmless type of craze, out of which the Doukhobors must be led by reasoning. The embarrassed Quakers begged the Canadian government to show patience. And Herbert Archer found a political motive in the pilgrimage, suggesting that the Sons of God hoped that 'the march would so inconvenience the Government that it would concede their demands as to the land question and registration (enabling them to form a solid community of their own, independent of any but their own government), or would at once take means to transport them to a warm climate.' [27]

Since that time certain sections of the Doukhobors have so often used similar tactics to confound the authorities that it seems at least possible that such a thought of moral coercion did mingle with the genuine religious exaltation that inspired the marchers of 1902. The phenomenon was, as far as we know, new in Doukhobor history. The members of the sect had often threatened to march off on their own, but this was the first time they actually did it. The pilgrimage in fact marks the appearance of a new type of aggressive militancy among the Doukhobors, and it is no accident that among its participants were those who eventually became the first leaders of the radical Sons of Freedom.

8 PETER THE LORDLY

Even after the Doukhobors had left Russia, promising never to return, the tsarist government maintained an interest in them, as the Communist régime in that country still does, seventy years after their departure. In another way, by virtue of having become host to the greater part of Verigin's followers, the Canadian authorities acquired an interest in the few hundred who still remained in Siberia. At first this interest probably signified no more than a well-meant hope of making their promising new immigrants happy by reuniting them with their brethren. Later on, as the trouble over land entries developed and it began to appear that the Doukhobors would fit no more easily into a democratic Canada than they had into a despotic Russia, an incentive was added. Everyone—government officials as well as friends of the Doukhobors—began to feel that the only hope of an escape from the maze of misunderstandings lay in the direct leadership of Peter Verigin.

How actively the Canadian authorities intervened in Verigin's release from Siberia is a matter of speculation. Verigin himself in later years liked to create the impression that he was released through the efforts of influential persons, and some writers have suggested that the Canadian authorities acted through Lord Strathcona, then high commissioner in London, on behalf of all the Doukhobor exiles in Siberia. In accordance with Strathcona's request, the Foreign Office is said to have instructed the British Ambassador in St Petersburg to open the question with the Russian authorities, which was done without effect. It is not impossible that informal inquiries were made along these lines, but we have found no official records of any such transaction in the Foreign Office papers.

Verigin was released from his exile in the autumn of 1902 and told that he must leave for Canada. This could have happened entirely through the routine operations of the tsarist administration. Most of the Doukhobors in Siberia were there under long sentences, up to twenty years, and at this time, several years before the liberalization that followed the Revolution of 1905, the tsarist authorities appear to have had no intention of remitting any portion of their terms. Verigin, on the other hand, was legally in a different position, having been sentenced to a series of five-year terms; it was when the third of these expired that he was released. To detain him longer would have been internationally embarrassing to the tsarist government, but to let him go free in Russia might have led to trouble among the Doukhobors who had stayed behind in the Caucasus. It is significant that when he made a request to visit the Caucasus on his way to Canada, ostensibly to see his former wife Evdokiia and his son Peter, he was refused permission. To export him on release was thus a solution very agreeable to the autocracy.

At this point, the British mission in St Petersburg definitely entered the picture, since it had to make arrangements for Verigin's entry into Canada. By November the news that he had been released and was travelling westward across Siberia had reached his followers. They immediately dispatched funds to pay for his journey, and began to build a log house in Poterpevshee so that he could live in the same village as his mother and his brother Gregory, who had now reached Canada.

At Moscow Verigin was welcomed by Tolstoy. Verigin's impressions of this first meeting with the man from whom he had learnt so much are not recorded. Tolstoy, we know, was dissatisfied. There was something in Verigin's smoothness and poise that did not fit in with the image of the strong, wise peasant the novelist had coined. While he granted that Verigin was a good man and probably capable of wielding a sound influence on his people, he had doubts about his spiritual qualities. Tolstoy and Verigin apparently fell into a dispute over Verigin's insistence that it was just as bad to kill an animal as a man, and just as bad to eat animal as human flesh. Tolstoy, according to Paul Biriukov, *said that he disagreed with that, and that in all actions and in life one must know the sequence, what comes before and after. Thus one feels more pity for the man and his sufferings than for the sufferings of a horse, and more pity for the sufferings of a horse than of a rat or a mouse, while one does not feel sorry for a mosquito. This feeling of sequence constitutes true wisdom. One should not pity a mosquito and at the same time be severe with a man.*[1]

For this reason Tolstoy did not believe that the Doukhobors in Canada had acted sensibly in liberating their animals. 'They could and should have acted in a Christian manner in many things before doing what they did.' Verigin annoyed a woman friend of Tolstoy by asserting that man was created 'thousands of years ago from a warm protoplasm'; evolution had apparently been among the subjects in which he was instructed by the political exiles, though he never broached such a dangerous theory to his followers. Tolstoy's daughter Alexandra found in Verigin 'something narrow, limited . . . despite his power of body and personality.'[2]

Tolstoy's chief disciple in England, Vladimir Chertkov, appears to have been troubled by no such doubts. He welcomed Verigin exuberantly and chaired a meeting for him in Essex Hall, London, on 10 December. Opponents of tsarism were popular in England at this time, and a large, friendly audience came to hear Verigin speak in Russian, interpreted by Chertkov. Questions followed and Verigin showed no uneasiness in dealing with them. To one man who challenged his vegetarianism with the statement that Christ ate fish, Verigin gave a glimpse into Doukhobor theology by remarking that Christ had been a man living two thousand years ago and had only opened a door to truth through which later men were free to proceed farther. When asked to state what his people wished from the Canadian government, he answered that they wanted to live freely, without harming their neighbours, with enough land held communally so that each could work according to his strength, and with no one to force them to act against their consciences. And when a questioner challenged his theoretical anarchism by asking how a society could exist without government, he remarked that a herd of cattle must have a bull with larger horns than the rest to keep the herd together for its own good, but that men, having the powers of reasoning, could live without government.

To everyone in the audience that evening it was evident that they were in the presence of a man who, though he might not come up to the high standards by which Tolstoy judged himself and others, was nevertheless a powerful personality with a mind that was quick, subtle, and capable, even if it was not profound. Tempered in the trials of exile, more deeply and widely read than any of his followers, and confident in the role of leader for which he had been trained so long ago by Luker'ia Kalmykova, Verigin was well prepared for the task of plucking order out of chaos which awaited him in Canada. He was quite ready, if necessary, to play the part of the long-horned bull.

After the Essex Hall meeting and conversations with Aylmer Maude, who tried to enlighten him on the situation he would face in Canada, Verigin set sail, landing at Saint John, where he was welcomed by three Doukhobor delegates, Ivan Ivin, Paul Planidin, and Semeon Reibin. On 22 December he reached Winnipeg, where his sister, Anna Podovinni- kovna, awaited him; after he had greeted her, he went to the immigration hall, where he met Acting Commissioner Moffat and Crerar, the Yorkton immigration agent.

It was immediately evident to the Canadians that Verigin was a very different kind of man from the mainly illiterate Doukhobor peasants they had so far encountered. He was dressed impeccably and expensively in a short blue gabardine coat, and his trousers were encased in close-fitting grey leggings, piped with black cloth; from a silken cord around his neck hung a silver watch and a gold pencil, and a large fountain pen was secured in his coat pocket with loops of black cloth.

His voice is low and of a singular sweetness [gushed the correspondent of the *Manitoba Free Press*]. *Physically, Verigin is a spendid example of his race. Tall and strongly built, and of erect and graceful carriage, he would attract attention among hundreds of good-looking men. His hair and beard—which is luxuriant—are black as jet. His eyes are dark and thoughtful, and his whole expression that of a man who has suffered much, and has triumphed over everything through the force of kingly courage and constancy.*

To Moffat and the other officials Verigin was polite but noncommittal.

'You'll be glad to be in a country,' said Mr Moffat, 'where there is religious and individual freedom.'

'I haven't looked around yet,' answered Verigin, through his inter- preter, 'so I cannot tell whether this is a free country or not.'

'You know, however,' said Mr Moffat, 'that in Canada we do not put people in prison because of their political or religious views.'

'Oh, yes,' answered Verigin, 'I know that.'

He refused to make any statement about what he would do when he joined his followers, or even to admit that he had any special influence over them. 'I hope my coming may be good,' was all he would say. His attitude favourably impressed the officials. It seemed to them the caution of a man who would not commit himself until he had carefully examined the situation.[3]

The next day he went on to Yorkton, and seemed annoyed that a crowd of Doukhobors had gathered to meet him. He was anxious to see his mother and immediately drove by horse-sleigh to her village. Here he made his ceremonial return to Doukhobor life, standing bareheaded before the singing V of his followers while they chanted the psalm of welcome and bowed with their brows to the ground as they had done so many years ago when they chose him as their leader beside the grave of Luker'ia Kalmykova. To celebrate the reunion of people and leader, the name of the village was changed from Poterpevshee, meaning 'past suffering', to Otradnoe, meaning 'joy'.

For three days Verigin stayed there, while the delegates came in from the villages to talk of the doubts that afflicted them. He grasped the situation quickly, and framed an adept policy to draw all the disputing factions under the aegis of his will. His main objective was to establish the strong community organization of which he had dreamed in Siberia as the guarantee of autonomy for his people, and his answers were diplomatically framed to that end. On the dispute between the communitarians and the independent farmers, he declared that communal living was the best guarantee of peace, love, and brotherhood among the sect, but that those who wished to live separately must be free to do so. Without openly condemning those who wished to be independent, he had stated his preference for a communistic organization. He did not reject those who had gone on the pilgrimage of the previous autumn, but he reasoned with them, remarking that a cold and healthy country had advantages that counterbalanced those of a hot country where sickness was always a danger. Much better, he suggested, to settle down where they were and live as brothers and sisters. As for those other brothers and sisters, the animals, he blandly contradicted what he himself had said in writing by remarking that to use animals was not necessarily to enslave them. Men and horses in fact worked together for their mutual benefit. The horses received hay and oats and lived in buildings built by men, and so men served horses as well as horses, men.

These arguments he elaborated as he went on a satrap's progress through the fifty-seven villages of his domain, riding with a dozen of his relatives and favourite friends in a great sleigh drawn by six picked horses, and followed by other sleighs from which a choir sang hymns as the procession drove over the packed snow of the prairie trails.

Verigin realized that the problem needing immediate solution was that of the formalities concerning land entry, and on 7 January he held his first meeting with the government officials. At this point, possibly for the first time, Verigin was made aware of the details of the Dominion Land Act. He discovered that in fact its provisions would give the Doukhobors a breathing space of three years before they would be faced with what they regarded as the most objectionable clause of the act, the one demanding that they become naturalized and in the process take the oath of allegiance to the British Crown. Just over a month later, on 10 February, he called a gathering of two delegates from every village and invited to it the immigration agents from Swan River and Yorkton. The officials once again stated the government's arguments. Their attitude was conciliatory, and according to Gregory Verigin, who was present, one of them even said that the oath of allegiance was not obligatory. This version was later accepted by the Doukhobors, but it seems to have been a misunderstanding; what the official probably said was that there were provisions for those who wished to affirm their allegiance rather than swear it. The delegates were hesitant, waiting for the views of Verigin who, as in the sobraniia of the past, assumed the leader's privilege of speaking last. The important thing, he suggested, was not the act of entering for the land, which was a formality; it was the resolution, after entry had been made, to regard the land not as individual property but as owned by all. Unanimously the delegates endorsed his decision and proceeded—even those who came from the most individualist villages—to resolve that the land would in future be communally owned and that anyone who acted otherwise would be regarded as no longer a Doukhobor. A committee, to which the individual Doukhobors gave power of attorney, was established for making entries. It consisted of Reibin, Planidin, and Zibarov, representing the main trends in the Community, with Verigin as its chairman. By April entry had been made for more than 1,700 quarter sections, and in the end, by 1905, a total of 2,770 homesteads were registered, making almost seven hundred square miles, or more than half the area originally set aside in the three Doukhobor reserves. Only six dissidents refused to enter for the quarter sections allotted to them.

Thus, within a few weeks from his arrival, Verigin had united the Doukhobors, had solved the problem of land entry, and, to all appearances, had convinced all but a tiny minority of his followers to accept a communal form of organization and to co-operate with the Canadian government.

Whether his success would be lasting depended on a precarious balance of circumstances. In the beginning at least, a number of important factors were in his favour. His first acts gained him the immediate support of the Canadian authorities and the Canadian press, who hoped that his influence would keep the zealots in line more effectively than police action and that eventually, by an assimilative process, the Doukhobors under his influence would withdraw their objections to registration of births, deaths, and marriages, and to education. At the same time, except for a very few malcontents, his initial compromises did not lose him the loyalty of the Doukhobors. They respected and in many cases even worshipped him because of his position as hereditary leader. Their regard was enhanced by his record of steadfastness in exile; up to now he had shown none of the flaws in character that had marred the male members of the Kalmykov dynasty. Accordingly, no matter whether they were communalist or individualist in economic orientation, orthodox or radical in their interpretation of Doukhobor doctrines, they were all prepared to give him an opportunity to lead them and to shape their future. The most important result of this general co-operativeness was that the drift towards private farming was temporarily halted. A few individualists, the precursors of the Independent Doukhobors, refused to accept Verigin's communism and stood out on their own farms in the relatively isolated Prince Albert district; a few radicals refused to accept his apparent willingness to come to terms with the government. Altogether these original malcontents on both sides can have amounted to only a tiny fraction of all the Doukhobors in Canada, and Verigin obviously thought them unimportant enough to ignore.

Indeed, he had enough to occupy him in the congenial task of organizing the Doukhobor Community into a healthy economic unit. No sooner was the land question settled, at least temporarily, than Verigin began an elaborate process of reconstruction. He bought thirteen square miles of land outside the Community reserves, beside the Canadian Northern Railway. Here he established a completely new village, which he named Verigin and which became his headquarters on the prairies. At Verigin he built a large octagonal house which served the same purposes as the Orphan's Home in the Caucasus. It was the administrative centre of the whole Doukhobor Community in both the Assiniboia and Saskatchewan territories; it was also the palace of the leader, from which he would set out on his tours of the villages in all the state that had characterized the Kalmykov rulers in the Caucasus. Clad in the English style, wearing a silk hat, he would drive in summer in a phaeton, in winter in a sleigh, drawn by pure-bred horses; and whenever he reached a village, the people would welcome him with psalms and a vegetarian banquet. On these triumphal progresses he was accompanied by a choir of maidens who lived in the house at Verigin under the supervision of his aged mother and who, like their predecessors who had inhabited the Orphan's Home in the Caucasus, were expected to learn and transmit orally the psalms of their people.

A special place among these inhabitants of the great house at Verigin was occupied by Anastasia Golubova, the daughter of one of the leader's nieces, who joined his entourage when she was still a fresh, plump girl of eighteen, a blue-eyed brunette. From the beginning she was his favourite, and inordinately proud of the fact. For twenty years, until his death, Anastasia Golubova was his constant companion and his most intimate servant, often travelling with him in Canada and the United States; in later years, Verigin sometimes referred to her as 'my wife', and such, according to Doukhobor custom, she appears to have been. As a result of her position, she established a considerable influence among the Doukhobors, and even, in later years when it was felt that some of the glory of the leader had reflected on to her, a following of her own.

Most of the Doukhobors accepted as a matter of course the satrapal way of life that Verigin assumed. It was the style expected of a leader, and its splendour glorified the whole Community. They would have accepted it even if Verigin had been like his predecessor Peter Kalmykov, uninterested in anything beyond his own pleasure. But Verigin had an aptitude and a zeal for organization that in other circumstances might have made him an excellent business executive.

Since he must have some nominal office, he was made 'representative' of the Christian Community of Universal Brotherhood, a position analogous to that of 'manager' of the Orphan's Home, which had given the leaders in Russia a status vis-à-vis the tsarist authorities. He was assisted by a committee consisting of Paul Planidin, representing the more conservative Doukhobors, and Nikolai Zibarov, representing the radicals who had gone on the pilgrimage; Semeon Reibin also played an important role during this period as interpreter and external liaison man.

No relaxation in work must be allowed, Verigin decided, if the Community were to be built on a sound and progressive basis, and the temporary halting of the trend towards individualism gave him a large labour force that he could deploy in whatever way he chose. Capital was urgently needed if the Doukhobors were to abandon the peasant farming they had practised in Russia and substitute modern North American techniques in its place, and since they had no resources on which to raise capital but their strength, Verigin decided to treat this as a saleable commodity. Instead of being released from railway building to attend to their own farming, the Doukhobor men were urged to accept outside employment in larger numbers than ever before, so that during the summers from 1903 onwards more than a thousand men worked away from the villages. Once again the burden of work on the land rested on a minority of able-bodied men, assisted by old men, women, and children. With the money gained in this way Verigin planned to mechanize Community farming so that as much land as possible might be brought under cultivation with as little labour as possible. While the process of gathering capital and acquiring machinery was going on, the Doukhobors were expected to live a very frugal life. It was a process similar to that by which present-day ex-colonial countries have tried to modernize themselves by crash programs aiming at plenty tomorrow, based on sacrifice today.

The initial success of Verigin's program can be measured in material terms by the acquisitions of the Community by the end of 1903, a bare year after his arrival. Apart from the thirteen square miles of land by the railway at Verigin and another ¾ square mile elsewhere, the Community had bought more than four hundred horses, constructed flour mills and sawmills, and bought six steam engines at the cost of $15,290, as well as many ploughs, harrows, and other implements. Altogether in that first year $114,734 was spent on land, stock, machinery, and implements. On clothing and feeding some 7,500 people, as well as providing hardware, garden seeds, harness leather, oats for the horses and meeting minor expenses, only $86,908 was spent. This was considerably less than the Doukhobors brought back from their outside work. The rest of their upkeep came from garden and field crops grown in the Community, from their own dairy products, and from the labour put into weaving cloth and making clothes and shoes by hand. In matters of day-to-day living the Community was more self-sufficient than most prairie settlers; there can have been very few farmers in Canada even at that time who spent less than one dollar a month per member of family on outside purchases. At the same time, even though the Community was fighting hard to use every dollar in building up its capital and in paying off some of the loans from the Quakers, money was found to send to aged and sick brethren in Siberia and to Tolstoy in aid of another group of Russian sectarians, the

Pavlovtsy, who had been condemned to penal survitude for refusing military service.[4]

Yet by the end of this first successful year it was already clear that Verigin's attempt to put into practice his vision of a more or less autonomous communitarian society in the middle of the prairies was threatened in many ways, and that his own position was neither simple nor easy.

He was the centre of great and conflicting expectations on the part of both the Canadian authorities and his own followers. The government officials were anxious to rehabilitate themselves in the eyes of the Canadian public for what, since the pilgrimage of 1902, was regarded widely as the error of admitting the Doukhobors into Canada. At the same time the extension of the Canadian Northern Railway had attracted large numbers of individual settlers into the northern prairies, and among them the reservation of large areas for the Doukhobors was becoming a matter of vocal grievance. If only the Doukhobors could be persuaded to accept Canadian laws and become gradually assimilated, the officials believed that hostility towards them would die down, criticism of the government would diminish, and there would be less reason to complain that good land was being kept away from loyal Anglo-Saxons for the sake of unruly foreigners. Verigin was their great hope, and his easy solution of the problem of land entries made them rely more than ever upon him to break Doukhobor resistance to other government requirements.

Verigin, however, realized from the beginning the equivocal position in which too close a collaboration with the authorities might place him. His very influence over the Doukhobors depended on maintaining as long as possible that isolation from the world of the unfaithful in which they had lived since the first days at Milky Waters. Every demand of the government that was accepted would bring them nearer to assimilation into the aggressively individualist society of the prairies and progressively weaken their ties with Doukhobor traditions. Already the authorities were inclined to encourage those Doukhobors who wished to become independent farmers. Individual homesteads fitted more neatly into the pattern of settlement that had been envisaged under the Dominion Land Act, and, though Community farmers might help to fill an empty prairie, it was tacitly understood among the Canadian officials that they should encourage any tendency for groups of this kind to break up into separate family units.

It was Verigin's shrewd and immediate assessment of this situation that led him to buy time by agreeing to the land-entry formalities. After that he procrastinated on further concessions, and deliberately discouraged the registration of vital statistics. His purchase of almost fourteen square miles of land in 1903, when the Doukhobors were short of cash and in occupation of hundreds of square miles of free land, becomes comprehensible in this context. He was already beginning to provide for the day when the Doukhobors might have to reject the gifts of the government because of the conditions that were attached.

On the other side Verigin was sensitive to the varying pressures of his people. To outsiders he seemed to exercise 'unlimited one-man power',[5] as one immigration official remarked. Even those who were disposed to overlook Doukhobor faults agreed with this view: 'The sovereignty he exercises over them', said Hannah Bellows, daughter of the secretary of the Quaker Doukhobor Committee in London, who lived as a teacher among the Doukhobors on the prairies, 'is almost as absolute as that of the Tsar over his subjects.' [6] But in fact the Doukhobor leader was not a simple despot; in the curious reciprocity that we have already observed as existing between leader and sobranie, he was influenced by urges that came from below. The Doukhobor women and the older men, insulated in their villages from the influences of Canadian life, remained conservative, anxious to preserve the old traditional ways in the new environment. Life on the prairies, with few comforts, was difficult; outer society, filled with people speaking a strange language, was frightening; the familiar gave security. Thus a large section—possibly a majority—of the Doukhobors obeyed Verigin because they felt dependent on him to guide them through an increasingly hostile world. In submitting to him, they also compelled him, as the ruled so often compel the rulers; the expectations among his followers, their dreams of an autonomous Doukhobor society, free from all government interference, gave him no alternative, if he wished to retain the role for which he had been shaped from youth, but to pursue that aim.

But even this task, though he was supported in it by the mass of the Community, was made difficult by the re-emergence of the tendency, incipient during the last years in the Caucasus, for the Doukhobor sect to divide in three directions: a conservative centre, intent on communal institutions as a manifestation of the spiritual life; a radical left, intent on dramatic resistance to the world and on pursuing to a logical extreme the anarchistic implications of Doukhobor doctrine; and an assimilationist right, inclined, like the Small Party in Russia, to make its peace with authority and to revert to the individualism that characterized the laxer and more prosperous periods of Doukhobor history.

These tendencies had already manifested themselves in Canada before

Verigin's arrival. In the centre were the Doukhobors who tried to follow out Verigin's instructions to establish a communistic economy, on the left were those who liberated their cattle and took part in the pilgrimage, and on the right the independent farmers of the Prince Albert colony. In the first months of elation after Verigin's arrival in Canada the divisions seemed to have melted away almost completely, and it is possible that, if the Doukhobors had been able to live in the isolation they desired, a long period of harmony might have prevailed. But the alien world was always present; it surrounded and separated the three distinct colonies into which the Doukhobors were divided, and Verigin's attempt at instant self-sufficiency by accumulating capital resulted in a close and continued contact between the able-bodied Doukhobor men and non-Doukhobor Canadians on the railway grades. This contact was a source of continued attraction to those who had already felt inclined to adopt an independent way of life, and of continued aggravation to those who had already expressed their dissent from Canadian society by attempting to walk away to the mythical southern paradise.

Less than six months after Verigin's arrival in Canada, the more zealous of the former pilgrims began to show their dissent in a new and dramatic manner. Immediately after the spring thaw on the prairies, the small group who had refused to make entry for their lands began, as in the previous autumn, to wander through the villages preaching their doctrine of resistance to the temptations of this world. For the first time they began to call themselves Svobodniki, the literal meaning of which is 'Freedomites', though the more familiar label of 'Sons of Freedom' has passed into western-Canadian usage and is accepted even by the Svobodniki when they talk of themselves in English.

The Sons of Freedom were clearly puzzled by the discrepancy between Verigin's compromises with authority and the radical teachings that his published letters appeared to convey. Since he had not actually condemned the zeal that had led them to embark on their pilgrimage, they evolved a devious theory that the letters in fact still expressed Verigin's true wishes and that his instructions to comply with regulations were only meant to deceive the Canadian government. By a perversion of reasoning that was to become popular among Sons of Freedom in later decades, they argued that he meant his followers to understand precisely the opposite of what he said in public for the benefit of outsiders, and therefore if they continued to act in the radical spirit of the letters they would earn his approval.

They evolved a way of manifesting their beliefs quite novel in Doukhobor history. At first, as they walked through the villages, they repeated the old teachings of the previous autumn—that physical work was sinful and that the animal brethren should be liberated. Their preaching fell on the deaf ears of peasants busily engaged in ploughing the prairies or cultivating their gardens. Finding that few of their brethren were interested in learning 'how one should live rightly', the Sons of Freedom, who had now increased to fifty-two, including women and children, decided to march naked. As one of them, Alex Makhortov, put it: 'We went in the manner of the first man Adam and Eve, to show nature to humanity, how man should return to his fatherland and return the ripened fruit and its seed.'

The date of this new departure is set by a Mounted Police report on 11 May of a 'disgraceful exhibition of Doukhobor men and women.' The nudist pilgrims wandered through sixteen villages, impervious to the exhortations and mockery of their brethren. Finally, near the village of Nadezhda, they encountered Peter Verigin on his way from Otradnoe, where he was still living at this time, to Petrovka, twenty miles away. They stopped his trap and demanded that he set free his horse. Verigin replied that he fed and sheltered his horse, and had a right to use its services in driving from one village to another. The Sons of Freedom forcibly freed the horse and told Verigin that they were going to Otradnoe 'to destroy the throne of Satan'. Verigin managed to get to Nadezhda before them, and told the villagers to stop the pilgrimage from going any farther. The men of Nadezhda sallied out, armed with willow twigs, and when the Sons of Freedom refused to turn back beat them until they were covered in blood 'so that it was terrible to see us.'

Then we were surrounded by some twenty men, and were not allowed to enter the village. And night came on; the weather was bad, rain and snow and wind. Then we clustered into one heap, and lay on the ground one on top of another. And those who guarded us stopped for the night near us; they put on their sheepskin coats and cloaks. We remained naked; and really it was wonderful to us ourselves that in such a wind we were not frozen. Those who stood guard over us publicly announced that the cold that came on was a very great cold, but not one of the naked was frozen.[7]

In the morning the men from Nadezhda seized the women and children at Verigin's orders and took them into the village. The twenty-eight men were allowed to proceed.

While they were still on the Doukhobor reserve, the police observed them without interference. On one occasion the pilgrims invited a Mounted Police corporal to join them; he refused, but shrewdly commented that though 'the whole proceeding was thoroughly disgusting . . . there was not much immoral in their action outside the fact of their being naked.' [8] Two miles from Yorkton, when the Sons of Freedom were marching fully clothed and nibbling grass and young leaves like their brothers the animals, the police finally stopped them, and after questioning and counting them, ordered them to return to their villages. Instead, they stripped and proceeded towards the town; on the outskirts they were met by a posse of a hundred townsmen riding out on horses and in buggies, who seized the unresisting pilgrims and started to dress them. The Doukhobors were astonished at the agitation their nakedness caused among the Canadians.

In Yorkton the pilgrims were confined in the immigration hall, and the next day were convicted of indecent exposure—though exhibitionism in the ordinary sense had been far from their intent—and sentenced to three months' imprisonment. They were kept at Yorkton for several weeks in the hope that they would promise to keep the peace as a condition of release; but even Verigin's attempts at persuasion were unsuccessful, and on 9 June they were taken off to Regina Gaol, where all but three of them refused to work and insisted on living on a diet of raw potatoes, oatmeal, and grass, later supplemented by bread. According to Alex Makhortov, they were then beaten with ropes and reins and pulled by their beards; their arms were twisted and they were held up by their heels with their heads in buckets of water until they were almost suffocated. This accusation of barbarous acts on the part of the prison officers has never been proved or disproved, for the simple reason that, despite complaints, no official inquiry was held. Certainly two of the prisoners were afterwards certified as insane and sent to Brandon Asylum, where one of them died, according to a statement by Verigin (again supported by no proof), of starvation because he refused to eat meat. Eventually the prisoners agreed to do weeding in the Regina prison grounds, and late in the summer they were released.

Thus ended the first nude demonstration of the Doukhobors in Canada. The consequences—arrest, imprisonment, resistance, alleged ill-treatment —were to be repeated so often with dismal similarity that to record all the occasions in detail would be tedious, and we shall later confine ourselves only to those instances that have some special importance. On this first occasion, however, it is worth speculating on the origin of nudism as am means of manifesting faith among the Doukhobors.

There is no record or even hint of any such action while the sect remained in Russia, nor was there any disrobing during the first pilgrimage of 1902. Many millenarian sects in western Europe during the Middle Ages and the Reformation described themselves as Adamites and practised ritual nudity in imitation of the original man, usually in the privacy of their meeting-places, but we have no reason to suppose that the Doukhobors had any knowledge of these somewhat obscure passages of Christian history. Since nudism has no place in earlier Doukhobor tradition, V. A. Sukhorev suggests that the idea may have been introduced by a member of a nudist colony in Oregon who visited the Doukhobors shortly after their arrival in Canada and preached to them the necessity for men to resurrect the original paradise where the fathers of the human race went naked until their innocence was lost. However, the revelation may just as credibly have come to one of the Sons of Freedom in pondering over the enigmatic passages of Verigin's letters in which he talks of humanity 'regaining an earthly paradise' and in which—even more to the point—he says:

That the Apostles and Christ wore clothes and ate bread was natural, for there were plenty of clothes and bread, and (one must add) even Christ and the Apostles were not able, all at once, to go naked.[9]

Given the Doukhobor belief that men may develop spiritually beyond Christ, this passage could be interpreted as suggesting that nakedness is a desirable state at which the enlightened should aim. In this way it was evidently taken by Alex Makhortov and his associates.

Inevitably the incident stirred up once again the angry public debates concerning the Doukhobors, and whose who had a vested interest in refurbishing the image of the sect, like Clifford Sifton and his fellow Liberals, were just as anxious to mete out punishment to this small group of rebels as were their most rabid opponents. Tolstoy, almost alone, saw through the absurdity of the actions to the sincerity of the motive that might inspire them. His remarks can probably stand as the best defence that could be made of the early Sons of Freedom.

My view of this movement among the Canadian Doukhobors is that materially they have injured themselves. But this movement has shown that there lives in them what is most precious and important—a religious feeling, not passive and contemplative, but active, drawing them to the renunciation of material advantages . . .

One must remember that the material well-being they have now

attained thanks to communal life, rests entirely on the religious feeling
which showed itself in their movement to free the cattle; and that this
feeling is more precious than anything else, and woe not to them in whom
it shows itself in a perverted form (I refer to undressing when entering
villages), but to him in whom it has dried up.[10]

Tolstoy, far away and personally uninvolved in the great task of creating an economically and socially viable community on the prairies, could
afford such empathic understanding. Peter Verigin could not, as he
showed shortly afterwards. On their release from prison most of the
original group of Sons of Freedom returned peaceably to their fields and
gardens, but ten of them, including Alex Makhortov, remained true to
their vision of the pure and holy life. The Satanic element, they decided,
was science, which was now inspiring the efforts of their brethren. Sabotage seemed the solution, and they first flattened part of a field of ripened
wheat with a roller and then set fire to the cotton sack of a binder. They
also tried to set fire to a threshing machine, but were prevented by other
Doukhobors. All this they did so that men should trust not in science but
in God, showing, in the first instance of Doukhobor arson in Canada, that
concept of destruction as an agent of purification and renunciation that
since then has always been an element in the motives of Sons of Freedom who resorted to fire in the name of religion.

At Verigin's instance six of these men were arrested, and, though the
Mounted Police and the judge warned him of the probable consequences,
he insisted on prosecuting them for arson, with the result that they were
each sentenced to three years' imprisonment—for burning a small piece
of canvas. Later Verigin refused to petition for the men's release even
when he was urged to do so by Professor James Mavor at the instance of
the commissioner for immigration in Winnipeg.

Verigin's attitude cannot be justified. When even the Canadian officials
were inclined towards clemency, he went against all Doukhobor traditions by delivering his own followers up to be imprisoned by the very
earthly rulers his own religion condemned. At the same time, his motives
can be clearly understood. Not only were the actions of this small group
of zealots embarrassing to him when he was trying to weave a diplomatic
course in his relations with the Canadian authorities, but their assaults on
machinery dealt a blow at the very program of modernization by which
he sought to make the Community economically successful. If their
example spread, he would be faced with disunity and chaos within the
Community, and those who hated his communistic experiments would

be encouraged. He probably felt that the short-term effect of his severity was its justification, for, though there were several other attempts at pilgrimages and nude demonstrations during 1904 and 1905, they involved only tiny groups of people, and the Sons of Freedom movement did not at this time extend beyond a few dozen individuals.

Though less dramatic, the movement of the Independents, as they were called at this time to distinguish them from the Community Doukhobors, was in fact much more threatening to Verigin's plans. Many of the members of the Prince Albert colony had already made individual entry for their quarter sections before Verigin arrived, and, though they were swept along in the general enthusiasm for communistic organization at the beginning of 1903 and agreed to pool their work and resources with their brethren, by the end of harvest that year they began to withdraw into their former independence. Even in the South Colony there were individuals who rebelled, and in the village of Novotroiskoye feeling between the Community Doukhobors and the 'No Doukhobors', as they called the Independents, grew so high that on one occasion there was a fight with pitchforks and staves. Verigin ordered that all Independents should be expelled from the colonies, and threatened that their exemptions from military service would be withdrawn. To a certain extent he was successful in forcing dissidents in the North and South colonies either to submit or to seek homesteads of their own outside the Doukhobor reserves. Even in the Prince Albert colony he retained many faithful followers, and while he ruled on the prairies there were never so many Independents as there had been before his arrival, when Bonch-Bruevich counted 2,100 of them. In 1906 they numbered 849, as against 7,852 Community Doukhobors.[11] Thus the Independents made up about ten per cent of the Doukhobor population of Canada at that time, but they were only kept to this proportion by the most drastic treatment of dissidents by Verigin and his lieutenants. The Independents maintained the Doukhobor religion: it was the communist economic organization they rejected.

Yet, despite the divisive elements on both wings, the Doukhobor community on the prairies between 1903 and 1907 was a remarkable achievement for a group of illiterate people who had started out with no capital but their own strength and no previous experience of North American business methods or of modern farming. Out of the chaos that existed before Verigin's arrival was built up in a remarkably short time one of the largest and most complex of the many idealistic communities in North American history.

Some of its features will already have become evident. It was divided geographically into three widely separated colonies and organized in villages, of which by 1907 there were sixty-one, the railway village of Verigin and three other settlements having been added to the fifty-seven founded in 1899. In eight years the number of Doukhobors in Canada had increased from 7,300 to 8,700. There had been a number of new immigrants, but nearly one thousand of the new population were children born since the ban on sexual relations, imposed during the time of persecution in Russia, had been lifted when the Doukhobors came to Canada. This gave an average population of 142 per village.

In each village a headman or elder assumed responsibility for coordinating work and ensuring that the village sent its contributions to the general fund and received its quota of supplies from the central stores. Within the village the sobranie served as a means for reaching Community decisions. Attended by all the inhabitants, it was usually a combination of religious gathering and business meeting. Generally speaking, household goods were owned individually and each family provided its own meals. Except on individual garden plots, however, the work was done communally with communally owned implements. All livestock, even down to the hens, was owned and tended in common.

A regular pattern of life was imposed. Early in the morning a choir singing in the street would take the place of a waking bell, and at night the same choir would sing the equivalent of a vesper hymn to mark the day's end. The summer routine of work, as described by Professor James Mavor, who toured the Doukhobor settlements in 1904, resembled that so often portrayed in nineteenth-century Utopian romances.

Their working day is from five in the morning until eight in the evening. But this is divided in a fashion peculiar to themselves into three shifts of five hours each. One shift of men and horses goes to work at five, quitting at ten, for the five hours' rest, while another shift continues the work. At three, the first shift resumes work, and continues until 8 p.m. Thus, one shift of men and horses has had ten hours of work, broken by a period of five hours' rest, the other has had but five hours of work. The heavy and light shares of work are taken turn and turn about by the two shifts of men on alternate days.[12]

Most of the work was done in gangs, which marched singing to the fields each morning; but in each village there were full-time blacksmiths and carpenters, and other men were delegated to the special tasks of looking after the communal cattle shed, sheepfold, and stable, and of herding the animals in the fields. Visitors were impressed by the good care taken of the animals. Early in 1906 the chief forest ranger of the Department of the Interior visited the Doukhobor settlements and reported that 'the care of their livestock could not be excelled on the best thoroughbred stock farm in America. There is a man on duty in the stables night and day carefully watching the animals.' [13]

Half of the able-bodied male labour force of about two thousand worked through the summers on construction contracts for the extension of the Canadian Northern Railway and for branch lines on the Canadian Pacific. During the winters also many of them were away from the villages cutting lumber for the Doukhobor Community in government forests where they had logging permits. Their absence was made possible by the fact that in Doukhobor villages there were hardly any idle hands. From a comparatively early age, each child performed light duties around the house or in the field, or gathered berries or wild herbs. This early apprenticeship to life was and still is considered among Doukhobors at least as important an education as the formal training in the schoolroom. The women and children made an important contribution to the finances of the community by gathering the medicinal senega root, which grew wild on their reserves; in the three years from 1903 to 1905 almost $25,000 was earned in this way. Even the old women worked as long as they could move a limb—spinning, knitting, tending the garden plots. Undoubtedly, in these early years on the prairies, such universality of physical toil created a great bond among the people, and, except for the minority of Independents and the small fraction of those who were tortured by their zealotry, Mavor was probably not exaggerating when he described the Doukhobors then as 'comfortable and happy'.

While some Doukhobors adopted Canadian dress and rather superficially mimicked the habits of their non-Doukhobor neighbours, in general the social life of the villages did not differ much from that in the Caucasus. Food was still prepared in the Russian way. The central dish of every meal was the great bowl of borsch from which the whole family would eat together, each dipping with his own wooden spoon. The week was punctuated by routine events—the sobranie every Sunday and on Saturday the visit to the bathhouse to sweat out the dirt of the week's toil. The custom of early marriages followed in the Caucasus still obtained; girls were married at sixteen or seventeen, and boys often at fifteen, the age at which they were considered mature enough to go out and work among the men on the railway grade or in the fields. One particularly attractive feature of Doukhobor life was the respect shown to wild animals. Elk, antelope, and prairie chicken wandered unmolested over the land and into the villages. They were as much brethren as the cows and the horses.

Under Verigin the Community was much more centralized than it had been in the early years. From his headquarters at Otradnoe and later at Verigin he was able to co-ordinate efficiently the economic life of the villages in the North and South colonies. It was less easy to fit the Prince Albert villages into this arrangement; they were three hundred miles away and nearly half their inhabitants had become Independents. In the end Verigin gave up the attempt to discipline these distant settlements and urged his supporters in that region to abandon their land and join the South Colony, which they did eventually in 1906 and 1907.

In appearance the Christian Community of Universal Brotherhood was a democracy, governed by the Conventions that were held early each year to receive the annual report and financial statement presented by the Representative Committee and to vote on various matters of policy and practice brought before them. Originally two delegates from each village attended these gatherings, but in 1906 the special interests of the female constituency were recognized and one woman from each village was added to the delegation. In practice only the villages of the North and South colonies sent their representatives, and not even all of them; at the Convention of 1906 only forty-four out of the total of sixty-one Doukhobor villages were regarded as reliable enough to be represented. In theory the annual meeting was supreme. In practice, though Verigin's formal powers were small, his real influence was immense, and not merely because of his position as hereditary leader. Among the Doukhobors he had the most flexible imagination and the deepest understanding of the way in which the technology of his time could be adapted to serve a community of radical Christians, and in men like Planidin, Zibarov, and Reibin he was supported by able collaborators. Resolutions at the annual Conventions never went contrary to his advice, and during the twelve months that elapsed between meetings he and his four or five closest associates acted as an executive with sweeping powers to make almost any decision on behalf of the Community.

The General Accounts prepared for each Convention reveal a dual financial structure within the Community. The villages sent their members to work outside, collected their earnings and dispatched them to the central treasury. In 1905 these earnings varied, according to village, from $1,000 to $4,830, and totalled $114,136. Sales of produce and other general financial transactions were arranged through the central office in Verigin. The income from miscellaneous sources in 1905 was $75,646, but this included a bank loan of $50,500 that Verigin had been able to negotiate at the very advantageous rate of 4 per cent. During the same year great investments were made in machinery, so that there was a total expenditure of $249,963 and a deficit, not counting the bank loan, of $60, 180, covered by communal assets (quite apart from village property) of $61,925.[14]

These figures give an incomplete idea of the productiveness of the Community, which was largely self-supporting. In 1904 some 100,000 bushels of wheat were grown and ground into flour for the use of the villagers, while flax, grown as a first crop on the newly broken ground, as well as the wool of the 3,000 sheep in the Community flocks, was spun and woven into cloth by the women. The herds of communally owned cattle had increased to more than 5,000 and now provided an adequate supply of dairy products, while in 1906 there were 1,057 horses. None of this livestock was included in the assets of the Community. In land the Community had some 42,500 acres actually under cultivation.

By daring deficit financing Verigin was in fact building up the infrastructure of a self-contained community. While the villages owned their simple farm implements, such as ploughs, harrows, and horse-drawn mowers, the machinery and the industrial plant were in the hands of the Community as a whole. At the end of 1905 it owned sixteen steam engines, which went round the villages for ploughing in the spring, and eleven threshing machines. It possessed six flour mills and five sawmills. Two miles from Verigin a brickworks was established, making bricks and tiles for sale as well as for use in the villages, where some of the original sod or wattle houses were being replaced by more durable structures. At Yorkton there was a plant for making cement blocks, as well as warehouses and a home for sick Doukhobors. At Verigin, beside the railway, stood the great warehouses for storing goods that were bought wholesale for the Community from Winnipeg, Ontario, even Vancouver, and sent to the villages, where they were distributed according to need among the people.

These facts and figures leave no doubt of the extent of the achievements of the Christian Community of Universal Brotherhood on the prairies under Peter Verigin's leadership. But the statistics have a solid human foundation. The people were better fed and better cared for than they had been in the chaotic years before Verigin's arrival. Under the Community system the sick and the old were provided for equally with the rest, and though at the 1906 Convention the delegates decided to postpone the question of a hospital, items in the balance-sheet for drugs and even operations suggest that the members of the Community did in fact receive some orthodox medical treatment as well as the attention of their traditional bone-setters and of the old women who had brought from Russia their lore of herbs and spells. The insistence on a communitarian in preference to an individualist economy had prolonged the old Doukhobor way of life, which would have been more quickly eroded if the members of the sect had been thrust as individuals into the competitive world of the developing prairie society.

Nor were the achievements of the Community of benefit to its members alone. Arriving at a crucial time in the history of the prairies, the Doukhobors played a considerable part in the opening of the west, not only by breaking and cultivating large areas of land, but also by building many miles of the vital railway links, often under conditions that other workers were unwilling to accept. Though many Canadians were hostile from the beginning and others were rendered so by the eccentricities of the early Sons of Freedom, those who actually visited the Community and met Verigin were more inclined to be impressed than otherwise. They wondered at the ability of the Doukhobors to achieve so much in so little time, and particularly at the use of modern machinery, while Verigin's business acumen and his power of inspiring his followers drew him many admirers. Wherever he appeared in person he was the centre of interest, and often, as a typical Winnipeg newspaper report in 1906 suggests, of appreciation.

Both physically and mentally, he is perfectly equipped to be a leader of men. In height he is fully six feet, broad-shouldered, deep-chested, and perfectly built. He is swarthy in complexion, wears a dark moustache, and his dark hair is becoming thin. He is square-faced, and his normal expression is serious but kindly. . . . His conversation reveals a bright, keen, active mind, fully competent to deal with every problem which might arise among his people.[15]

Unfortunately this kind of interest was narrowly based. The people who visited the Community or met Verigin belonged to restricted classes; they were either sympathizers (Quakers, Tolstoyans, radicals of various kinds) or they were government officials, academics, and publicists. From the ordinary people of the prairies the Doukhobors kept aloof; they were disinclined to learn the English that would have enabled them to communicate, and they were by tradition suspicious of outsiders. Other settlers were often resentful of their clannishness or jealous of their landholdings, and the Doukhobors made no overtures likely to soften their

neighbours' prejudice. In the prairie towns the goodwill they had originally built up among the merchants by their trustworthiness was turned
into hostility when the Community began to buy goods wholesale and to
cut itself off completely from local markets. This meant that when they
came to need them the Doukhobors found themselves almost without
friends or defenders in the prairies.

Given Verigin's brilliant leadership, the loyalty of the great majority
of his fellow Doukhobors, and the expansion of the Canadian economy,
which was to continue until 1913, the Community might have continued
prospering in the prairies, provided only that it had been left alone by the
authorities or that some imaginative compromise had been worked out
between the government and the Doukhobors. The compromise over the
land entries in 1903 merely delayed a confrontation, and by the beginning
of 1906 it was already evident that both sides would soon have to face the
difficult question of the oath of allegiance. The actual crisis did not
mature until the autumn of 1906, but already in 1904 and 1905 there
were a number of events that ominously reminded Verigin and his closer
advisers of the difficulties of their situation. On 15 December 1904, the
Doukhobor reserves were abolished. All the homesteads that the Doukhobors had not entered were opened for public entry, which meant an
immediate influx of non-Doukhobor settlers into the neighbourhood of
the Community villages and a breaching of Doukhobor isolation. In 1905
the two territories of Assiniboia and Saskatchewan were absorbed into
the new province of Saskatchewan, and Clifford Sifton, who had a pro-
prietary interest in the Doukhobors, resigned as minister of the interior
on a difference of opinion with Sir Wilfrid Laurier over the education
clauses in the law establishing the province. His place was taken by Frank
Oliver, who had no prestige at stake in the question of Doukhobor immigration and who before long displayed marked hostility towards the
sect. From that time relations between the Doukhobors and the authorities steadily worsened.

Meanwhile, in 1905, Peter Verigin had further reason for disturbance
when two new groups of Doukhobors arrived in Canada. One consisted of
the exiles from Yakutsk and the other of a small family group—Peter
Verigin's divorced wife Evdokiia, his son Peter, now a young man of
twenty-five, Peter Petrovich's wife Anna, and their two children, one of
whom was also a Peter Petrovich. Anastasia Verigina had died early in the
year, and Verigin had felt a sentimental desire to be reunited with his
family and to see his son who, according to Doukhobor custom, would
eventually succeed him as leader of the sect. He wrote to Evdokiia and,

from curiosity rather than affection, she and the younger Peter accepted his invitation. They were accompanied by Alesha Vorob'ev, the leader of the Middle Party, who came to survey the possibilities of immigration for his own group.

This was the only occasion on which the three Peter Verigins who were accepted as leaders by the Doukhobors of Canada were ever together: the father whom his followers called Peter the Lordly, the son who succeeded him as Peter Chistiakov (the Purger), and the grandson who a generation later was to be the Doukhobor 'king across the water', living and dying in a Stalinist prison camp but still reverenced by his Canadian followers as Peter Iastrebov (the Hawk). The meeting, from all accounts, was not a success. Peter Petrovich had been influenced by the hatred that his mother's clan, the Kotel'nikovs, bore towards his father. Having received something of an education, he was a rather opinionated young man and quickly showed himself intent on exposing the human weaknesses of Peter the Lordly. He flaunted his independence, talking bawdily, smoking, and gathering around him an admiring circle of young men who were tempted by the ways of the world outside the Community. He told the Doukhobors that his father was fooling them, robbing them and keeping them in ignorance. On more than one occasion he bearded Peter the Lordly in public, calling him a cheat and a bandit, and denouncing his elaborate way of living. Evdokiia, who may have hoped to win back her former husband's affection, became jealous of the ascendancy of Anastasia Golubova in Peter the Lordly's household and, far from offering him any consolation over the hostility of Peter Petrovich, withdrew into her own resentment. Mortified at the scandal his son had created, Verigin watched his visitors return to Russia at the end of six months with relief. To save his own face, he gave Peter Petrovich, according to the latter's account, a special mission.

Father said to me that there remained in the Caucasus brothers and sisters who in their hastiness and scepticism did not join the movement. He said I should return, find the Doukhobors, and unite them. Father gave the example of potatoes that are left after the harvest and which a good farmer gathers.[16]

In the following year Peter Petrovich did in fact return to Canada for a brief period, looking for land to settle Doukhobors from the Caucasus, but his father, anxious not to repeat the experiences of 1905, told him the time was not opportune and sent him back. He did not return to Canada during Peter the Lordly's life.

The arrival of the brethren from Yakutsk was hardly more satisfactory from Verigin's point of view. They had been released during the summer of 1905 and made a long journey, on horseback, by cart, by boat, and eventually by train, to St Petersburg. In August they reached London, where they charmed the English with their good temper and their simplicity, and amazed them with their robustness. 'Several of the women turned the scales at more than 180 lbs.,' reported the *Daily News*, 'and many of the men at over 200 lbs.' [17]

Verigin was neither charmed nor impressed. He had heard from his brother Gregory and from Ivan Konkin of the independent spirit that had developed among the Yakutsk exiles, and his temper was already frayed by the experience with his family. The exiles, though they were welcomed by their relatives in the villages, entered the Community under a cloud of official disapproval. To make matters worse, instead of visiting Verigin immediately to make their submission, they spent their time arguing with the Community members about the kind of respect that should be allowed to Verigin, whom they regarded as a mere manager, and about the intolerance they found among their brethren. They even dared to object to the persecution of those who wanted to be independent, and, having lapsed from vegetarianism, they complained of the food in the Community. Above all, they put forward the extremely heretical idea that salvation could be attained by other people as well as Doukhobors. The old people were shocked and antagonistic; the young, who had already been subjected to the iconoclastic talk of Peter Petrovich, were inclined to agree, and began talking among themselves in the same rebellious manner as the men from Yakutsk.

Verigin recognized the threat such newcomers posed to his authority and felt that by dealing with them severely he might recover some of the prestige he had lost through the antics of his son. Accordingly he not only refused to receive the representatives of the exiles when eventually they went to see him, but ordered the villagers to discipline these refractory brethren by depriving them of food and, if they remained obstinate, expelling them from the Community. Some of the villages obeyed and starved their Yakutians; others did not, and many of Verigin's own followers were disturbed by his actions. As this treatment did not appear to be very effective, Verigin ordered that the exiles must be forced to give up their money. A few complied, and an entry of $303 duly appeared on the balance-sheet as a 'contribution from the Yakutsk brethren', but many refused; they were already beginning to see that there was no future for them in the Community. In the end, a minority of the Yakutsk exiles submitted and remained in the Community, but most of them departed. A few, like Vasilii Pozdniakov, joined the tiny group of Doukhobors in California; the majority found work on the prairies or took up land and swelled the number of Independents. Verigin's Community had shown itself too rigid to allow for variant opinions; like most religious brotherhoods, it equated conformity with survival.

9 STRIFE WITH THE STATE

The crisis between government and Doukhobors, which brought a virtual end to the communitarian experiment in the prairies, must be seen against the changing demographic and political background of the Canadian west in the early nineteenth century. In 1898 a total of 31,900 emigrants entered Canada; more than an eighth of these were the first two shiploads of Doukhobors, who thus formed a valuable part of the new population that during the next four or five years opened the prairies, built the railways, and proved by practical experiment that a farming life was possible in the regions to the north of the Canadian Pacific Railway.

By 1905 the situation had changed radically as Sifton's policy of encouraging immigration showed its maximum effect. In that year no less than 146,266 immigrants entered Canada, and in 1906 there were 189,064 of them. The majority of these people, as well as many land-hungry Canadians from Ontario, found their way to the prairies, and free homestead land was in great demand.

Added to the pressure of population were other considerations that appealed especially to the politicians. The new settlers in the prairies were either British subjects or intended to take out naturalization papers as quickly as possible; they were, in other words, potential voters, as well as the kind of future citizens, devoted to the doctrines of free enterprise, whom Laurier's Liberal government and his new minister of the interior, Frank Oliver, particularly desired. Large numbers of individual farmers would promote retail trade, which in turn would develop the small towns of the prairies, and placate the local business communities whose members had lost trade through the wholesale buying and selling practices of the Doukhobors.

In contrast to the immigrants who were entering the country in 1905 and 1906, the Doukhobors, from the point of view of the average Canadian, had proved a disappointing experiment. Their very real pioneering achievements had become obscured in the popular eye by the eccentricities of their behaviour—the mass pilgrimage of 1902 and the nude demonstations, beginning in 1903, which were to become a subject of prudish yet fascinated attention on the part of non-Doukhobor Canadians for the next sixty years. Few people paused—as few of them do even today—to reflect that these vagaries of behaviour were the actions of a minority of the sect, and, in the case of the nudists at that period, of a tiny minority. They condemned the sect *en masse*, and from 1902 onward the name 'Doukhobor' became almost synonymous in the popular Canadian mind with bizarre and shocking manifestations of religious fanaticism.

Underlying this more sensational aspect of the Doukhobor situation was the conflict between the sect and the government, which, despite Verigin's apparent efforts at conciliation in 1903, grew steadily more acute. As we have already seen, Verigin's behaviour in 1903 was more equivocal than it appeared on the surface. On his way from Siberia to Canada in 1902 he had told Paul Biriukov that he agreed with his followers in refusing to comply with the land regulations and to furnish vital statistics, 'because such demands of a government are against the freedom and independence of man.' [1] When he reached Canada he conveyed the opposite impression not only in his conversations with government officials, but also in his statements to the newspapers. In January that year the *Manitoba Free Press* carried reports that the Doukhobors now intended to comply fully with the laws regarding registration of vital statistics,[2] while Verigin's surrender on the question of land entry was widely accepted as the sign of a new era in relations between the sect and the government.

For a while Verigin carefully concealed from the outside world his real views on these subjects. But in all the directions in which the state, or conventional society, sought to persuade the Doukhobors into conformity, a growing obstinacy among the sect became evident, and it was only the unwillingness of Sifton to push matters to the point of crisis that postponed a final confrontation until Oliver, his successor, had settled into office and was ready for decisive action.

There were several points of crucial disagreement, but in 1906–7 the issue of the Doukhobor lands was the most important one; the three other issues—registration, taxation, and education—which aroused much bitterness in later years, now assumed only subsidiary importance, though their presence certainly helped to condition the attitude of the officials and the public towards the Doukhobors.

At this time the sect complied only sporadically, if at all, with the regulations regarding registration. Though they were counted on several occasions in connection with the allocation of lands, this was done by government representatives visiting the villages, not by Doukhobors themselves reporting births or deaths. The visiting officials often found that the Doukhobors either refused to give information or lied to them in the traditional manner of Russian peasants dealing with feared and resented outsiders. In 1905, when the Census Commission's enumerators toured the Doukhobor settlements, the people in villages sympathetic to the Sons of Freedom refused to give their names. Later in the same year, the Homestead Inspectors tried to check on the exact number of men over eighteen in order to decide the validity of land entries, but the women, fearing that information was being collected for military-service purposes, gave false ages for their sons. Yet no serious attempt was made to enforce the registration of vital statistics, and no Doukhobor at this early period was prosecuted for failing to comply.

The situation with regard to marriages was somewhat different. There was no penalty in law for failing to register a Doukhobor marriage, for the simple reason that their form of marriage, admitting no participation of the civil authorities, was not recognized. Doukhobor couples were not officially regarded as married until the law was changed in 1959. Their children were technically illegitimate, but this was unimportant to the Community Doukhobors, since it carried no moral stigma among them and questions of inheritance were not involved as long as property remained communal.

Like all functions of the state, taxation was repugnant to the Doukhobors, but in Russia they had paid their dues as a kind of tribute to the authorities in the hope of buying peace and seclusion. This compromise was made at Milky Waters, and in the Caucasus under the Kalmykov dynasty, though some of Verigin's followers in Russia during the early 1890s began to manifest their new-found militancy by refusing payment.

When the Doukhobors reached the Canadian prairies, the system of taxation in the west was still rudimentary; it was only after they had been there for two or three years that they were asked to make their first payments to maintain the public roads. Many resented this tax, and even disapproved of the existence of public roads in the reserves, which they had come to regard as Doukhobor domains to be guarded jealously against intrusion. At the Convention of the Christian Community of Universal Brotherhood of 28 February 1904, the delegates resolved to pay all the land taxes that were due, but in future to build their own roads, and they petitioned the officials of the Territory of Assiniboia to exempt them from road taxes. When their pleas were unsuccessful, they accepted the fact, and in 1905 paid $1,506 in road taxes for the North Colony and $1,192 for the South Colony.[3]

The situation regarding education was at this time rather complicated, since the Doukhobors had to deal not only with the state, but also with the Quakers, who were extremely eager to promote education among them. Though Verigin had spoken in favour of literacy in the letter he wrote from Obdorsk on 6 January 1899, neither he nor the majority of his followers showed in practice any eagerness to accept the opportunity of education when it arose in Canada. It is difficult to document Doukhobor opinions regarding schools at this period, but their action—or rather their avoidance of action—speaks eloquently enough. For the majority, the lore transmitted through psalms and hymns was sufficient, if it were combined with the practical knowledge of farming and craftsmanship that could be learnt by practice and example. For Verigin, while he needed a small minority of literate men to act as interpreters, clerks, and managers and to ensure the smooth running of the Community and its relations with the outside world, there were advantages in keeping the majority of his followers within the confines of their traditional oral education. Literacy might make them susceptible to negative influences from the outside world, and might weaken not only his own influence but also the solidarity of the sect as a community. Education provided by the state was further suspect because it might involve patriotic and militaristic teachings repugnant to Doukhobor pacifism, while schools run by Quakers, though unexceptionable on these grounds, might attempt to substitute the written Bible for the oral Living Book in the minds of Doukhobor children, and thus weaken their religious loyalties. Moreover, those Doukhobors who visited the Quakers in the United States were distressed to find that they were almost all merchants, and were appalled by the materialism of their daily lives.

There was no law requiring education in the Northwest Territories, and, though the province of Saskatchewan was established in 1905, it was only in 1916 that the legislature passed an act that made school attendance compulsory. Where the Doukhobors did come into conflict with the authorities was over the question of taxes raised by established school districts. Under the laws of the Northwest Territories the residents of any area could set up such a district, provided there were sufficient pupils to justify a school; they could then claim financial assistance from the government of the Territories, and levy local taxes to make up the remainder of the costs of maintaining the school. At Devil's Lake near the South Colony the local ranchers had created a school district that included part of the area settled by Doukhobors. The ranchers, who wanted the school, began to levy taxes on the more numerous Doukhobors, who did not. Quite apart from the unwelcome taxation, the latter feared that the trustees would force their children to attend school, and the disputes between them and the ranchers eventually led the Territorial government to intervene, suspend the powers of the trustees, and appoint a commissioner, who persuaded the Doukhobors at least to pay their taxes. From this time they paid regularly towards the school at Devil's Lake, and in 1905 they also paid taxes in the school district of Fort Pelly, but very few sent their children to either of these government-subsidized schools.

The Quakers were much more persistent than the government authorities in trying to spread education among the Doukhobors. Already, in 1900, an article in *The Friend* (London) had pointed out the seriousness of the problem. There were, it estimated, an average of forty children in each of the fifty-seven villages then existing, and the most desirable plan would be to bring them all together into a central school where they could be taught English.[4]

The early Quaker experiments were in fact on a much less ambitious scale, mainly because the British and American Societies of Friends had devoted the major part of their funds to feeding and clothing the Doukhobors and to helping them establish their communitarian economy by gifts of livestock and equipment. The first school was a very modest effort. In the summer of 1899 Mrs Eliza Varney, a Canadian Quaker, set up a dispensary at Devil's Lake (or Good Spirit Lake as it was also called), and in the following summer (1900) she was joined by her cousin, Nellie Baker, a graduate of Queen's University. They pitched three tents, one for living quarters, one for the dispensary, and one for a school which Nellie Baker conducted, improvising magnificently. She knew no Russian, but in little more than two months her older pupils had learnt to write and were already beginning to speak English. Possibly in the spirit of Verigin's letter of the previous year, the local Doukhobors welcomed her efforts, and even offered to pay her when they heard that her work was voluntary. But when she departed there was no one to take her place immediately, and so her work was largely wasted.

In 1901 the Russian expatriate nobleman Michael Sherbinin was sent by the Doukhobor Committee of the Society of Friends in London to the Prince Albert colony. Sherbinin went to the village of Petrovka, where he taught first in villagers' houses and later in a lean-to attached to the home he built for himself. His classes were small, rarely more than a dozen children, whom he taught to read and write in English, with a little simple arithmetic and much reading of the New Testament. Most of his students were the children of Independent Doukhobors, but even these drifted away in 1903 under Verigin's influence, and after three years Sherbinin was forced to close his school and take to farming.

But the Quakers persisted. In 1902 Helen Morland, who had been educated at Newnham College, Cambridge, came from England under Quaker auspices to take up the work started two years before at Devil's Lake. She found it far more difficult than Nellie Baker had done to assemble a class. In the autumn of 1902 she was teaching six boys, and the correspondent of the *Frankfurter Zeitung*, who visited the Doukhobors at this time, remarked that she was less busy than her companion, the Irish nurse Sarah Boyle, whose services were much in demand. Helen Morland may have antagonized the Doukhobors by tactless leisure activities, for the same correspondent remarked that 'the young lady, who finds her time lie heavy on her hands, amuses herself by shooting ducks and prairie-hens . . .'[5] During the following winter she was more successful, and by the spring of 1903 she had twenty-two boys in her school but no girls. Even though Sherbinin was teaching in Petrovka at this time and Herbert Archer was also being paid a modest salary by the Doukhobors themselves to teach English to a few boys in the North Colony, the number of Doukhobor children receiving some kind of formal education in 1903 cannot have been more than fifty.

The Quakers were fully aware of the unsatisfactory nature of the kind of schooling that temporary teachers provided in makeshift quarters, and in 1903 the Society of Friends in Philadelphia offered to build and staff a school, at the cost of $15,000, partly from the royalties on Joseph Elkinton's book *The Doukhobors*, which was published that year in the United States, and partly from a legacy left by a Quaker woman interested in the sect. Elkinton, whose father welcomed the first shipload of Doukhobors at Halifax in 1898, had visited the prairie settlements in 1902 and even then expressed concern at the lack of schools. The Doukhobors told him that they intended to build their own schoolhouses as soon as they were able to do so. The Quaker offer to build a school was considered by the Convention of the Christian Community of Universal Brotherhood, held in February 1904, and declined with thanks, since 'it is not necessary because we will build our own schools.' Apart from Verigin's own reasons for keeping the opportunities for education within narrow bounds, the Doukhobors appear to have been suspicious that the Quakers would attempt to convert their children. Nor can one dismiss the possibility that the Quakers offended their protegés by a display of what Bonch-Bruevich called 'arrogant benevolence'. Seen from Philadelphia, the Doukhobors were among the underdeveloped peoples of their day, and the American Quakers appear to have moved among them with an ill-disguised contempt for their religious beliefs and orally transmitted culture.

The Quakers had no intention of abandoning their efforts to bring the English language and Bible training to Doukhobor children. In 1903 Hannah Bellows, the daughter of John Bellows, secretary of the Doukhobor Committee of the Quakers in London, came out to take Helen Morland's place in the South Colony. Like her predecessor, she seems to have been a rather opinionated young woman, for the comments she later made in *The Friend* about her experiences showed shrewd observation of the Doukhobors in general and of Verigin in particular, whom she obviously disliked, but little real sympathy for the outlook of the people she had gone to help.[6] She had even fewer pupils than Helen Morland— sixteen boys at the peak of her activities—and her school was soon closed.

This appears to have been the last effort on the part of the British Quakers. But their American brethren persisted, concentrating on the Prince Albert colony where they had hopes of winning pupils among the Independents. In 1903 they persuaded a number of parents to allow their children to be educated in the United States; one of these was Peter Makaroff, who later became a lawyer—the first Doukhobor professional man—and eventually an active promoter of the Co-operative Commonwealth Federation. In 1906 they finally carried out their plan of establishing a permanent school for Doukhobor children. A two-room school was built in Petrovka of sections prefabricated in British Columbia. It was run by Hermann Fast, a Russian-speaking pacifist from Rumania. He was assisted by a Canadian woman teacher, Eleanor Martin, who had already gained some experience teaching among the Mennonites, and later by Vilma Moore; both were Presbyterians. As the land crisis developed in

1906 and 1907, the Community Doukhobors left this district for the colonies near Yorkton or for British Columbia, and the Independents, left to themselves, sent their children to be educated by Fast and his assistants; in 1908 the school had sixty-seven pupils, seventeen of them Stundists (members of another sect of Russian dissenters) and the remaining fifty Doukhobors, including some girls. It was the first successful educational enterprise among the Doukhobors, and it represented a major change in attitude so far as the Independents were concerned.

The rest of the sect were to accept education only after many years and much strife; the history of that struggle will be told later. To all intents and purposes, by 1906 there was no educational activity in the conventional sense among the Community Doukhobors. Though, for the sake of form, 'schools' were built in a few of the villages, the buildings were never used for that purpose, but lapsed into cow barns or storage sheds. From 1906 onwards the Saskatchewan government set up school districts in the areas inhabited by Doukhobors. This began in the Prince Albert region and it was one of the reasons why Verigin persuaded his followers to leave that area. The same pattern was shortly followed over the whole inhabited section of the province, so that very soon, though attendance was still not compulsory, there were schools available to which Doukhobors could, if they wished, send their children. At this time, apart from the Independents, none of them did.

Though in different ways it troubled Doukhobors, Quakers, and Canadian authorities, the education question had at this time no drastic consequences. The differences between the government and the sect regarding the formalities of land-holding were, on the other hand, to destroy the community that Verigin had attempted to create in the prairies, and to implant among the Doukhobors deep and bitter grievances, which have shaped their attitudes and dominated their lives from that day to this.

For the first year after his arrival in Canada, Verigin was careful not to make any public statements that might reveal to the Canadian authorities his true feelings on the problem of the oath of allegiance that, within three years, would confront the members of his sect. On 15 April 1904, however, he wrote a letter to Vladimir Chertkov which, knowing Chertkov's itch to print anything that fell into his hands, he must have realized would not be kept secret. It duly appeared in *Svobodnoe Slovo*, the periodical that the Tolstoyans published in England. Verigin was careful to talk obliquely and to attribute the feelings he expressed to his followers. Since his followers tended to wait for his advice before expressing themselves in any way, it seems obvious with whom the feelings originated.

According to the Canadian laws all immigrants who receive grants of land, have to sign an attestation of allegiance to the English King. Privately, agents of the Government have already two or three times proposed this to the Doukhobors, but most of them do not at all wish to, and apparently will not, become subjects; and, in the future, troubles with the Doukhobors may arise here. The law is that, from the day of entering for the homestead three years should pass; then the Government gives a titledeed of ownership of the land, for which the oath of allegiance must be signed. In principle, this term has not yet passed, as the Doukhobors only entered their names for the land when I arrived last spring, but practically the Government fully acknowledges the Doukhobors to be reasonable, and are not unwilling to accept them into the bosom of citizenship . . . There is yet two years' term, and time will show what will then happen. To speak openly, many of the Doukhobors are now dissatisfied with the climate and with cattle breeding. And taking all things together, whether it will not compel the Doukhobors to emigrate from Canada, cannot be guaranteed.[7]

This statement made clear for the first time Verigin's own inclination to abandon the prairie lands rather than accept the oath of allegiance, and it may have been intended as a veiled warning to the government of the strength of Doukhobor feelings on this matter. If so, it came too late; with the tide of immigration running so fast, the Canadian authorities were no longer likely to be disturbed by the thought of losing a few thousand settlers who could easily be replaced by others more willing to conform.

At about the same time, on 7 May 1904, the *Winnipeg Telegram* published the text of a catechism said to have been circulating in the Doukhobor villages since the previous March. The most significant part of the catechism was a series of questions and answers relating to political loyalties.

Q. *Why do you not wish to become subjects?*
A. *The teaching of our Saviour forbids it.*
Q. *Of what kingdom are you subjects?*
A. *Of that which has no bounds.*
Q. *To what law are you subject?*
A. *To that which has no bounds.*
Q. *Of what faith are you?*
A. *Judge by our deeds.*
Q. *To what society do you belong?*
A. *To the Universal Brotherhood.*

Q. *In what land do you live?*

A. *In the world, temporarily.*

Q. *Wherein has the love of God revealed itself to us?*

A. *In that God has sent into the world a son of like substance, that through Him we might be saved. Kings! You exist for men who like yourselves are men of war. Peoples! As Chistians we cannot take part in any conflicts and dissensions, and therefore you may leave us in peace . . .*[8]

The origin of this catechism still remains something of a mystery. It has the form and much of the content of Pobirokhin's catechismal psalm defining the nature of Doukhoborism, and it accords with the traditions of the sect. It was, perhaps inevitably, attributed to Verigin; but Verigin publicly denied authorship. Aylmer Maude, who received a separate version (from which we have quoted), attributed the reports of the circulation of the catechism to 'some anti-Veriginite Doukhobors' and refused to pass judgement on its authenticity. We can do no more, though our suspicions are provoked by the suggestion that a written catechism was passed round to be memorized by mainly illiterate people with magnificently trained powers of remembering orally transmitted material. But, even if the catechism was not—as his enemies suggested—intended by Verigin to instruct his followers in the answers they should give to officials who questioned them about homestead formalities, it certainly represented basic Doukhobor beliefs. Its appearance, in whatever way it may have originated, was symptomatic of the unrest and apprehension that, after the time of tranquillity following Verigin's return, were spreading once again among the Community Doukhobors.

Quite apart from their religious beliefs, there were good historical reasons why Doukhobors should be suspicious of the oath they were called upon to swear. In tsarist Russia, the attempt to impose the oath and the attempt to impose conscription had been closely associated, and Doukhobors had resisted both. How could they be sure that in Canada also the oath of allegiance would not lead to conscription? To peasants ignorant of Canadian history the question seemed an obvious one, and their inbred suspicion of all governments made them reluctant to accept any assurance to the contrary.

In the spring of 1906, after Oliver had taken over as minister of the interior, there were two developments that inevitably enhanced the fears of the Doukhobors and provoked their defensive stubbornness. Responding to the signs of a new dispensation on the prairies, land-hungry men from eastern Canada, from Manitoba, and even from the United States began to squat on unoccupied Doukhobor lands, in the expectation that they would soon be thrown open for public entry.

At the same time the authorities began to pursue a new policy deliberately aimed at encouraging individual farming by the Doukhobors and at breaking up the large aggregations of community land. In spite of Sifton's assurances in 1902 that the Doukhobors would be allowed to live in villages, and would be exempted from the obligation to cultivate individual quarter sections provided they tilled an adequate proportion of their communally held lands, Frank Oliver reinterpreted the Dominion Land Act and in March 1906 issued instructions that Doukhobor land entries were to be 'dealt with in all respects as ordinary homesteads.' [9] Every quarter section was to be inspected individually; where no improvements had been made and no residence duties carried out, the entry was to be regarded as subject to cancellation. Later in the year Oliver told Verigin personally that, though Doukhobors could live in villages, they could not get patents to their land by living in villages; in other words, each would have to move out to the quarter section entered in his name and actually put up a dwelling there, an interpretation of the Hamlet Clause that could hardly have been sustained had it been brought into the courts.

Acting on this dubious interpretation of the law, Oliver sent out his Homestead Inspectors, who discovered that more than a hundred entries were irregular, mainly because of discrepancies between the age of the applicant as shown on the entry and that given when the inspectors toured the villages. These entries Oliver ordered to be cancelled immediately, doubtless to warn the Doukhobors that he would very soon insist on the rest of the land's being patented according to the absolute letter of the law, including the oath of allegiance.

Having shown his intentions and evoked no response from the Doukhobors, Oliver appointed a special commission under the Rev. John McDougall, a Methodist missionary who had long been active among the Indians of the Canadian west. McDougall was assisted by Dr E. L. Cash, MP for MacKenzie, Homestead Inspector M. G. McCallum, and Michael White, who acted as interpreter. For almost three months they toured the Doukhobor settlements, visiting all sixty-one villages and compiling careful statistics of population, livestock, land cultivated and uncultivated, and the numbers and attitudes of Community and Independent Doukhobors.

The commission was still far from having completed its work when Peter Verigin decided to absent himself from the scene of impending crisis by going on a trip to Russia. He gave two ostensible and seemingly incompatible reasons: to find out whether, in the slightly more liberal atmosphere that followed the 1905 Revolution, the Doukhobors might possibly return to their homeland; and to recruit ten thousand Russian peasants to take up construction contracts on the Canadian railways. The timing of his departure, however, suggests that his real motive was to evade open responsibility for the persistent refusal of his followers to comply with the requirements of the Dominion Land Act as interpreted by Oliver. Since he not only talked of the sect's returning to Russia but also interrupted his journey in Chicago to inquire into the possibility of settlement in California, one may fairly assume that he had already become reconciled to abandoning the farming empire he had built up with so much effort over the past three years and to finding some place where the Doukhobors would be masters of their own land on their own terms. In Winnipeg, on his way to Chicago, he met Frank Oliver on 15 October and tried to persuade him to relax his policy. Oliver was inflexible, and Verigin realized that little would be gained if he returned to Saskatchewan. When he did come back in March, Oliver's policy had already led to its expected consequences. Verigin has often been accused of disloyalty in leaving his followers at this extremely difficult time; and on these grounds his conduct seems to deserve criticism, though he was by no means the first ruler by divine right who deserted his people in the hour of need.

McDougall's commission discovered that, so far as the Community Doukhobors were concerned, only an average of 21.8 acres per quarter section entered had in fact been cultivated. The Independents had cultivated rather more than double this proportion of the homesteads for which they had entered; they also owned proportionately almost twice as many livestock as the Community Doukhobors.

The commission found that the Community Doukhobors were irrevocably opposed to the idea of naturalization, and that they would not accept assurances that the Canadian government had committed itself to exempting them from military service.

When we continued to reason with them they repeatedly told us 'We do not want to own the land—all we want is to be permitted to make a living thereon'. And this was the invariable answer of the Leaders and representative men of these strange people on this question of land ownership, dependent as it is upon naturalization.

The Independents in their turn complained not only of boycott and persecution, but also of being 'robbed by the Community'. The latter accusation was based on the fact that when they left the Community, 'years of labour and shares in plant and stock have been kept from them.' The commission appears to have accepted this particular claim as reasonable, but one may question whether a man who retires voluntarily from a group experiment has individual rights over what has been produced by collective effort. The Independents, like the Small Party in the Caucasus and the rich Doukhobors who stayed behind at Milky Waters, seem to have tried to curry favour with the authorities as a reward for abandoning communal farming. All the evidence suggests that most of the Independent Doukhobors were richer from the start than their Community brethren, and that in the long run they profited financially from breaking away.

The commission recommended that everything should be done to assist the Independents in obtaining title to their lands. As for the Community Doukhobors, it suggested that the government 'concede to their desire and relieve them at the present from the necessity of citizenship by cancelling all their entries to homesteads.' However, McDougall and his associates clearly foresaw the difficulties that might arise if almost eight thousand Community Doukhobors were left landless to fend for themselves on the prairies, and it recommended that government-owned reserves be established around the villages, allowing seventeen to twenty acres per person; a reasonable period should be allowed to give Verigin's followers the choice of whether to become naturalized or to lose their lands.[10]

In mid-December McDougall was given a second commission to investigate land claims, with full power to cancel entries at his discretion, and in January 1907 a circular in Russian and English was distributed in the villages. Its contents showed that the government had now developed an open bias against communal ownership, and that Oliver had definitely broken Sifton's undertaking, made at the time of the arrival of the Doukhobors in Canada and confirmed in 1902, that communal cultivation would be allowed. The circular begins:

The Government . . . is very sorry to see that after having been in Canada for seven years, the large majority of the Doukhobors still cultivate their land in common and refuse to become citizens of the country. They have left large areas of land which the Government has permitted them to hold in their names without cultivation and improvement. The law is that a man must cultivate his own land or he cannot hold it. The people who are not Doukhobors now demand that Doukhobors be no longer allowed to hold land without cultivating it and becoming citizens of the country.

Even cultivating the land in individual quarter sections was not enough. The government clearly wished to break up the village pattern as far as possible, and as a first step it specified that :

If any man who lives in a village cultivates his land more than three miles from the village in which he lives, his entry will be protected for six months to enable him to build and live on the land. If he does not build and live on the land within that time the entry will be cancelled.

To each Doukhobor, once the land entries had been cancelled, fifteen acres would be allocated, but this land would be 'held by the Government for the protection of the community Doukhobors' only 'during the pleasure of the Government.' [11]

The demands of political expediency, represented by the masses of voters clamouring for land, are clear in this document, as are Oliver's legalistic inflexibility where the Doukhobors were concerned and his remarkable elasticity when it came to breaking his predecessors' promises. Even more equivocal appears the attitude of Sir Wilfrid Laurier, who had supported Sifton's indulgence while the Doukhobors were needed in the prairies and now, when their usefulness was ended, supported Oliver's rigidity.

Since the Doukhobors had farmed communally and lived in villages with the approval of the Ministry of the Interior for the seven years up to Oliver's appointment, the only legal excuse for depriving them of their lands was in fact that they would not take out naturalization papers because of a simple technicality: an oath of allegiance was required and this was contrary to their principles. If the Canadian authorities had familiarized themselves in the most general way with the history of Doukhobor disputes with tsarist authorities, they must have been aware of this difficulty from the beginning; yet they took no steps to devise a formula that would accommodate itself to the peculiar beliefs of their new immigrants. Since they had made such an accommodation on the question of military service, it could hardly have been difficult for them to yield gracefully on this further point, particularly as the oath was in practice no more than a formality. Instead, the Liberal ministers used the issue of the oath as an excuse to seize land for which there was public demand. It is hardly surprising that in later years the Doukhobors came to believe that their land on the prairies had been stolen from them. In law, it was not; but the moral case is different.

The Doukhobors submitted petitions against government action to the prime minister and the minister of the interior. At the same time, Professor James Mavor came to their defence and, with an intimate knowledge of the conditions under which the Doukhobors had been brought to Canada, protested to Laurier and to other cabinet ministers at such a patent breach of faith. The Doukhobors gained little other support. They had failed to cultivate friends, and in the prairies there were too many people who stood to gain by the new policy. On the whole, the press was uncritical of Oliver; journalists tended to regard the assimilation of the Doukhobors as a desirable end. Typical were the remarks in an article in *The Canadian Courier*, which appeared in April 1907, the month in which Mavor made his protests.

The Doukhobor is physically the superior of the average settler in the Canadian West . . . hardworking and economical . . . moral by inclination . . . When the Doukhobor shall put away Veriginism and substitute for it Canadianism, there is every reason to believe he will be a credit for the country.

Neither the appeals of the Doukhobors nor the protests of Mavor and their few other friends had any effect on the actions of the government. McDougall, the Christian minister, went about his task with an imperturbable pitilessness. In the spring he announced his dispositions. Some 235 Independents made legal entries, and these, together with 136 who had already taken the oath, received a total of 59,360 acres. A further 122,880 acres were reserved for the Community Doukhobors in the sixty-one villages. But well over half the land entered by the Doukhobors between 1903 and 1905 was taken away from them completely, and on 1 June, 258,880 acres were made available to the general public, resulting in a land rush such as had never before been seen in the Canadian prairies.

By now Verigin was back from his tour of the United States, western Europe, and Russia. Though he made no public pronouncement on his return, it was evident to him that the Doukhobors had no longer any great future on the prairies. Most of the land the Community now farmed was vested in the government, and the Doukhobors were at the mercy of official caprice. Moreover, the loss of the confiscated homesteads not only reduced their pastures, but also meant that agricultural expansion was impossible.

The majority of the Community Doukhobors were dispirited and discouraged, and, as had always happened at times of crisis, the conservative and the radical wings of the sect revived. There were now more than a thousand Independents, and when Verigin withdrew his Community followers from the Prince Albert colony, the Doukhobors in that region reverted to individual farming. In the summer of 1907 there was a further outbreak of activity on the part of the Sons of Freedom.

In August some seventy of these fanatics set off from the villages, led by Ivan Kislin and clad—men and women alike—in long blue gowns and wide-brimmed straw hats. They reached Yorkton and then started along the railway line for Winnipeg, chanting, begging from the people they met on the way, and announcing their intention of going to a warmer land where Christ would await them. Everything else had to be set aside in order to pursue this great aim, they told the other Doukhobors; as for Verigin, they denounced him as a 'machinery man'. In Winnipeg they stayed at J. S. Woodsworth's mission, and invited him to join them. Woodsworth declined, but a Tolstoyan watchmaker, Boris Sachatov, attached himself to the company and, from all accounts, behaved as eccentrically as his companions.

Into the woodland country of eastern Manitoba they wandered, halting for a while beside the Lake of the Woods, and then on through the forests to Fort William on Lake Superior, where they rented a tumbledown former vicarage and on New Year's Day paraded nude through the snowy town. The police behaved sensibly, draping them in horse-blankets and taking them back to their house, where they were in the habit of sitting naked on the floor around common piles of fruit and nuts, their main diet. When Ivan Kislin died in the middle of a fast, they took his body out on a sleigh, intending to dump it unburied in the cemetery. Eventually, when the spring came, many of them burnt their clothes, and their nude walks in the streets around the parsonage became so frequent that the police finally arrested nineteen of them, who were sentenced to six months' imprisonment. Eventually, after disputes over jurisdiction between the Dominion government and the provincial governments of Ontario and Saskatchewan, they returned, via various prisons, to their home villages. A whole year had passed since they first set out on their pilgrimage.

While such amiably bizarre happenings were taking place on the wilder fringes of his movement, Verigin settled down to plan for the future. In material terms, all that the Community Doukhobors now actually possessed was about fourteen square miles of land that Verigin had been shrewd enough to buy, plus the buildings in Yorkton and Verigin and some equipment. He immediately decided that the only way to gain economic security and political freedom was for the Community to increase its holdings as quickly as possible, and in the summer of 1907, as the land-grabbers settled in on former Doukhobor homesteads, he bought ten acres near Yorkton and set up a second brick-factory. The largest enterprise of its kind west of Winnipeg, it was capable of turning out 50,000 bricks a day.

Meanwhile, he advised his followers that they must work even harder and live more frugally. The largest possible crops must be grown on the land that remained to them, so that they could sell even more than the 150,000 bushels of wheat and 100,000 bushels of oats they had marketed from the previous harvest. The young men must all work outside the Community and turn every dollar back into the fund. All livestock beyond the necessary minimum must be sold. 'Luxuries' like tea, coffee, and sugar should no longer be bought. The Doukhobors must live sparsely once again, as they had done in times of crisis, for the sake of a more abundant future.

As in the Caucasus, such instructions were the prelude to an exodus, the traditional Doukhobor solution to an insufferable situation. At some time late in 1907 the delegates of the North and South colonies, plus those of the few Prince Albert colonists who had now joined them, assembled to discuss the future. Since Verigin had been unsuccessful in arranging for a return to Russia, the attention of the delegates turned to the warmer lands beyond the Rockies. Verigin and his trusted lieutenants, Nikolai Zibarov and Semeon Reibin, were appointed to inspect possible areas of settlement. California had already attracted the Doukhobors, and they had heard of Oregon from some of the religious enthusiasts of other faiths who had visited them. Verigin and his companions made their plans to tour these western American states. But before they could cross the border an opportunity presented itself that was to keep their future within Canada.

10 THE SECOND COMMUNITY

West of the Rockies, into the valleys of the Selkirks and the Monashees, the gold miners had penetrated during the 1860s, and there had been brief unprofitable rushes to places like Wild Horse Creek and Big Bend. After that, for three decades the area was largely abandoned to the Indians and the trappers, until, in the 1890s, the real rush came to the Kootenay and Boundary areas, sparked off by the discovery, not of gold, but of silver and base metals. Mines were opened, smelters built, and raw shack settlements sprang up around them, later dignified by the name of cities. When the mines gave out, some of the miners' cities were deserted and swallowed up by the returning bush; some, like New Denver, shrank into peaceful villages. But others retained a certain life and importance, either, like Trail, as metal-producing centres, or, like Nelson and Grand Forks, as the transport, marketing, and administrative centres for the mixed farming, lumbering, and mining economy that survived the passing of the great Kootenay boom in the opening years of the present century.

It was into this area of high mountains and narrow damp valleys that Peter Verigin came in the spring of 1908, the year after the seizure of the Doukhobor lands in the prairies. As he and his companions travelled through the Rockies, still densely under April snow, they must often have been reminded of their old home in the Caucasus, though here were dense coniferous forests, broken by stands of cottonwood in the valleys, instead of the bare grasslands of the Wet Mountains. By now the great mining boom had already declined. Nelson, where the Doukhobor delegates left the train, had sobered into a somnolent and isolated town among the mountains, and on the flat benches above the great rivers of the area— the Kootenay and the Columbia—land was being logged and the first of the fruit farmers, mostly immigrants from Britain and Germany, were planting their orchards. But the cultivated areas were still minute clearings in the sombre vastness of the great forests. Compared with the prairies that Verigin and his companions had left, the whole region seemed a new frontier waiting for a pilgrim people to liberate it from the wilderness.

At Nelson the Doukhobor delegates were met by Claude Laing Fisher, a man of all trades—chemist, engineer, lawyer, and real-estate speculator— who had bought or taken out options on several square miles of land on the western side of the junction of the Kootenay and Columbia rivers. Hearing of Verigin's desire to acquire land over which the Christian Community of Universal Brotherhood would have complete control by means of ownership, Fisher had already sought out the Doukhobor leader on the prairies, showing him the survey maps of the parcels he had to offer and talking in glowing terms of fertility, climate, and water for irrigation. From Nelson he took Verigin and his companions twenty-five miles down the Kootenay to the abandoned gold-mining camp of Waterloo. There he not only showed them the land, but, when their enthusiasm flagged at the thought of the labour involved in clearing the forest, demonstrated, by means of his own carefully prepared drawings, how they could build an inexpensive gravity-operated irrigation system to carry water from the mountains and feed their fields and orchards throughout the growing season.

Verigin decided to buy 2800 acres of land at Waterloo. He also bought, across the mountains in the Kettle Valley, another 2700 acres on the outskirts of Grand Forks. Returning to the prairies, he told his people that at last they would live on land that was their own, in a region where fruit— the natural food of natural men—would grow abundantly. 'In British Columbia it is possible to grow fruits of nearly all kinds—apples, pears, plums, cherries, etc.' he reported. 'Small fruits and vegetables are grown wonderfully well.' There was plenty of excellent timber for building purposes, and 'the air and waters are similar to those in Switzerland in nature, and even much healthier.' [1]

Preparations for the exodus began immediately. Barely a month after Verigin had decided to purchase the lands in British Columbia, pioneer parties were sent out, as they had been in the prairies, to clear land and build houses for the farm workers. Once again Nikolai Zibarov led the most advanced patrol, at Grand Forks, where the Doukhobor lands were named The Valley of Fruit. At Waterloo, whose military associations were erased by renaming it Brilliant, from the glitter of its waters, John Sherbinin and a group of eighty men moved into the abandoned buildings of the gold-mining camp and built the first sawmill.

Meanwhile, Verigin set about financing the migration in his characteristic way, obtaining short-term credit and paying off the Community's debts by a program of hard work and austere living by his followers, in exchange for the promise of freedom from outside interference and of better times ahead. The arrangement he made with Claude Laing Fisher was typical. The agreed purchase price for the land at Brilliant was $150,000. At first it was proposed that this be covered by a mortgage. Verigin, however, devised a method that would keep him out of the hands of the trust companies. He arranged with Fisher for the title deeds to the land to be placed in escrow with a bank. Each fortnight he would deposit to Fisher's credit the pay cheques of six hundred men whom he intended to send out on labouring jobs. By this means the debt was paid off in less than eighteen months instead of the five years specified by the agreement.

Perhaps the most significant fact of this agreement was that the lands were bought, not by the Christian Community of Universal Brotherhood, but by Verigin personally, and they were registered, with the consent of his followers, in his name. By a will written at this time, he bequeathed the lands to the Community as a whole, and prominent members were named as trustees. At no time was there any serious suggestion that Peter Verigin made this arrangement for his own profit, though it obviously reflected his desire to keep control of the Community in his own hands. He was anxious to prevent the possibility that ambiguity about the ownership of the land might allow new groups of Independents to defect from the Community; one of the main aims of migrating to British Columbia was to preserve the Christian Community of Universal Brotherhood intact, and in Verigin's view every precaution must be taken to this end. Furthermore, the Community was not yet established as a body with corporate rights under Canadian law. Its hold over the lands in British Columbia would therefore be more secure if they were vested in a single individual, and Verigin, identified by Canadians as well as Doukhobors as the symbolic head of the Community, was the obvious person. Later on, in 1917, when security appeared to rest in giving the Community legal status by transforming it into a limited liability company, Verigin was quite prepared to abandon title to the lands.

The lands bought in 1908 at Brilliant and Grand Forks were only the beginning of Doukhobor acquisitions in British Columbia. By December the Community owned some 8,800 acres—2,800 at Brilliant and 2,700 at Grand Forks, together with 2,200 acres at Pass Creek, fifteen miles north of Brilliant along the Kootenay, and 1,100 acres at Slocan Junction. By 1910 it owned about 10,000 acres; some of this consisted of already planted orchards purchased from English farmers, from which the first harvest of fruit was gathered in that year. By 1912 the total properties in British Columbia had reached 14,403 acres;[2] and by the time of Peter Verigin's death in 1924, they totalled 21,648 acres.

This appears a small area in comparison with the 400,000 acres the Doukhobors had once held on the prairies. But the foothold on the prairies was never entirely relinquished. Gradually, as Community Doukhobors migrated to British Columbia, the reserves of fifteen acres per person allotted in 1907 were taken up by the government and opened for public entry as homesteads (often going to Independent Doukhobors), but in 1918, when the Dominion government finally abolished these reserves, a residual area of 7,892 acres was left, and this was sold to individual Veriginite Doukhobors who turned it over to the Community, which had financed the purchase through a loan of $71,445 from the Sun Life Assurance Company. The Community also retained the land originally purchased at the village of Verigin, and other areas of prairie land were bought at Kylemore and Kelvington in Saskatchewan, at Benito in Manitoba, and at Cowley and Lundbreck in Alberta. In all, by 1924 the Community held 49,947 acres on the prairies, much of it purchased during Verigin's last years. Its total holdings, including both British Columbia and the prairies, amounted to 71,587 acres of land, or about 112 square miles.[3] It was less than a quarter of the area of the prairie lands held by the First Community in Canada, but it was on the average much better land, and it was certainly more thoroughly cultivated.

We have glanced ahead to the extent of the Second Community at its peak, just before Verigin's death, in order to show the kind of kingdom he was trying to create and the results he obtained. The Second Community as it evolved from 1908 was geographically even more fragmented than its predecessors in the early prairie days and in the Caucasus. Benito, the easternmost outpost, was a thousand miles from Grand Forks, the westernmost, and Verigin's followers were scattered at more than a dozen points over this great area of prairie and mountain valley. From 1909, when eight hundred Doukhobors left the prairies, they came in steady relays over the mountains to take up work and residence on the cleared lands of British Columbia, until, according to a special census of Doukhobors in the province taken on 22 October 1912, there were 3,988 people in the settlements there;[4] very shortly afterwards this increased to 5,000. Well over half the Doukhobors who accepted Peter Verigin's communitarian leadership moved to the valleys of British Columbia; the denser population in relation to the area of land was justified by the more intensive cultivation possible in a climate adapted to the growth of fruit and vegetables.

If the Community became more scattered, which increased the possibilities of disunity, it also acquired the potentiality of greater diversification. Verigin's retention of land on the prairies, and his subsequent addition to community holdings there, were calculated to create a situation in which the Doukhobors would not only be largely self-supporting in agricultural produce, but would also develop a variety of means by which cash could be earned. Grain grown by Doukhobors on the prairies could be exchanged for fruit and timber from the British Columbia settlements. The development of the orchards would encourage such pursuits as the production of honey; no less than six hundred colonies of bees were eventually set up. And, apart from their prime money-earning commodity of labour, the Doukhobors would be able to trade with the outside world in fruit and fruit products, in lumber, and in grain. Cattle rearing had declined considerably, partly because of the pressure of the Sons of Freedom but also because, in a community that did not eat meat, the cost of feeding cattle would not have fitted in with Verigin's austere economics. In 1917 the Community Doukhobors in British Columbia and the prairies owned together only 450 cattle and 540 horses.

This varied and largely self-sufficient community was a bold plan, and though it involved much self-sacrifice on the part of the individual members it was, until its originator's death, more successful than most North American communitarian experiments on a similarly ambitious scale.

The new settlements in British Columbia continued to be financed by a combination of mortgages and contract work. The expenses were extremely high. In four years, by 1912, Verigin had committed himself to $646,000 for land purchases alone (of which about $359,000 had already been paid). To transport five thousand people from the prairies to British Columbia cost, even at the reduced fares that Verigin obtained from the CPR, more than $200,000.[5] In addition, though some equipment in use on the prairies could be sold and some transported to British Columbia, a large expenditure was necessary on the different kinds of machinery needed for lumbering and land clearing, while the establishment of extensive orchards necessitated the bulk purchase of fruit trees. By 1912 some 70,000 had been planted, quite apart from the trees already growing in the established orchards purchased by the Community.

The finances of the Community at this period are somewhat obscure. Bonch-Bruevich preserved detailed accounts up to 1905, but from that time until 1912 information is meagre and vague. Verigin certainly raised a bank loan of $100,000 on properties in Saskatchewan, and sold a considerable proportion of the moveable assets—valued at about $400,000— that the Doukhobors had accumulated in the prairies. The rest of the money appears to have been raised mainly by outside labour. The men who went out to work were instructed, after paying their expenses, to bring a certain sum back to the treasury. At first this was $100 per man per season, later $200. In 1911 alone this assessment brought $214,000 into the funds of the Community.[6]

An abundance of willing labour, men, women, and even children, who would work during summer through the long hours of daylight, was in fact the great advantage possessed by the Community over the non-Doukhobors who at this time were endeavouring to set up individual farms in the Kootenays. It enabled them to manipulate gang labour for clearing the forests, creating the irrigation systems, tilling the ground for the first crops, and planting fruit trees. It provided a pool on which local farmers and sawmill-owners could draw at a time when casual hands were scarce in the interior of British Columbia. It provided men who worked on the railways and on construction jobs, as they had done in the prairies, and labour for the contracts into which the Community entered to provide railway ties and telegraph poles from the timber on its lands.

By the end of 1909 James McDougall, the clergyman who had carried out the dispossession of the Doukhobors in the prairies, was moved by curiosity to see how they were faring over the mountains in British Columbia. At Brilliant he found some seven hundred already settled. They had made several miles of roads, built two sawmills and a number of communal houses, stables, and out-buildings, cleared five hundred acres of forest land and planted it with fruit trees, terraced hillsides to form vineyards, and constructed a concrete reservoir with a capacity of a million gallons, linked with a number of irrigation channels. In addition to these considerable tasks, on their own account they had managed during the summer to earn thirty thousand dollars from outside employment. It was an excellent achievement for a first season's work.[7]

As in the prairies, Verigin combined the deployment of mass labour with the use of machinery. Steam engines and mechanical stump-pullers helped in clearing the forest. At Brilliant a pumping plant was erected on the Kootenay River to raise water into the reservoir and also to generate electricity. The sawmills were extended and planing machinery was added, so that the Community not only provided lumber for the settlements on the prairies and in British Columbia, but also made furniture for them. A brickworks was established at Grand Forks, and, despite their objections to earthly rulers, the Doukhobors were willing to sell their surplus production of bricks to the provincial government for its new administrative buildings at Grand Forks. Two large modern flour mills were erected on the prairies, at Cowley and Verigin, producing flour for Community use and also for sale, while six grain elevators with capacities varying from 75,000 to 100,000 bushels each were erected at various points on the prairies to handle Doukhobor-grown wheat. Finally, in 1910 Verigin bought the jam factory operated by the Kootenay Preserve Company in Nelson. Shortly afterwards a larger and more modern factory was built at Brilliant, with production for outside sale of sixty carloads of jam a year; canning and fruit-packing plants were also established at Brilliant and Grand Forks.

By 1917, when Peter Verigin decided to relinquish direct financial control and the Community was finally incorporated as the Christian Community of Universal Brotherhood Ltd, it was capitalized at one million dollars, with the shares held by fourteen shareholders, including Verigin (who became perpetual president), Michael Cazakoff and J. P. Shoukin, general manager and secretary-treasurer respectively, and, not surprisingly, Anastasia Golubova.[8] Vasilii Sukhorev, who in the later twenties was treasurer of the Community and automatically became a shareholder, told one of the writers that, on the reverse of his share certificate, 'I had to sign that I keep this share in trust for the people actually members of the Christian Community of Universal Brotherhood. That's how the corporation was based.'[9]

At this time the property of the Christian Community of Universal Brotherhood was assessed at $1,985,748, with outstanding debts of $563,226. Its value rose rapidly until Peter Verigin's death in 1924. An assessment in 1923 placed the Community's assets at $5,752,479, while, according to Sukhorev, in 1924 the corresponding figure was $6,410,822; the unpaid mortgages at this time amounted to $1,113,300.[10] The increase in seven years was due partly to the acquisition of further land and plant, but also reflects the sharp rise in prices during the years immediately after the First World War. Although throughout Peter the Lordly's reign the steady increase in the physical holdings of the Community was accompanied by an equally steady increase in its debts, which almost doubled in seven years, there is little doubt that, as a commercial empire, the Second Community in 1924 was a great deal more impressive than its predecessor that came to an end in 1907. How far this affected the actual lives of the six thousand adults who formed the membership of the Community at its peak is another matter which we shall discuss later.

Undoubtedly Verigin and his associates, while theoretically denying the validity of material achievements, were proud of the success of their venture as an industrial, agricultural, and trading enterprise, and this was reflected in the organization of the Community. Old forms still remained important: there were elders in the various villages, and the sobraniia at both village and Community levels remained important vehicles of communication between the leader and the membership. But parallel with this traditional hierarchy, and to a great extent replacing it, was a managerial hierachy headed by Verigin (transfigured from living Christ to company president) and staffed by members of his family and by his trusted associates. Cazakoff and Shoukin became steadily more influential in administration and policy-making because of their positions as general manager and secretary-treasurer, while at Brilliant, Grand Forks, Cowley, and Trail there were branch offices with managers and secretaries. Larion Verigin, Peter's nephew and secretary-treasurer of the jam factory, and John Sherbinin, manager of the largest sawmill, in the Slocan Valley, were also important members of the hierarchy. In addition to these officers there were ten directors of the Community, including in 1917 Zibarov, Ivan Ivin (who had been one of the first two delegates to Canada), and another member of the ruling dynasty, Peter J. Verigin. Among the directors the women were well represented; there were three of them, including Anastasia Golubova.[11]

Most of the hierarchy were chosen from the minority of literate Doukhobors, and there is no doubt that a natural peasant shrewdness and a certain organizational skill helped them in their business dealings. The rank-and-file Doukhobors, in their turn, appear often to have shown the ability to pick up practical skills that one sometimes finds among illiterate people, and some of them became efficient sawyers, steam-engine operators, or brickmakers. On the other hand, there were many who still found it difficult to cope with the demands of a life so different from that of the Caucasus.

The combination of Verigin's powers of large-scale organization and the inevitable shortcomings of his half-educated followers produced varying impressions of the quality of the Community's achievements. Some of its industries, where the energy and efficiency of a single capable manager could influence a relatively small group of workers, were highly successful; 'K. C. Brand' (Kootenay Columbia) jams, produced at the factory in Brilliant, gained a reputation throughout western Canada for their high quality, and the demand for them was always more than the supply. But in the field of agriculture, opinions on the achievements of the Doukhobors have differed considerably.

Visitors who arrived at Grand Forks or Brilliant in the spring, when the great orchards were full of blossom, or in the late summer when the valleys were busy with fruit pickers, tended to be impressed by what they saw and to talk highly of the Doukhobors as farmers. People who watched them through the years, or looked at their achievements with a more expert eye, tended to criticize them. These remarks of a retired Grand Forks farmer, who for almost fifty years had worked land next to Community property, are typical:

We never thought they were good farmers. They looked to us as if they just took everything off the land they could. They had some good land and a lot that was very, very poor, and they tried to farm it all. But the great thing about them, they had unlimited labour supplies. They wanted to do a job, and the women and the children and everybody would go out and work in the fields. That's why they were so much better off than the rest of us.[12]

This view was supported by the report of the University of British Columbia's Doukhobor Research Committee of 1952, whose findings suggested that Doukhobor farming in British Columbia was never completely efficient. With one exception, the committee recorded, 'all the orchards noted were planted with poorly chosen varieties arranged in a very haphazard and unsatisfactory manner, which alone must have made them very inefficient.' The committee was also highly critical of the irrigation systems established by the Community. Many, they pointed out, had never been satisfactory.

One of the main reasons for this was their apparent construction without technical advice and proper design. For example, some $230,000 was *devoted to an irrigation system to pipe water from Pass Creek to the villages at Brilliant and across the Kootenay River to ten villages at Ooteshenie. The scheme was of unsound design and got no water to Ooteshenie, a costly and tragic failure which could have been avoided had competent advice been sought.*

Reaching the general conclusion that 'the land was not . . . being utilized effectively', the committee nevertheless made an exception for the 'small intensively cultivated gardens' that were to be found in every village and next to every Doukhobor house, and, despite its other criticisms, admitted the value of the farming operations in 'providing food and shelter for the inhabitants.' [13]

But if, as a business organization, the Community failed to make the best use of all its assets, how did it succeed as an experiment in a religious and communitarian way of life? We may begin by describing the community organization that ran parallel to the managerial structure. Verigin was at the head of both. If he was now the company president, he was still the spiritual head of the sect as well, and as he travelled from village to village, inspecting, negotiating, exhorting, leading prayer meetings and choirs, he represented to the ordinary Doukhobor the combination of mundane action and spiritual thought that inspires Doukhobor Christianity, with its slogan of 'Toil and peaceful life'. It was he who set the keynote for the general life of the Community and represented in his person the significant changes that had taken place since 1907.

The days of a semi-oriental kind of leadership, his actions seemed to indicate, were at an end. The proliferation of managers and secretaries suggested that, even if a democracy in the genuine sense had not emerged, at least the Doukhobors had reached the condition of an Orwellian oligarchy in which all were equal, but some more equal than others. The concept of the role of leader had subtly changed, and Verigin altered his ways and his appearance to suit. He abolished the custom of bowing to the ground before him. The luxurious coach with which he had toured the prairie settlements now rotted in a storehouse. Instead, he drove around in a simple buggy with a single horse, unattended by choirs, and dressed like a labourer, with an old straw hat and trousers bound at the bottoms with binder twine. He represented in his person the universal austerity that was the keynote of the Second Community.

That austerity was expressed in every detail of daily life. In one major respect the Community in British Columbia now departed from Russian peasant traditions and adopted the traditional Utopian arrangement, sketched out originally by Sir Thomas More and practised by the Phalansterian and Icarian colonists in mid-nineteenth century America, of large groups of people inhabiting common houses and sharing not only in work, but also in food or possessions and in the daily domestic routine. To this day, in the valley lands that were once cultivated by the Community, one still sees the large, gaunt, square houses, designed by Verigin himself and built with Grand Forks bricks, standing in pairs in the middle of the fields, with outhouses of various kinds clustering around them, and perhaps the dying remnant of an orchard climbing up the hillside behind. These are the houses where, for a quarter of a century, the Doukhobors tried to live as the inhabitants of More's Utopia had done.

Each house contained between thirty and fifty people; a pair of houses formed a village, with a population of between sixty and a hundred. The house had its own organization, with a communal kitchen and a cashier who would go each month to the warehouse of the settlement in which the village was situated and receive the provisions apportioned to the people under his care.

The village formed a commune that was responsible, apart from any outside work its members might do, for tending the hundred acres of fields or orchards in which it stood. For this purpose it possessed its own pair of horses, its ploughs, wagon, and sledge.

From the descriptions that have survived of the communal houses and from our own visits to them in their present rather decrepit state, it is evident that life in them was very austere and lacking almost completely in privacy. On the upper floor of each house there were eight small bedrooms, with curtains instead of doors; the furniture was simple in the extreme—board beds with feather mattresses, tables and chairs, no pictures or any other decorations on the walls. Normally a family occupied one room, the father and mother sleeping in one bed, the younger children in the other. Children over ten were usually placed in another room. To people accustomed to Russian peasant life, such conditions did not offer great hardship, and it was only in the beginning, when the first community houses were built, that their inhabitants complained of overcrowding. Later, as more villages were built, the population of each house decreased, and during the 1920s the average was not much higher than thirty-five. On the ground floor of each house was a large common livingroom with a table in the middle and benches around the walls, and a kitchen with a big Russian oven in which large square loaves were baked every day and much of the other cooking was done. Attached to the community houses were wooden verandas, annexes that contained bath-houses, store-rooms, and guest rooms that were also used for sick people who needed quiet and seclusion. The houses were clean and neatly arranged, and the main criticism that outsiders were inclined to make was that they lacked adequate ventilation, a common enough fault in the homes of European peasants, who spend their working days out of doors.

Life in such houses was very similar to that in a modern Asian joint family. The lack of privacy was balanced by the feeling of being supported in all one's daily activities by a close group of fellow believers. The old were automatically cared for by the young, and the children grew up, as they do in joint families, in a permissive and affectionate environment. Many Doukhobors have recollections like those of the artist, William Koochin, now absorbed into the wider Canadian world, who remembers his upbringing as 'almost a group effort'.

As a young child I felt a lot of freedom—I mean before the age of ten. We lived in a village where there were many other families and we had such free rein. There was no boundary. There was as far as we could walk and back in a day, all community lands, and we were welcome to go anywhere. So that the restrictions were very limited at that time, and also I think because of the numerous grandmothers and aunts and so on that each child had at that time, there was a feeling of comfort in the sense that you were always looked after no matter what village you went into.[14]

As Koochin's account suggests, the organization of the houses and villages took on a strongly matriarchal character. This was mainly because most of the men of working age were either earning money by outside work or were employed in a community enterprise away from their own villages. This pattern persisted among the Doukhobors after the Community disintegrated in the 1930s, and even today a large proportion of the men spend the greater part of the year away from home on seasonal work or on construction projects. This is one of the main reasons for the persistence of conservative attitudes among the Doukhobors, since in Canada it has always been the women, living in far greater isolation from the outside world than the men, who have played the dominant role in shaping the attitudes of the children at a formative age.

The community of domestic life, which became for almost thirty years the dominant Doukhobor pattern in British Columbia, was not the only area in which Verigin's experiment paralleled those of the Tolstoyans and of the Utopian socialists about whom he had heard from the political exiles who were his companions in Siberia. An attempt was also made to create a completely moneyless internal economy. Theoretically at least, the principle of 'To each according to his needs' was established. Many needs were met by the Community members themselves, who cultivated vegetables, berries, and other fruits in the gardens attached to the houses, and also kept bees; they themselves consumed some of the products of these activities, but the surplus had to be turned over to the warehouse or the nearest jam or canning factory belonging to the Community, since no individual trading was allowed. Their other needs—flour, salt, kerosene, and clothes—were met from the communal warehouses situated at strategic points like Grand Forks and Brilliant. Since all the essential needs were met, there was, according to Verigin, no reason for Community members to buy goods individually, and no cash allowance was made to them. Men who worked outside on behalf of the Community in British Columbia were expected to turn into the treasury every cent they earned—until 1916, when there was a return to the assessment system. Some in fact kept back a few dollars, but the majority of the Community members, during the reign of Peter the Lordly, did not handle a coin from one year's end to the next and yet were provided with the means for a simple life.

How abundantly these means were provided is difficult to say, since the degree of austerity varied from period to period. Certainly throughout the life of the Community its ordinary members were allowed nothing that might remotely be called luxuries. Musical instruments, bicycles, personal ornaments, even the cheapest kind of jewellery, were all forbidden, as was expenditure on travel: Doukhobors were expected to remain on the Community lands unless they had been instructed to go outside for the purpose of work. Clothing was as simple and inexpensive as possible; Verigin himself introduced the custom of going bareheaded, and in the summer all the children and many adults went without shoes. Except in winter, the children wore only a single garment—the girls a long dress and the boys under twelve a shirt reaching to the knees. The women were encouraged to cut their hair short, and to wear short skirts reaching to the mid-calf; these were economical in cloth and more practical for field work. Later, after the First World War, when short hair and short skirts became fashionable, the Doukhobors felt they had once again proved themselves pioneers.

Such austerities were encouraged partly because Doukhobor religion places a special value on the simple life and partly for reasons of economy. Verigin and his assistants wished to spend as little as possible on living expenses so that the greater part of the money earned by the Community could increase the capital assets and pay off principal and interest on the mounting debts. These considerations affected even the kind and quantity of food that the members of the Community received. In good times this was probably adequate, though rather monotonous because of the vegetarian diet and the limitation of outside purchases to a few essential staples. An insight into Doukhobor eating habits in the early years in British Columbia was given by a teacher named Beulah Clarke, who lived among them for a few months in 1912. As she recollected it a short time afterwards, an average day's menu would run thus:

Breakfast—Excellent bread, butter, a glass of milk, soup made of potatoes, onions, butter and a grain something like oatmeal. Potatoes and onions fried in butter. Baked apple or preserves. Dinner—Bread, butter, milk, vegetable soup. Beans, peas and cabbages boiled together. Pancakes, made very thin and usually without baking-powder. Melted butter is poured over them and I ate them either with sugar or jam. Supper—Bread, butter, milk, 'lapshe'. This is made from flour and water. It is rolled very thin and then shredded and put into boiling water; butter is added, and very often there are small pieces of potato with it. Preserves, turn-overs; these are made from bread-dough, rolled very thin. Mashed potatoes are put in some, and rhubarb and sugar in others. They were put in the frying-pan and baked in a brick oven.[15]

While Doukhobors always provide well for passing guests, even when they have little for themselves, there is no suggestion that Beulah Clarke at this time was very much better fed than the people among whom she lived; on the contrary the fact that she went without meat, eggs, and tea, of which they also were deprived, suggests that in 1912 what she ate was the customary diet. At other periods, and particularly during the First World War, food was cut to a very low minimum. For a whole year no salt was available, and there are stories current among present-day Doukhobors of times during 1914 when a slice of bread and a helping of flour and vegetable soup for each person was all that was available on many Community tables.

For all these hardships there were compensations. There was the sense of exaltation and community when the people came together in a hillside orchard to sing their rich harmonies for hours together under the open sky. There were the Sundays, when work was abandoned and the whole day would be taken up with singing and talking. The members of the Community would gather in the dawn to begin chanting and praying;

if Peter the Lordly were present, he would address them later in the day, and long discussions would follow on theology and politics and on the nostalgically remembered past in the Caucasus. There was that consciousness of working for a religious society that has sustained monastic ascetics in even worse austerities than the Doukhobors accepted. And there was the feeling of safety that came from living in the bosom of the group while 'They'—as the ordinary Community members respectfully called Peter the Lordly—looked after all one's affairs and dealt with the threatening outside world.

For many, particularly among the women and the old, these consolations were sufficient, except at times of acute shortage, when complaints often became loud, particularly if the women felt the children were not sufficiently fed. On the whole they were simple people who felt that hard work and sacrifice were expressions of the inner religious urge and the means by which a better way of life would eventually be built. Whether they sought it by going on pilgrimages or by 'Toil and peaceful life', such people were led by an almost superstitious belief in the possibility of attaining the kingdom of heaven on earth, and when their vision of the Community was broken, as happened during the 1930s, many of them were to follow the chiliasts among the Sons of Freedom, who offered an alternative apocalyptic vision.

These were the true believers. But already, during Verigin's life, there had developed two classes who did not share either the faith of the believers or the visions of Peter Verigin. These the Doukhobor historian Peter Maloff has called 'pseudo-believers' and 'non-believers'.[16] The 'pseudo-believers' were the considerable group of managers and clerks, including some of Verigin's own family, who had acquired power and a degree of comfort not shared by the ordinary Community members. Many of them, as a result of their privileged intercourse with the outside world, no longer believed in the ideals of the Community, and, while presenting a pietistic exterior, they were interested only in personal material gain. They supported Verigin as long as it was in their interests, but even in his lifetime some of them withdrew to use their acquired business skills more profitably in private enterprise.

The 'non-believers' were those younger men who lacked the religious impulse and resented the narrowness of Community life. In British Columbia, under the strict eye of the leader, it was difficult for such Doukhobors, who as yet were comparatively few in number, to give expression to their opposition. The majority in the communal meetings was effectively controlled by Verigin, who enjoyed the loyalty of the women and the old, and even those who criticized him privately were prevented by his overbearing personality and the respect accorded to his rank from opposing him publicly. Besides, the Community had its own miniature criminal code for dealing with those who were regarded as disloyal. Public censure was the lightest punishment. More serious offenders would be deprived of their flour ration for anything from three days to a month. The gravest punishment was expulsion from the Community, and few were willing to risk this, since they were turned away without any means whatsoever and lacked the skills or the linguistic ability to live in the outside world as anything better than casual labourers. Moreover, there was no free land on which to make a start in southern British Columbia as there had been in the prairies.

In consequence, though discontent increased among the Community members, there were, during Peter the Lordly's life, comparatively few desertions in British Columbia; nor did the opposition movements of the Independents and the Sons of Freedom acquire any real importance west of the mountains until very shortly before his death.

In the prairies the situation was somewhat different. There, when the Community members began to leave in 1908, more than a thousand Independents were left in the Prince Albert district. They still retained the essentials of their religion and particularly that faith in pacifism that is possibly the most durable of all Doukhobor beliefs, but they no longer accepted the divinity of leaders, and they had abandoned the communal way of living so decisively that by 1910 most of them had left the villages and were living on their quarter sections. Under the influence of the Independents, many Community Doukhobors whom Verigin had left behind in the prairies broke away from his leadership after the main exodus to British Columbia and had no difficulty in getting homesteads from a sympathetic government. By 1913, when only about thirty Community members had dared to break away in British Columbia, the number of Independents in the prairies appears, from several estimates made at this time, at least to have doubled, so that a quarter of the Doukhobors had moved away from Verigin's leadership. When the railway town of Blaine Lake was founded in the middle of their territory, the Independents acquired a centre around which they began to develop institutions of their own, culminating in the founding in 1916 of the Society of Independent Doukhobors. The secretary of this society was Peter Makaroff, who had now graduated from the University of Saskatchewan and was practising as a lawyer. Without adopting any of the pretensions of the traditional leaders, he became the intellectual guide to those Doukhobors who had chosen the path of opposition to Peter Verigin but were not prepared to abandon entirely their loyalties to the past of the sect.

Peter the Lordly was acutely conscious of the danger that the growth of the Independent movement in the prairies presented to the Christian Community of Universal Brotherhood. The more numerous, prosperous, and united the Independents became, the greater would be the temptation for the younger men in Brilliant and Grand Forks to follow their example. Accordingly, in 1913 he forbade intercourse with Independents under penalty of expulsion from the Community. Families had become divided in their allegiances, and Community members were expected to give up contact even with their relatives when these lapsed into heterodoxy.

But the establishment of a *cordon sanitaire* of boycott and ostracism was not enough to still Verigin's fears, and he awaited the opportunity to attack the Independents directly. It came with the First World War and the National Service Act of 1917. The authorities accepted the original exemption of the Doukhobors as valid in wartime and agreed that Independents would be covered in the same way as Community Doukhobors. Verigin, however, viewed the situation in a rather different way. To him the Independents were not Doukhobors at all. They had deserted their divinely inspired leader; they had abandoned the communal way of living that he had declared essential to the faith. He saw a chance of strengthening his own hand, and resorted to the power of the state, as on an earlier occasion, to serve his own theocratic ends. He began to warn Community Doukhobors that the exemption did not apply to their former brethren; this had the effect of knitting his followers more closely together at a time when he was imposing considerable hardships upon them, and it also induced a few recently converted Independents to hurry back to the Verigin fold. But its only effect on those Independents who had established themselves as individual farmers and were prospering as a result of the wartime boom was to scare them into founding the Society of Independent Doukhobors to protect their interests.

Having failed by these means, Verigin now approached the minister of justice in Ottawa, informing him that, as 'representative' of the Doukhobors, he regarded the Independents as 'liable to be conscripted for military service on the same basis as other citizens of Canada',[17] since they had accepted homesteads and therefore must be called upon to defend them. In bitter press controversies he and Joseph Shoukin, the secretary-treasurer of the Christian Community, accused the Independents of abandoning all the principles of their faith by keeping firearms in their houses, eating meat, smoking, and drinking. There may have been, in certain cases, a degree of truth in these accusations, but Verigin was attacking the mere externals of the situation. The real sin of the Independents was disobedience, and for this he was willing to see inflicted on them the very persecutions that his people had left Russia to avoid.

The authorities in Ottawa were unaffected by Verigin's demands, and there is no evidence that they ever contemplated breaking their undertaking regarding military service with regard to any section of the Doukhobor movement. One difficult incident took place, but that appears to have been the result of an excess of patriotic zeal among local officials rather than of any failure on the part of the federal government to keep its promises. At Blaine Lake a Mounted Police sergeant (later hanged for murdering his wife) arrested a number of Independents, including Peter Makaroff, for failing to present themselves for military service, and an equally zealous magistrate refused to recognize their exemption, sentenced them to short terms of imprisonment, and informed them that on termination of sentence they would be handed over to the military authorities. The angry Independents marched on Blaine Lake and threatened to burn their farm machines and destroy the ripe wheat standing in their fields. The prisoners were released by telegraphed orders from Ottawa, and during the short remainder of the First World War the Doukhobors had no further trouble about military service.

If Peter Verigin failed in his efforts to break the Independent movement, there is little convincing evidence that before his death the Community actually dwindled appreciably. In 1912 some 8,000 people, including children, were living in its various settlements west and east of the Rockies. In 1917, when incorporated as the Christian Community of Universal Brotherhood Ltd, it contained about 5,880 members, but as these were adults, the total number of people living communally, counting children, was about the same as it had been in 1912.[18] In other words, a number roughly equivalent to the natural increase over this period had found their way into the ranks of the Independents.

During Peter the Lordly's life the example of the Independents remained a constant but not acute danger to the integrity of the Community. The same might be said of the Sons of Freedom, who were confined to the prairies until 1918, when the newspapers reported their first sporadic acts of nudity in British Columbia, and who contented themselves with a few minor demonstrations until in 1923 they began the course of dramatic and destructive protest by fire and dynamite that they were to follow for the next forty years.

The rise of the Sons of Freedom from a tiny splinter group of a few dozen zealots to an important wing of the Doukhobor movement is a story that we shall later tell in detail. At present it is sufficient to remark that as a phenomenon it was linked intimately with the renewal of the struggle between the Doukhobors and Canadian society that began very shortly after the emigration to British Columbia.

It is doubtful if Peter Verigin really believed that immunity from outside interference could be bought by purchasing land any more than it could be received as a gift. Most probably he hoped to buy time rather than isolation, to build up the Community as an agricultural and industrial organization until it became so successful that its members would no longer be tempted to leave it. Then a few compromises with the authorities would not have been important; even in Kapustin's day the Doukhobors had been willing to pay taxes provided they were left alone in other ways.

But, while this may have been his long-term aim, in seeking it he had to follow a short-term policy of encouraging his people in the belief that isolation was both possible and desirable. The conservatism of the majority of the Community members, and their fears of the world outside, made this policy internally feasible. Externally it broke down because the Interior valleys of British Columbia did not long remain the frontier that they appeared to Verigin and his companions when they first travelled into these unpeopled forests in the spring of 1908.

Even then all the valley lands had been in private hands and they had been forced to buy where they could, so that if one travels by modern highway from Grand Forks eastward over the mountains to Brilliant and then north into the Slocan Valley, one finds the sites of the former Community settlements scattered over a distance of more than a hundred miles in a dozen pockets varying in size from more than four thousand acres at Grand Forks to small parcels of less than four hundred acres in the Kootenay Valley. Not only were the Doukhobor settlements fragmented and separated in this way, but the very narrowness of the valleys, and the relatively small size of the farms compared with those in the prairies, brought them into even closer contact with non-Doukhobors than had been the case in Saskatchewan.

Other factors militated against any hopes the Doukhobors may have nurtured of being left for long to themselves. Unlike the prairies, where mass immigration was encouraged and a growing proportion of the new settlers were of central and east European origin, British Columbia had been settled mainly by people of British descent, with a despised Asian minority, and the Doukhobors were distrusted not only because of their peculiar beliefs, but also because of their ethnic origin. Very soon after their arrival in the Kootenay and Boundary areas the derisive epithet of 'Douks' was applied to them, while their neighbours referred to themselves, in relation to the Doukhobors, as 'white men'; this custom still persists in the valleys of the Interior.

Furthermore, the political atmosphere in British Columbia was strongly unfavourable to dissident minorities. The prairies, when the Doukhobors arrived in 1898, were ruled by a loose territorial adminstration, but British Columbia had existed as a political entity since 1858, first as a Crown colony and later as a province of Canada. The mining discoveries, creating the need for law and order even in relatively isolated districts, had brought into being an administrative system and a provincial police that established effective control over the southern interior more than a decade before the Doukhobors arrived. Rigorous education laws and taxing regulations existed, and behind the local adminstration stood a provincial government little inclined to understand or to show patience towards a group of Russian sectarians who wished to be a law unto themselves. Whatever party happened to be in power, the political climate in British Columbia was afflicted by a moralistic and parochial conservatism that had not changed greatly since colonial days. The Doukhobors were not to be without defenders west of the Rockies, but the general feeling of the people and of the authorities turned against them after the curiosity aroused by their first arrival had worn off.

It was not very long before anti-Doukhobor feeling began to find expression in the local press, which faithfully repeated accusations of neglecting local trade that had been brought against the Doukhobors by retail merchants in the prairies and were raised even more vehemently by the same class in British Columbia.

The interior towns were in fact—and they have continued to be—the centres of anti-Doukhobor feeling. The farmers who employed Doukhobors or had some kind of business relations with them were inclined to be much more tolerant. Doukhobor labour was cheap and efficient, and when the jam factory was started the Community established excellent relations with many independent growers by buying fruit crops on the trees for a good price and then sending their members in to do the picking. In this way the middlemen were eliminated to the benefit of both sides. But this merely gave the businessmen in the towns a further reason for hating the Doukhobors, and, since they wielded more political influence than the isolated fruit farmers, the local politicians of both the Conservative and the Liberal parties were inclined to take their side against the non-voting Doukhobors.

It was not long before the British Columbia government also focused its attention on the Doukhobors, who discovered that even if they had shed the problem of oath-taking by buying their land, this did not protect them from the three other civic obligations they were anxious to avoid— education, registration, and taxation.

The first pressure was applied by the education authorities, who in 1911 calculated that there were seven hundred Doukhobor children between the ages of seven and fourteen in the various Doukhobor settlements. To them the situation seemed a matter of routine. The law required that these children should be sent to school, and the law must be obeyed. Out of such simplistic reasoning were created the problems that have surrounded the Doukhobors for sixty years in British Columbia.

In the autumn of 1911 a school was built near the Doukhobor lands at Grand Forks and the members of the Community were urged to send their children there. There was a slow but steadily increasing response, and in 1912 Peter Verigin fulfilled a long-made promise by building a school on Community land at Brilliant. Beulah Clarke was engaged as teacher. For a brief period she found the people interested and hospitable and the children receptive. Verigin appeared pleased with the experiment; he proposed to extend the school and engage more teachers.

Unfortunately, having won an apparent victory on the education issue, the provincial authorities assumed that in other directions the Doukhobors would be an easy people to bully into submission. Acting with incredible clumsiness, they suddenly arrested four men for failing to register a death; the prisoners were sentenced to three months' imprisonment in Nelson Gaol. Immediately the Doukhobor children were withdrawn from the schools at Brilliant and Grand Forks, and the Community, in a specially convened sobranie, decided on mass refusal to comply with the registration laws.

Bombarded with official reports of Doukhobor civil disobedience and with complaints from the citizens of Grand Forks and Nelson, the Conservative government of Sir Richard McBride finally decided to institute the first of a long series of Commissions inquiring into Doukhobor affairs. They chose a man who seemed politically reliable, an English mining engineer named William Blakemore. A local pillar of the Conservative party, he had for the past seven years been editing a newspaper in Nelson called *The Week*. In August 1912 Blakemore became a one-man investigating team, travelling and staying for almost four months among the Doukhobors in British Columbia and the prairies, visiting all the settlements, holding long public hearings, and in the end producing a report that, quite apart from its recommendations, is an invaluable document on the Doukhobor Community during its first years in British Columbia.

Blakemore was an impressionable man. The industry of the Doukhobors stirred his admiration, and he fell heavily under the personal spell of Peter Verigin. The chapter in the report that is devoted to him is the most favourable description of a Doukhobor leader that ever appeared in an official document.

His personality is both attractive and impressive. He is a big man in every sense of the word—tall, muscular, massive, with a fine head, great natural dignity of carriage, and the very atmosphere of strength exuding from every pore. Yet, like many such men, he has a remarkably gentle manner. He speaks in a low tone of voice, but it is so musical and sweet as to be almost seductive.

His every movement is marked by a natural courtesy and simple dignity that would signal him out for notice anywhere. . . . His eyes are dark and thoughtful, and in moments of excitement shine with hidden fire. His whole expression is that of a man who has suffered much, and has triumphed over everything through the force of courage and constancy.

No man can be in his presence long without believing in his benevolence. It is his nature to be kind, and no man can be kinder to those who obey him.[19]

That there was a sterner side to Verigin, Blakemore was well aware, and he also noted perceptively the difficult situation in which the leader found himself:

He has fought before against persecution; he is fighting now against environment, and against the other disintegrating influences which have already made serious inroads on his Community, and which threaten to overwhelm it.[20]

Blakemore listened with sympathy to Verigin's account of the dispossession of the Doukhobor lands on the prairies, and dismissed as insubstantial the objections of the businessmen of Grand Forks. There was no evidence, he decided, that the Doukhobors were likely to 'swamp' the local communities either by acquiring a major part of the land or by a great increase of population. He produced facts to show that if the Doukhobors did buy from wholesalers, most of these were now situated in British Columbia and some actually in Nelson. Far from agreeing that the presence of the Doukhobors would retard the development of the region, he argued that

the evidence is all the other way. Witness after witness holding large areas of land declared that he regarded the Doukhobors as desirable neighbours, because of the high-class cultivation of their lands and their peaceable, quiet habits. As to the effect upon land-values, while there were a few witnesses, especially in Grand Forks, who claimed that the Doukhobor holdings tended to lower the land-values, there were many more witnesses who thought otherwise; and in this connection the fact must not be overlooked that in the Grand Forks District land-values have continued to advance.[21]

Like the Russian investigators of Alexander I's reign, Blakemore found the Doukhobors a people of excellent and moral character, industrious and sincere, even in their objections to Canadian laws. He found mitigating factors in their misunderstanding of those laws, and in the fact that they were under the illusion that by buying their land in British Columbia they were exempt from certain laws they found objectionable. But this was as far as Blakemore, a Conservative and the appointee of a government, could go. He could not take the Doukhobor side on such questions as education and registration, but at least he investigated their attitudes thoroughly and brought out clearly the nature of their objections to education, allowing their own statements to appear verbatim in his report.

The basic objections are worth restating, since they form the grounds on which many Doukhobors resisted school education from that time to the beginning of the 1960s. First came the ideological argument. Canadian schools teach children things that Doukhobors regard as immoral. 'The school education', remarked Blakemore's Doukhobor informants, 'teaches and prepares the people, that is children, to military service, where shed harmless blood of the people altogether uselessly.' School teaching was not adapted to the needs of 'working-class people', as the Doukhobors regarded themselves; 'we try by the path of honest labour, so we may reap the necessary maintenance, and to this we adopt our children to learn at wide school of Eternal Nature.' This argument has always occupied an important part in Doukhobor polemics against conventional education; real education, they contend, must be practical, and this attitude is undoubtedly related not only to their peasant traditions and to their particular mystique of 'Toil and peaceful life', but also to the expediency of training children to share in the Community work at an early age. Finally, education was a disintegrating influence. 'Just as soon as the person reached read and write education, then, within a short time leaves his parents and relations and undertakes unreturnable journey on all kinds of speculations, depravity and murder life.' Clearly, behind this argument lay the fear of education as an assimilative process that would lead to the disintegration of the Community. At the same time, the writers of the note could not resist assuming an air of moral superiority because in their Community life they sustained the brotherhood of man, while 'crack-brained people . . . in highest royal universities . . . swallow down all the national peoples power and the capital.'

In parenthesis one may remark that on this occasion it was not the Doukhobors alone who seemed lacking in formal education. The eccentricity of their English was balanced by the Commissioner's ignorance of Russian, which resulted in the names of the signatories to the document we have just quoted being transcribed so strangely that they read like those of citizens of Lilliput.

> CEAMUR BECUNBELURC BEPENGARNR.
> ANAEMACUR MEPEMEVURA.
> UBAN EBC. KON-KUN.
> FLAGBUNA X CEMENEBNA BEUKUNA.
> (NEYANAYUAL).[22]

Blakemore ended his report with an extraordinary mixture of recommendations. He suggested that no drastic immediate steps should be taken to force compliance with the education and registration laws, that the government be patient with the people and put pressure only on the leaders, and that, when action had to be taken, fines rather than imprisonment should be imposed. He suggested the appointment of a Doukhobor sub-registrar and of Russian teachers, and a simplification of the curriculum to arouse Doukhobor confidence.

All these were, in the circumstances, excellent recommendations, but Blakemore was moved by his Conservative background to end with a suggestion that, once it was made public, undid all the good his patience and sympathy might otherwise have achieved. Giving no reasons at all, he expressed the view 'That it is in the best interests of the country that the Order in Council granting exemption from military service should be cancelled.' As soon as the literate Doukhobors read these words, it seemed to them and all their brethren that their suspicions that the Canadian authorities intended to break their word on this vital question had been justified. More strongly than ever, conscription seemed to them the likely consequence of conformity, and their obstinacy hardened.

Blakemore was a well-meaning man who honestly desired to reach a solution, but who in the end pleased neither side. Before his report appeared it was evident to the authorities, and particularly to the provincial police, that his sympathies were deeply engaged with the Doukhobors, and even as he was carrying on investigations the police—in defiance of his request—brought up at least one other Doukhobor for trial in Nelson on a registration charge. The local Conservative leaders and the businessmen's associations, annoyed at Blakemore's rejection of their charges, renewed their agitations as soon as his findings were published. The police in their turn began to exhume Doukhobor bodies in order to gain evidence. In August 1913 they raided a Doukhobor village in an attempt to seize witnesses, and were driven away by rioting women who attacked them with fence rails.

Blakemore, highly conscious of the responsibility laid upon him by his commission, tried to stem the rising flood of popular prejudice. He protested in the columns of his own newspaper, and in the end, despairing of any action other than crude coercion on the part of the government of British Columbia, he turned to the Quakers in England and communicated with them through a Victoria estate agent named Mitford Abraham. In October 1913 Abraham wrote to Isaak Spark, Secretary of the Central Office of the Society of Friends in London :

Of late there has been some outrageous conduct on the part of the Grand Forks police and public . . .

Mr Blakemore tells me that the public in Grand Forks are doing all they can to drive the Doukhobors away and get back the land which they (the public) had previously sold to the Doukhobors, who have by their great industry enhanced the value of the land very considerably. The Grand Forks people do not like the Doukhobors, simply because they do not conduct their business in the way they would like and are extremely jealous of the very successful colonisation ways of the Doukhobors.

Blakemore had asked Abraham to submit his report to the London Quakers and ask their support on two questions. He believed that the Doukhobors had a just claim for compensation from the Dominion government for the improvements they had carried out on the lands lost in the prairies. (Through Cazakoff, the general manager of the Christian

Community, the Doukhobors had already claimed the highly unrealistic sum of $11,400,000.) He asked the British Quakers to raise this matter in Ottawa, and also to protest to the government of British Columbia against 'the very unjust and outrageous conduct on the part of the police and public of Grand Forks, B.C.' [23]

The Doukhobors' claims to compensation were ignored by the Dominion government. The provincial government continued in its policy of coercion. There is no record that even the Quakers interfered on behalf of their former protégés. And William Blakemore fades from the scene, leaving in one's mind an impression of fair-mindedness that at this troubled period was rare indeed among those who had official dealings with the Doukhobors.

As the government's attitude grew more threatening, the Doukhobors began to talk in traditional terms—of emigration and sensational protest. Verigin started to make inquiries about land in Colorado. And in March 1914 a group of Doukhobor elders sent a long list of grievances to Attorney General William Bowser in Victoria, ending with a threat of a kind soon to become familiar in Doukhobor-government disputes.

There are 6,000 people in the Doukhobor Community, who will take off their clothes—these being all that is left after the robbery committed by the Government in Saskatchewan—and will deliver them up to your officials in Nelson and Grand Forks, and will themselves remain naked in the streets . . . Do you want people to wander about naked? [24]

A few days later, writing to the minister of the interior in Ottawa, Cazakoff, the general manager of the Christian Community of Universal Brotherhood, repeated the threat in a slightly more veiled form; Verigin remained silent, but these statements can hardly have been made without his approval. In other words, the first threats of mass nude demonstrations as acts of protest rather than as Adamite demonstrations of the ideal life came from the orthodox Community Doukhobors and not from the Sons of Freedom. Admittedly, the Sons of Freedom were to take the initiative in such action when it later happened, but the fact that statements of this kind were uttered in 1914 by Verigin's officials illustrates how narrow at times of crisis were the boundaries that divided the various strands of the Doukhobor movement. The attorney general was not intimidated, and with the rough arrogance that earned him the name of 'Napoleon' Bowser among his political opponents, he not merely threatened to imprison them all for indecent exposure, but went ahead with the preparation of the first specifically anti-Doukhobor legislation to be enacted in Canada. This was the Community Regulation Act. It repeated the obligations under law to provide vital statistics and send children to school, and it specified the fines to be levied. It differed from previous legislation in adding a clause that allowed distraint on the possessions of the Community for the offences of its members.

During the summer of 1914 Bowser travelled to Brilliant and delivered a threatening address to the assembled Community members, but the Doukhobors ignored his warnings. Through the winter from 1914 to 1915 no children returned to school. In August 1915 the government finally decided on legal action against the Community, only to come up against the difficult technical point that the property of the Doukhobors was at this time vested in the name of Peter Verigin and might not come under the new legislation after all. However, the law officers were preparing for a test case when, with the abruptness that often characterizes the relations of two opposing authoritarians, the whole situation was resolved. Bowser took it upon himself to guarantee that no paramilitary exercises or religious education would be forced on Doukhobor children, and Verigin promised to enrol enough pupils to fill the completely inadequate schools that then existed. This compromise solution lasted for seven years, until 1922. The Doukhobors built nine schools on their own land in the Kootenay area, and sent their children in Grand Forks to schools provided by the local school district. During this period their compliance with the education regulations was never complete. The peak enrolment in 1921 reached 414, about two-thirds of the children of school age. Those enrolled attended only about half the time (average attendance in the same year was 209),[25] but they did receive some education, and the first real break in traditional illiteracy was made among the Community Doukhobors.

Verigin's decision to conform was doubtless linked with the peculiar opportunities and pressures of the war situation. During the wartime boom the farmers of British Columbia prospered, and the Community was no exception. The young men, exempted from military service, were in great demand among outside employers, and the saleable produce of the Community—increased by Verigin's austerity program—found an immediate market. It was like the old days in the Caucasus when the Orphan's Home filled its coffers as a result of the Russo-Turkish war, and in 1914–18, as in the past, the Doukhobors were not entirely happy in their role.

In a number of ways they tried to assuage their uneasiness. During

1917 and 1918 they passed resolutions, at Verigin and Grand Forks, to practise economies in order to send money to war sufferers, though there is no evidence that any money was sent. But they did donate jam to the value of five thousand dollars to the Red Cross for the families of soldiers, and Verigin proposed to the government a special scheme for growing more wheat. The Doukhobors, he insisted, were unalterably opposed to war service of any kind, but they wished to help those suffering the effects of war, and if the government would only purchase a hundred thousand acres of prairie land and a hundred steam engines, he would provide Doukhobor working men to grow the wheat.[26]

The offer was never taken up. On the other hand, the authorities appear to have been conscious of the expediency of keeping the Doukhobors working hard on their own lands, both in British Columbia and the prairies, and once the schools issue was settled in 1915 the Community endured surprisingly little interference. There were a few prosecutions for failing to register, and on one occasion nine Sons of Freedom were imprisoned for letting loose a farmer's horses and burning down his stables in an obscure surge of protest; but, apart from the abortive effort to conscript the Independents at Blaine Lake, there appears to have been no attempt to enforce military service. The principal way in which local pressure was applied during the war years was through attempts to force Doukhobor contributions to the Patriotic Fund, and even these did not produce very spectacular results. In December 1916, Verigin agreed to give a hundred dollars a month on behalf of the Grand Forks Doukhobors, but in 1918 this modest contribution was suspended. In 1919, when the provincial committee of the Patriotic Fund demanded $75,000 from the Community, Verigin gave $10,000, which he claimed he had been forced to borrow from the bank. He apologized in the *Nelson Daily News* for the smallness of the amount.

But I must explain that the Christian Community of Universal Brotherhood Ltd., has about 700 men from 18 years of age to 60, and the balance are all elderly men, women and children, and in such a heavy timbered and stony place as British Columbia it is very difficult to make a living.[27]

It is hard to accept Verigin's low estimate of his effective labour force, or his pleas that 1918 had been a bad year and 1919 not much better. In fact the Community had excellent markets for any produce or lumber that it could produce throughout the war, and it emerged at the end with more assets than before. The fact that it had also amassed more debts merely indicated that at this time its credit was still as good as it had been ever since Canadian bankers recognized in Verigin a man whose business instinct they could safely trust.

If the Doukhobors had been relatively unmolested during the war, they were the victims of a rising resentment immediately after it ended. The demands of the Patriotic Fund were only one symptom of this. The idea of conscientious objectors making money during the war aroused in an intensified form the patriotic and militarist sentiments expressed when the Doukhobors first arrived in Canada, and the provincial government joined the populace of the interior towns in a new anti-Doukhobor campaign. In March 1919 members of the sect were deprived of the right to vote in provincial elections, and later in the same year the minister of public works toured the areas they inhabited, arousing public feelings by speeches in which he exaggerated the non-co-operation of Community Doukhobors and shouted 'Doukhobors should be made to live up to the law!' [28]

The old enemies of the Community in Grand Forks and Nelson wanted something more than a mere insistence on observing the law; they wanted to expel the Doukhobors from their district, and to this end they worked on the feelings of the returned soldiers. The soldiers asked for land; to the businessmen of the Kootenays the obvious solution seemed to be to give them the land of those who had not gone to fight. In February 1919 a meeting of returned soldiers in Nelson demanded that all Doukhobors be deported to Russia and their lands given to veterans. In a highly emotional meeting a few days later in Brilliant the Community members, led by the women, resolved to abandon their lands and go wandering again. Their sense of martyrdom had been aroused. Verigin quickly repudiated the proposal, and in April a meeting of Grand Forks citizens passed further resolutions demanding deportation and expropriation of lands. Immediately afterwards a squad of twelve ex-soldiers went to Brilliant to force their demands on Verigin; moved by his inclination towards grand gestures, he signed an agreement to dispose of the Doukhobor lands to the Soldiers' Settlement Board. The local officials actually sent out surveyors and appraisers. In a few days Verigin had changed his mind and wired to Arthur Meighen, then minister of the interior, claiming that he had signed the agreement under duress. In the meantime, news of the situation had reached Canadians who viewed the problem less narrowly than small-town merchants. A strongly critical editorial appeared in the *Manitoba Free Press*.

There is considerable suspicion that the pressure under which the Doukhobors made the offer to sell their lands in British Columbia was applied by persons anxious to exploit their known determination not to 'resist evil' or go to war. Thus their dispossession would be a form of persecution.[29]

Professor James Mavor once again sprang to the defence of the Doukhobors, writing a long Open Letter to Sir Thomas White, the acting prime minister. In the end Arthur Meighen, the Conservative minister of the interior, who consistently proved fairer to the Doukhobors than his Liberal predecessor Frank Oliver, ruled that the Soldiers' Settlement Board had no right to carry out expropriations, and there the matter ended.

In other respects the situation of the Community deteriorated sharply after the war. The year 1921 was particularly difficult. There was too little rain in British Columbia and too much in Saskatchewan. Crops were small, prices began to fall, and less outside work was available for members of the Community. Yet the interest and principal on the great loans Verigin had obtained had to be paid, and a further period of austerity began as Verigin's officials reduced the amount of cash spent on supplies for Community members to ten cents per person per day.

Discontent sprang up immediately throughout the settlements in British Columbia. The members began to complain that they did not have enough food while Verigin lived in comfort. Verigin himself chose the moment for one of his most dramatic gestures. On 21 February 1922 the *Vancouver Daily Province* came out with banner headlines.

HAS VERIGIN GONE CRAZY?
HORRIBLE SCHEME OF DOUKHOBOR LEADER IS FRANKLY ADMITTED
TO SLAUGHTER WOMEN AND AGED SO
MEN MAY ROAM ABOUT

It seems to have been a case of macabre humour rather than insanity. In discussing the economic situation of the Community and the burden of taxes, Verigin had indeed remarked, with due appearance of solemnity, that it was pointless to carry on any longer, and that the members of the Community might just as well kill the old people and the children, throw the bodies into the Columbia, sell their lands to pay off the debts, and go wandering off to preach the gospel of Christ and join the proletariat. Newspapers all over the country picked up the story, and for a few days the Kootenays were crowded with officials and police from Ottawa and Victoria questioning hundreds of Community members, until Verigin decided that the joke had gone far enough and grandly agreed to use his influence to save the threatened victims. He had obtained what he wanted—a stage—and the elaborate public apologies he made through the press were accompanied by statements of grievances and demands for help. The *Vancouver Daily World* of 27 February 1922 reported that:

> He states that the Doukhobor children are deprived of milk because all milking cows were sold in 1920 to pay taxes, and last year the fruit crop went for the same purpose. *Collection of $4,000 income tax from the Community he declares 'contradicts the king's law', the earnings of indi-vidual members all being far within the exemption limit.*
>
> Specifically, Mr Verigin asks for a commission of inquiry and that the province reimburse the community for the roads it built, including a $30,000 bridge, which was the community's invested capital, and also that a loan of $50,000 be provided, for irrigation.

The demand for an inquiry, the request for help from a government rejected by Doukhobor principles—these, accompanied by theatrical gestures aimed at arousing public attention, were to become regular features of Doukhobor activity from this time onward. By 1922 they aroused no response on the part of the provincial government and, with rising discontent in the Community, familiar symptoms began to appear. There was renewed talk of leaving Canada, and Verigin actually went down to Oregon and bought eight hundred acres of land at Eugene, on which he established a few families from Brilliant. Then, after seven years of compliance with the education requirements, Doukhobor parents began once again in the fall of 1922 to withdraw their children from school. The precise reason for this change of attitude is not clear, though it appears to have been a result of instructions from Verigin.

The authorities acted quickly. In December eight parents were fined, and when the police prepared to seize Community goods the fines were paid. In April the next year a similar incident happened, with the same result. A motor truck was seized by the police and released after payment of the fine. But the apparent triumph of the authorities in this case was followed by the first act of arson connected with the Doukhobors in British Columbia. In May 1923 a school was burnt to the ground by unidentified arsonists, and in the months that followed a total of nine schools in the Brilliant district were destroyed, the burnings in each case coinciding with some attempt on the part of the police to seize property in payment of fines.

Verigin emphatically denied any connection on the part of the Community with these burnings. He attributed them to 'Nudes', 'Anarchists',

'Outlaws', to a group of twenty or thirty malcontents who were hostile to him and who thought he had collaborated with the Canadian government. There is good reason to believe him, since by this time not only schools, but also Verigin's own house at Brilliant and other Community property, including a sawmill and a poleyard, had gone up in flames. We shall discuss this question further when we deal in greater detail with the Sons of Freedom movement; for the present it is sufficient to point out that past manifestations of fanaticism had stemmed from situations of discontent and frustration similar to those that existed in the Community during the early 1920s.

The last school burnt in February 1925. There followed two months of angry dispute between the Doukhobors, who refused to send their children to school, and the authorities, who demanded not only that they do this, but also that they pay for the rebuilding of the schools that had been destroyed. When the premier, John Oliver, visited Grand Forks, eight hundred Doukhobors demonstrated outside the house where he was staying. A stormy exchange followed in which the Doukhobors claimed that their laws were better than Canadian laws and Oliver shouted hysterically, 'The laws would be more right if you were dead than as you are now!'[30] Later, when the Doukhobors invited him to visit Brilliant for a personal discussion, he refused, but reiterated the hard policy laid down by his predecessors McBride and Bowser. The Doukhobors must obey the laws; otherwise they had better go elsewhere. He indicated the official line of action when he remarked that he was not going to use taxpayers' money to keep Doukhobors in jail. Little serious attempt was made at this time to find the arsonists who had burnt the Doukhobor schools. The levying of penalties seemed much more attractive to the authorities, not only because it would save taxpayers' money, but also because it would be a means of weakening the Community by diminishing its physical assets.

During the spring of 1925, school and police inspectors visited the Community, and on 5 April they addressed a mass meeting of 2,500 Doukhobors at Brilliant. When the question 'Will you obey the school laws?' was put directly to the meeting, there was a great shout of 'Nyet!' The loudest voices were those of the women. Four days later a magistrate in Grand Forks levied fines totalling $4,500 on thirty-five parents who had not sent their children to school. Inspector Dunwoody of the provincial police thereupon mounted a small invasion of the Doukhobor settlements, leading—on horseback—a force of ten constables and a hundred road-gang navvies, who forced their way into the Community warehouses at

Grand Forks and seized office equipment, supplies, and lumber that the Community had cut for sale. The goods were sold for $3,360, undoubtedly below their value, but not so far below as the Doukhobors—who claimed a loss of $20,000—suggested. The action appeared to be effective, for the Community paid the remaining portion of the fine, the children began to return to school, and during the summer of 1925 Doukhobor carpenters started work on new schools in place of those that had been destroyed. A further campaign in the long struggle between the sect and earthly government had ended in temporary truce.

By this time Peter the Lordly's reign over the Doukhobors of Canada had come to an end. He died, with eight other people, early on the morning of 29 October 1924, when the railway coach in which he was travelling was blown to pieces on its way through the mountains between Brilliant and Grand Forks. The story of this tragedy has been told in sensational detail by other writers on the Doukhobors, so there is no need for us to repeat it *in extenso*, particularly as none of the clues that were revealed has led to a solution of the mystery. The evidence points to a deliberately planned explosion rather than an accidental detonation of illegally carried dynamite, but identifies no assassin.

With a controversial figure like Verigin, who had accumulated enemies both within and outside the Community, the range of possible culprits is considerable, and the ingenuity of the investigators and writers who have speculated on the issue has produced a wide range of candidates with various motives. Mary Strelioff, one of his female companions, was killed with him, and it has been suggested that a rival handmaiden, or possibly even a lover of one of the girls he gathered around him, planned the murder because of jealousy. The Sons of Freedom, who later took with great fervour to dynamiting, have been obvious suspects, particularly as Verigin's house had been burnt down shortly before he died; however, there is no other clearly proved case on record in which they used explosives with the primary intent of killing, and no known facts link them with Verigin's death. A CPR investigator, James Johnston, linked the murder with the presence among the Doukhobors from 1924 to 1930 of a watchmaker named Metro Grishen, who came from Soviet Russia and apparently returned there after his departure from Canada. Johnston, assuming that Grishen had planted the bomb, suggested that it was a plot by Verigin's son, Peter Petrovich, to get rid of his father.[31] If—and here we are talking only in conjectures—a man from Soviet Russia did kill Verigin, then it would seem much more likely that he came as an emissary of the Bolsheviks and that Verigin was killed for the same reasons as many other Russians who opposed the Communist régime. Many Doukhobors, annoyed at the failure of the police investigations, believed and still believe that Verigin was actually a victim of the government, but here they were endowing Canadian authorities with the characteristics of their Russian counterparts. The likelihood of such action seems too remote to be worth considering. On the other hand, Verigin had many non-Doukhobor foes in the Kootenay and Boundary areas, among them men who would have easy access to dynamite and a knowledge of its use.

There also remains the chance that Verigin was not in fact the intended victim. The member of the B.C. legislative assembly for Grand Forks, John A. Mackie, was sitting in the same coach, just across the aisle from Peter the Lordly, and, like him, was close enough to the centre of the explosion to be killed immediately. It is not impossible that he was the intended victim, killed by some crank with a political grievance.

After Verigin's death legend quickly clustered around the event. His followers believed that he had the gift of prophecy and foresaw his own death, to which, as a Christ, he went a willing sacrifice. Little incidents were remembered: his invitation to drink fruit juice with him on the evening of his departure; his last remark—'Farewell and forgive me, brothers!'—as he got into the day coach. The feeling of something preternatural about his death was increased by the fact that for the preceding year his thoughts had turned more frequently than usual towards religious matters. In the winter of 1923–4 he had held almost daily meetings at Brilliant in which he discoursed on questions spiritual and moral, and shortly before his death he not only wrote a treatise on ways of life— 'Allegiance to the Devil'—in which he reiterated emphatically the traditional Doukhobor objections to smoking, drinking, and meat-eating, but also composed a devotional hymn.

> Oh Lord, Thou art the life of my life,
> And Thee I wish to praise for ever.
> From earth Thou hast created me
> And blessed me with a reasoning spirit.[32]

He had even gone outside his own sect to carry the Doukhobor message of non-violence and the simple Christian life. He visited the Mennonite settlements in the prairies, telling their members not to forget the importance of the commandment 'Thou shalt not kill', and in California he urged the Molokans to unite with the Doukhobors, give up eating meat, and abandon the corrupting city life that so many of them were leading. These preoccupations led some people later on to suggest that his death may in fact have been an act of suicide because he felt that the Community was declining economically and spiritually.

Considered even outside the divine context in which many of his followers wished to place him, Verigin was remarkable. His formal education was slight, but he learnt much from reading and from contact with more cultured men than himself. He had a strength of character that was tempered rather than ruined by exile, and his assumption of effective leadership on arriving in the new and very different environment of Canada was a mark of his capabilities. He knew neither the language nor the customs of North America, and he had never lived outside a basically peasant and pre-industrial society, yet he realized almost immediately how he could turn the machinery and the financial habits of the New World to the end of creating a religious Utopia. Against considerable geographical and political odds, he created within one decade a very successful community on the prairies and a moderately successful one in British Columbia. For more than thirty years, from the time of his reforms in Russia, he inspired his followers to great efforts and great sacrifices, and he averted, up to his death, the failure that the Community's many enemies had sought to promote. He commanded respect far beyond his own following, and even his most bitter opponents angrily admitted that he was an extremely able man. His epithet of 'Lordly' was in many ways deserved.

Perhaps his greatest fault was his refusal to acknowledge the power of time and change. He wished to use just those elements of modern progress that he chose, and otherwise sought to keep his followers in the mental state of another time and another land. By cloistering them as far as possible within the Community, he deprived them of the ability to compete in the harsh outside world. His failure to create a proper educational system—even a system of vocational training that would have been acceptable to Doukhobor principles—left the young Community members unfitted for anything beyond a simple life of manual toil, so that their wills were stunted and they became dependent on authoritarian leadership.

In the final analysis, Verigin sought to give shape to a personal vision. He was incapable of delegating decisions, and while he had agents who sustained the pyramid of power he had no associates. He trained no successor and named no heir.

To the funeral of Peter the Lordly, Doukhobors of all factions came, many of them travelling from the prairies. Seven thousand of the faithful, Community members, Independents, and Sons of Freedom, marched in chanting formations to the hillside overlooking Brilliant where he was buried. It was evident even on that day that his failure to name an heir threatened a repetition of the strife that had followed Luker'ia Kalmy-kova's death. Among the older people, there was no doubt that the hereditary principle should be followed and that Peter Petrovich, away in Russia, should reign in his father's place. Others, Independents and Sons of Freedom, went among the crowd saying that Peter the Lordly was the last of the leaders—the Independents because they thought leadership was no longer necessary, and the Sons of Freedom because some among them believed the time had come for the Tsar of Heaven to rule over the whole earth. A powerful pretender arose in Peter the Lordly's companion, Anastasia Golubova. Around her clustered the Community officials—Cazakoff, the general manager, and Shoukin, the secretary-treasurer—and the members of Verigin's family, his brothers Gregory and Vasilii and his nephew Larion. All of these men, powerfully entrenched in the affairs of the Community, felt they had more to lose than to gain by the arrival of Peter Petrovich, and all of them believed that Anastasia would be malleable. There were six weeks between the funeral and the ceremonial in which the new leader would be chosen at the old leader's grave. The interlude was as busy as an election campaign, with Anastasia travelling with a choir from settlement to settlement and her opponents holding their own meetings. At last, on 10 December, four thousand people gathered at Peter's grave. Only five hundred of them voted for a second woman leader. The rest bowed their heads to the name of the absent Peter Petrovich. A week later Cazakoff and Shoukin were appointed to run a caretaker government and at the same time two representatives of the Community Doukhobors, Nikolai Plotnikov and Gabriel Vereshchagin, set off for Soviet Russia to bring the new leader to his waiting people.

11 LINKS WITH THE FATHERLAND

According to a legend that is still current among the Doukhobors, Luker'ia Kalmykova foretold that, though her people would in time flourish in Canada and live in houses of glass, all except those who had become too attached to material comforts would eventually return to their fatherland. Whether or not Luker'ia actually made such a prophecy, the fact that it persists is evidence of the nostalgia Doukhobors still feel for a land many of them have never seen. It is a nostalgia linked intimately with their religion, with its ideal of a life based on Russian peasant ways and its music derived from the Russian liturgy. A manifestation of this nostalgia is the strong feeling Doukhobors retain for their native language. In the 1960s there are still Doukhobors who, though born in Canada, can speak hardly any English. Most third-generation European immigrants tend to lose their native tongues and become assimilated linguistically as well as culturally into Canadian life, but many Doukhobors still teach their children Russian and most of them speak the language among themselves. While members of other ethnically oriented sects, such as Lutherans and Mennonites, often carry on services in English, Doukhobor sobraniia are always conducted in Russian, and any change in this respect would be unthinkable to the average member of the sect. Doukhobors often say that without Russian their religion would die.

It is certainly true that a Doukhobor can only cease to speak Russian if he cuts himself off from his community.

This strong feeling of identity with the Russian past is linked with an interest in the Russian present, which waxes at periods when the Doukhobors feel particularly unhappy in Canada and wanes when relations between them and their neighbours are relatively calm. Thus the Doukhobor feeling for Russia is not merely a sentimental longing for a lost fatherland. It also provides, on occasion, the vision of an alternative way of life. Until the 1960s the Doukhobors in the Interior of British Columbia remained mentally unassimilated, retaining with extraordinary tenacity the sense of being transients who have paused—though it has been for sixty years—on their pilgrimage from one destination to the next. Among the lands to which they might go when their stay in Canada ends Russia has naturally figured prominently.

Not least important, they have never forgotten the brethren they left behind them in their fatherland. Doukhobors may, like other sects, have the tendency to divide into bitterly warring factions, but the divisions are never complete or permanent. Canadian observers have often been puzzled by the way, in times of high emotional fervour, Independents, Community Doukhobors, and Sons of Freedom tend to exchange roles, so that divisions that appeared clear-cut suddenly become blurred. In the same way, though the split between Verigin's followers and the Small Party in 1887 seemed final and irreversible, both family ties and a shared consciousness of the unique character of the Doukhobor faith kept alive the links between members of the two groups. The idea of a reunion, in Canada, in Russia, or elsewhere, did not seem impossible either to those who had emigrated or to those who had stayed behind.

If the Doukhobors in Canada continued in this way to look back to their ancestral land and their brethren there, this interest has been reciprocated not only by Russian Doukhobors, but also by many non-Doukhobor Russians.

Prominent among these were the Tolstoyans, and particularly Vladimir Chertkov in England and Paul Biriukov in Geneva, who continued to act as links between the Doukhobors and the Tolstoyans in Russia. The interest was natural, in view of the assistance the Tolstoyans had given to the Doukhobors during the persecutions of the 1890s in the Caucasus and at the time of their departure to Canada. The early stages of Doukhobor life on the prairies had been recorded in Chertkov's publications, particularly the various editions of his *Christian Martyrdom in Russia*, his short-lived periodical, *News of the Doukhobortsi*, and his more regular magazine, *Svobodnoe Slovo*. Before the arrival of Peter the Lordly from exile in 1902, the Tolstoyans who went to Canada made a determined attempt to shape the Doukhobor Community according to their own conceptions of peasant communism, which they believed the Doukhobors shared. They were opposed to the tendencies of the Kars and Yelizavetpol refugees to farm individually, and some of them—Sulerzhitskii for example—worked very hard to get the Doukhobors settled in Canada and to get the communal organization established. Others, like Bodianskii, were interested in the anarchistic elements in Doukhoborism, which all the Tolstoyans overemphasized: by encouraging rebellion where it was inappropriate, they caused great confusion.

To this confusion Chertkov undoubtedly added by his publication of Bonch-Bruevich's collection of Verigin's letters, and also by bringing out a *Handbook* in Russian and English that he prepared specially for the use of the Doukhobors so that they might learn the language of their new homeland. The *Handbook* was a great deal more than a language manual; it was intended also to give moral guidance. It encouraged the Doukhobors to oppose registration and oath-taking, and even suggested the appropriate phrases to use when doing so.

We are quite willing to answer accurately when asked. But we cannot promise anything. A promise is the same as an oath. Our religion forbids us to take an oath. Christ said, 'Do not swear.' A man must be free. A promise ties the conscience and actions of a man. Even in little things we want to be free.

The *Handbook* also provided a view of Canadian society compounded of half-truths and hardly calculated to create trust between the Doukhobors and their new neighbours. The Canadian population, according to Chertkov, consisted of Red Indians, emigrants from Europe, Doukhobors, and 'nigroes'.

The Indians and nigroes are very badly treated in the lands that belong to the Europeans. The poor Indians have been hunted towards the north and deprived of their rights. They are gradually dying out. And yet they are a very noble race. They are honest, truthful, and hospitable. They are a nomadic tribe and live in tents. There was a time when the Indians were a great and powerful people. They had great intellectual development. And the rules of their morality were very elevated. They did no harm to anybody. And in their own way they served God, whom they called the Great Spirit. Then the greedy Europeans came and began to destroy and take away their land. The Indians were exasperated and revenged themselves cruelly upon the 'white people' as they called the Europeans.[1]

Evidently the Tolstoyans' views of Canadian history were as highly oversimplified as their image of the Doukhobors. Much of the *Handbook* was later incorporated into the ideology of the Sons of Freedom.

With the departure of most of the Tolstoyan volunteers in 1900 and 1901 and the reimposition of Verigin's direct influence over the Doukhobors, the connections between the two groups became looser; but a certain mutual interest remained, and until the end of the 1920s various followers of Tolstoy played their brief roles in Doukhobor history.

Other Russian radicals also retained an interest in the Doukhobors until after the Revolution of 1917. They were drawn to them as victims of tsarism, and interested in their pacifism and particularly in their religious communism. Ever since Herzen and the Narodniks, many Russian intellectuals had sustained the idea that out of the *mir*, the traditional village organization, might be developed a rural communitarianism quite different from the communism based on the industrial proletariat that was advocated by the Marxists. Up to the time of the October Revolution, the Socialist Revolutionary movement, with its stress on peasant communalism, was numerically more powerful (though organizationally weaker) than either the Bolsheviks or the Mensheviks. To the members of this movement who read the books by Biriukov, Sulerzhitskii, Bodianskii, and Bonch-Bruevich that appeared in Russia between 1905 and 1909,[2] the experiments of the Doukhobors were very attractive. Even some Marxists considered the Doukhobors the most promising Russian peasants from their point of view, and Bonch-Bruevich long sustained his interest.

One result of this interest was that Russian intellectuals and semi-intellectuals continued to visit the Doukhobors and even in some cases to live among them for fairly long periods. Some, like Michael Sherbinin with his school at Petrovka, tried to help constructively, and some, like the watchmaker Boris Sachatov, were attracted to the innocent vagaries of the early Sons of Freedom. Another watchmaker, Sergei Petrov, settled among the Doukhobors in Saskatchewan, and his home became a centre where dilettantes interested in the sect would gather. The tiny group of Sons of Freedom basked in the interest they created among these strangers, but the visitors were encouraged neither by Verigin nor by the Community Doukhobors, who merely gave on occasion the hospitality that custom demanded.

Verigin appears to have been somewhat more cordial towards certain

Americanized Russians who came from New York to British Columbia at the time of Blakemore's Commission in 1912 and intervened on behalf of the Doukhobors. One of them, Alexander Evalenko, testified before the Blakemore Commission and later published in New York a highly partisan book, *The Message of the Doukhobors*, which accused the Canadian authorities of deliberate persecution. Somewhat more moderate was Voldemar T. Kruglak, the editor of the *Russian-American Echo* in New York, who lived in Castlegar, close to Brilliant, during 1912 and 1913 and organized a number of petitions, signed by New Yorkers, calling on the British Columbia government to leave the Doukhobors unmolested for the time being and allow the forces of assimilation to work quietly upon them. 'Red tape and reprisals', he remarked prophetically, 'will but feed and inculcate antagonism even in the rising generation.' [3]

This interest on the part of expatriate Russians has never completely died down, and even in the present decade one hears of individual Russians who are attracted for various reasons to the Doukhobors in Canada. On a recent visit to Grand Forks one of the writers encountered a United Church minister and an evangelical preacher, both of Russian birth; the first was trying to establish an ecumenical link between the Doukhobors and Canadian Protestants, and the second was frankly seeking converts. The most striking example of this kind of intrusion was that of the evangelist Stefan Sorokin, who in the 1950s played an extremely controversial role among the Sons of Freedom; to his story we shall return.

Even the tsarist authorities did not entirely lose interest in the Doukhobors. The publicity surrounding their departure had caused a great deal of mortification in government circles, and among the higher bureaucrats there was at least a pretence of concern for these immigrants who, so long as they refused to become naturalized in Canada, were still technically Russian subjects. When, at Verigin's insistence, the six Sons of Freedom were imprisoned in 1903 for burning the canvas on a binder, reports of their ill-treatment in prison spread to the delighted ears of the Russian foreign minister in St Petersburg, who immediately lodged a protest with the British ambassador. Undoubtedly there was a feeling of satisfaction in St Petersburg that the Canadian government, which in Sifton's day had sympathized with the Doukhobors in their persecutions in Russia, was at last finding them difficult guests.

Apart from posing as the protectors of the Doukhobors from their democratic tyrants, some members at least of the government in St Petersburg appear to have considered the possibility of bringing them back to Russia. It would, after all, be a great propaganda victory for the tsarist government, while the Doukhobors could always be used in their old role of colonizers on one of the seemingly endless frontiers of the Russian Empire. It was with this in mind that in 1904 a very different figure from the shabby radical expatriates who clustered around the Sons of Freedom came to visit Peter Verigin on the prairies. The visitor was E. E. Ukhtomskii, who in 1898 had tried to arrange Doukhobor emigration from the Caucasus to Manchuria. In the intervening years Ukhtomskii had risen further in the world. The paper he edited was one of the leading organs of the Establishment, and he himself was a friend of Nicholas II. He was in the strategic position of being a member of the inner tsarist circle without holding any official position, and his visit to Verigin may have been inspired by a great deal more than personal curiosity. He urged upon Verigin the desirability of returning with his followers to Russia. He told him that the minister of the interior in St Petersburg was in favour of a resettlement of the Doukhobors on Russian soil, and that the tsarist government would pay the expenses of their return. Verigin appears to have discussed the suggestion seriously with Ukhtomskii, and even to have considered the most desirable region for Doukhobor colonization. Since experience had taught him that remoteness from metropolitan centres and railway lines was the only condition under which the Doukhobors could sustain for any appreciable period their freedom from interference, he decided that nowhere in European Russia would be satisfactory; he favoured instead the mountainous region of Minusinsk on the Upper Yenisey River in Siberia. At the time nothing came of Ukhtomskii's proposal, but the suggestion that the tsarist government might be happy to get its Doukhobors back lodged in Peter the Lordly's mind and was to influence his actions a few years later.

In the meantime, the younger Peter Verigin and his mother paid their visit to Canada in 1905 in the company of Alesha Vorob'ev and another Russian Doukhobor named Baev. Both of the latter were members of the Middle Party from the village of Orlovka in the Wet Mountains, and, apart from acting as escorts to Peter's divorced wife Evdokiia and her family, they were greatly interested in the possibility of acquiring land in the prairies. At first Peter the Lordly was extremely cordial to both Vorob'ev and Baev, taking them on trips around the Doukhobor villages, with the usual accompaniment of female choirs and feasting, while Evdokiia, Peter Petrovich, and the rest of the visiting relatives were expected to stay at home and even to work in the fields like the ordinary Community Doukhobors. Peter the Lordly evidently hoped to incorporate the Middle Party into the Christian Community of Universal Brotherhood if only he could persuade them to take up land in the right areas of the prairies, but very soon he and Vorob'ev began to cool towards each other. The ostensible cause of their disagreement was Anastasia Golubova, who accompanied them in all their triumphal progresses through the villages, acting with queenly ostentation. Vorob'ev criticized Verigin openly for his relationship with Anastasia, and Vorob'ev's frankness, together with his reluctance to accept Peter the Lordly's spiritual leadership, soured relations between the two men to such an extent that when Vorob'ev left Verigin did not even bid him farewell.

Having cooled towards Vorob'ev, Verigin turned his attention to Baev, the other Middle Party representative, who was apparently of a somewhat more pliable character, and told him that it was his duty to bring his brethren from Russia to join the Community in Canada. Since he apparently gave very similar instructions to his son, Peter Petrovich, confusion ensued as soon as the visitors had returned to Russia. Baev went around the villages in the Caucasus attempting to recruit emigrants, but Peter Petrovich and Vorob'ev, both of whom were more influential in the region, proclaimed that they alone represented Peter the Lordly, so Baev was unjustly discredited and his efforts bore no fruit. Having defeated his rival, Peter Petrovich persuaded a number of the brethren to accept the idea of emigration to Canada, and in 1906 returned briefly to the prairies to make the necessary arrangements, only to be informed by Peter the Lordly that the time was premature.

However, the idea was not forgotten. Peter the Lordly now knew that others of his sect were interested in coming to Canada. He also believed, after Ukhtomskii's visit, that there was a good chance of returning to Russia under favourable terms. Either course might be manipulated in such a way as to increase his influence, but only if he kept the control of events firmly in his own hands. This, undoubtedly, was why he decided not to accept an emigration arranged by his son and why he did not avail himself of Ukhtomskii's offices as a go-between. In the slightly more liberal political climate that prevailed after the 1905 Revolution it was reasonably safe for him to return to Russia, and he decided to go there with a number of his followers and explore the possibility of reuniting in Canada all factions of the Doukhobors or, alternatively, of taking his own followers back to Russia. The outlook seemed propitious, for the Russian consul in Montreal made no difficulty about issuing passports to Verigin and the party of Doukhobors who would accompany him. Frank Oliver, whom he met in Winnipeg on his way east, warned Verigin that with such a passport he would not be entitled to British protection while in

Russia, and suggested that he become naturalized; but Verigin cannily recognized this as the narrow end of a very large wedge to be driven between him and his people, and refused.

He made a leisurely progress, leaving in the autumn of 1906—just in time to avoid the unpleasant situation that arose when the government put pressure on the Community Doukhobors to take the oath of allegiance as an alternative to losing their lands. He was accompanied by Paul Planidin, Dmitri Gridchin, and Ivan Makhortov, the aged naval veteran who had been the friend of Peter Kalmykov and the first to bow down before Peter the Lordly at Luker'ia's tomb nearly twenty years before; the Doukhobor women were represented by Mavra Dymovskaia and, perhaps inevitably, Anastasia Golubova.

In its early stages the journey was punctuated by a series of encounters with those to whom Verigin and the Doukhobors owed a debt of gratitude for help in the past. In Toronto they called on Professor James Mavor and in Philadelphia visited the Quakers; Peter the Lordly and Ivan Makhortov orated to the assembled Friends, and there was an uncomfortable interview with Joseph Elkinton Jr, who tried and failed to commit Verigin to a definite program of education among the Doukhobors.

Finally, after a brief interlude in New York, whence Semeon Reibin, who had accompanied the party as interpreter, returned to the prairies, Verigin and his companions sailed for Europe. They stopped in London to meet Chertkov. In Berlin, as in New York, they contented themselves with the role of sightseers, but created a minor scandal by starting to sing psalms in the Reichstag, which the Germans regarded as a marked breach of decorum.

In St Petersburg the party halted while Verigin, according to his own account, saw 'several ministers and many generals'. All of them, he claimed in a letter to the brethren in Canada, expressed their regret that the Doukhobors had left Russia, and so did the tsar himself, to whom Stolypin, the minister of the interior, spoke on the telephone in Verigin's presence. According to Doukhobor traditions, Verigin tried to see the tsar but was refused an audience because a recent visitor had made an attempt on the autocrat's life.

Stolypin was the minister with whom Verigin discussed the possibility of the sect's returning to Russia. If the latter's account is correct, the matter must have been considered seriously by the tsarist authorities, for when the question of free land came up he was assured that it could be made available in the Altai Mountains, on the frontier between Siberia and Mongolia. The possibility of a settlement in the Amur was also discussed. Evidently the authorities intended, once again, to keep the Douk-hobors well away from Orthodox Russians who might be influenced by their example, and to use them as pioneers. On the question of exemption from military service, Stolypin apparently promised that no compulsion would be applied to the Doukhobors if they returned to Russia.

By this time, however, Verigin had absorbed enough of the atmosphere of St Petersburg between 1905 and 1917 to be doubtful whether, even if the tsarist authorities agreed to it, a return to Russia would be sensible or practicable. The heritage of the Revolution of 1905 was still strong, and the country was in considerable disorder. Political murders and military courts were the two complementary aspects of a violence that pervaded Russian society. Walking through the streets of St Petersburg, Verigin was depressed by the poverty constantly before his eyes; and the very taste of the adulterated bread seemed to symbolize the decay of a country. He suggested to his followers that they should send five thousand dollars to aid the hungry in Russia; he himself would give a thousand dollars that he and his companions had saved by being economical on their travels. Meanwhile, having given up the idea of taking his followers back to Russia, Verigin continued from St Petersburg the negotiations he had already started with Morse, the president of the Grand Trunk Railway, for the importation of ten thousand Russian peasants on a two-year contract for railway work. Where he would recruit all these peasants is not clear, but he was probably relying on the Middle Party to provide the nucleus—though there is no evidence that he actually negotiated with their spokesmen during his visit.

From St Petersburg the party travelled inland, through the deepening winter, to Yasnaya Polyana, where they stayed for four days with Tolstoy and his family. It was a somewhat stormy visit. Not only were the differences between Tolstoy and his children evident even to the Doukhobors, but Tolstoy and Verigin disagreed more sharply than they had done on Peter the Lordly's first visit in 1902. Tolstoy was at last becoming enlightened about the real nature of the Doukhobor theocracy, and he did not disguise his disillusioned anger. He had heard, he said, that Verigin claimed to be a Christ and a divine leader, that he lived like a tsar, and that he shirked physical labour. Verigin listened uncomfortably, particularly when Tolstoy revealed that he had heard of the whipping of the naked Sons of Freedom outside the village of Nadezhda in 1903 at Verigin's bidding. 'How is it that you have changed from a martyr for the truth into a despot?' shouted Tolstoy.

Verigin took refuge in a complete denial of the charges, which he de-

clared were slanders put out by envious people. Tolstoy was rightly skeptical, and the argument became so heated that eventually he picked up his
hat and walked away for fear their dispute would develop into an irreconcilable quarrel. The next day he returned to the charge, demanding that
Verigin give up his position as a 'lord and master' and start serving God
by living humbly.[4] It was a bitter lesson for a man of Verigin's pride, but
he took it to heart, and from the reflections provoked by this incident
originated the simpler way of life that differentiated the Verigin of British
Columbia from the Verigin of the prairies.

Nevertheless, Peter the Lordly was glad to leave the chiding presence of
his rival prophet and set off on a southerly pilgrimage that took him and
his party first to the Ukraine, where they met Khilkov and Bodianskii;
two other veterans of the early days of settlement in Canada, Bonch-
Bruevich and his doctor-wife, they had already visited in St Petersburg.
Then they went on to Milky Waters, of which Ivan Makhortov had childhood memories. He showed them the site of the old Doukhobor cemetery,
but there was nothing left there or anywhere else in the area to remind
them of the mild Eden from which their fathers had been exiled more
than sixty years before.

Why Verigin did not go on to the Caucasus, as Makhortov and all the
other members of the party urged him to do, is not certain. He himself
attributed it to the great cold, but the explanation is unconvincing; he
must have endured lower temperatures in both Siberia and Canada than
he would have encountered even in the bleak Wet Mountains. Perhaps he
remembered the rebellious contempt with which his son Peter had treated
him, the quarrels with Vorob'ev, the coldness in which Evdokiia had
draped herself before her departure from Canada, and, after his encounter with Tolstoy, did not wish to face these hostile faces. Perhaps he
feared that, among the Small Party and the Middle Party, he would not
receive the adulation he felt was his due. Perhaps he was moved by one
of those Proustian intuitions that restrain the wise from the disillusioning
experience of visiting the scenes of their fortunate youth. Whatever may
have been the reason, he led his party out of Russia through Constantinople and the Balkans and into Switzerland, where they stopped in
Geneva to visit Paul Biriukov. They went on to London for a second
meeting with Chertkov, and then, in March 1907, returned to Canada.

The generally disillusioning effect of Verigin's trip can be gauged by the
fact that, though he returned to find the Community in the prairies
threatened by destruction through the loss of its lands, he no longer
thought of Russia as presenting any possible solution to the Doukhobor

predicament, but turned instead to British Columbia. As for the scheme to bring his ten thousand Russians to Canada for work on the railways, this too proved a disappointing failure; after further negotiations following Verigin's return to Canada, the Grand Trunk Railway finally declined to sign the contract for which he had hoped. Both the aims of his journey had been frustrated. The Doukhobors would be reunited neither in Russia nor in Canada.

After Verigin's return in 1907 the links between the Doukhobors in Canada and their friends in Russia became more tenuous. The problems of emigration to British Columbia preoccupied Verigin and his followers, while the Tolstoyans in Russia had their own problems as tsarist rule after 1907 entered into a new phase of reaction. Far away in Canada, and apparently permanently settled there, the Doukhobors also ceased to be of much interest to Russian newspapers and, except by a few radicals like Bonch-Bruevich, who retained personal memories of them, they were almost forgotten.

Over Russian expatriates in the United States, however, they continued to exercise some fascination, doubtless because they were the largest group of Russians in North America still living in a more or less traditional manner. The Russian-language papers run by various émigré socialist and anarchist groups, and after 1917 by the White Russians, frequently published items concerning the Doukhobors, while the editor of *Novoe Russkoe Slovo* found them interesting enough to pay a visit to British Columbia some time before Verigin's death. As literacy spread among the Doukhobors, these papers were read fairly widely, particularly by the Independents. In time—though rarely before the 1930s—individual Doukhobors began to write for them. Some of these papers, particularly the New York *Ruskii Golos*, were highly critical of Verigin and his Community system, and the attack on his dynasty was to be taken up later by the Communist-oriented Canadian-Russian periodical, *Kanadskii Gudok*, which in the middle thirties ran a regular column on Doukhobor life. Such papers acted as a disrupting influence on the Community, even when their overt aim was not to win converts to their own political philosophies.

Meanwhile, those Doukhobors who remained in Russia retreated, so far as the historian is concerned, into an obscurity almost as deep as that in which their ancestors had lived before the Milky Waters settlement. By conforming to the requirements of tsarist law and abandoning their communal customs, they seemed to the Tolstoyans and other radical intelligentsia to be losing the basic beliefs of Doukhoborism and therefore to be no longer of any interest. Bonch-Bruevich was the exception. Though he had no longer any hope of converting Doukhobors to the class struggle, he retained a genuine sociological interest in them and liked to compare the conditions he had seen among Verigin's followers in Canada with those of their brethren who had stayed in Russia.

Three years after Verigin's trip to Russia, Bonch-Bruevich travelled down to the Caucasus to visit Vorob'ev and his Middle Party. What he saw there may explain why Vorob'ev's interest in emigration to Canada waned so quickly on his visit to the prairies in 1905. The Doukhobor farms were prospering, granaries were full and enormous haystacks stood in the yards. Experimentation in seed strains had enabled wheat to grow in mountain areas where formerly only barley and oats had ripened. Horse-breeding had developed so far that for several years the Doukhobors had won the first prizes in the agricultural fair at Tiflis. They had also learnt from German immigrants the art of making cheeses that Bonch-Bruevich regarded as not inferior to those of the Swiss. In comparison with other Russian peasants, and with the average members of the Christian Community of Universal Brotherhood in Canada, these Doukhobor farmers in the Caucasus were financially well off and relatively unmolested by the authorities. There was a demand for their produce, and they shared in the expansion of the Russian economy that continued from the turn of the century up to 1914. Presumably the farmers who belonged to the Small Party were in the same position as Vorob'ev's followers.[5]

Yet the prosperity that Bonch-Bruevich described was not enjoyed by all the Doukhobors who had stayed behind. Whenever the ideal of religious communism was relaxed among the Doukhobors, differentiations between rich and poor peasants emerged once again. Bonch-Bruevich met a number of Doukhobors who were emigrating to Canada, where their relatives had already preceded them. These may have well been poorer brethren who had little to lose by leaving the Caucasus. They were probably some of the two hundred non-Veriginite Doukhobors who arrived in Alberta in 1911, took up homesteads in the Langham area and, while avoiding any entanglement with Peter the Lordly, established close contacts with the Independents in the Prince Albert district of Saskatchewan.

Bonch-Bruevich's observations bear out the thesis of the Soviet historian, A. I. Klibanov, who claims, on evidence gathered from tsarist records, that the Doukhobors in the Caucasus were at this time better farmers than the other Russian peasants and that they acted as the pioneers of advancing capitalism in the countryside. According to Klibanov's evidence, which applies mainly to the Doukhobors who had remained in the Yelizavetpol district after the emigration to Canada, almost every household in 1905 possessed an iron plough, which in tsarist Russia was a very important criterion of peasant wealth and agrarian progress. In other respects the Doukhobors were not so advanced. At the same period, less than a third of the male Doukhobors in Yelizavetpol were barely literate and all the women were completely illiterate.

In 1909, according to official estimates, there were approximately fifteen thousand Doukhobors in the whole of the Russian Empire. The sect had ceased to make conversions and had begun to lose adherents because of the proselytization of other sects and of the Russian Orthodox Church. The conversions to Russian Orthodoxy took place mainly among isolated Doukhobors in the central, northern, and eastern regions of Great Russia, where, between 1907 and 1914, some 447 Doukhobors returned to the traditional church. In the Ukraine, the original home of Doukhoborism, it was the Baptists, the Stundists, and the Molokans who were gaining most of the Doukhobor converts. The Baptists, whose evangelistic methods were extremely aggressive in the decade preceding the Russian Revolution, even gained adherents in the Doukhobor heartland of Transcaucasia; in 1905 there were 172 Baptists living in the Doukhobor villages of Yelizavetpol, forming almost a tenth of their population.

Of the fifteen thousand Doukhobors estimated to be living in Russia in 1909, thirteen thousand were in the Caucasus. The extent of erosion by conversion in the other regions is suggested by the figure of two thousand given for the Doukhobors in 'the Voronezh, Samara, Kiev, Irkutsk and several other gubernias, and in the Amur region.' The latter estimate may be low, however, in view of other information about the number of Doukhobors on the Amur alone.[6]

Because of their remoteness, the Doukhobors on the Amur had always been less well known than their Caucasian brethren. They had taken no part in the dispute between Peter Verigin and the Small Party, but they may have maintained some connection with their brethren in Canada, since there is an oral tradition among the Doukhobors of Grand Forks that representatives from Siberia arrived in search of land before the First World War but decided not to emigrate. Their numbers were small, but almost certainly not so small as the tsarist estimate of 1909 suggested. A Soviet census of 1926 reported that they had ten villages with 2,311 inhabitants,[7] and we can assume a population during the early years of the century of about two thousand. The difference between rich and poor members of the sect was less marked on the Amur than elsewhere, since the Doukhobors there had taken advantage of the availability of cheap Chinese labour and had become lazy and prosperous. Among them, apparently, communal institutions were minimal.

The early years of the First World War made the links between the Canadian Doukhobors and their fatherland even slighter as communications grew more difficult. Naturally, they opposed the war itself. In August 1914 they issued a manifesto from Brilliant demanding the immediate cessation of hostilities and putting forward their own proposals for a peace. France should be granted Alsace-Lorraine and Belgium should become a neutral republic like Switzerland. (The king of the Belgians, 'a great fool', should be stripped of his offices.) The Balkan states should become a confederation of republics and Constantinople an international free port in a demilitarized area. Russia should be granted Galicia, but, in her turn, should unite the Poles and grant them full self-government. To these rather sensible proposals was added a crudely anti-Semitic comment that reflected traditional Russian peasant attitudes towards the Jews. The Jews, the manifesto suggested, can be compared to 'unhealthy microbes spread throughout the human organism' or to 'nomadic gypsies'; they should have settled down long ago and learnt something better than 'trading in needles and small buttons'.[8]

Some of the Russians who had lived among the Doukhobors went home in 1914, and others followed in 1917 to take part in the work of the Revolution. The Doukhobors also were stirred by the events taking place in Russia at that time; they were appalled by the news of bloodshed but elated by the thought of the passing of tsarism and the dawning of an order that—they hoped—would favour those who had been persecuted in the past. In March they sent a telegram to Rodzianko, chairman of the Duma, asking him to transmit their thanks to Nicholas II for his willingness to abdicate and thus end the bloodshed incurred in the February Revolution. The hope of returning to Russia flared up again in their minds after having lain dormant for the decade since Verigin's visit, and shortly afterwards Peter the Lordly sent a telegram to Prince L'vov, prime minister of the Provisional Government, informing him that the ten thousand Doukhobors in Canada were anxious to return; since his own followers at this time numbered no more than eight thousand, he had taken it upon himself to speak for the two thousand Independents as well.

L'vov did not reply. The Provisional Government was still thinking in terms of pursuing the war with Germany to a final victory, and it needed soldiers rather than pacifist farmers. However, this did not lessen the interest of the Doukhobors in what was happening within Russia. Verigin realized the potentialities for indiscriminate violence the situation contained, and there was an almost prophetic note in the telegram he sent to the Provisional Government on 30 April 1917 pleading that the lives of ex-Tsar Nicholas and his family, of the former ministers, and of the Russian Orthodox clergy, should be spared, provided they bowed their heads before 'the truth'. 'The truth' Verigin did not define.

On 9 November, two days after the news of the Bolshevik seizure of power had been telegraphed across the world, Peter the Lordly put forward his own proposals for a new Russia. Military service, that nightmare of the Doukhobors, stood at the head of the list: it must be abolished, and soldiers and militia recruited voluntarily for use only in dealing with criminals. Fortifications should be destroyed and Russia become a neutral state. Taxes should be reduced. Factories should be nationalized and built in the countryside rather than in the towns, which should be reduced and gradually abolished. Industrial production should be increased and an end put to the export of raw materials. These proposals contain many echoes from the Utopian Socialists and from writers like Kropotkin—in his *Fields, Factories and Workshops* (1898)—and little from traditional Doukhobor peasant thinking; they remind one of the extent to which Verigin had been schooled in such matters during his exile in Siberia and give substance to the stories that, while his followers were discouraged from educating themselves, he himself kept a modest library of nineteenth-century political classics, including not only Tolstoy but also Marx and Engels. His proposals aroused the criticism of Soviet scholars, who branded them as an example of 'pastoral capitalism' inspired by the 'patriarchal prejudices' of his followers. In our view, however, they show a realistic grasp of the needs of Russia at that time and, far from being reactionary, are in accord with the best of Russian nineteenth-century radical thought.

As his proposals made clear, Verigin's ideas of communism were very different from those of Lenin. Yet in the beginning he and other Doukhobors were inclined to hope much from the Bolsheviks. They were ignorant of the record or aims of the party, and Lenin was unknown to them, but at a distance there were certain apparent resemblances between Bolshevik and Doukhobor ideals. Both were opposed to tsarism; both were opposed to the First World War, and the insistent Bolshevik demand for the end of hostilities impressed the Doukhobors. Finally, the institution of the Soviets appealed to them, for these councils of workers and peasants seemed to resemble their own sobraniia.

What they did not realize at the time, but learnt later, was that Bolshevik Communism was based on the calculated use of violence and on a form of earthly government more all-pervading than that of the tsars. Peter the Lordly and his son Peter the Purger were often accused of being Bolsheviks or Bolshevik agents, and sometimes the accusations came from their own relatives. Larion Verigin, for example, levelled the latter charge against Peter the Purger, his cousin. But in fact there was little in common —except their authoritarianism—between these theocrats aiming at religious communism as a setting for the spiritual life, and the commissars creating a monolithic secular society based on industry, centralized control, and state socialism. As we have seen, it is possible that Peter Verigin, like Trotsky, was sought out and killed by a Bolshevik agent; certainly both his son and his grandson, Peter Iastrebov, suffered at the hands of the Communists.

In the early days of the Revolution it is doubtful if the Doukhobors, far away from the centres of immediate action, entered greatly into the thoughts of the Bolsheviks. Lenin never mentioned them in his writings, though he showed interest when Bonch-Bruevich told him of the Living Book. Under the Bolsheviks, the Doukhobors were better off with regard to military service than they had been under most of the tsars. During the wartime period of 1914–17 they had been subject to conscription, and a number of them had refused service; some were imprisoned. In January 1919, however, Lenin promulgated a law that exempted sectarians from armed service in the Red Army. Throughout the Civil War Doukhobors in Bolshevik territory were allowed to serve in labour battalions. A special commission dealt with the cases of religious conscientious objectors, and one of its members, who made a point of assisting Doukhobors, was their old friend Vladimir Chertkov.

However, at the time such exemptions meant little to the major groups of Doukhobors in the Caucasus and Siberia, who came relatively late under Bolshevik control. In 1921 the Soviet régime took control of Georgia, but until that date the situation in the Caucasus was extremely confused, with Georgian and Armenian nationalists, White Guards, Moslem tribesmen, and the Red Army all struggling for power. Banditry was rife in the region, and one Bolshevik writer asserts that the Doukhobors bought two hundred rifles from the Armenian refugees and used them to protect their property and their herds, remaining under arms until, in 1927, the region was finally pacified.

There are indications that at some time before the First World War, Peter Petrovich Verigin attempted to re-establish a theocratic leadership among the Doukhobors who remained in Russia and thus become a rival to his father. At this time he was very close to Vorob'ev and appears to have wielded a considerable influence over the Middle Party. Whether any members of the Small Party accepted his leadership is not known. The leaders of this group certainly maintained their opposition to the Verigin clan, and the Orphan's Home at Goreloye appears to have remained in the hands of Michael Gubanov at least until 1914.

Even after the Revolution the Russian Doukhobors, whose numbers had now increased to almost twenty thousand, lived in a defensive isolation. Their world had become static and withdrawn. Unlike their Canadian brethren, they were hostile to the Soviet régime, which they saw at close quarters in all its materialism and political ruthlessness; but they did not oppose it actively and in no way formed a threat to it, for they had long before lost the urge to proselytize. During the reforms that followed the Civil War they lost some of their land to their Armenian neighbours, but by Russian peasant standards many of them were still prosperous, and they could afford to employ not only Armenian shepherds, but also labourers from among their own poorer brethren.

As far as possible the Doukhobors in the Caucasus avoided co-operating with the Soviet government. According to a Communist writer,[9] the administration of the villages remained in the hands of the elders, who were, in practice, the richest and the most conservative peasants in the locality. Disputes among the Doukhobors were settled by the elders at village level to avoid recourse to the Soviet courts, and only a minority of the sect, including very few of the women, took part in the elections to the rural Soviets. Up to 1927 there were no members of the Communist Party at all among the Doukhobors in the Caucasus, and only two members of the Komsomol, who kept their association with that organization secret because they feared the hostility of their brethren. Only two Doukhobors had accepted official positions under the Soviet government.

At the end of the Civil War there was very little communal organization among the Caucasian Doukhobors. In 1919 a few villages, caught up in the spirit of the times, attempted to re-create peasant communes, but the experiment collapsed in 1920. After that the only strictly communal institution was the Orphan's Home, still operated in Goreloye. Cheese and milk co-operatives had been founded in some of the villages, but there was no communal work on the land and there were no communal workshops. Trade unions of agricultural labourers had reached the Caucasus, but their membership was entirely Armenian; even the poorest of the Doukhobors kept aloof from them.

For the gifts of education, medicine, and technical assistance the Bolsheviks tried to press upon them, the Caucasian Doukhobors had little use. Like their brethren in Canada, they still felt that the Living Book, orally transmitted, contained enough of wisdom, and teachers were not encouraged to stay among them. Their literacy rate was about one in six, and even those who could read took no interest in newspapers or any other literature that might subject them to outside influence. According to one Communist account, which is possibly exaggerated, they were so ignorant that they believed neither in the villainy of Rasputin nor in the death of Nicholas II, whose photograph they still displayed on the walls of their houses.[10] It is evident, even if one discounts many of the official Soviet statements as mere propaganda, that there was little in common between the Doukhobors and the Communist Party and that their distrust was mutual.

By the early 1920s the Caucasian Doukhobors began to feel the pressure of land shortage, and in 1922, as soon as the Civil War was ended, a new series of migrations began. Many of the Middle Party trekked northward, some returning to the Milky Waters area and others proceeding farther into the Ukraine. A large group, led by Peter Petrovich Verigin, obtained permission from the Soviet authorities to settle in the Don region. They found land in the Sal'sk district, a hundred miles to the southeast of Rostov. It was flat, fertile steppe country, deserted and treeless; once again the Doukhobors were fulfilling their role of pioneers.

Altogether some four thousand of them migrated to Sal'sk and organized themselves into twenty villages, each of two hundred people. At first communal farming was attempted, but soon this was abandoned and the settlements were divided into individual farms. The Sal'sk colonists chose Peter Petrovich as their leader, and the Bolsheviks, still anxious to placate minority groups by making suitable concessions, confirmed his appointment; so that he was a Divine Leader and almost a Bolshevik commissar at the same time, a fitting counterpart to his father, who combined the roles of Divine Leader and company president. Several thousand of the brethren stayed behind in the Caucasus to till their old lands.

During this period the interest of the Canadian Doukhobors in the new Russia had not diminished. They were shocked by the bloodshed during the Civil War and the ruthless elimination of opponents of the Soviet régime, and in 1921 they gathered at Cowley in Alberta and at Verigin in Saskatchewan to burn arms symbolically in protest. A meeting at Brilliant called upon the workers in Russia to withdraw their support from the Communists because of their indiscriminate use of violence, and collections were made to send aid to the victims of famine.

But still the vision of Russia as a homeland to which they might return hovered tantalizingly in Doukhobor minds. In 1922, barely a year after they had protested against the activities of the Bolsheviks, they heard that the Soviet government was inviting sectarians who had fled because of persecution under the tsar's régime to return to Russia. Immediately a telegram was sent on behalf of the Community to the commissar for agriculture in Moscow, asking for land in a good region, where it was proposed to establish wheat-growing and fruit-growing communes and an agricultural implement factory valued at a million gold roubles. The Doukhobors undertook to pay the expenses of their return to Russia and the cost of building the factory. They asked for tax exemption for twenty years and for what had by now become the three Doukhobor freedoms—freedom from military service, from registration, and from the obligation to send their children to school. There is no record of any reply to this approach, but one can easily imagine the response such demands would arouse among the victorious Bolshevik leaders.

Nevertheless, the idea of a return to Russia remained alive until Verigin's death. In January 1924, according to Peter Maloff, Peter the Lordly was seriously negotiating with a syndicate in Chicago for the sale of the Community lands and other assets in British Columbia at a price of two million dollars (considerably less than their assessed value).[11] Verigin proposed immediately to send representatives to Russia for talks with the Soviet government; if these worked out satisfactorily, two thousand Community members would leave in the autumn of 1924 to prepare the new home for their brethren.

Like so many Doukhobor plans for migration, this scheme seems to have dissolved into thin air. When Gabriel Vereshchagin and Nikolai Plotnikov did eventually go to Russia in 1925 it was after Peter the Lordly's death, and not to find land, but to bring their new leader out of the Soviet Union.

The two delegates had no difficulty in entering Russia and making their way down to Rostov-on-the-Don, where they met Peter Petrovich Verigin and accompanied him to the settlements at Sal'sk. In middle age Peter the Lordly's son was an impressive-looking but difficult man. His height (he was well over six feet tall), his heavy moustaches, and the expression of distinguished anger that lingers in his photographs, gave him the look of a retired tsarist colonel. He had inherited his father's intelligence and sharpened it with a better education than any of his predecessors in the

Doukhobor leadership; he attended a village school and completed his courses in a technical institute in Tiflis, so that he was familiar with city as well as village life, and combined a wide general knowledge with a great interest in Doukhobor traditions. He lacked, on the other hand, his father's good sense and steadfastness of purpose. There was an erratic impulsiveness in his nature, manifested in violent rages and an uncontrollable weakness for vodka. His father's imperiousness was complicated in him by a strain of cruelty which emerged not only verbally, in the bitter tirades that he would deliver against his followers, but also in physical violence.

When Vereshchagin and Plotnikov arrived he was on his best behaviour, delighted at the thought that he would now be the leader of all the Doukhobors, in Canada as well as Russia, and full of what appeared to be sound and balanced opinions. One of his first acts was to send a message telling his people in Canada that it was good to attend school; as a result of this advice the dispute with the British Columbia government over education was temporarily settled in 1925.

But Peter Petrovich was not yet ready to depart for Canada, though he admitted that life might be better there than in Russia. His people in Sal'sk needed him, he claimed, until their communities were really established. But he was ready to send his mother, and late in 1925, after pleading with him in vain for several months, the delegates were forced to accept this arrangement. They returned to Canada with the aged Evdokiia, who was welcomed enthusiastically at Brilliant by a vast crowd of Doukhobors. As the mother of the incumbent leader she played the same symbolic role in the Community as Anastasia Verigina had played a quarter of a century earlier while the Doukhobors waited for the arrival of Peter the Lordly from Siberia.

It seems probable that Peter Petrovich delayed his arrival in Canada for diplomatic reasons. He had learnt from Plotnikov and Vereshchagin of the divisions among the Canadian Doukhobors, and he wished to arrive as the accepted leader of all factions. Accordingly, he opened a correspondence with a number of leading Independents, who were inclined to listen favourably to what he had to say, for the very reason that twenty years before he had shown himself opposed to his father and critical of the Community. Soon a metallic clink entered into his letters. His resources were limited. To depart quickly he needed money. He demanded five thousand dollars of the Independents, more of the Community Doukhobors. 'Your help will bring great relief to our cause, which is not personal,' he told one of his correspondents. 'The sum should not alarm you, nor should return of the money worry you.' [12] The Doukhobors in Canada responded fervently; it was an honour to help the new leader rejoin his people. And so an often-to-be-repeated pattern was established. The exact amount Peter Petrovich collected on this occasion is not certain, but the more conservative estimates place it at around eighteen thousand dollars. Nor is it known how all the money was spent. Peter Petrovich's critics—and they are many—assert that all but a small proportion went on drinking and gambling. But he himself claimed in a Canadian court-room in 1932 that Soviet officials exacted their share as part of the price for letting him go. It is possible; Russia was short of hard currency when Peter Petrovich left in 1927.

His departure was, to say the least, melodramatic. He had spent 1926 trying to consolidate his Russian domain before leaving for Canada, and in January 1927 he presided over a meeting at Milky Waters attended by Doukhobors from that region, from Sal'sk, and from the villages in the Caucasus. Some Canadian Doukhobors are also said to have been present; only the brethren in Siberia did not send delegates. The gathering was intended to promote unity among Doukhobors of all regions and all trends, a favourite theme with Peter Petrovich. A United Community of Doukhobors would be set up to embrace the brethren in North America as well as in Russia. It would be co-ordinated by a central executive committee, located at Milky Waters, under the guidance—presumably from a distance—of a president who would, naturally, be Peter Petrovich Verigin. Each region inhabited by Doukhobors would have a common chest for the support of poor families, but the brethren could live as they wished, either in community or individually. These plans were not carried out in Russia, because the Doukhobors there did not feel strongly enough about their principles to resist the Soviet authorities, who had no inten-tion of allowing the successful operation of an organization that they would not in effect control. However, the concept of a united organiza-tion of communalist and individualist Doukhobors was to remain the most constant theme in Peter Petrovich's policies after he eventually reached Canada.

Since official Soviet documents are not available, it is difficult to tell how far the plans worked out at Milky Waters were responsible for the difficulties with the Bolshevik authorities that Peter Petrovich experienced almost immediately afterwards. Accused of drunkenness and brawling, he was first stripped of official recognition as leader of the Sal'sk communi-ties and shortly afterwards taken before a Workers' Court and tried for counter-revolutionary activities, namely habitual intoxication, beating up two of his followers, and endeavouring to extort money from the Community funds. He was imprisoned, allegedly in order to cure him of his alcoholism.

As soon as the news reached the Doukhobors in Canada that their leader was in prison instead of being on his way across the Atlantic, and might even be exiled to Turkestan, they began a series of frantic appeals on his behalf. They not only telegraphed the Central Executive Committee of the Soviet Union on 15 May, assuring the Bolshevik officials that Peter Petrovich could not be an enemy of the régime since, like all Doukhobors, he believed in his own kind of communism, but they also sent appeals to Bonch-Bruevich and to the leading Tolstoyans.

Bonch-Bruevich did not intervene, and in a letter he wrote later in the same year to V. I. Treglazov in Los Angeles he defended the actions of the Soviet authorities regarding Peter Petrovich.

You are asking me why P. P. Verigin, who is now in Canada, was arrested. I know that many in Canada consider that Peter Petrovich was arrested because of some idealistic matter, because he and his followers did not want to bear arms and they were compelled to do so. That is not true. It is all lies spread by those for whom it is convenient to present Peter Petrovich in a better light so as to proclaim him the successor to the deceased Peter Vasil'evich and to proclaim that a new Christ has appeared among those who are expecting him. I know Peter Petrovich well, and get on well with him, and wish with all my heart he would correct himself, that he would be like his father in his best years after the burning of the arms in the Caucasus when, suffering himself, he led men through sufferings to a better life as he understood it. Peter Petrovich was arrested by the Soviet authorities for unbelievable hooliganism, for drunkenness . . . The Soviet authorities behaved towards him in the kindest manner, and in no way wished to shame him before others, although they had the necessary legal grounds for doing so . . .[13]

It was one of the Tolstoyans who had visited the Doukhobors long ago in the Caucasus, Ivan Tregubov, who eventually intervened. He was not well liked by the Bolsheviks, since his ideas of communism did not agree with theirs, and he probably risked a great deal in making the appeal. Nevertheless, he was well known and respected, and the Stalinist shadow was not dark enough in 1927 for the words of such men to go entirely unregarded.

Tregubov made his appeal early in June, when Peter Petrovich had been transferred to the notorious Butyrskaia prison in Moscow prior to the final decision whether he should indeed be sent to Turkestan. The Bolsheviks were persuaded that it would not only be less expensive but also less troublesome if Verigin were sent across the Atlantic, where he would no longer form a rallying point for Russian Doukhobor sentiment. He was granted a passport, and the Canadian authorities, aware of his action during the education crisis, decided—as they had done in the case of his father—that he might be a moderating influence on his followers and was therefore worth admitting into the country. Finally, at the end of August, Peter Petrovich was able to depart from Russia. He left behind him his wife and his children, including the young Peter who was now heir to the leadership of the Doukhobors. Instead, as his companion, he chose the eighty-year-old Tolstoyan veteran, Paul Biriukov, who joined him in Paris, attracted by great promises of the educational work he would be allowed to do among the Doukhobors. They sailed on the *Aquitania*, and on 16 September 1927 landed at New York, where Michael Cazakoff, the acting chairman of the Christian Community of Universal Brotherhood, was waiting to welcome his new leader.

12 PETER THE PURGER

When Peter Petrovich Verigin landed in New York, his first words were for the reporters at the dockside. Asked if he intended to send Doukhobor children to Canadian schools, he replied, 'Yes, we will take everything of value that Canada has to offer, but we will not give up our Doukhobor souls.' Then, indicating his companion with a wave of the hand, he added: 'We will educate our children in the English schools, and we will also set up our own Russian schools and libraries, for which purpose I am bringing with me Paul Biriukov, the friend of Tolstoy.' Michael Cazakoff, the one-man welcoming committee from the Christian Community of Universal Brotherhood, was impressed by the ease with which the new leader behaved as he stepped on to the continent where he would live out the rest of his stormy life.

Later, in the hotel, a different Peter Petrovich revealed himself. He began pressing Cazakoff for details about the financial status of the Community. Already, from his correspondents among the Independents, he had heard rumours about its enormous debts, but he was apparently unprepared for the news that they had now reached almost a million and a quarter dollars. He demanded to see the books, and when the unhappy general manager confessed that he had not brought them, Peter Petrovich burst out in anger and accused Cazakoff and Shoukin, who had been chosen in December 1924 to manage the Community until his own arrival, of 'banditry' and incompetence.

The situation of the Community had indeed deteriorated sharply since the death of Peter the Lordly. The outbreaks of incendiarism that continued from 1923 to 1925 and the seizures of Community property by the British Columbia government combined to lower confidence in the solvency of the Community. Neither Cazakoff nor Shoukin had the financial panache with which the departed leader had charmed businessmen and bankers, and short-term creditors were beginning to demand payment. Over the winter of 1924–5 the Community held a series of agonized meetings in which Cazakoff lamented the situation without suggesting anything more constructive than a return to Saskatchewan, where the government had handled the education problem without distraining upon Community property. In the hope of gaining enough cash to satisfy pressing demands, the Community desperately appealed to the provincial government in Victoria to repay them $150,000 that they had spent on building roads now in public use. The appeal was ignored, and Cazakoff decided that yet another long-term loan was the only solution, in the hope that sooner or later the general economic situation would improve and the Community would earn enough to pay off all its indebtedness.

A loan for $350,000 was negotiated with the National Trust, representing the Canadian Bank of Commerce. In the general meetings at which it was discussed many members were opposed, since the conditions were extremely onerous. The National Trust would obtain a mortgage on all land and all buildings—including the Brilliant jam factory—on which no other creditors held liens. This meant that everything owned by the Community would now be encumbered with debt, an eventuality that Peter the Lordly had always been careful to avoid, while the interest of 7½ per cent would be a heavy drain on future income. However, the other officers of the Christian Community supported Cazakoff, and the transaction was completed. The $350,000 was used to pay off taxes and the more pressing short-term debts. When everything had been settled, the Community was even worse off financially than it had been when Peter Verigin died. By 1928, on the eve of the Great Depression, its debts had reached $1,202,579 [1] and its credit had vanished because there was nothing left to mortgage.

Peter Petrovich saw clearly that to repeat the policies of his father in a changed situation would be disastrous. His aim, he quickly decided, must be to free the Community of its burden of debt. And, though the methods he employed were sometimes bizarre and led to widespread doubts about his financial integrity, the fact remains—as we shall see—that by his death in 1939 he had cut in half the debt that, as the new president of the Christian Community, he inherited when he came to Canada in 1927. We stress this achievement now, since it is bound to affect one's judgement of many of the events that intervened.

From New York Peter Petrovich travelled to Ottawa, where he met officials of the Dominion government and promised that under his leadership the Doukhobors would obey the laws of Canada and send their children to school. He was eloquent and well-behaved, and his gentlemanly appearance aroused the same hopes as his father's commanding presence had done twenty-five years before in 1902. The Verigins—father and son—possessed a flair for the theatrical that they could use to great effect in inspiring loyalty or trust.

Peter Petrovich used his histrionic talents to telling effect as soon as he reached his followers on the prairies. At Winnipeg there were only the reporters to deal with, and he fielded their questions with bland remarks. 'We are willing to give the government our energies and our brains, but not our souls.' At Yorkton a tiny group of Independents met him; they included Peter Makaroff, who was puzzled by the mixture of sound sense and extravagance in the new leader's conversation. It was at Verigin, the village built by his father, that he stepped into his kingdom, as thousands of his followers ranged themselves in a great V before the towering grain elevators and sang the psalms of joyous welcome. Standing on the balcony of the leader's house, he began the first address to his people, a long sermon lasting for two hours in which quotations from the New Testament jostled with lewd quips, and advice on farming with ambiguous flights of mysticism. Beneath the pyrotechnical flourishes ran the double theme of unity and reform. The divisions among Doukhobors must be healed, and their backslidings from the true way of life must be corrected. This was the mission of Peter Petrovich. 'I am Chistiakov [the Purger],' he shouted. 'I shall divide lies from truth, and light from darkness.' He had given himself the name by which all Doukhobors would henceforward know him.

From the village of Verigin, the Purger continued to the other Doukhobor settlements of the prairies, not neglecting the Independent stronghold of Blaine Lake. It was October before he finally made his way over the mountains into British Columbia, where the officials of the Christian Community of Universal Brotherhood awaited him at Nelson. From Nelson he drove in a triumphal progress to Brilliant, knelt weeping before the grave of his father, and then joined his mother Evdokiia and the thousands of Community people who had gathered outside the jam factory to meet him.

There followed another of his rambling, colourful speeches, which left his followers puzzled and wondering over the meanings that lay concealed. He had come, he declared, not to destroy the Community but to strengthen it by purgation, and to bring unity among all Doukhobors. In the prairies he had been inclined to show his friendliness to the Independents. Now it was the turn of the Sons of Freedom. 'Sons of Freedom', he shouted, coining one of the slogans in which he delighted, 'cannot be slaves of corruption.' Far from it, with their enthusiasm they were the 'ringing bells' that would keep the ears of other Doukhobors open to the truth.

The other new slogan he brought forward at the Brilliant meeting was so reminiscent of the musings of Ivan Karamazov that one must assume Peter the Purger had read not only his Tolstoy, but also his Dostoevsky. 'The welfare of the world is not worth the life of a single child.' By following these two slogans, he declared, and by educating their children ('Let Doukhobors become professors'), they would begin the new era. He ended by warning his followers that he was nothing more than a man; if his actions seemed praiseworthy, let them give the credit to the voice within him.

That night his followers saw another and more disquieting aspect of Peter Petrovich. He had gathered a group of the more prominent Doukhobors for a supper in the Community residence and requested that a choir sing outside the building. The room became stuffy. Peter rose to open the window behind him. He tried repeatedly, but it would not move. Then all at once his geniality vanished, his face contorted with rage, and he smashed his elbow through the window; the glass fell on the heads of the choir below. As the singing died down, the Purger's voice rose in a crescendo of obscenity.

A few days later the faithful at Grand Forks also received a lesson on what it meant to have a purger for a leader. The day Peter Chistiakov was expected, they gathered early in the morning outside the meeting-house and chanted hour by hour, standing without food through noon until sunset, and long into the night. At midnight, when they had decided to go home to sleep, their leader, who had idled the day away in his father's house in Grand Forks, suddenly appeared, shouting reproaches, and preached till three in the morning about the Day of Judgement when the Doukhobors would act as a jury in the great trial of all mankind. These exhibitions were clearly intended to keep his people alert by inculcating a dread of the unexpected and the capricious; he varied them with dawn inspections of the fields and workshops in which he criticized indiscriminately, and with long nagging sessions with Cazakoff and Shoukin over the Community's books.

These tactics undoubtedly had the effect—if only a temporary one—of inspiring his followers to work more diligently; but inspiration by fear is rarely lasting, and as his people began to know their new leader more intimately, the more discreditable aspects of his nature were revealed. He began to get drunk with increasing frequency. He would brawl not only with his own followers, but also with strangers in the hotels of Nelson and Saskatoon and Yorkton. He gambled at cards, extravagantly and unskilfully. For these escapades he excused himself with rationalizations reminiscent of his predecessor, Peter Kalmykov. As the Purger, he was obliged to degrade himself, partly to test his followers and partly to deceive his enemies who, whenever they saw him intoxicated, would be led to underestimate his powers. His followers should do as he said, not as they saw him do. The faithful—those for whom Doukhoborism was synonymous with obedience to a divinely inspired leader—accepted everything, the abuse and the obscenity, the drinking and the physical maltreatment that occasionally followed, as a primitive pagan might accept the caprice of the gods. To such believers, the sheer irrationality of the Purger's behaviour set him aside from ordinary beings and therefore proved his divinity. But there were others—most of the Independents and a growing number of the Community members—who wondered whether a man so distant in behaviour from the ideals of Doukhoborism could be a true leader.

Yet Peter the Purger was no mere drunken fool. He had as much intelligence and energy as his father, though they were manifested in different ways; he possessed a fertile and often lurid imagination; he knew the psychology of the true believer. He saw before him two immediate tasks, to establish solvency and to establish unity, and he set about them in his own dramatic way.

First came unity. All the main Doukhobor factions had accepted him on his arrival—the members of the Christian Community, about 5,500 adults; the Independents, by now somewhere over 2,000 in number; and the Sons of Freedom, still a small group of zealots to be numbered in the scores rather than in the hundreds.

One group alone stood aloof in that autumn of 1927. This was the Lordly Christian Community of Universal Brotherhood, the tiny following of Anastasia Golubova, which claimed to carry on the true teachings of the first Peter Verigin and which rejected Peter Chistiakov as a charlatan and a Bolshevik. Through Larion Verigin, Anastasia had followed the method used by the Small Party in Russia, appealing to the British Columbia government for protection and also for financial aid in establishing her community, since she and her followers had been turned off their land at Cowley. Premier John Oliver refused, remarking that 'the whole lot of them are a nuisance',[2] and Anastasia then persuaded twenty-six families (sixty adults) to pay a hundred dollars each for the purchase of land in Alberta. She no longer laid claim to be a holy leader, but wished merely to teach the children and transmit the psalms, of which she had a great repertory. However, like Peter the Lordly many years before, she bought the land in her own name and kept the conduct of community affairs in her capricious hands. The stories of her follies are manifold. In one year she is said to have sold all the wheat put aside for next year's sowing, and in another to have forbidden the mowing of hay so that during the following winter the half-starved animals were hungry enough to eat the people's washing. She never posed any real threat to the Purger's authority over the Doukhobors in general, and her following quickly diminished, until by the mid-1930s she was left with the land and a single servant, with whom she lived on into old age, a pathetic relic of the period of Peter the Lordly.

Peter Chistiakov started his unity program with a reorganization of the Christian Community of Universal Brotherhood. A few days after arriving in British Columbia, he met his principal lieutenants in a Trail rooming-house patronized by Doukhobors who worked for the Consolidated Mine and Smelting Company. There, importing the terminology he had learnt in Communist Russia, he transformed them into a Supreme Council of Community Economics, in which they held positions as commissars in charge of various phases of activities. These roles ran parallel to the posts they retained as legally appointed officers of the Christian Community of Universal Brotherhood Limited. The only appointment that lay outside the existing organization was that of Gabriel Vereshchagin as director of education, with Biriukov as his assistant, and this was a mere gesture, for Vereshchagin was given no funds with which to operate and Peter the Purger later showed no interest in the schemes for Russian schools with which Vereshchagin and Biriukov approached him.

The Supreme Council quickly faded away. More important in the long run was the decentralization of the Christian Community that Verigin planned and to a great extent carried out. The geographical difficulties posed by holdings spread over a thousand miles were recognized, as, by implication, was the fact that most members were tired of the rigidity of Peter the Lordly's communitarian economics: the organization was divided into eighty 'Families', each of up to one hundred men, women, and children, responsible for the cultivation of their lands, for the collection of the assessed earnings of their members, and for selling (not giving) their surplus products to the Community factories or grain elevators. This meant that, though trading was still in the hands of the Community, the old inhibitions on the handling of money were abolished, and men who worked outside were allowed to retain anything they earned over and above their assessments.

At first, in 1928, the assessments were based on a flat rate of forty dollars for all members of the Families, whether working or not. From 1930 onwards they were based in British Columbia on the number of working men and their ages. In that year a man between 20 and 45 was expected to provide two hundred dollars; a man between 45 and 50 a hundred and fifty dollars; and a youth between 16 and 20, a hundred and twenty dollars. The highest assessment was in 1932, when men between 20 and 45 were expected to pay three hundred and fifty dollars; but as the depression deepened, the assessments declined, until in 1936 and 1937 they were as low as sixty dollars. In Saskatchewan and Alberta, from 1930 onwards the assessment was based on acreage, at the rate, in that year, of $1.75 in Alberta and $1.90 in Saskatchewan.[3] In effect, if not in theory, the status of the Community members was changed into that of tenants paying yearly for the land they used.

In addition to the Families, which maintained a direct connection with the central administration, provincial branches of the Christian Community were set up to operate business enterprises in the various areas, such as grain elevators, flour mills, and brickyards on the prairies, and jam and canning factories and sawmills in British Columbia. These provincial branches also operated Community stores, selling for cash, in place of the former warehouses from which rations were handed out to the members according to need. Finally, at the apex of the pyramid, stood the central management of the Christian Community, which collected tribute from the Families and the provincial branches, paid the taxes, assumed responsibility for maintenance and capital improvements, and carried out the vital task of manipulating the complicated debt structure by keeping up interest payments and reducing the principal whenever possible. Peter Chistiakov appointed himself auditor, with full supervisory powers over the Community's financing, and invented a bookkeeping system that some Doukhobors who entered private business follow to this day, maintaining that it is greatly superior to any orthodox system.

These changes represented a considerable shift from the kind of communitarian system that Peter the Lordly had tried to sustain. Now the only real difference between the Community members and the Independents was that the former owned no land, buildings, or equipment of their own; they had acquired rights of use and even profit, but not of actual proprietorship.

Having reshaped his father's work according to his own conceptions by reforming the Community, Peter Chistiakov turned his attention to the wider problem of unification. On 27 June 1928 he called sixty delegates to a meeting on the farm of the Independent Vasilii Popoff, near Kamsack in Saskatchewan. The conference founded a new, all-embracing organization, the Society of Named Doukhobors. The resolutions of the conference, drawn up in a document that Doukhobors generally call The Protocol, were studded with the Purger's slogans and padded out with reverberating generalizations about non-violence and Christian doctrine. But they also contained a number of very specific statements that marked out the policy favoured by the new leader. All internal disputes should be settled through arbitration by the society's executive committee. Doukhobor marriages should be based on love; where it was found that love did not survive, the union should be dissolved by written consent of both parties. In their relations with the outside world, Doukhobors should make all concessions consonant with their beliefs. There was no reason to object to registration or to education in the public schools, provided the teaching of imperialism or hatred were avoided. Those who committed crimes would automatically be expelled from the Society of Named Doukhobors.

These resolutions were planned to please the Independent Doukhobors, who were willing to make compromises with the state. The Sons of Freedom, feeling that they had their own instructions from Peter the Purger and could place their own interpretations on his statements, stood aloof from the Named Doukhobors. This was the time when the famous 'upside-down' method of explaining the instructions of leaders by their opposites first came into fashion among them, and in that same year, 1928, they began new demonstrations against education, considering that, whatever the resolutions of the Named Doukhobors, they were carrying out their duties as 'ringing bells'. Peter, however, had inserted the clause regarding the expulsion of criminals quite deliberately to give him a means of dealing with the 'ringing bells' in case they jangled out of tune.

An executive of seven members was chosen for the Named Doukhobors. To bring the Independents into line with the Community members, they were organized into 'Hundreds', corresponding to the Community 'Families', but these units were very loose, having no economic purpose, and it is likely that in actuality they were unimportant. In fact, Peter Chistiakov quickly narrowed the functions of the Society of Named Douk- hobors until the organization, apart from symbolizing a unity that in practice was little more than sentimental, fulfilled a single function: raising money.

The financial relations between Peter the Purger and his followers were so complicated and so bizarre that he has often been accused of mis- appropriating funds on a colossal scale. It is not easy to find the true facts, since there are great gaps in the records, and we have not discovered evidence that conclusively shows what really happened. That he lived extravagantly there is no doubt; the eye-witness accounts of his drinking and gambling, from Doukhobor and non-Doukhobor sources, are too numerous to be discounted. Since he reached Canada with no money of his own, he must have obtained whatever he wasted in this way from the Doukhobors, either as a community or as individuals; that he stole it in the sense of taking it from unwilling people is not proved. The true be- lievers among his followers undoubtedly expected him to take whatever he might consider appropriate to his inexplicable needs as a divinely inspired leader; it was the Doukhobor custom, and only those influenced by Canadian ideas saw anything wrong with it. That Verigin himself, under the guise of simple Christianity, should have taken advantage of the credulity of his followers is reprehensible, but no more so, in a legal or a moral sense, than the practices of early twentieth-century industrialists who considered themselves justified in gaining the maximum possible profits at the expense of their workers, or of trade union bosses who lived high on the contributions of their members. He was an exploiter in a world that favoured exploiters.

The transactions on which the strongest criticisms of the Purger have centred are the series of loans that he commandeered from his followers. The first of these, raised shortly after his arrival in Canada, was intended to reduce the Community's massive debts. Peter Chistiakov shrewdly calculated that many members who worked outside during the moder- ately prosperous years after Peter the Lordly's death must have accumu- lated savings after they had paid their assessments, and this money he sought to charm from them by a letter in which he urged them to help the Community emerge from its financial crisis. They responded; as much as $350,000 was raised in this way and used to pay off the more urgent debts.[4] But this was still not sufficient, and in 1929 Peter Chistiakov hit upon a plan so extravagant that in most circumstances it would merely have aroused derision. Among the vision-ridden Doukhobors it succeeded.

He played upon their ancient mystique of pilgrimage by announcing that the time had at last come when they must leave Canada. Canada had not honoured the pledge of ninety-nine years' freedom from the law that he claimed Queen Victoria had made to Peter the Lordly, and now they must leave such a dishonourable country. A white horse would take them into a faraway land where the days of sorrow and persecution would at last come to an end. The symbol of the white horse caught the imagination of his followers, and they spent much time debating whether a miraculously gigantic steed would indeed appear out of the heavens or whether the Purger really meant a great white ship that would transport them to the earthly paradise.

While Peter Chistiakov chose to keep the true identity of the white horse in the misty realms of fantasy, he left his hearers in no doubt of its most important peculiarity. While other horses ate hay and oats, the white horse had a voracious appetite for dollar bills. The Purger called upon his people to provide this necessary fodder. Those who kept back their money would not be true Doukhobors, and would find no room on the white horse. But their money would avail them nothing, since after the true Doukhobors had left, the Canadian financial system would fall into chaos and money would lose all value. As for those who went where the white horse led them, they would need no money, for in the earthly paradise everything would be naturally provided.

The Sons of Freedom were the first to contribute, breaking off a campaign of nude marches, which had occupied the summer of 1929, to become devotees of the white-horse cult. In the end, to be on the safe side, most of the Community Doukhobors also gave, and there were even some Independents who advanced money, as an investment, when Verigin privately promised them interest. In all, $525,329 was collected.[5]

The fodder of the white horse did not all go, as certain writers have insinuated, into Verigin's feed-bag. Treating it as a personal loan to himself, he loaned it in turn to the Community to pay off debts, interest, and taxes. He charged six per cent interest—just a little less than the trust companies—and out of this he paid interest to the Independents. Eventually, he repaid about $160,000, and by 1938 the indebtedness of the white-horse fund was reduced to $365,000,[6] which was inevitably lost in the ultimate collapse of the Community. Nevertheless he made at least

$46,431 personal profit [7] out of the interest during a period of three years. It seems to have been a heartless transaction in which the Purger deliberately profited from the needs of his community and the credulity of its members. In practice, it meant that the corporate debts of the Doukhobors were reduced and the leader's extravagances subsidized by extracting from the members whatever individual profits they had made from the assessment system. The effect was to return them to the moneyless state in which they had lived under Peter the Lordly.

Peter the Lordly had kept his followers happy—or at least resigned—with promises of a better life in Canada when the Community had become solvent and self-sufficient. Peter Chistiakov continued to play on the theme of the white horse. Once he had extracted his half-million dollars out of the secret stores of the faithful, he kept their minds occupied by announcing the destination of the great exodus. It was to be Mexico. One of the solicitors who from time to time handled Peter Chistiakov's complicated legal affairs was a Russian Jew living in Winnipeg, Philip Ney, who had contacts with American land speculators. One of the speculators was Senator Joseph Hackney, who had options on large tracts of Mexican land. As bait, Hackney offered to pay the expenses of sending a group of Doukhobors to view the lands he had to offer, and in January 1930 Verigin called a special conference in Saskatchewan to choose the delegates. Three Community Doukhobors and three Independents were picked, for Peter Chistiakov wished to make this a mass migration that would bring together all Doukhobors. In February he set off with them for Tampico in Mexico.

The fertile lands of Mexico have long been over-occupied, and all that Hackney had to offer was a waterless, rocky waste, inhabited by a few mestizos who reminded the Doukhobors, unpleasantly, of the Tartars they had left in Russia. The delegation went from site to site. In some places there was a little more water than in others, but that was the only difference; nowhere did the Doukhobors see anything that looked half as enticing as the Saskatchewan wheatlands or the green hills of the Kootenays. However, with characteristic secretiveness they kept their thoughts to themselves, and Hackney gained the impression that the dollars he had been pouring into the Purger's hands had been well spent.

On 31 March, Verigin and his companions reported to a mass meeting of several thousand Community Doukhobors assembled at Brilliant; among them were fifty delegates from the prairie settlements. Senator Hackney and Philip Ney were in attendance. The leader began his oration with one of his familiar pleas for Doukhobor unity, and proceeded to a denunciation of the rottenness of Canadian society. He had just started on a visionary peroration describing life in the new land, when six naked Sons and Daughters of Freedom appeared on the stage behind him. Verigin stopped in mid-course and, after volubly cursing the intruders, declared the meeting closed and stalked from the hall.

Next morning the people gathered again, and the delegates were allowed to make their reports in peace. It was evident that most of them were not impressed by what they had seen in Mexico, but the meeting, as was customary, awaited the leader's opinion before it reached any conclusion. As soon as Peter Chistiakov walked in, the Sons of Freedom appeared again, to the annoyance of the Purger. Blows were added to curses, and again the meeting was closed. Afterwards he told a bewildered Hackney that everything would work out satisfactorily; the Sons of Freedom would be left behind and the good Doukhobors would leave for Mexico. But he declined to sign any formal agreement, and one is left to speculate on how far the curious events of those two days were carefully stage-managed at the leader's instructions in order to keep both his people and the land speculators in a stage of profitable expectation.

Senator Hackney hoped to gain $750,000 from the sale of his Mexican lands, and he was understandably reluctant to believe matters were quite so unpromising as they appeared. He handed out advances to Verigin for yet more inspection parties, until in the end he had parted with more than ten thousand dollars. Hackney also drew others into the vortex of Peter the Purger's fantasies. He aroused the interests of an International Colonization Company and of the president of a Mexican railroad, and these eager speculators busily sold shares in the scheme for selling useless land to the elusive Purger.

Peter Chistiakov continued to elaborate his scheme in ever more megalomaniac forms. Not only the Canadian, but also the Russian Doukhobors must gather in the new paradise, and in May 1931 he selected a delegation of six Community members to return to Russia and liberate their brethren. The delegation sailed from New York to Germany in the middle of June. At Bremen they were met by Valentin Bulgakov, Tolstoy's former secretary and friend, with whom they travelled to Berlin. There they applied at the Soviet consulate for permission to enter Russia.

The situation had changed greatly since Gabriel Vereshchagin, who headed this group, had come six years before, to invite Peter Chistiakov to Canada. No visas were granted, despite interviews with leading officials in the Soviet Embassy, and as they waited in Berlin the delegates began to hear disquieting news from Russia. Chertkov advised them not to come. Their friend and Tolstoy's disciple, Tregubov, had been arrested. They failed to establish proper communication with the Doukhobors in Russia; all they received were unsigned letters that made it clear their brethren were in great difficulties.

From 1929 the Russian Doukhobors had been enduring the sweeping agrarian collectivizations initiated by the Communist government. Members of the sect in all regions suffered, and official Soviet statistics for the villages in Siberia give some idea of the pattern of oppression and dispersion. Five out of the ten Doukhobor villages on the Amur disappeared completely between 1926 and 1932, and the total population of these communities declined during the same period from 2,311 to 207;[8] in other words, ninety per cent of the Siberian Doukhobors were either dispersed or killed off during the collectivization drive or had abjured their religion under pressure. Since appreciable numbers of Doukhobors were left in the Don and Transcaucasian regions, the action of the Communists in these areas cannot have been quite so drastic, though many of the more prosperous or more obstinately religious went into exile and some villages were particularly hard hit. Goreloye, the centre of the Small Party, must have been largely depopulated when eighty families were sent into exile in an operation involving a battalion of Red Army soldiers; it is possible that this was the occasion on which the Orphan's Home was destroyed. In the Sal'sk settlement, some 120 Doukhobors had been exiled by 1931.[9] However, the majority of the Doukhobors in both these regions, and also in the Ukraine, conformed to the collectivization scheme, and it is possible that some of the poor Doukhobors, with little or no land, actively collaborated with the authorities in setting up the kolkhozes. There were petitions to the Kremlin from the Sal'sk Doukhobors, asking for their brethren to be released from exile and putting the traditional requests for internal autonomy or, alternatively, migration abroad. They also wished to carry out communalization on their own traditional terms. All these requests were firmly refused, and the leading petitioners went to join their brethren in exile.

The effects of collectivization were twofold. The Doukhobors were dispersed as never before; after Stalin's death, when Russian Doukhobors began once again to write to their relatives abroad, it became clear that collectivization and purges had spread the members of the sect more widely over the country than had happened at any time during the tsarist régime. Even more important, their traditional way of life was irretrievably destroyed. A few religious observances lingered, but these no longer retained the corporate force they had possessed in the past. The old systems of sect and village government had completely vanished; and, as we shall later see, the members of the Verigin clan who were left in Russia either died in detention camps or survived precariously in confinement until the post-Stalin period began.

This process was already far advanced in 1931 when the delegates from Canada reached Berlin. Eventually, at the end of July, they were categorically refused visas and told that the Soviet government had no intention of releasing its Doukhobors. After further fruitless negotiations they were able, with the help of Tolstoyans in western Europe, to organize a petition to Kalinin, Chairman of the Supreme Soviet, which was endorsed by such habitual signatories as Albert Einstein and Romain Rolland. It also failed. The reason, according to Bonch-Bruevich, was that the Soviet government believed that Peter the Purger intended to 'sell' the Doukhobors to the capitalists of Mexico.

The delegates returned to Canada to find that their leader had created a nine days' sensation by prematurely announcing the forthcoming arrival of between twenty and thirty thousand Russian Doukhobors. Gone were the fantasies of settlement in Mexico; Verigin now proposed that the hypothetical newcomers should be settled throughout the Canadian west. The government of British Columbia took him seriously and made frantic representations to Ottawa. Quite apart from the unpopularity of the Doukhobors, the depression was already an inescapable fact and the economy of the west was unable to absorb its growing masses of unemployed voters.

From 1931 to the end of the decade, the story of the Doukhobors in Canada is woven of three different strands. The personal actions of Peter Chistiakov follow a frenzied pattern that runs ever closer to insanity. The Community, hampered by outside hostility and internal disunity, fights a losing battle against the depression. And the Sons of Freedom grow in numbers and aggressiveness until they develop from a leavening of zealots into a small-scale mass movement. This development will be treated separately in the next chapter; but it cannot be entirely ignored in dealing with the general record of the Doukhobors in the 1930s, since the Sons of Freedom gained numbers from the disintegration of the Community and encouragement from the example of the Purger's erratic behaviour, while they in turn played an important role in precipitating the Community's final end.

During the last seven years of his life, Peter Chistiakov carried on a battle with Canadian society that was quite different from the struggle of a religious or social idealist fighting against a corrupt or tyrannical society. There had been times, particularly in Siberia, when Peter the Lordly had stood out as the representative of a minority defending its right to be different from the accepted norm. But his son fought a personal battle; and if any consistent thread can be seen in his actions, it is that of nihilism in the strictest sense. There is little evidence that he held anything sacred. An irresponsible and unprincipled use of power seems to have characterized his relations with his followers, and a similar arbitrariness, a temperamental lawlessness, governed his relations with Canadian society. Inevitably, Canadian society fought back, and the melodrama of Peter the Purger became increasingly a matter of law courts and prisons.

The trouble began in 1931. By this time the Community was raising money by allowing some of its prairie members to opt out and buy their own land. One of them, George Chutsoff, had already received the title to his land in Saskatchewan when Verigin demanded a further thousand dollars that he claimed was still owing. Chutsoff disputed the claim, and Peter Chistiakov, forgetting the resolution of the Named Doukhobors to settle all such disputes through their executive committee, took him to court. Verigin lost the case and, dipping further into the morass of litigation, accused Chutsoff of perjury. Chutsoff was duly arrested. The case came up in the May assizes and ended, ironically, in Verigin himself being charged with the crime of which he had accused Chutsoff. On 5 May 1932 he was sentenced to three years in Prince Albert Penitentiary. In June the sentence was reduced by the Saskatchewan Court of Appeals to eighteen months. There was little protest outside Doukhobor ranks, and it looked as though Peter Chistiakov would sit out his term without interruption.

Government stupidity, however, turned this rather sordid incident into a major skirmish in the struggle for civil liberties. Verigin's trial had been attended by a series of nude demonstrations by British Columbia Sons of Freedom. These began on 1 May, four days before he was convicted, and continued for almost the whole month. It is by no means certain that there was anything more than a fortuitous link between the two events; the Sons of Freedom appear to have been demonstrating, not on behalf of, but against the Purger and his policy of evicting their members from the Community. But the Dominion government, which in July 1931 had passed an act making public nudity punishable by three years' imprisonment, was now faced with the problem of finding penitentiary room for several hundred convicted Sons of Freedom and making some provision for their children. The temptation to find a scapegoat was overwhelming, and the Conservative prime minister of Canada, R. B. Bennett, succumbed. Only remove the evil genius Verigin, he decided, and the whole trouble would come to an end.

Accordingly, in January 1933, before his sentence was half completed, Verigin was secretly pardoned, and two plainclothes men from Ottawa arrived to set him free from the Prince Albert prison and re-arrest him on a deportation order from the Department of Immigration. He was refused permission to see his lawyer. His guards had orders to take him to Halifax with the utmost possible secrecy, so that when his deportation became known he would be on his way back to Russia where, in view of the political climate of 1933, a place in a concentration camp was the best treatment he could expect. This attempt at arbitrary government action, worthy of tsarist or Communist Russia, failed because the secret was not well kept and a local correspondent of the *Saskatoon Star Phoenix*, Mrs J. D. Rose, learnt that Verigin had been removed from jail. She telegraphed the city editor who in turn informed the Independent Doukhobor lawyer, Peter Makaroff.

By this accidental chain of events the plans of Prime Minister Bennett were eventually frustrated. Makaroff telephoned Bennett and his minister of immigration, Wesley Gordon, asking that Verigin be held in Winnipeg for him to interview. Both of them refused his request. A Winnipeg lawyer, B. C. Dubienski, met the train on which Verigin was being taken east, and was denied access to him by the guards. Meanwhile Makaroff travelled by train to Winnipeg and, with Semeon Reibin, flew east to Boston, where they met Joseph Shoukin. There Makaroff again telephoned Bennett, pleading for a delay in the deportation, but received a categorical refusal; Verigin would sail next morning on the *Montcalm*. Risking their lives in a chartered plane in bad weather, the three Doukhobors flew to Halifax and recruited a local lawyer, Lionel Ryan. The immigration officials refused to say where Verigin was detained, but eventually Ryan discovered him in the immigration sheds, waiting to be hurried on board ship at the last moment before sailing. Serving writs of habeas corpus on the captains of the Europe-bound liners that were preparing to sail, the two lawyers frustrated the government's plan for immediate and secret deportation and brought the case before the Nova Scotia courts. Arbitrary deportation was becoming a favourite device of the Bennett government; it had been used widely as an economic expedient to rid the country of unemployed men who had not been in the country long enough to establish domicile, and the news of a legal fight centring on a figure so colourful as Peter the Purger attracted country-wide attention.

The lawyers for the Crown and for Verigin put their cases, and while the court considered its decision Verigin was released on bail; his first act was to write to his followers in British Columbia, instructing them to be calm and not to listen to Sons of Freedom agitators. He was still in a cowed mood. On 25 February, Judge Mellish of the Nova Scotia Supreme Court ruled that he had been detained unlawfully and that he could not be deported. Deportation was not legal until a jail sentence had terminated, and a pardon could not be used for the purpose of deportation because a conditional pardon was valid only if the prisoner accepted the conditions. A higher decision, in the Supreme Court of Canada on 29 March, ruled that deportation after a pardon was indeed legal, but the law officers of Nova Scotia maintained that Verigin's release was still valid within their province. It was a moot point, but the government did not attempt to test it further, since by this time newspapers and public figures across the country had expressed their repugnance for its actions and, without defending Verigin as a person, had praised the principle that his resistance to deportation involved. For a brief season he appeared as a hero in the struggle for civil liberties which became steadily more intense as the depression deepened and popular discontent with the Bennett government increased.

It is doubtful if Verigin was much concerned with the general principles other people saw in his case. A growing paranoia seemed to dominate his actions, and, having been extricated from one legal scrape, he quickly became involved in others. He sued one of his solicitors, J. M. Patrick of Winnipeg, for seven thousand dollars that he claimed he had been overcharged in connection with the perjury trial of the previous year; later in 1933 he himself was sued by Senator Hackney, who by now realized that the Mexican immigration scheme had collapsed like the bubble of fantasy it always was. He demanded the whole $750,000 he had expected to gain. The case dragged on for five years, ending in 1938. Hackney, ruled Judge Embury in the King's Bench Court at Yorkton, had seen the chance of making a great sum of money and had gambled on it. He awarded him $11,300 to reimburse him for the amounts advanced to Verigin, but ordered him to pay the general costs of the case, which meant that the land speculator in fact received nothing, while Verigin paid to lawyers the amounts he had pocketed from Hackney during that strange transaction.

By this time the Purger had gone through a further series of undignified encounters with the law. In February 1934 he was involved in a beer-parlour brawl in Nelson and was lucky to escape with a fine for drunkenness. In November of the same year he was imprisoned for two months in Winnipeg for assaulting a non-Doukhobor interpreter. In April 1937 he harried a couple driving on the road to Nelson by persistently overtaking them, obstructing the road with his car, and cursing them bilingually. He was charged with vagrancy, fined seventy-five dollars and sent to Nelson jail for three months. His one really successful fight in the courts was a fratricidal one against a former member of his own Community, a building contractor named Cheveldaev. In Yorkton Cheveldaev had constructed six houses for Verigin, which the latter let for his own profit. When Peter was sent to prison for perjury in 1932 he transferred legal title to Cheveldaev in trust. Cheveldaev decided to keep the houses for himself. Like other disputes involving Verigin, the case reached the King's Bench Court in Yorkton, and in 1935 judgement was passed in his favour. But his success gained him little credit, since Doukhobors and non-Doukhobors alike wondered where he had got the means to pay for property that was valued at $27,000.

Throughout these excursions into misdemeanour and litigation, Community Doukhobors complained that Peter Chistiakov was being persecuted by a hostile government, and his own pastoral letters from prison confirmed this view with pietistic claims that he was 'partaking of the suffering of Jesus Christ'. But, except for the attempt to deport him, it is hard to find any justification for such an attitude. The courts in fact treated Verigin no worse than they would have treated any other offender in similar circumstances, and the Supreme Court of Nova Scotia admirably defended his personal rights as a victim of arbitrary government.

Verigin's escapades brought extremely bad publicity to the Doukhobors in general and helped to destroy the unity that he so zealously promoted during his first years in Canada. The Community, the loyal heart of Doukhoborism in Canada, shrank steadily in membership throughout the decade. In 1928 there were 4,326 members in British Columbia; by 1936 the number had fallen to 3,083. In the prairies the decline was even more striking—from 1,149 in 1928 to 386 in 1936.[10] Some of the lapsed members drifted away of their own accord; others were expelled for failing to meet their assessments. Many of these dispossessed people, particularly in British Columbia, swelled the settlements that the Sons of Freedom began to form around 1932. In the prairies the tendency was for the lapsed Community members to join the Independents, but an increasing number began to move completely out of the Doukhobor orbit into the wider Canadian society, where they would slowly lose their cultural identity and bring up children who did not speak Russian.

If the Community was slowly declining during these years, so were its relations with other Doukhobors. From 1929 onwards Peter Chistiakov systematically evicted the Sons of Freedom from the Community. His personal attitude towards them may have been more ambivalent than his public actions suggested, but there is no doubt that their expulsion drove a wedge between the Community 'haves' and the Sons of Freedom 'have-nots'.

The unity of his Society of Named Doukhobors was also threatened from the political left. This was the age of Communist front organizations, and it would have been surprising if a people of Russian extraction like the Doukhobors had been left untouched. The Russian-language Communist paper *Kanadskii Gudok* had prepared the ground by its articles discussing Doukhobor affairs and criticizing the Purger, and in June 1934 a small group in Saskatchewan defied Peter Chistiakov's threats of excommunication and formed the Progressive Society of Doukhobors, with an anti-militarist, anti-capitalist program couched in orthodox Marxist rather than traditional Doukhobor phraseology. The society survived into the early 1940s, but its membership was always small and concentrated in the prairies; the Community influence was still too strong in British Columbia for such a dissident group to have any success there.

This rebellion on the left alarmed Peter Chistiakov, who denounced its adherents as 'Bolsheviks and No-Doukhobors'; it was one of the reasons why, in July 1934, he called 250 delegates to the second convention of the Society of Named Doukhobors. The other reason was the enactment by parliament of a flagrant piece of discriminatory legislation : the amendment to the election laws by which Doukhobors in British Columbia (where they were numerous enough to hold a balance of power in certain constituencies) were deprived of the federal vote. In a ringing declaration, the Named Doukhobors made a virtue out of necessity.

The modern world—mankind—has scattered and divided itself into countless numbers of groups—following the watchwords and programmes of the various political parties. Every political party struggles against others not for the good and benefit of the people but for dominance over them . . . Members of the Union of Named Doukhobors have never recognized and do not recognize any political party. They have never entered nor will they ever enter into the ranks of any political party. They have never given nor will ever give their votes during elections; thereby they are free from any responsibility before God or man for the acts of any government established of man. Members of Named

Doukhobors essentially are above party politics; they not only gave their votes but their bodies, blood and souls, to the One and Unreplaceable Guardian of the hearts and souls of men, the Lord Jesus Christ, whereby we have obtained perfect freedom by egressing from the slavery of corruption into the freedom of glory of the children of God.[11]

This declaration represented the socially-withdrawn attitude of the Community Doukhobors. The Independents, on the other hand, were establishing more complex contacts with the world around them. Education was one of the means by which they were doing so. The example of Peter Makaroff was being imitated, and, at a time when Community Doukhobors rarely completed primary schooling, a number of Independents were already studying at universities; by the end of the 1930s there were Doukhobor doctors, engineers, dentists, and chartered accountants, though the Community did not choose to benefit from their services. In politics also the Independents increasingly followed their own course, which led them away from traditional apoliticism and towards the parties of the left and centre. Most of them gravitated towards the CCF and voted for Peter Makaroff when, in 1933, he stood as that party's candidate in the Saskatchewan provincial elections.

Since the Independents paid little heed to the antipolitical manifesto of the 1934 convention of Named Doukhobors, this event seems to mark the beginning of their rapid withdrawal from Peter the Purger and his policies. The Society of Independent Doukhobors began to reassert itself, and with each revelation of Peter Chistiakov's irresponsibility it moved farther away from him, until, on his final imprisonment in 1937, the Independents dissociated themselves publicly from him, denouncing the cult of leadership and declaring that they no longer recognized the Verigin dynasty. This did not cut all the tenuous ties of sentiment between the various groups of Doukhobors, who were united by faith and family, but it meant that the Purger's dreams of a united Doukhobor movement in Canada had been destroyed, mainly by his own hand.

Yet the most important event of the decade was not the collapse of the Society of Named Doukhobors, which had been an artificial construction of Peter Chistiakov, but the downfall of the Christian Community of Universal Brotherhood.

It began in 1937, when the Community went into bankruptcy, and it was consummated in 1938 when two major creditors, the National Trust and the Sun Life Assurance Company, won foreclosure proceedings that allowed them to issue eviction notices early in 1939. To the National

Trust was owed $168,283.13 in principal and interest, and to the Sun Life Assurance Company, $192,297.51; for a total debt of $360,580.64,[12] these two companies destroyed an undertaking whose assets were worth —even at the depreciated prices of 1938—between three and four million dollars and on which several thousand people depended for their living.

Whether the Community would have survived if this action had not been taken by these two creditors is not an easy question to answer. In some directions it was showing alarming symptoms of decay. Not only its membership but also its cash income was falling rapidly. Work became so scarce that the assessments on the working members had to be cut back year after year, while the proportion of unproductive old people steadily increased. During the five years from 1928 to 1932, the total assessments were $1,070,000 and they seem in the main to have been met. During the next five years, from 1933 to 1937, the assessments were only $344,000, less than a third of the total for the preceding period, yet even at this level they were beyond the resources of all the members and $69,000 was unpaid.[13] Even more catastrophic was the fall in the price of wheat and other produce. The Community also suffered greatly during the decade from fires of various kinds, some at least of which were set by Sons of Freedom arsonists. In terms of capital assets this meant a loss of $437,000 by 1938,[14] but more important to the economy of the Community was the loss of earning power, since the fires destroyed several sawmills and the big flour mill at Verigin. The lack of cash in its turn disrupted the balance of the Community economy, as it was now no longer possible to pay the freight charges on shipping produce between the fruit and timber areas of British Columbia and the wheatlands of the prairies.

Undoubtedly there was also considerable mismanagement. While Peter Chistiakov's mishandling of the Community funds has certainly been exaggerated by hostile writers, his erratic methods can hardly have been conducive to business efficiency. It is true that an élite of managers and clerks had arisen over the thirty years since the migration from the prairies to British Columbia, but the best of them left the Community for private business and the others worked under the capricious supervision of the leader, who was company president as well.

Considering all these circumstances, the actual record of the Community during Peter Chistiakov's reign was in some ways rather impressive. Even if his means of raising money were unorthodox and calculated to bring him a modicum of personal profit, Peter Chistiakov did pay off by 1938 some $704,243 of the debt of $1,202,000 that he inherited in 1927. He also paid $543,661 in interest and $301,949 in taxes. There was even an expansion of capital assets. New lands were purchased to the value of $161,839, buildings were erected to the value of $221,671, and $220,147 was spent on the clearing of land.[15] All this was achieved in a decade when only one full year (1928) lay outside the depression era. It hardly gives the impression of a moribund organization.

Yet by 1938 the Community was in fact barely clinging to life. The new buildings had been constructed and the land bought and cleared before the end of 1933; no new capital assets were acquired after that time. Most of the liquidation of debts took place during the same period. The steadily falling cash income from 1933 onwards would have made any further progress in this direction impossible. On the other hand, if the Community had been left unmolested until 1940, the wartime expansion of the economy might have saved it.

In the long run the Community probably suffered as much from Peter the Lordly's methods of deficit financing and ambitious expansion as from his son's extravagances. Peter Chistiakov realized the dangers that faced the Community because of its burden of debts, and in his own way he tried to stave off disaster. The situation would have been much different if, in 1929, the Community had carried only a manageable burden of debt; its varied economy might have enabled it to retreat into self-subsistence and sit out the depression with comparatively little reliance on cash income.

The dismantling of the Community had different results in the prairies and in British Columbia. In Alberta and Saskatchewan the creditors sold the lands to individual members of the Community on agreements for sale, and so created a new group of Independents. In British Columbia a receiver was appointed and the moveable assets of the Community were sold for cash. Money was still scarce in 1938, and the implements, machinery, lumber, etc., were sold at derisory prices. Machines were broken up and sold as scrap. Many non-Doukhobors were anxious to acquire the Doukhobor farms and orchards at similar knock-down prices, and early in 1939 Sun Life and the National Trust were about to start evicting the members of the Community preparatory to putting its properties up for auction.

Up to this time the provincial government had watched without interference the dismantling and dispersion of the Community's assets. When the courts refused protection against foreclosure under the Farmers' Creditors Arrangement Act, on the grounds that as a limited company the Community could not be considered a group of farmers, it took no emergency action. But once the foreclosure had been authorized and it was certain that the Community as a business concern was destroyed and stripped of all its property, the authorities acted to prevent the disorder that would arise if several thousand Doukhobors were evicted without resources. Before the eviction notices could go into effect, the government entered into negotiations with the National Trust and the Sun Life Assurance Company by which it acquired for $296,500 [16] the Doukhobor lands and buildings in the Kootenays and Grand Forks. The Community holdings, which were now the property of the province, were administered by the Land Settlement Board, and the former members were allowed to remain on payment of nominal rents. In this respect, their position did not differ greatly from what it had been in the final days of the Community, when they had to pay a fixed assessment; indeed, the Land Settlement Board was rather less strict in collecting rents than Peter the Purger had been in collecting assessments. But the whole business superstructure of the Community was destroyed, and most of its plant had been taken away, so that in effect its members were reduced to individual tenants without the capital or the machinery or the incentive to make proper use of land that they now inhabited on sufferance.

To the Doukhobors this situation seemed like a repetition of what had happened in the prairies in 1907. Again they had lost their lands, and again a government had played a significant part in the transaction. To them it appeared to be a plot between the authorities and the financiers, and even now they talk of the 'stealing' of their land. There is some justification in their resentment, for the timing of government intervention was significant. Had the $296,500 been offered to the Community as a loan before the foreclosures, it might have saved it from disaster; by waiting until the Community had been dispossessed, the government made sure that there would be no resurrection of a communitarian enterprise that was resented by politically powerful local interests. If the government did not kill the Community, it deliberately neglected to keep it alive.

The leader died with the Community. Since early in 1938 Peter Chistiakov's vitality had been declining; he had suffered from pains in the lungs which he tried vainly to dull with heavier drinking. Troubled by the situation of the Community, which he realized could not be saved by his efforts or those of his followers, he called a convention for 1 August to consider how the sect might be reorganized to survive under the new conditions. When the time arrived he was too ill to attend and went instead to Vancouver, where the doctors recommended an immediate operation.

He refused and returned to Brilliant where, in the middle of November, he conducted his last convention. At this convention the economic organization of the Christian Community of Universal Brotherhood officially came to an end and the Union of Spiritual Communities of Christ arose in its place. The USCC was based on common religious beliefs and formed of some thirty-seven communities in British Columbia and the prairies.

On New Year's Day Peter went to the hospital in Saskatoon, where three infected ribs were removed from his chest. He was nearer to death than even the doctors suspected. On 2 February he went back into hospital, and on 11 February he died of cancer of the liver and stomach that earlier had been mistakenly diagnosed as an ulcer. He died as he had lived, cursing his followers.

Few among the Independents mourned him, and probably nobody outside the Doukhobor sect; but his personal followers wept at his grave, and to this day one meets intelligent Community Doukhobors who, admitting all his faults, still defend him as a man of misjudged idealism. A man of contradictions he certainly was, and to understand him thoroughly one needs the insight with which a Dostoevsky could portray such a tempestuous and divided nature. Peter the Purger would have fitted splendidly into the world of the Karamazovs.

He was buried at Brilliant in the same tomb as his father, and six weeks later the assembled people elected his son, 35-year-old Peter Iastrebov (the Hawk), as their leader. But Peter Iastrebov was in Russia; no one knew where. Until he was found, another member of the Verigin dynasty was chosen to act as a kind of regent. This was Peter Chistiakov's eighteen-year-old grandson, John Voikin, who was born at Orlovka in the Wet Mountains and came to Canada to join his grandfather in 1928, when he assumed the name of John J. Verigin. As secretary of the USCC, John J. Verigin carried on many of the practical functions of leadership; but he was not yet recognized as possessing the charisma of the true leader, and for many years his followers' thoughts turned towards the distant Peter Iastrebov, the Hawk, silent behind the walls of Stalin's Russia.

13 THE SONS OF FREEDOM

The Second World War affected the Doukhobors far more profoundly than the preceding conflict had done, since its outbreak almost coincided with the collapse of the one organization that had provided them with a strong communal structure, based on the economic and social as well as the religious aspects of the Doukhobor faith. From the beginning, the Union of Spiritual Communities of Christ was a less ambitious organization than its predecessor, and it owed its survival during the first crucial years after the dissolution of the Christian Community of Universal Brotherhood mainly to the fact that many Doukhobors felt it prudent to pay the annual dues of twenty-five dollars as a safeguard against military callup. Thus, while the membership of the Christian Community had fallen in 1938 to 3,157, that of the USCC had by 1940 risen to 3,563.[1]

If the outbreak of the war helped to preserve the main Doukhobor organization, it also saved individual members of the sect from the acute distress that seemed about to engulf them when the liquidation of the Christian Community was completed. They had been left on their farm lands, but they had neither equipment nor working capital. Buildings, irrigation facilities, and orchards were all, by the end of the thirties, showing severe deterioration, for once the land passed out of their actual possession, the Doukhobors no longer felt any incentive to carry out the necessary maintenance.

Even the poorest of subsistence farming would thus have been difficult on the former Community lands, if the war had not offered alternative means of survival. From the end of 1939 the demand for unskilled and semi-skilled workers steadily grew, and the Doukhobors, whether they belonged to the USCC or the Sons of Freedom, found no difficulty in obtaining employment as sawmill hands, rough carpenters, or railroad maintenance workers. For those who preferred to work on their own, there was a steady demand for lumber in its various forms, and many Doukhobors who later became prosperous contractors started their business careers at this time. The attraction of outside employment drew almost all the Doukhobor men away from the fields and orchards, and in a few years one of the strongest traditions of the sect had been broken. Though they continued to pride themselves on being 'sons of the soil', and still do so on occasion, by the middle of the Second World War the Doukhobors had ceased to be peasants and were much more like a semi-rural proletariat. Only the meticulous and productive Doukhobor gardens, largely cultivated by women and children, remained as concrete survivals of the peasant past that still occupied so large a place in Doukhobor tradition.

Such a transition brought inevitable communal and personal stresses. Some gladly accepted the new situation as a liberation from the suffocating conformity of the old Community life. Others—particularly among the old people, the women, and the strongly religious—clung to the ideal of Doukhoborism as an exclusive, messianic religion, and fought against that assimilation into Canadian society which would become inevitable if they and their brethren accepted the values of the acquisitive environment into which their new employment pattern increasingly drew them.

If the war situation encouraged the breakup of accepted Doukhobor attitudes, it also strengthened by reaction both the traditionalist and the radical elements within the sect and united them into a growing resistance movement. In 1940 parliament passed the National Resources Mobilization Act, which required universal registration, as a prelude to conscription, and in 1943 this was followed by the Selective Service Act, which brought the principle of compulsion into all fields of employment. Some political leaders actually demanded the revocation of the Doukhobor exemption from military service. One of these was John Diefenbaker, who argued in 1943 that the exemption granted in 1898 referred only to the immigrants who had landed at that time and should not cover their descendants.[2]

Mackenzie King's government acted in the spirit of the pledge given in 1898, and it was left to the Doukhobors to choose whether or not they would enter the armed forces. A few did in fact volunteer, and among these a surprisingly high proportion were Sons of Freedom. For the remainder there was, under the National Mobilization Act, the possibility of non-combat service as conscientious objectors. But registration was obligatory for all residents of Canada; and it was on this initial step that many Doukhobors, with their ingrained distrust of regimentation, chose to refuse co-operation. Among those who declined to register in 1940 were members of the USCC and even a few Independents. But the most determined resistance came from the Sons of Freedom, to whom the initiative within the Doukhobor sect shifted with the death of Peter Chistiakov and the collapse of the Community. For the next twenty years a radical, activist minority was not only to shape the image of the Doukhobor in the Canadian mind, but also largely to determine the relations between the sect and the assimilationist society around it.

Until almost the end of Peter the Lordly's reign the constructive impetus of the Community and the dominating personality of the leader had left little room for the development of a strong or active radical movement. The original Sons of Freedom, with their abortive pilgrimages and their nude parades intended as manifestations of Adamite innocence rather than demonstrations of protest, had dwindled to a sprinkling of diehards who sought to re-establish the simplicity of Doukhobor existence. Their aims ran counter to those of Peter the Lordly, with his efforts at mechanization and business efficiency. Gradually their traditionalism led them to question the motives of the leaders. Even if they did not actually reject Peter the Lordly or, later, Peter Chistiakov, they assumed that the leaders' overt statements did not convey the real teachings of Doukhoborism, and the search for hidden meanings, the impulse to turn upside-down whatever they might be taught, led them to emphasize the anarchistic elements in their creed. They defied earthly government, but they did not accept their own theocratic government at its face value. This impatience with authority produced an intolerance of orderly patterns that left the Sons of Freedom for long periods without either leaders of their own or any formal organization. Their emphasis on the sudden inspiration, the spontaneous, unpremeditated act was in time to have dramatic consequences.

The zealots who kept the attitudes of the Sons of Freedom alive during the greater part of Peter the Lordly's reign were probably no more than a hundred in number, and their achievements were not spectacular, though one rather prophetic incident occurred shortly after Peter the Lordly had begun to transfer the Community from the prairies to British Columbia. While the leader was at Brilliant, Alex Makhortov, one of the heroes of the first nude march, led a score of chanting men and women to the big octagonal house Peter had built at Verigin. They set it on fire and then stripped off their clothes, threw them into the leaping flames, and stood singing hymns while the Community Doukhobors angrily whipped them and summoned the Royal Canadian Mounted Police. The motives of the act were clear. Verigin's house represented the material things of this world. By burning it, the Sons of Freedom were doing him a kindness, since they were divesting him of corrupting material possessions; but they themselves, in performing the act, were also symbolically renouncing wealth, and as a sign of this they threw the clothes they were wearing into the flames and stood in the nakedness of holy poverty.

In 1923 a significant change became evident in the tactics of the Sons of Freedom. This was a time of general discontent among Doukhobors; the Community was already in economic difficulties, austerity was the rule, and the education question had been aggravated by the government's distraints upon Doukhobor property. It was in these circumstances, as we have seen, that the first school in a Doukhobor region was burnt, and this was followed by other similar incidents until, in 1925, Peter Chistiakov's instructions from Russia led to an acceptance of the government's demands.

Though the incendiaries were singularly elusive, nobody has seriously doubted that the schools were burnt down by Sons of Freedom. The interesting aspects of this campaign are not merely its extensiveness—in effect it destroyed all schools accessible to Doukhobor children in British Columbia—but also the aims and methods of the arsonists.

Up to now the Sons of Freedom had been intent on converting their fellow Doukhobors to a more religious way of life by examples of renunciation—giving up the exploitation of animals, throwing away articles of leather or metal, undressing to display Adamite simplicity, or publicly destroying Doukhobor property to protest against the encroachments of materialism. In the case of the school burnings, the intent was quite different. It was one of protest and challenge against a seemingly hostile government. The burnings were, in their own way, acts of war, skirmishes in the long guerilla struggle that the Sons of Freedom were to carry on for the next forty years to halt the process of absorption into Canadian society. And, like men at war, the incendiaries inverted earlier Sons of Freedom methods by acting in complete and efficient secrecy.

From 1923 onwards the activity of the Sons of Freedom was to take several forms. Mass nude demonstrations expressed the solidarity of protest. The ritual burning of one's own house or that of another Doukhobor, accompanied by stripping and singing, still expressed renunciation of material things. Such actions were carried on openly and often provocatively, to court arrest and martyrdom. At the same time, a minority within the Sons of Freedom minority became dedicated to secret acts of destructiveness aimed at the property of Canadian government agencies, railway and power companies, and other organizations manifesting economic or political power, and also at the property of the Community Doukhobors. Such activity became known among the Sons of Freedom as 'black work', and, though it was carried out by individuals and small groups, there seems little doubt that it was approved by the movement in general and gave prestige to those who performed it.

The attitude of Doukhobor leaders to the Sons of Freedom has often been questioned. How far did Peter the Lordly and Peter Chistiakov in fact encourage them? There is no really convincing evidence that Peter the Lordly encouraged them at all, except fortuitously, before his arrival in Canada, through the publication of the letters that he had not intended for Doukhobor eyes. Subsequently he appears to have regarded them as an impediment to his work, and his willingness to have them beaten and imprisoned leaves little doubt that he was completely out of sympathy with them. During 1914, it is true, he allowed his officials to threaten nude parades in the Sons of Freedom manner, but nothing of the kind materialized, and when the schools were burnt he disowned the arsonists; there is no reason to suppose that he was insincere in this, since he obviously realized that if arson were encouraged, Community property would eventually suffer.

Peter Chistiakov is a more problematical case. When he arrived in Canada he flattered and encouraged the Sons of Freedom, calling them his 'ringing bells' and inventing for them the slogan that they have proudly brandished ever since, 'Sons of Freedom cannot be the slaves of corruption.' During the later 1950s certain Sons of Freedom terrorists claimed in their confessions that he had encouraged them and even commanded them in their 'black work', while in bitter polemics that took place at the same time between various factions among the Sons of Freedom his name was often used to justify the actions of both sides. This evidence, however, is highly suspect. The confessions, as we shall later

see, were made at times of mass emotionalism, when the Sons of Freedom were offering themselves for punishment under the influence of the
slogan 'migration through the prisons'. Whether or not Peter Chistiakov
could be construed as encouraging individual acts of terrorism depended
entirely on the interpretation placed on his words; once the 'upside-down'
manner of interpretation came into fashion, almost everything he said
might be given the meaning his hearers desired. The claims of the factions
are similarly suspect; groups of traditionalist Doukhobors would naturally seek to show that they had worked in accordance with the will of
the leader. Apart from such suspect statements, there is little to show that
Peter the Purger actually had any hand in the terrorist activities of the
Sons of Freedom. A residual doubt remains, however, inspired by the
character of the man rather than by any deeds he can be proved to have
performed or commanded. He was erratic, capable of supporting secretly
a mode of action of which he did not approve publicly, and there was a
strain of violence in his own actions that he might easily have projected
onto others. But even if we are to infer that he was a kind of Jekyll
and Hyde in his relationships with Canadian society, openly counselling
obedience to laws while secretly ordering his followers to destroy
schools and other government property, are we to assume that while he
made some effort to save the Community from bankruptcy, he also encouraged the arsonists who destroyed Community property and thus
weakened its economic position? In the lack of clearer evidence, we must
be content to accept Peter Chistiakov's public attitude. From 1929 onwards this led him to condemn the Sons of Freedom and to seek their
expulsion from the Doukhobor fold.

The differences between the Sons of Freedom and Peter Chistiakov became evident very shortly after his arrival in Canada. In 1928, after three
years of peace, the fires began to burn again in the Kootenays, and the
Sons of Freedom openly declared their opposition to compulsory education for Doukhobor children. In March a group of zealots at Grand
Forks wrote to the prime minister: 'We will make our children the
servants of Christ, but will not allow them to enter public schools which
could turn them into slaves of corruption.' In May seventy Sons of
Freedom paraded through the streets of Nelson, calling on the people to
prepare for the Second Coming, and Peter Maloff, at that time one of
their leaders, made a speech proclaiming that Canadian civilization was
the work of the Devil and the public schools were turning Doukhobor
children 'into the children of Satan'.[3]

In June the Sons of Freedom in Saskatchewan issued a manifesto to the Doukhobor sect that found a simple explanation for the succession of wars, revolutions, and other calamities that had been plaguing the world for the last half-generation.

The cause of all this is the SCHOOL *with its wrong orientation, thrusting sadism upon the youthful generation. Especially when a person partakes of higher education, or attends military academies, does he become a truly insane animal. Sometimes, through oversight on the part of a common soldier to salute a general or a lesser officer, the unfortunate is beaten half to death and oftentimes to death.*

The clergy, upon graduation from the institutes of higher learning, i.e. the universities, under the pretext of religion and fanaticism, inveigle the unwary, bless them in the churches and then send the young people off to war, to kill their own brothers and themselves in the name of their fatherland.

They called upon their brethren to avail themselves of 'an inner ticket, given freely to all and without reproach, to enter the abode of Our Father, and thusly save your children and yourselves'. The 'inner ticket', they explained, was their motto, 'Sons of Freedom cannot be the slaves of corruption.' [4]

By 1929 some of the Community Doukhobors were beginning to avail themselves of the inner ticket. Since Peter Chistiakov's arrival the Sons of Freedom had increased modestly, to about two hundred activists, but their influence grew to such an extent that in January 1929 the attendance at the schools in Grand Forks began to fall rapidly. The zealots demonstrated before the schools and went in to lead the children out. The police attempted to arrest the defaulting parents, and provoked a nude demonstration that was eventually dispersed by tear gas. As one of the participants was convicted, she shouted 'I find Magistrate Cantwell guilty!' 'I think I will let myself go,' replied the magistrate.[5]

Peter Chistiakov dissociated the Community from these disturbances, writing letters to the press condemning the 'dirty bandits and provocateurs'. This did not prevent the Sons of Freedom from issuing in March a further manifesto, studded with references to Tolstoy, Shaw, Tagore, and Gandhi. 'It was the same kind of government as the Canadian', they announced, 'that crucified Christ two thousand years ago.' [6]

The emotions of martyrdom were being whipped up, and on 29 June three of the schools that the Doukhobors had built in 1925 were burnt to the ground. Early in August three other schools went up in flames, together with the Community flour mill and warehouse at Grand Forks. Paul Vlasoff, a Sons of Freedom leader, was arrested and committed for trial. The Sons of Freedom threatened demonstrations, while Peter Verigin held a meeting in which he compared the zealots to 'the Black Hundreds of Tzarist Russia' and reiterated the threat that those convicted of crimes would be expelled from the Community.

It was a point of challenge, and the Sons of Freedom used it to reveal that a year of agitation had brought them recruits. Earlier, in July, 150 Sons of Freedom in Kamsack, Saskatchewan, had stripped in the streets and been dispersed by fire-hoses. A few weeks after, in Canora, thirty demonstrated nude. Then, during the last week in August, the zealots of British Columbia began to march down the Slocan Valley upon Nelson. At first there were only a hundred of them, and these were turned back on the edge of the city. They camped by the roadside, and soon their numbers grew to three hundred. On 29 August the provincial police went to the camp, accompanied by Peter Chistiakov, who tried to persuade the campers to withdraw to the nearest Community settlement. They refused and immediately began to strip; 104 of them were arrested and each was sentenced to six months' imprisonment. Eight children were among them; these found their way to the government industrial schools, where they passively resisted any attempts to educate them. By the time they were sent home on the release of their parents in February 1930, it was evident that this method of dealing with recalcitrant Doukhobor children could produce only negative results. During September 250 zealots engaged in further demonstrations in Saskatchewan, and altogether at least six hundred people manifested their adherence to the radicalism of the Sons of Freedom. At the same time Peter Chistiakov drew a clear line between the Doukhobor factions by insisting once again, in September, that those who took part in Sons of Freedom demonstrations would be rejected by the Community.

This threat was put into effect when the 104 imprisoned in 1929 were released. Homeless, they began to drift to those marginal lands that had been unsuitable for cultivation by the Community, and particularly to a dry plateau overlooking the Slocan Valley that was known as Krestova —the Place of the Cross. Peter the Lordly had built community houses there and installed pump-operated irrigation, but the system had never worked and the people of Krestova had always found difficulty in meeting their assessments and even in feeding themselves. Consequently, of all the Community Doukhobors they were the most inclined to discontent with the leadership, and they gave a welcome to the homeless Sons of

Freedom, who built their wretched shacks on this bleak upland at the edge of the Verigin domains. Krestova began its long career as an arsonists' sanctuary in 1930, when more schools and sawmills were burnt, and the first dynamiting since Peter the Lordly's death took place at the fireproof school that the government had built at Glade in the Kootenay Valley.

As the depression settled down over the Community, Peter Chistiakov extended the policy of expulsion to cover those who failed to pay their assessments. Many of these drifted into the Doukhobor Alsatia of Krestova, and the Purger eventually recognized the fact by withdrawing all the Community Doukhobors in good standing and leaving the plateau to those who could not fit into the Community but were too set in their extremism to be absorbed into Canadian society.

In Krestova a new kind of life began to emerge, revolving around minor and temporary leaders, like the autodidactic intellectual, Peter Maloff, or the eccentric Louis Popoff, the self-styled Tsar of Heaven who on occasion paraded in a white robe with a crown of ripe oranges upon his head. There were others, deliberately more obscure, who engaged in the 'black work' with matches and kerosene or with home-made infernal machines of stumper's dynamite. Most of the inhabitants lived by cultivating their small gardens and by a little casual work. The men in particular had much time on their hands, now that they were no longer working for the Community, and this was spent in long discussions on the state of the world and the role of the Doukhobors as its spiritual saviours. Like the poor at all times in Doukhobor history, the people at Krestova were not only the most pietistic but also the most fundamentalist of Doukhobors. Among them the ceremonial life of sobraniia and psalm-singing was richer than elsewhere, and they developed the strongest resistance to any concession to the materialism of non-Doukhobor life. In fact, the more fanatical of the Sons of Freedom were willing to attack such concessions wherever they found them, and on 24 April 1931 they dynamited, for the first of many times, the pompous marble edifice that covered the tomb of Peter the Lordly.

The growing activity on the part of the Sons of Freedom aroused the Canadian authorities to punitive action. The federal government had stood somewhat aloof from the Doukhobor question after the seizure of the prairie lands in 1907; now, in 1931, it decided to take a direct hand by securing an amendment to the Criminal Code that provided a mandatory penalty of three years' imprisonment for nudity in a public place. Such a savage penalty, for what is at most a minor peccadillo, was a startling revelation of the strength of Canadian prudery, particularly

when one considers that the maximum penalty for an intentionally indecent act remained at six months' imprisonment. But it was not merely
a question of prudery. To make Doukhobor offenders serve in federal
penitentiaries, where convicts with sentences of more than two years
are sent, was the only way in which the Dominion government could
share the task of the provinces and show a united front of official opposition to Sons of Freedom activities.

As a deterrent, the new penalty proved useless. The Sons of Freedom
were not ordinary peace-breakers. They were religious fanatics thirsting
for martyrdom, and less than a year after the new legislation had
appeared on the statute books there were greater nude demonstrations
than ever before. They began on 1 May 1932. It was the time of Peter
Chistiakov's imprisonment for perjury, but this, it appears, was coinci-
dental; those who took part in the demonstrations claimed—and still
claim—that they were protesting against the evictions from the Community. 'It was a protest', one participant told Koozma Tarasoff, 'against
land ownership and all ownership, against Caesar's injustice that he has
taken the whole cosmic property into his own hands.' [7]

The first group of 117 men and women gathered in Thrums, in the
Kootenay valley, and were arrested marching nude along the highway
towards Nelson. A mass trial followed; all were sentenced to three years
in prison. This merely encouraged their brethren, and Sunday after
Sunday further contingents of the Sons of Freedom converged upon
Thrums. On 8 May, 209 were arrested, including children as well as
adults. Further mass parades took place on 15 and 24 May. By the
end of the month 745 men, women, and children were living in an improvised detention camp of tents and makeshift buildings within a
barbed-wire enclosure at Nelson. Smaller demonstrations continued
until almost the end of June, and in all some six hundred adults were
sentenced to the mandatory term of three years' imprisonment. In
addition, 365 children had been arrested or were left uncared for when
their parents were sentenced. The total of almost a thousand shows how
rapidly the movement had increased in the hothouse of discontent
created by economic distress and by Peter Chistiakov's growing failure
to lead and inspire the Doukhobors in British Columbia.

The authorities put on a brave front. R. H. Pooley, the attorney general,
went into the Kootenays and threatened to arrest *five or six thousand*
Doukhobors if necessary; he is said to have fled in consternation when
a mere six Daughters of Freedom pulled ingeniously contrived draw-

strings on their garments so that all at once they stood before him in their sturdy nakedness.

The federal penitentiary at New Westminster would not hold even the mere six hundred new prisoners, and it was decided to establish a special penal colony for the Sons of Freedom. Deserted Piers Island, in Haro Strait, two miles off the nearest tip of Vancouver Island, was chosen as the site, and workmen were sent out to build two enclosures, one for each sex, with barbed-wire fences twenty feet high and tarpaper-covered buildings. In November the first prisoners arrived. The camp was run by the deputy warden of the penitentiary at New Westminster and staffed by temporary guards and wardresses hired rather indiscriminately on Vancouver Island. No rehabilitative treatment at all was attempted during the 2½ years the prisoners remained on the island, and their worst affliction was undoubtedly the boredom of inactive days. The only work they were expected to perform was to prepare their own food and mend their clothes. At first they refused; but when they found that nobody else would cook for them, most of them shared in the normal tasks of the camp. Only about thirty obstinate passive resisters consistently refused to work. The Piers Island prison camp was closed early in 1935, when the majority of the prisoners were released.

The expedient of Piers Island was successful as a means of temporarily removing the Sons of Freedom from the environment of the Kootenays, where their activities had further angered their neighbours and provoked new threats of vigilante action, but their attitudes were unchanged; in fact, their resolve to disobey the state was enhanced by a consciousness of martyrdom achieved at comparatively little personal discomfort, and a further chapter of grievance was added to the living book of their complaints against Canadian society.

Most of the adults bore their imprisonment with a rather stolid sang-froid and emerged little harmed by the experience. The same could not be said of their 365 children, who spent their first year away from home either in orphanages or, in the case of almost half of them, in industrial schools intended for delinquent children. The action of the provincial government in seizing them was of dubious legality, since it was based neither on parental consent nor on court orders. Furthermore, the children were removed from the peculiar warmth and closeness of the Doukhobor family to the coldness of impersonal institutions where they thought of themselves as prisoners, and an abiding resentment was built up. From among the boys who were immured in the Provincial Industrial School came many of the post-war generation of arsonists and dynamiters. By the spring of 1933 the stringencies of depression finances led to a change in government policy. The children were taken away from the institutions and, again without the consent of their parents, placed in the care of Community and Independent Doukhobors. By this time the emotional damage had already been done.

Adults and children alike, the Sons of Freedom who were liberated and reunited in 1935 found themselves homeless and unwanted, for Peter Chistiakov had forbidden their return to the Community. Those from the Kootenay and Slocan valleys gravitated to Krestova, where a thousand people now tried to gain a living from the arid, ungrateful soil. Others, who had lived originally in the Kettle Valley, were put off the train at Grand Forks and herded by the police to a piece of government-owned waste land on a cliff overlooking the Kettle River. Here they built their huts and started to dig their geometrically precise gardens beside the tracks of the Great Northern Railway. The village became know as Gilpin, deriving its incongruous name from the railway halt on the other bank of the river. Living henceforward in their own villages, the Sons of Freedom steadily grew farther apart from their Community brethren.

This did not prevent the two groups from being confused in the public mind, and newspaper accounts of the burnings that in 1936 followed the return of the Piers Island prisoners usually attributed them to 'the Douks' without any qualifying epithet. As the toll of depredations rose (by the end of 1937 it had reached 153), politicians became increasingly prone to blame the whole sect for the deeds of a minority. In November 1937 a Liberal member of the British Columbia legislature came forward with a proposal strangely reminiscent of tsarist methods. The sectarians should all be sent to the Peace River in the far north of the province. There they should be confined to their own settlements and debarred from cutting timber on government lands or from operating businesses. Such proposals led Peter Chistiakov to suspect that a further attempt might soon be made to deport him, and in his turn he became more vehement than ever in his denunciation of the Sons of Freedom, publicly demanding stronger government action and declaring that he feared for his own life.

As the Community collapsed in 1938 and 1939, the activity of the Sons of Freedom diminished. Now that their brethren were dispossessed, landless, propertyless, they appeared to feel that their own violent protests were less necessary. Arson and dynamiting almost disappeared during the first four years of hostilities and during the whole six years of war there were only 44 incidents, as against 118 in the two years

(1946 and 1947) immediately after peace was declared. The horror at the actuality of war seemed to enhance the pacifistic as opposed to the nihilistic element in the philosophy of the Sons of Freedom.

During the First World War the Doukhobor movement had been disunited by Peter the Lordly's campaign against the Independents. During the Second World War the process was reversed; the bitterly divided factions of the depression years drew together under the pressure of outside hostility. Wartime circumstances not only consolidated the newly born Union of Spiritual Communities of Christ; they also brought about a *rapprochement* between the USCC and the Society of Independent Doukhobors, so that during the war these organizations issued joint manifestos. In 1945 they came together to form the Union of Doukhobors of Canada, with an initial membership of eight thousand.

This unity among Doukhobors, into which even the Sons of Freedom were accepted, did not long outlast the war. Soon afterwards the USCC withdrew from the Union of Doukhobors, which in turn expelled the Sons of Freedom. Yet, while it lasted, the urge to unity was genuine and effective. The Independents withdrew their support from the CCF, which backed the Canadian war effort, and returned to the traditional non-political attitude of the Doukhobors; the members of the USCC refused to be tempted by government offers to sell their land back to them in individual lots on favourable terms, and in this way reaffirmed their adherence to Peter the Lordly's communitarian ideals. It was a time when old Doukhobor ideals were revived, and in no way more strongly than in the growing resistance to those moves of the government that the members of the sect interpreted as leading to conscription.

Most Doukhobors were willing to accept the national registration of 1940. It did not, after all, go far beyond the registration of vital statistics and the census enumerations, which all but Sons of Freedom had been accepting ever since the accession of Peter Chistiakov. Some of the Sons of Freedom were arrested and imprisoned for failing to register, and resistance was carried a stage further when the government tried to implement the provisions of the conscription laws requiring that conscientious objectors of military age should perform alternative service. In practice this was attempted, so far as the Doukhobors were concerned, only in Saskatchewan; and there it provoked strong resistance among Independent and Community Doukhobors as well as among the Sons of Freedom. At the Lac La Ronge road-building project, especially designed for Doukhobors, only seventy members of the sect put in an appearance, while ninety-two were imprisoned for refusing to report; the experiment was abandoned after one season.

Resistance became almost universal when the Selective Service program was implemented at the end of 1943. This meant nearly complete industrial as well as military regimentation, for the authorities were given power to direct almost any individual to any job. Efforts were made to get the Doukhobors to accept the scheme. In November their leaders met with government representatives in Ottawa and failed to reach agreement. Then, on 12 December, Major J. N. Bowell and another officer of the local military command visited Brilliant to present an ultimatum. Three thousand five hundred Doukhobors gathered to meet them. The affair was finely stage-managed. As Bowell was about to begin his speech, the crowd parted and the astonishing figure of twenty-two-year-old John J. Verigin appeared, clad immaculately in morning coat and striped pants, with a flower in his buttonhole. 'The answer of the Doukhobors', he said in clearly enunciated tones, 'is No!' And the crowd shouted in chorus. As Bowell ruefully admitted on his return to Vancouver, 'Thirty-five hundred people make a NO sound pretty loud!'[8] The Sons of Freedom took it upon themselves to underscore the negative answer; that night the jam factory at Brilliant, once the glory of the Christian Community and now government-owned property, sent its flames leaping high into the winter sky.

The meeting at Brilliant and its aftermath served as a warning which the government heeded. From that time little pressure was applied to make the Doukhobors keep to the letter of the Selective Service regulations. The officials turned a blind eye to the many sawmills that employed Doukhobor labour, and behaved as tactfully as possible in order to avert repetitions of incidents like the strike of 650 Doukhobor carpenters and labourers who, in 1943, walked off the Brilliant dam project, which was of vital importance to provide hydro-electric power for the metalworks lower down the Columbia valley at Trail. By that time the interior valleys of British Columbia had become so stripped of manpower that Doukhobor labour played a vital part in keeping the local economy alive.

The burning of the jam factory was also the beginning of a new wave of direct action by Sons of Freedom. It was followed, in January 1944, by demonstrations at Krestova in which women's clothes and jewellery were burnt as symbols of the vanity of modern civilization. At the end of the month, John J. Verigin's house at Brilliant was burnt. Next, the schools in the Sons of Freedom settlements at Krestova and Gilpin were destroyed, as well as the CPR station at Appledale. In February the Sons of Freedom began wandering through the Doukhobor villages col- lecting registration and ration cards and Bibles to feed ritual bonfires. In April the spring's activities rose to a crescendo, with nude parades in Nelson and an invasion of Vancouver by twenty-five enthusiasts who preached in Stanley Park against the war and on 7 May climaxed their campaign by stripping before a large crowd. Sixteen were arrested; in the magistrate's court, as they were being sentenced, six of their com- panions started to strip. They in turn were brought up for sentencing. One woman flourished before the magistrate the picture of a nude woman torn from a girlie magazine. 'What did she get?' she asked. 'She didn't appear before me,' said the magistrate. Looking at the photograph, he added, 'She should have received life!' If the magistrate was joking, Attorney General Maitland was in dead earnest when, in the same month, he called for whipping as an added punishment for those convicted of disrobing in public.

On the surface the outburst of Sons of Freedom activity in early 1944 appeared to be a wave of protest against government action in attempt- ing to impose Selective Service. In fact, its motivations were a great deal more complicated. Four years of wartime employment, with no need to turn their wages in to a central fund, had made Community Doukhobors and even Sons of Freedom a great deal more prosperous individually than they had ever been before. Their standard of living rose; they began to desire and often to attain the material benefits enjoyed by their non-Doukhobor neighbours. The old Community houses were divided up, and the individual homes that resulted were at least a little less austere than the bare rooms of Peter the Lordly's days. The younger women began to visit hairdressers, to wear high-heeled shoes, to pay some attention to fashion. Above all, Doukhobors became addicted to the automobile, and every man who could possibly afford it—even among the Sons of Free- dom—bought a car or a pickup truck. This tendency to compromise with the values of a materialistic society led the Sons of Freedom to believe that their brethren were indeed becoming 'slaves of corruption', and the series of outbreaks that followed each other every few years, from 1944 to the last important acts of arson and dynamiting in 1962, can be interpreted not merely as protests against the activities of the state, but even more as battles against the tendency towards assimilation among the Doukhobors themselves.

A further complication was introduced by the bitter struggle for leadership that began in 1944 and whose repercussions continued to disturb the movement for almost twenty years. Until 1938 the Sons of Freedom had at least nominally accepted the leadership of the Verigins. Immediately after Peter Chistiakov's death, the figures who rose to prominence among the zealots were spokesmen rather than leaders in the traditional sense. Of them, Peter Maloff, later a Doukhobor historian, found his intellectualism dividing him from the obscurantism of the more traditional Sons of Freedom, and in 1940 he parted with them completely and became an Independent. Louis Popoff was too eccentric even for the Sons of Freedom to accept him in the role of Paul, Tsar of Heaven, which he claimed; he was arrested in April 1944 for appearing in Nelson garbed only in his crown of oranges, and shortly afterwards he died mysteriously in prison.

By the early 1940s it was evident that a power vacuum existed within the sect. Peter Iastrebov, the acclaimed leader, was lost in the *terra incognita* of Stalin's Russia, and though the Community Doukhobors accepted John J. Verigin as a substitute, he was much too colourless a figure for the tastes of the Sons of Freedom. The first person who attempted to move into the vacant seat of power was John L. Lebedoff, a farmer from Saskatchewan who enjoyed a certain reflected glory as the descendant of Matvei Lebedev, the first Doukhobor soldier to obey Peter Verigin's call to refuse military service in Russia in 1893. After the death of Peter Chistiakov, John Lebedoff moved to Krestova, where he stirred the imagination of the Sons of Freedom by declaring mysteriously that he had a message from 'the Master', whom everyone assumed to be the missing Peter Iastrebov. Lebedoff, a lean, gaunt, untidy little man, made a special appeal to the women of Krestova, and surrounded himself with courts of sturdy female companions.

Very soon, however, his domination over the dreary little Rome of Krestova was challenged by a rival who could claim authentic Verigin blood. This was another Saskatchewan farmer, named Michael Orekoff, third cousin of Peter the Lordly in the female line of the dynasty. Orekoff, regarded as an Independent, seemed to move out of Doukhobor circles during the 1930s, when he left the prairies and set up in Vancouver as a boarding-house keeper. An obese, gross-looking man, he had none of the handsomeness of the two Peters to whom he was related; but he had a vein of shrewdness that he had used in his business affairs, and he possessed a fertile and plausible imagination.

Orekoff had claimed since boyhood to be a visionary. Long ago in Russia, he said, the Archangel Michael had appeared to him, and for this claim he himself became known as 'Michael the Archangel', a title whose connotations he subtly changed until it suggested that in him the Archangel was actually incarnate, as Christ was incarnate in other members of his clan.

By 1940 he had assumed the prestigious name of Verigin, and on 11 February of that year he appeared at Brilliant and laid claim, before a large assemblage of Community Doukhobors, to have received special messages from Peter Chistiakov and even from God the Father. According to Michael, among other instructions given by the Purger prior to his death was the order that henceforward the affairs of the Community must be managed by a triumvirate led by the Archangel himself. God, whom he met face to face, had revealed that he had three sons—and three sons only—Jesus Christ, Peter the Lordly, and Peter Chistiakov. The first was crucified on the earth; the second died on the air into which the bomb had thrown him; the third died by water, in the sea of human wickedness. The Doukhobors themselves, by their failings, had helped to destroy their holy leaders. The implication of all this was that if they followed the will of God, as relayed to them by 'Michael the Archangel', they might yet atone for their wickedness.

The Community Doukhobors paid no attention to the new prophet. John J. Verigin's direct descent from both Peter the Lordly and Peter Chistiakov impressed them more than Michael's revelations. But the Archangel's brand of visionary prophecy appealed strongly to the Sons of Freedom. He maintained close contact with them, and in January 1944 appeared in Krestova as a serious contender for leadership.

Michael the Archangel was a chiliast who brought back into Doukhobor discussions the idea of the approaching millenium. He taught that the Second Coming was near at hand, and having—like the Doukhobor leaders of old—appointed twenty-four elders, he proceeded to teach the return to religious communism, the breaking up of possession, not only of goods but also of persons. The time had come to end that atrocious manifestation of property relationships known as marriage. Michael also called for a suspension of the 'black work' and declared that indiscriminate nakedness must come to an end; nudity should be used for religious purposes, he maintained, and his enemies accused him of strange mate-rotating celebrations in the name of God. He was in favour of education, provided it was Christian, and he set up a school in Krestova. He also established a store there, and, with a curious disregard for his own teachings about 'mine and thine', made himself its proprietor.

At first Michael's teachings of the close proximity of the kingdom of God were attractive to the people of Krestova. He enjoyed a brief ascendancy. Opposed to him were the hard core of Lebedoff's followers, and also those radical terrorists who, except for a nominal allegiance to the absent Iastrebov, acknowledged no leader. These extremists began to destroy the houses of Michael Verigin's supporters, and, whether by design or accident, a woman follower named Mary Nazarov was burned to death when kerosene was spilt on her dress as her house was exploding into flames. The Archangel's store, an offense in fanatical eyes, was also burnt, and he and his very much reduced following were forced to move a mile away to Goose Creek. There Michael's enemies followed him and in broad daylight burnt all the buildings down and stripped the struggling Archangel to the skin. In June 1946, with his voluble lieutenant Joe Podovinikoff, he abandoned the Kootenays for Vancouver Island. There, in the wide, beautiful valley at Hilliers, a little way inland from the seaside resort of Qualicum Beach, they came to a spot revealed to Michael in a dream, and bought the land for the community in which they would await the Second Coming. It was the westernmost point of Doukhobor emigration.

When one of the writers of this book visited Hilliers in 1949, about a hundred people were gathered there, living in two old farmhouses and in a little hamlet of cedar-wood huts, with the usual neat gardens, fields of corn and tomatoes, and some cattle. Total communism had been reestablished, and, theoretically at least, marriage had been brought to an end, but the indiscriminate promiscuity that the shocked inhabitants of nearby Victoria envisaged did not in fact take place. Like Peter the Lordly before him, Michael the Archangel had declared that until the community was properly established sexual intercourse must lapse. This presented no great difficulty, for the greater part of the Community consisted of old people and children, with very few men of working age. (This incidentally made it a poor economic undertaking from the beginning.) One woman who gave birth at this time was punished by ostracism, but the child was nevertheless accepted as the son of the Community in general and, in an open-air ceremonial, was incorporated into the sectarian hierarchy by being christened Gabriel the Archangel. This little community, preached Michael the Archangel, would become the site of the New Jerusalem; the hundred and forty-four thousand of the elect mentioned in the Book of Revelation would be drawn there by occult forces. Michael the Archangel, in other words, came after the era of the Christs and was the herald of the direct reign of God on earth.[9]

Meanwhile, in the Kootenays his admonitions against the 'black work' went unheeded. From April to August, 1947, the terrorists were on the rampage, burning schools and attempting to dynamite the suspension bridge at Brilliant, but concentrating their attention mostly on Doukhobor property. That year the Union of Spiritual Communities of Christ took a step back towards communitarian organization by establishing the Sunshine Valley Consumers' Co-operative at Grand Forks. During the summer the building was destroyed, as were brick community houses up and down the Kootenays, together with many of the shacks at Gilpin and the house of John Lebedoff at Krestova. Feeling ran high in the region, among Community Doukhobors and non-Doukhobors alike. The USCC and the Union of Doukhobors of Canada issued statements condemning the Sons of Freedom, as did Michael the Archangel in Hilliers. On 21 August John J. Verigin publicly asked for police protection for his followers, and on 25 August he demanded the removal of the Sons of Freedom from the Kootenays. Non-Doukhobors began to talk of direct action, and on one occasion a group of men from Castlegar organized a march through the Doukhobor settlement at Brilliant as a warning that they might form vigilante groups in the future.

Finally, on 12 September 1947, the government of British Columbia appointed Judge Harry Sullivan as a one-man commission to inquire into the cause of the disturbances in the Doukhobor settlements and to recommend remedial measures. The hearings began on 14 October, with the lawyer for the USCC presenting a brief that stressed the need for security. It argued that until security was actually established in Doukhobor villages, the members of the former community could not go ahead with any plans for buying back their lands. But the peaceful majority of the Doukhobors played a very small part in the remainder of the hearings. They were disinclined to give evidence against their wayward brethren of the Sons of Freedom, perhaps from fear, perhaps from a feeling that their opposition to earthly government might be compromised if they actively supported the forces of the state.

The Sons of Freedom were eager to talk, and Judge Sullivan's hearings began an epidemic of true and false confessions, of accusations and counter-accusations, that brought an atmosphere of pseudo-religious hysteria into the courtrooms of the interior of British Columbia lasting more than a decade. One of the leading terrorists, Peter Swetlisoff, led the chorus before Judge Sullivan by publicly confessing to participation in twenty-five acts of depredation, either individually or with small groups of accomplices, including the destruction of the Brilliant jam factory in 1943. Florence Lebedoff submitted a list of 364 individuals who had taken part in acts of violence. And witness after witness from

Krestova and Gilpin accused Michael Verigin of having ordered the deeds of violence. The Archangel denied all the charges, and at least one outside observer, the reporter for the *Vancouver Daily Province*, thought he was being deliberately framed. The mainland Sons of Freedom, he reported, were trying to get Michael imprisoned so that the scandal would bring about a general deportation of the sect to Russia.[10]

After wrangling for days on end with the Sons of Freedom over conflicting views of the rights of governments, Judge Sullivan finally adjourned his hearings in exasperation, concluding that the depredations of the Sons of Freedom were the acts of lunatics and criminals, and recommending drastic penal action against them.

The accusations against Michael Verigin had a delayed effect; not until 1950 were he and Joe Podovinikoff arrested on Vancouver Island and taken to Nelson to face charges of 'seditious conspiracy' to promote burnings, dynamitings, and public nudity. Shortly afterwards the same charge was levelled against Michael's great rival, John Lebedoff. All three were found guilty and sentenced to long terms of imprisonment, but Lebedoff's sentence was drastically reduced, and Verigin and Podovinikoff were released when the Court of Appeals ordered a retrial on the grounds that the judge had failed to instruct the jury properly on the fact that the witnesses were self-confessed accomplices whose evidence had not been corroborated. The Archangel died in 1951. The case against Joe Podovinikoff was so insubstantial that in the end the Crown entered a stay of proceedings.

How far these Sons of Freedom leaders were directly responsible for the burnings and dynamitings that took place at this period, and how far anything in the nature of an organized conspiracy existed among the zealots, have been questions of debate. Certain police officers and crime reporters believe that such a conspiracy, directed by successive leaders since Peter Chistiakov, did in fact exist, and that in its existence lay all the explanation of Sons of Freedom depredations, including such public activities as nude parades. It is significant, however, that the attempts of the Crown to prove the existence of a conspiracy have regularly failed.

In our view, the theory of an organized and enduring terrorist conspiracy, lasting over many years and involving all the 2,500 people who by the 1950s formed the Sons of Freedom movement, stems from the attempts by police officers and lawyers to impose a convenient logical structure on an illogical situation. The erratic nature of Sons of Freedom activity, the waves of depredations followed by periods of calm, the bitter internal feuds, the surges of mass emotion that can equally well bring about floods of confessions or sudden protest marches, all suggest a group fighting against logical organization, which is an attribute of the world they hate. Sons of Freedom leaders may have been able to cultivate certain climates of feeling within their group, but there is no real evidence that they are responsible for every action of every follower. If one ignores the confessions of the arsonists and looks at the actions themselves as described in court hearings, it is evident that in most cases the acts have been plotted and carried out by small groups, or even by individuals, acting autonomously. In discussions with members of the USCC, who were nearer to the problem than most outsiders, yet strongly critical of Sons of Freedom methods, we found a general agreement that the idea of an organized terrorist conspiracy was entirely false. They divided Sons of Freedom acts into two classes. There were the acts of mass protest, with hundreds of people involved, such as nude parades and burnings of their own houses. But there were also the terrorist acts, the 'black work', perpetrated by gangs of youngish men driven into tense psychological states by the atmosphere of fanatical communities like Krestova and Gilpin, by traditional winter idleness, and by an enduring sense of grievance—all complicated by competitiveness between gangs. In other words, Sons of Freedom violence has been a product of alienation, and, like the violence of city youth, it is inclined to be unplanned in its manifestations.

Only one leader succeeded for a period in giving a semblance of organization to the Sons of Freedom movement. He was Stefan Sorokin, who was not a Doukhobor. He was a former member of the Russian Orthodox Church who had fled from his homeland in 1929 and had spent twenty years wandering over Asia Minor and Europe, shifting allegiance from the Plymouth Brethren to the Lutherans, from the Baptists to the Seventh Day Adventists. He entered Canada as a displaced person on 26 March 1949, and after a few months proceeded to the Doukhobor regions of Saskatchewan. He had already read about the sect and his curiosity about them may well have been genuine. Nevertheless, in this as in all his earlier enterprises, the elements of power and material gain entered. He liked to dominate people; he liked also to live comfortably.

Among the Independent Doukhobors in Saskatchewan he gathered information, learnt some of the Doukhobor psalms, and enjoyed the hospitality that would have been given to any stranger speaking the Russian language. But he did not find any greater encouragement, and as spring broke he travelled over the mountains, arriving in Grand Forks on 7 April, a striking figure with his long black beard and hair, his flashing Svengali eyes, and the harp, designed by himself, to which he would sing in a deep, harmonious voice. By now his plan was formed. He had heard of Peter Iastrebov, and, while he never claimed explicitly to be the lost Doukhobor leader, he hinted expressively at the possibility. His hints did not impress the Community Doukhobors, whom he joined in their Easter Youth Festival, but they did interest John Lebedoff, who happened to visit Grand Forks at the time.

After Michael the Archangel departed in 1946, Lebedoff had regained his influence in Krestova and consolidated it by the tried method of starting a migration myth. In January he founded the first abortive formal organization among the Sons of Freedom, which he called Spiritual Communities of Christ. He himself was the divinely appointed chairman of the Interim Committee, which was to lead the people to that new home for which the Doukhobors had always longed. Though John J. Verigin mocked Lebedoff's schemes, thirteen hundred Sons of Freedom expressed their willingness to depart, and Lebedoff with his wife Florence set off to Ottawa to make inquiries. They thought of Turkey, a country that had exercised a certain fascination over the Doukhobors in the preceding centuries, and, of course, of the Soviet Union. But, though the Canadian authorities expressed their eagerness to help the Sons of Freedom depart, neither the Turks nor the Soviet authorities showed any readiness to accept the aspiring immigrants. The scheme appeared to be foundering, and Lebedoff's authority with it. The arrival of the mysterious bearded stranger seemed a godsend. If the Sons of Freedom accepted him, perhaps Lebedoff might still rule, as the Grey Eminence of Krestova.

Lebedoff was a successful king-maker, but, like many who pursue that role, he gained little advantage from it. Sorokin had no intention of becoming a puppet. He charmed the Sons of Freedom with his singing and intrigued them by the mysterious possibilities that were suggested by his carefully learnt fragments of Doukhobor lore. To many of them it seemed that Peter Iastrebov, the Hawk, had indeed arrived; and when Sorokin denied in public that he was or claimed to be the lost leader, they were inclined to accept this as an answer intended merely to hoodwink the authorities. Certainly, whether or not Sorokin actually posed among his followers as the third Peter Verigin, he assumed the position and prerogatives of a traditional Doukhobor leader. Lebedoff went to prison in July 1950 and did not emerge until 1952. Sorokin used the providential interim to consolidate his power, and only a tiny minority among the Sons of Freedom did not accept his dominance.

He had arrived at the peak of a new outbreak of Sons of Freedom activity. Stimulated by Lebedoff's migration projects, the people of Krestova were impatient to depart; and when John J. Verigin spoke contemptuously of the scheme in public, a band of them went down to Brilliant to burn his home once again. This time there was no secrecy. They waited until the police arrived to arrest them. The arrests were the signal for the people of Krestova to start burning their own houses; nude and chanting, they watched the wretched huts collapsing into the flames. In the subsequent roundup, four hundred people—most of them men—were arrested on charges of arson or nudity, and eventually they reached the penitentiary at New Westminster.

Like Michael the Archangel, Sorokin preached an end to the 'black work'. He toured the Freedomite settlements, joined the Doukhobor Consultative Committee that the provincial government set up in 1950, and visited Sons of Freedom prisoners in Nelson jail and in the penitentiary. By August the imprisoned arsonists had accepted him as their leader, and the people back in the villages followed suit. Imitating Lebedoff's example, Sorokin set up a committee (which later became the Fraternal Council) to manage the affairs of the group, and he persuaded his followers to give themselves yet another of those resounding and wordy titles to which Doukhobors are prone: Christian Community and Brotherhood of Reformed Doukhobors (Sons of Freedom).

When, as a result of the recommendations of the Doukhobor Consultative Committee (to which we shall return), some 395 arsonists were released on a mass amnesty, leaving only a hard core of a few dozen intransigents, Sorokin claimed the credit, and some of it at least he deserved, for if he had not persuaded them to sign pledges of good behaviour, the amnesty would have been impossible. A few extremists objected to this solution, and a few fires were set after the prisoners returned, presumably in an attempt on the part of a small minority to discredit Sorokin with the authorities, to whom he presented himself as a man of peace. But in general his popularity increased. When one of the writers stayed in the Sons of Freedom village of Gilpin in the winter of 1950–1, shortly after the amnesty, all its inhabitants were full of praise for Sorokin, whose photographs decorated the walls of their austere cabins; the young men who had just been released from prison seemed the most devoted of all.

Sorokin did not value his services lightly. The photographs that hung in his followers' cabins were sold to them at a profit. They also built him a cottage, bought him a car, and in general kept him in the style appropriate to a Doukhobor leader.

In the end, like other leaders before him, he struck that never-failing bonanza, the migration scheme. A plan to relocate the Sons of Freedom in a remote part of British Columbia had been one of the proposals of the Doukhobor Research Committee in 1950, and it was in this connection that Sorokin began to charm from his people the savings put aside from their summers of logging and fruit-picking. (Latter-day Sons of Freedom, unlike their predecessors in 1902, do not include money among the objects of renunciation.) When the scheme for resettlement in Canada failed, Sorokin proposed a migration to South America. In February 1952 he left via the United States for Uruguay, ostensibly to find land for his followers. With him he took the money he had collected; the amount has been variously estimated, but accounts agree that it was more than ninety thousand dollars. In July he came back to Canada and, according to his followers, returned the funds collected for migration. In October he went again to Uruguay. No land was located, except that which Sorokin, a poor man when he first reached Canada, bought for himself in the environs of Montevideo. There he settled down to live prosperously; his followers did not deny that the gifts they sent allowed him to do so. His case seems to be very similar to that of Peter Chistiakov. He did not defraud his followers in a legal sense; he merely took advantage of their traditions, which instructed them to give to a chosen leader so that he could live in lordly style. He had enough moral elasticity to do so without any perceptible qualms of conscience.

Hardly had Sorokin departed than the pillars of flame and smoke began to rise again towards the skies of the Kootenays. The terrorists were free from a leader's restraint, and more houses were to burn in 1953 than in any year before.

14 THE DOUKHOBORS TODAY

To anyone observing the Doukhobor situation in 1950, or even in 1960, any lasting peace between the more radical members of the sect and the rest of Canadian society seemed remote. In 1950 the most extensive of the Sons of Freedom demonstrations of protest against assimilation were still in the future; even in 1960 one could look forward to more sensational acts of terrorism than had taken place ever before, and to the great march of 1962, when the inhabitants of Krestova and Gilpin travelled to the coastal metropolis of Vancouver to bare their grievances to the world at large.

No one at that time realized that the march on the coast marked the end of an era; no one expected that in 1967, at the time of completing this book, Canadians would be able to look back on five years of uneasy peace among the mountains of British Columbia, five years of adjustments on the part of both Doukhobors and their neighbours which seem to hold a promise of concord—though admittedly it is a concord paid for by the surrenders of a people who have long lived out of time and place and now yield unwillingly before the pressures of the majority.

From the vantage point of 1967 one is able to perceive that this development was in fact maturing throughout the 1950s and the early 1960s. Violent and intransigent though the desperadoes of Krestova may have seemed, with their ingenious wristwatch-operated bombs and their Molotov cocktails, they never represented more than a minority of the Doukhobors as a whole or even of the Sons of Freedom. When one of the writers interviewed Robert Bonner, the Social Credit attorney general of British Columbia, in 1963, he admitted that the core of 'trouble-makers' whom the RCMP had constantly under observation numbered no more than eight hundred, less than a third of the twenty-five hundred people who identified themselves as Sons of Freedom and less than a twentieth of the whole Doukhobor population of Canada.[1] Even among these eight hundred there were many whose deeds of defiance never went beyond exhibitions of nakedness and the burning of their own shacks, after they had carefully removed the furniture and in some cases the doors and the window frames as well. The real terrorists, who destroyed public property and attempted to instil fear into other Doukhobors, probably numbered no more than two hundred, a black élite belonging to a few families among whom, in the forty years of continuous incendiarism from 1923 to 1962, a tradition of destructive action had grown up.

While these obsessive actors who performed violent acts for the glory of God illuminated with flames and explosions the corruption of the world they saw around them, more than nine-tenths of the Doukhobor sect were already accepting the inevitability of living at peace with that world. The Independents, the members of the Union of Spiritual Communities of Christ, and even the more moderate of the Sons of Freedom differed from each other only in the degree of their acceptance; and it is possible to interpret even the acts of protest and terror on the part of the more extreme minority as a desperate last-ditch action against a process of inevitable change. By 1950 all Doukhobors in Canada, with the exception of the small, dwindling company of the Archangel's followers on Vancouver Island, had abandoned the communistic economic system that, more than anything else, differentiated them from the general population of Canada.

It was because they were daily assuming more of the protective colouring of assimilation that the peaceful majority of the Doukhobors attracted far less attention from the news media during the 1950s and 1960s than their more irreconcilable brethren, who fought the established society with all the bitter passion that characterizes men who know in their hearts that they defend a lost cause. Yet the very passivity of the Independents and the Community Doukhobors during the past two decades has affected Doukhobor life as profoundly as the dramatic deeds of the zealots.

Not least important, the Independents and the Community Doukhobors ceased during this period to be impervious to the attempts at reconciliation on the part of those members of the wider Canadian community who questioned the wisdom of an approach to Doukhobor problems based entirely on coercive methods and a legalistic interpretation of social relations.

For their first forty years in Canada, any *rapprochement* between the Doukhobors and their more tolerant neighbours was made difficult by the suspicious attitude towards outsiders the leaders fostered. The Independents, led by men like Peter Makaroff who participated fully in Canadian public life, were the first to escape from the magic circle of isolation drawn by Peter the Lordly. Then, when the Christian Community died as an economic entity, the gradual dissolution of its social self-sufficiency inevitably followed. Families became individual and self-contained; every man earned for himself and his immediate dependents, and this forced him into closer relations with the world outside. Children attended school fairly regularly, and in localities where Doukhobors were only one element in the population, this brought the children as well as their parents into closer contact with their neighbours. By the 1950s the majority of Doukhobors were inclined to accept the material essentials of the modern North American way of life. Their houses, their dress, their means of transport approximated ever more closely to those of their non-Doukhobor neighbours. They bought radios and, later, television sets, and the supermarket and the cinema have become part of their culture.

Doukhobors were slow, however, to join non-Doukhobor associations. For a long time they were the despair of union organizers in the woodworking industries, but by the 1960s even this reservation has tended to break down; in both British Columbia and Saskatchewan, Doukhobors serve on school boards and hospital boards and have taken a steadily more active part in the activities of the wider local community, particularly in towns like Grand Forks and Yorkton where they live in close proximity to people of other ethnic origins.

The tardy involvement in Canadian community life was at least partly due to the fact that the Doukhobors were not always welcomed by their neighbours. In the Interior of British Columbia there are still vestigial resentments on the part of small-town shopkeepers, and there is a lingering habit of regarding Doukhobors as an inferior race: the 'Douks' as opposed to the 'white men'. The failure of acceptance was intensified by the fact that many people blamed the Doukhobors in general for the depredations committed by a minority of the Sons of Freedom, and this error was perpetuated by the tendency of the local newspapers to refer to all such acts of violence as 'Doukhobor' outrages without qualifying adjectives. In the prairies, where the mosaic of ethnic origins is more varied than in British Columbia and where the impact of zealot violence has been less severe, Doukhobors have been more readily and naturally accepted, and are themselves less inhibited in their participation in local community life. But wherever the Doukhobors find themselves in 1967, and whether they are Independents, members of the Union of Spiritual Communities, or Sons of Freedom, the barriers between them and their Canadian neighbours have undoubtedly diminished during the five years of peace that have followed the last great outburst of zealot violence in 1962.

If any single event marks the beginning of this change in relationships, it is the request that Attorney General Wismer made to President Norman MacKenzie of the University of British Columbia in April 1950, asking him to establish a research project that would investigate the Doukhobor situation and suggest how it might be improved.

The request was made at the suggestion of two unusually enlightened police officers who had come to the conclusion that something more imaginative than a rigid enforcement of the law was needed to bring an end to the pattern of violence, which by 1950 was threatening to spread through the possible adoption of vigilante methods by the non-Doukhobors of the Interior of British Columbia. In 1949 Colonel F. J. Mead, the deputy commissioner of the Royal Canadian Mounted Police, had been asked by the federal government to act as its observer in Doukhobor affairs, and in December of that year he and John L. Shirras, the retired commissioner for the provincial police, received a similar request from the provincial government of British Columbia.

Mead and Shirras travelled into the trouble areas of the Kootenay and Kettle Valleys, and on 19 December 1949 they visited Krestova, where they held discussions with a four-man delegation of the Sons of Freedom and later addressed a general meeting attended by a hundred and fifty inhabitants of the village. 'We are not here to bargain with you in any way,' warned Shirras,[2] and he and Mead both emphasized obedience to the laws of the land as the minimum requirement before any progress could be made towards solving the Doukhobor situation. The Sons of Freedom, as was their custom, solemnly promised obedience; but the police officers departed with the feeling that they had achieved nothing, and that nothing would be achieved while the government's representatives talked to the Doukhobors only with the voice of compulsion. It was necessary for an independent, scientific study to be made of the problem. With this idea in mind they returned to Victoria.

It was perhaps providential that their return was almost immediately followed by the great outburst of arson in the spring of 1950. The Liberal-Conservative coalition government of Byron Johnson was willing to consider new approaches, and for the first time since the Doukhobors reached Canada a group of non-government experts was given exceptional powers of investigation and recommendation. Unlike the earlier investigations of Blakemore in 1912 and Judge Sullivan in 1948, the Doukhobor Research Committee, which President MacKenzie gathered together as soon as he received the attorney general's request, was not given the status of a Royal Commission. It was felt that a less official standing would inspire more trust among the Doukhobors and give the investigators more freedom and flexibility of operation. The chairman, Dr Harry Hawthorn, was a well-known social scientist and head of the Department of Anthropology at the University of British Columbia; members of the Departments of Psychology, Economics, and Slavonic Studies, and of the Faculties of Law, Social Work, and Agriculture also served, together with scholars from the University of Washington, the American University at Beirut, the Bank Street College of Education in New York, and the Sefton Institute of Baltimore, as well as Hugh Herbison, a member of the Wider Quaker Fellowship and an expert on Doukhobor religion.

Most members of the Research Committee spent the summers of 1950 and 1951 in the field collecting information, and the autumns and winters collating it; only a few were able to devote longer periods to field work. Not only did they investigate exhaustively the reciprocal attitudes of the Doukhobors and their neighbours; they also studied Doukhobor social patterns and the psychological attitudes that resulted from them, considered the economic basis of Doukhobor life both before and after the collapse of the Community, prepared an elaborate survey of the former Doukhobor lands in the Kootenay and Kettle Valleys, and carefully scrutinized federal and provincial laws insofar as they affected members of the sect. It was by far the deepest and most elaborate investigation of the Doukhobor situation yet undertaken.

Two years was the minimum time that could be allowed for such a project, but the provincial government, once it had become conscious of the need for special treatment of the Doukhobor problem, was anxious to solve quickly a situation that had arisen through the imprisonment of four hundred Sons of Freedom in the spring of 1950. The local jails were overcrowded, and the authorities had no desire in 1950 to repeat the Piers Island experience by setting up a special prison. They looked to the Research Committee for immediate guidance. The members of the committee, however, felt that, in the words of its chairman, Dr Hawthorn, 'if the pressures of action had descended prematurely on the research staff, their primary function of research could not have been carried out.' [3] Accordingly, a separate Consultative Committee was formed under the chairmanship of Dean Geoffrey Andrew, Deputy President of the University of British Columbia. The new committee established its own staff of field representatives, including Hugh Herbison, and Emmett Gulley of the American Society of Friends, and drew from time to time on the resources of the Research Committee. Its most important task was to act as a kind of parole board and to make recommendations regarding the hundreds of Doukhobor prisoners, many of whom had been convicted for relatively minor offences, such as nudism or small-scale arson, that carried disproportionately heavy sentences. The committee proceeded to screen the prisoners individually and to suggest an amnesty for those who pledged themselves to peaceful behaviour; in this work they were materially assisted by the emergence of Stefan Sorokin as leader of the Sons of Freedom. By the end of 1950 all but seventy of the Sons of Freedom prisoners had been set free.

Eventually, in May 1952, the report of the Doukhobor Research Committee was published. It was the first really intensive report on the Doukhobor situation and contained not only a great deal of information about areas of tension between Doukhobors and other Canadians, but also a detailed picture of Doukhobor life as it existed in British Columbia during the years immediately following the Second World War.

The recommendations reached intelligently into every cause of friction between the Doukhobors and other Canadians. The committee did not pursue a 'soft line'; on the contrary, it suggested that there should be more rigorous prosecution for such offences as habitual truancy, and that conviction of a crime of violence should incur the loss of exemption from military service. Yet its recommendations studiously avoided the assumption that coercion was the only way of dealing with Doukhobors, and sought means of establishing trust through justifiable concessions. For example, it recommended the recognition of the Doukhobor form of marriage and the repeal of all legislation aimed specially at the Doukhobors, such as the law excluding Doukhobors from participation in provincial and federal elections, and the section of the Criminal Code applying the special penalty of three years' imprisonment for parading in the nude.

The report recognized that there might be some justification for the sense of grievance that Doukhobors had long harboured regarding the loss of their lands; it suggested selling back to individual members of the sect the former Community properties administered by the Land Settlement Board. No mention was made of the transfer of the land on a communitarian basis, and it is not clear whether the committee disapproved of the idea of reviving the Christian Community or merely thought this an unlikely eventuality. There were other recommendations suggesting programs of assistance in rehabilitating Doukhobor lands and in providing improved welfare and nursing services.

The recommendations specifically devoted to the Sons of Freedom were described by the committee as involving 'a balance of pressures and inducements'.[4] What strikes one now is their reliance on a considerable degree of segregation to lessen contacts between the zealots and other Canadians, both in prison and outside. A special detention unit should be built so that Sons of Freedom could be housed apart from ordinary criminals and given appropriate rehabilitative treatment. Efforts should also be made to find some isolated area in which the Sons of Freedom might be relocated *en masse* and assisted to establish themselves as self-subsistent farmers. The last recommendation curiously echoed, in the words of non-Doukhobor experts, the old sectarian ideal of a Doukhobor state within the state, isolated physically from the corrupting contact of those outside the faith.

Finally, the committee recommended that a Commission for Doukhobor Affairs should be appointed 'to coordinate the activities of all levels of government as they relate to Doukhobors, and to give leadership in new approaches in meeting the problems of the group'.[5]

In these recommendations the wisdom of delegating the investigation to a non-official committee became evident. While the unorthodox attitudes of the Doukhobors frustrated government officials and exasperated judicial investigators like Judge Sullivan, they aroused the interest and often the sympathy of the researchers; and from the beginning the committee was concerned, not only with the difficulties that policemen and officials encountered in keeping order and making sure that regulations were obeyed, but also with the much more concrete problems the Doukhobors themselves faced as a result of the breakup of their communal way of living. The tone of the report was humane and constructive, and its recommendations placed reconciliation and assistance at least on a level with the enforcement of the law.

At first it seemed as though the conclusions of the Research Committee would be submerged in a flood of adverse events. Politics intervened catastrophically. When a remote area of land around Adams Lake was chosen as suitable for settlement by the Sons of Freedom, the proposal became an election issue in Kamloops, the nearest town (a hundred miles away), and the residents objected so vigorously that the plan had to be abandoned.

Then, among the Sons of Freedom, leadership disintegrated and chaos followed. By April 1953 it became evident that Stefan Sorokin would not be returning from Uruguay and that he would not be calling his followers to join him in South America. Once again a leader-inspired emigration, in which the faithful had placed their money and their hopes, had failed. John Lebedoff, recently returned from prison, tried to regain the leadership by reviving his own emigration scheme, but this merely resulted in quarrels between his followers and those of Sorokin. In the renewed atmosphere of dispute and disillusionment, the old slogan of 'migration through the prisons' began to sweep the Sons of Freedom villages, and the terrorists with their Molotov cocktails fanned out through the Kootenays, burning. As feeling whipped up into hysteria, the Fraternal Council of the Sons of Freedom denounced the Doukhobor Research Committee because of the failure of the Adams River plan, and before the summer was over the rash of secret fires set by the terrorists had produced a reaction among the mass of the Sons of Freedom. The makeshift huts that the people of Krestova had put up on their return from prison in 1950 became torches of protest in a series of demonstrations. By the summer's end the site of the village was chequered with charred ruins. Then, early in September, the homeless people began to move down from the plateau of Krestova into the Slocan Valley, singing of the great pilgrimage they were about to begin. At Perry's Siding, twenty-five miles away, they established a temporary village which they called Polatka (tent).

The more radical Doukhobors showed by their actions that they had rejected the hopes of reconciliation that were implied in the findings of the Research Committee. They recognized that such a reconciliation could only be bought at the price of a degree of assimilation, and they were not prepared to pay that price.

Their actions resulted in a confrontation with the provincial government, which also was unwilling, for the present, to grant the concessions necessary for reconciliation. The political climate of British Columbia had changed considerably since the coalition government called the Douk-hobor Research Committee into being in 1950. In the elections of 1952 the Social Credit Party emerged as the largest group in the legislative assembly; it formed a minority government under W. A. C. Bennett. In 1953 a new election was called; Social Credit gained an absolute majority and returned to power with a militant urge to solve, by drastic measures if necessary, the outstanding problems of the province.

High on their list of priorities was the Doukhobor question. Social Credit relied for its strength on the constituencies of the Interior and made its principal appeal to those rural conservatives who had consistent-ly been the enemies of the Doukhobors. The election campaigns in the Kootenays and Kettle Valley had stressed the adoption of a hard line to-wards the Sons of Freedom. In April the attorney general, Robert Bonner, threatened to deal with mass demonstrations by wholesale arrests and with lapses in school attendance by seizing the children and placing them in the care of a welfare agency. Bonner also paid tribute to the work of the Research Committee and announced that the government was consi-dering the implementation of some of its proposals, specifically recogni-tion of Doukhobor marriages and the resale to Doukhobors of the former lands of the Christian Community of Universal Brotherhood. But action of this kind lay in the indefinite future, and for the present the Social Credit government intended to define its attitude by a show of force. The research committee's suggestion of proceeding by 'a balance of pressures and inducements' was clearly to be ignored.

How far the element of calculated provocation entered into the new policy it is difficult to determine. The threat of harsh treatment was tan-talizing to those among the Sons of Freedom who were obsessed with the idea of martyrdom, and it was undoubtedly largely responsible for the burnings at Krestova during the summer of 1953 and the subsequent migration to Perry's Siding. The attorney general instructed the Mounted Police to watch the campers at Perry's Siding and to move against them immediately there was any sign of illegality in their actions.

On 9 September the Mounted Police carried out a carefully planned foray. Forty of them surrounded the tent camp and arrested all its in-habitants. The excuse was that some of the Sons of Freedom had been contributing to juvenile delinquency by parading nude outside the little one-room school at Perry's Siding. The zealots denied the charge. The adult prisoners were loaded on to a special train standing on the siding and taken immediately to Vancouver, where the next day they were car-ried, passively resisting, into a specially convened court in a Vancouver community hall and sentenced to the customary three years in jail. The whole operation had a suspiciously streamlined quality.

But the arrest and imprisonment of the 148 adults played a minor part in the plans of the authorities. The children, who had not entered school for the autumn term, or for many terms before that, were the real quarry of this particular manhunt. One hundred and four of them, together with thirteen mothers whose children were still infants at the breast, were loaded into buses and taken up the Slocan Valley to the old mining town of New Denver, where the buildings of a sanatorium stood unused on the shores of Slocan Lake. There, invoking the Children's Protection Act, the government made them wards of the provincial superintendent of Child Welfare. Once again the operation had been planned. The committal of the children was covered by warrants issued by Magistrate William Evans of Nelson; unlike the seizure of the children at the time of Piers Island, it was technically legal.

For the next six years the population of the institution at New Denver was fed by periodic police raids on the Sons of Freedom settlements. The first took place at Gilpin in November 1954. Most of the children of school age fled into the woods surrounding the village, and only three were trapped. More successful was a dawn raid by fifty officers who seized forty children at Krestova in January 1955. Subsequent raids picked up individual children when they reached the age of seven; these continued until the institution was closed in August 1959, after the mothers had appeared before Magistrate Evans in Nelson and promised to send their children to school if he would order their release. The order was given, and the promise has since been kept; from 1959 onwards there have been no major difficulties over the education of Doukhobor children belonging to any faction.

During the six years of its existence, a total of 170 Doukhobor children passed through the institution at New Denver. Some reached school-leaving age and were released before 1959; the rest went on to day schools like Mount Central High School at South Slocan where, having learnt from experience, the authorities offered special curricula, including vocational training and the teaching of Russian, that met at least some of the criticisms the Doukhobors had made of Canadian educational methods.

Opinions were and continue to be divided about the value and the justification of the New Denver institution. The Sons of Freedom protested to the local authorities, to the provincial and federal governments, and even to the United Nations, always without success. The mothers of the children, forgetting their pacifism, almost succeeded in stripping Miss Ruby

McKay, the superintendent of Child Welfare, in her office in Victoria, while the Quaker Emmett Gulley was rescued with difficulty from involuntary nudity on a Nelson street; he was regarded as partly responsible for the government's action. One mother committed suicide. For other Sons of Freedom the institution became a centre of pilgrimage, where the parents would gather outside the tall wire fence and sing psalms expressing their sorrow and their solidarity with the children whom they regarded as the prisoners of a wicked government.

Many non-Doukhobors, concerned for civil liberties, were disturbed by the arbitrary use of compulsion at a time when the Doukhobor Research Committee had recommended a tactful and conciliatory handling of the situation. Opinions on the treatment of the children differed considerably and tended to divide along political lines. Newspaper reporters who approved of the hard policy of the Social Credit government saw the New Denver institution as a valuable means of conditioning the children to accept the Canadian way of life. Journalists from outside British Columbia, who viewed the experiment apart from the local context of chronic strife between Doukhobors and non-Doukhobors, were inclined to be critical from the moment they saw the high fences that gave the institution the appearance of a miniature concentration camp.

Any situation in which human beings who have committed no crime are coerced is of course distasteful to anyone who values freedom. New Denver was in this respect as much a prison as any Borstal institution. The children were robbed of the warm, close environment of the Doukhobor home and brought into perpetual contact with strangers who, though they may have been worthy individuals and excellent teachers, were still, according to Doukhobor beliefs, representatives of that hostile and evil entity, the government. In the beginning many of the children resisted passively, stripping and refusing to move unless carried. Classes were eventually established, and the staff attempted to evolve a curriculum that would arouse the children's interest without offending the religious principles inculcated in their homes.

Some children, particularly the older ones, remained sullen and withdrawn throughout their period at New Denver; these, like their predecessors of the Piers Island period, became recruits to the ranks of the terrorists in the early 1960s, some of them finding their way into prison, and one at least, Harry Kootnikoff, blowing himself up with a home-made bomb in 1962 at the age of seventeen. But the example of Harry Kootnikoff does not tell the whole story of New Denver. Many of the younger children responded to the treatment they received there and developed a genuine thirst for knowledge. Teachers who have dealt with these children since their release are inclined to praise the institution for laying the foundations of real education among the Sons of Freedom. The results of the experiment, in other words, are mixed; and one's view of whether the good results were worth while must rest on one's willingness to accept a government's right to coerce people for what appears to be their own good. In our view, that right is unacceptable.

In fact, the government of British Columbia was not thinking only of the good of the Doukhobor children. The establishment of the New Denver institution had also a political motivation. Education was seen as a means of weaning the children from the rebellious attitudes inculcated in their homes and in the makeshift Russian schools run by the Sons of Freedom in their own villages. In other words, the New Denver institution was in part a deliberate attempt to break up the separateness of the Doukhobor community, a stage in the long campaign of forced assimilation that began when the prairie land of the Christian Community was seized in 1907.

The events of 1953 suggested the triumph of nihilistic rebelliousness on the part of the Sons of Freedom and of calculated coercion on the part of the government. But once the Research Committee had carried out its scientific study of Doukhobor affairs and brought forward a series of constructive recommendations, it was impossible for any government to depart entirely from the path of reconciliation without appearing reactionary and irresponsible. In spite of the apparent retrogression that immediately followed the assumption of power by the Social Credit Party, most of the committee's positive recommendations eventually became matters of government action.

In August 1954, Judge Lord of Vancouver was appointed as a commissioner to investigate the sale of Doukhobor lands. In 1955 the federal parliament amended the Criminal Code so as to delete the penalty of three years' imprisonment for nude parading, and in 1957 the franchise in both federal and provincial elections was restored to the Doukhobors. In 1959, seven years after the research committee's report, the provincial government at last recognized Doukhobor marriages.

The implementation of the new marriage regulations was placed in the hands of William Evans, who from this point became a key figure in mediating differences between the Doukhobors and the authorities. As stipendiary magistrate of Nelson, he had accumulated many years of experience in dealing with Doukhobor problems; and he had often acted

344 / THE DOUKHOBORS

with a Welshman's respect for the rights and idiosyncracies of eccentric minorities.

Most important, he was ready to improvise flexible formulae that allowed for Doukhobor scruples. One of the main obstacles to the registration of Doukhobor marriages was an item on the form requiring the married person's citizenship. In 1947, when the Canadian Citizenship Act became law, John J. Verigin had protested to Mackenzie King on behalf of the Union of Spiritual Communities of Christ.

On the basis of our principles and religious convictions in the faith of Jesus Christ, we consider ourselves to be citizens of the whole universe; Christ is the King of all Kings, therefore we are his citizens. We categorically proclaim that we cannot be automatically citizens of this or any other country.[6]

Evans recognized the conflict of attitudes and devised a reconciling formula. The Doukhobors became, in citizenship, 'Canadian, subject to the law of God and Jesus Christ'. As a result almost twelve hundred Doukhobor marriages—some of them dating back for nearly sixty years—were legally recognized; and thousands of children were legitimized.

The resale of the Doukhobor lands proved the most stubborn of all the outstanding questions. The investigatory commission made slow progress, and this was not entirely the fault of the Commissioner. By 1957 the land had been surveyed, subdivided, and appraised, and an Applications Board had been set up, including a prominent Independent Doukhobor. Finally, on 9 October the plots were formally offered for sale.

At this point the slowness of government procedure was paralleled by the reluctance of the Doukhobors to commit themselves. This was due in part to the uncertainty about leadership. Only on 14 November 1957 did the USCC learn, through the Red Cross, that Peter Iastrebov, the leader they had only seen when he came as an infant to Canada in 1906, had died in a Russian labour camp.[7] His followers were unwilling immediately to accept the information, though it was confirmed by the Canadian Ministry of External Affairs in December 1957.[8] Not, in fact, until Anna Markova, sister of Peter Iastrebov, arrived in Canada in June 1960 was his death formally acknowledged. On 16 August 1960, the traditional ceremony to commemorate the passing of his soul was held at the tomb of the Verigins in Brilliant, and the assembled members of the Union of Spiritual Communities of Christ recognized John J. Verigin as their leader. Only then did he have sufficient status to influence major decisions within the sect.

The other reason for reluctance was the continued hostility of the Sons of Freedom to the repurchase of the land, a hostility expressed first by threats and later in action. Throughout 1958 the people of Krestova and Gilpin had been in a state of renewed migration fever. This time the objective was Russia. Already in 1957 the project was being discussed fervently in the Sons of Freedom villages, and by the winter the Fraternal Council had selected a four-man delegation to visit the U.S.S.R. and negotiate with the Soviet authorities for land grants and permission to enter the country which, since most of them were now Canadian-born, was no longer their fatherland.

The delegation consisted of Joe Podovinikoff, former lieutenant to Michael the Archangel, William Moojelsky, the favourite of Stefan Sorokin, John Chernoff, and Nick Kanigan. This was the era of Khrushchev's expansive gestures, and the visitors received visas without difficulty; the desire of people living in the democratic world to migrate to Communist Russia seemed an excellent propaganda point that could be exploited but that laid the Soviet government under no obligation.

In the Soviet Union the experiences of the Sons of Freedom appear to have been similar to those of Peter the Lordly in 1907. They talked to officials in Moscow, though evidently not to the highest of them, and apparently received assurances that if they did come to the U.S.S.R. their pacifist convictions would be respected to the extent of their being allowed to choose alternative service, presumably on the lines of provisions made for conscientious objectors during the Civil War. They were allowed to travel into Siberia and visit the Altai region that Peter the Lordly had merely discussed with Stolypin. By March 1958 they were back in Canada and announcing to a large open-air meeting in Krestova that the way was now open for migration. The meeting decided by acclamation in favour of leaving for Russia as quickly as possible.

In May negotiations were started with the Canadian authorities. They continued until August, when a formal agreement was announced. Provided the emigrating Doukhobors would sign away their claims to Canadian citizenship, and provided the Soviet government agreed to accept them, the federal government agreed to assist with transportation and resettlement costs. By November some 2,440 forms provisionally renouncing Canadian citizenship had been signed by the Sons of Freedom. A considerable sum of money was collected from among the faithful to finance the emigration. Missing was the final, formal agreement of the Soviet government to admit the Sons of Freedom. It never came.

One is left to speculate on what actually happened in Moscow. There is no reason to doubt that the delegation was politely received and that its members did gain the impression that they and their people would be welcome back in Russia. If anyone enacted a comedy of deception, it was probably the Soviet authorities. Presumably they expected the Canadian government would regard the eager departure of a few thousand of their citizens as a major loss of face; when the Canadians welcomed the idea of losing the Sons of Freedom and even offered to assist their departure, the Soviet government lost interest in a group they had never intended to accept. This, after all, was the Khrushchev era, the age when bluff dominated Soviet diplomatic practices; as soon as the Canadians refused to be embarrassed, the Russian bluff was called.

The whole period while the migration to the Soviet Union seemed possible was one of intense agitation among the Sons of Freedom. Dynamitings succeeded one another throughout the summer of 1958. The outrages spread beyond the Doukhobor regions, and bombs exploded in the Okanagan and even as far away as Princeton, some two hundred miles west of Krestova. The element of major sabotage entered for the first time into the pattern of depredations. Railway lines, power poles, and the lake ferry at Kelowna were among the objectives of the terrorists, and for the first time human lives were directly endangered, for bombs were planted in hotels and in the bus depot at Nelson. The campaign came to a climax in August when a young Doukhobor fruit-picker, Philip Pereversoff, was killed by his own bomb. After that, for a period, the wave of destruction subsided.

But it left the Doukhobors of the Union of Spiritual Communities of Christ nervous about buying land when the threat of violence hung so formidably over them. In 1959 Judge Lord recommended that a cut-off date should be applied beyond which the land would no longer be available. Having second thoughts about the value of compulsion, the attorney general was reluctant to agree. When no progress had been made with the sale of the lands by the summer of 1961, Magistrate Evans was again called in to solve the deadlock. John J. Verigin expressed his willingness to support him with his new-found authority as leader or 'Honorary Chairman' of the Union of Spiritual Communities of Christ. Evans then wrote directly to Stefan Sorokin in Uruguay. Still recognized by the majority of the Sons of Freedom as their leader, Sorokin ordered his followers not to interfere with the land purchase, and the obedient Fraternal Council in Krestova immediately issued a statement that they had no intention of preventing the members of the Union of Spiritual Communities of Christ from buying the former Community properties.

On 22 July an extraordinary convention of the Union of Spiritual Communities gathered at Grand Forks and decided in principle to buy the land. A committee of eight was set up to investigate various forms of ownership, and as a symbolic gesture John J. Verigin made the down payment on the white clapboard farmhouse, on eight acres of land on the outskirts of Grand Forks, that is the traditional home of the Doukhobor leaders.

Sorokin's word may have been good enough for the Sons of Freedom in general, but clearly even he had no remaining control over the terrorists. Within a few days of the decision to repurchase the Community lands, yet another bomb had shaken the tomb of the Verigins, and two USCC community halls had been burnt down. These depredations were followed on 20 August by the worst of all the outrages in the one-sided civil war between the terrorists and the Community Doukhobors. In the middle of that night a gang led by Sam, Peter, and Paul Konkin, a family noted for its interest in incendiarism, crept on the village of Ooteshenie with their bombs and Molotov cocktails. By the time they left, twenty-six buildings were in flames. A whole village was destroyed, and forty people had narrowly escaped death by burning.

These were the acts of desperate men. They suffered from an ideological desperation in seeing their brethren performing fateful acts of compromise. But another kind of desperation also raged in men like the Konkin brothers. They were not merely fighting a last-ditch stand for a threatened faith; violence had become for them, as for other men who acquire the habit of guerilla warfare, a vocation in itself, and by the end of the 1950s they had ceased to care for the consequences of their actions. The exciting break of fire as a kerosene-soaked house burst into flame, the deep thud of exploding dynamite, carried an irresistible excitement, and the kind of acts—such as the Ooteshenie outrage—that were perpetrated by the terrorists between 1958 and 1962 have a quality of cold-blooded monomania that had not before characterized the actions of the Sons of Freedom. Had the terrorists deliberately fought to kill, it would not have seemed so horrifying as the utter indifference to life that characterized the burning of Ooteshenie. Fire had become its own end, a passion that excited some of the arsonists to the point of orgasm as they watched the deadly splendour of their handiwork bursting out against the night sky.

Before 1961 the other Doukhobors had moved in constant fear of the terrorists. But once they had made up their minds to buy back the Community lands, the outrages only seemed to stiffen their resolve. Out of

750 parcels of land, 180 had been bought by the end of October 1961, and by the end of 1963 all the former Community lands in British Columbia except those at Krestova were once again in Doukhobor hands. The members of the USCC bought their plots individually, but, as a concession to their nominal adherence to the communitarian ideal, they named the Union of Spiritual Communities as trustee.

At last the Doukhobor lands had returned to the descendants of the men and women who toiled and suffered in the days of Peter the Lordly to build the great Community. But the Community itself remained a ghost. From 1961 to 1963 elaborate plans were worked out for a gradual return to a communal way of living, based on a revival of the traditional link between the Doukhobors and the land. It was proposed that the USCC should undertake the rebuilding of the ruined irrigation systems, as a community service. The brick factory would be re-established, and there would be communal pastures, gravel pits, and dairy farms.

None of these plans has yet materialized. The former Community members and their descendants had not, up to our last visit in August 1966, shown any signs of a mass return to the land. The irrigation systems remained derelict, and no attempt had been made to replant the orchards. On the other hand, stylish modern private houses were rising on the plots the Doukhobors had purchased. Though in sentiment the dwellers in these houses were still communalists, in practice they lived a life quite as individualistic as that of the other men with little pieces of land up and down the Kootenay and Kettle Valleys who commuted to their work in sawmills, on the railway, and in the great damsites of the Columbia Valley.

A liking for mildly co-operative institutions was all that remained of traditional Doukhobor communism. The consumers' co-operatives run by the Doukhobors at Grand Forks, Brilliant, and in the Slocan Valley were now large businesses patronized by almost all the members of the sect living in their localities, and this, of course, was a relic of Peter the Lordly's habit of buying wholesale and circumventing the retail merchants. The only other institutions that might be regarded as vestiges of the communal way of life were a small flour mill, employing one man, which was operated communally to grind Doukhobor wheat (grown without fertilizers or pesticides), and a co-operative implement pool to help USCC members till their newly acquired lands; in 1966 this pool possessed equipment worth only eight thousand dollars, a very modest achievement compared with the great mechanization programs of Peter the Lordly.[9]

In other respects, conformity now reigns in settlements like Brilliant and Grand Forks. The typical member of the Union of Spiritual Commu-

nities of Christ pays his taxes regularly, registers his marriage, and shares
to a large extent the pleasures and communal activities of his non-Doukhobor neighbours. His children and those of his brethren in the 1960s
attend not only primary but also high schools, and some of them are at
last following the example of the Independents on the prairies and attending the universities in the coastal cities of British Columbia. Young Doukhobors dance, play instrumental music, and in general live a much freer
life than would have been possible even ten years ago. The dietary taboos
die hardest. Few Doukhobors who remain among their co-religionists
smoke, drink, or eat meat, and those who do usually feel guilty about
their lapses.

The Doukhobors of the USCC claim to carry on most faithfully the
traditions of Peter the Lordly and Peter Chistiakov. Yet it is now only
their religion that still distinguishes them emphatically from ordinary
Canadians. Even there, changes are taking place. It is not likely, for example, that John J. Verigin, who worked for so long among them as a
substitute for the absent Peter Iastrebov, enjoys the same kind of reverence that was accorded to his formidable predecessors, Peter the Lordly
and Peter the Purger. His people respect him because of his office and his
lineage; they realize that he has often shown good judgement in dealing
with their affairs and has given the right leads on such issues as Doukhobor marriages and the land question. He has also emphasized the importance of pacifism as the central core of the Doukhobor creed, and in
this way he has done his best to redress in the public eye the image of the
Doukhobor as a fanatic concerned only with bombs, burnings, and bare
bodies. Even so, one has only to see John Verigin among his people to
realize that very few of them view him as a holy leader of the traditional
Doukhobor kind. Nor does he himself aspire to that role. He sees himself
in more modern and constitutional terms as the symbolic head whose
presence assures the cohesion of the organization over which he presides.

If the concept of leadership has evolved with the times, so have other
aspects of Doukhobor religion; and in particular its music. In the reign of
Peter Chistiakov, Gabriel Vereshchagin was responsible for the introduction of more complicated counterpointing, and now the styles of Doukhobor singing are changing again as the younger choirs pick up by ear the
manner of singing one associates with the Red Army Chorus and similar
choral groups from the U.S.S.R. In addition, hymns of non-Russian evangelical sects are being translated and absorbed into the oral tradition, so
that one is sometimes surprised to hear tunes like 'What a Friend We

Have in Jesus' mingling with the complicated harmonies of the Doukhobor psalms.

With the form of leadership and the styles of music changing, with the communal way of life thinning down almost to vanishing point, Doukhobor religion has in fact been stripped to its bare essentials among the USCC Doukhobors, and even more so among the Independent Doukhobors. Yet the differences between Independents and the so-called Orthodox Doukhobors are now in practice very slight. The Independents do not recognize the hereditary leadership of the Verigins, and, while the members of the USCC tend towards passive and sometimes grudging acceptance of Canadian ways, the Independents are more inclined to active participation, as is shown by their greater interest in public life and by the larger proportion of their members who go to universities and who follow professional or business careers or even, in some rare cases, enter the civil service. At the same time there are, surprisingly enough, a number of ways in which the Independents are closer to the Russian past than either the USCC or the Sons of Freedom. More of them have remained working farmers, so that in the prairies the old Doukhobor association with the land is much more of a reality than it is in British Columbia. They have also retained more of the folk songs, largely of Cossack origin, that their fathers brought with them from Russia in the 1890s; Peter the Lordly discouraged the use of such 'worldly' songs, and for this reason they died out among the Community Doukhobors in British Columbia, who were most directly under his influence.

Between 1961 and 1963, when the members of the USCC were performing a major act of reconciliation with the Canadian world by regaining their old lands, the Sons of Freedom embarked on the most dramatic and possibly the last of all their great campaigns against that 'corrupt' North American culture that has both repelled and tempted them by its materialism.

The year 1961 had ended with a grand total of 106 bombings and burnings; 1962, which was to become the classic year of terrorist activity (with an estimated total of 274 depredations), opened with a series of mass arrests. Sixty-nine alleged terrorists were rounded up by the RCMP. The arrests resulted from an unexpected confession by Mike Bayoff, a mentally unbalanced man who had already spent several years in the provincial mental hospital at Essondale, B.C. Bayoff not only confessed his own deeds; he also turned mass informer. What followed was even stranger, for no sooner had the men he accused been lodged in Nelson police station than they in turn began to imitate him and made their own confessions in an extraordinary atmosphere of mass euphoria. In the past, the terrorists had always clothed their activities in the utmost secrecy and had denied any charges laid against them, so that this *volte face* should have been regarded with suspicion. However, the RCMP officers enthusiastically recorded the confessions.

Shortly afterwards the trials began, in an atmosphere whose tension was heightened by a fire-bomb attack on the Nelson court house and an attempt to blow up the annex to the jail, followed by the death of Harry Kootnikoff, one of the terrorists still at large, through the accidental explosion of a home-made bomb. The scene in the courtroom was one of total confusion, since all the accused now withdrew their confessions, claiming, through their counsel, that they had been threatened by the police officers, by Mike Bayoff, and by the deposed leader of the Sons of Freedom, John Lebedoff. Some said they had confessed because of the prophecy of 'migration through the prisons', and others that they had confessed to protest against unjust arrests. Before the long weeks of the trials had ended, John Lebedoff was accused by his enemies in the dock not only of extorting confessions (how he was supposed to have done this was never made clear), but also of instigating arson, because when he went to Krestova to tell the people to abandon fire-raising he wore a disarranged tie, which was interpreted as an 'upside-down' instruction to do the opposite of what he counselled! These charges were balanced by others made by certain prisoners who claimed that all the acts of arson and bombing had been instigated by Lebedoff's rival, Stefan Sorokin.

As the months went on even the court displayed its bewilderment by the variety of sentences it imposed. Some men, against whom their own repudiated confessions were the only evidence, were acquitted. In other cases the prosecution entered stays of proceedings, hence admitting the flimsiness of its charges. Yet other men, including those accused of the destruction of Ooteshenie, were sentenced to periods of up to twelve years in the penitentiary. Most of these were probably real terrorists, but it is possible, given the general confusion, that some were not guilty of the crimes for which they were actually convicted.

It is very hard to say how seriously these confessions and accusations should be taken. Where they concerned only the individuals who made them, one has to remember the high value the Doukhobors traditionally place on martyrdom. Where they involved others, one has to remember the bitter factional disputes between the followers of Sorokin and the followers of Lebedoff that plagued the Sons of Freedom at this period; as Peter the Lordly showed in Canada and the Small Party long ago in Russia,

Doukhobors have not always been above using the despised forces of government authority to fight their fratricidal battles. Finally, where Sons of Freedom terrorists asserted that they received their instructions by esoteric signs from leaders or elders, one has to remember first the dependence upon authority that the institution of theocratic leadership had inculcated among the Doukhobors and secondly the right to interpret any statement or any gesture in any way that was conferred on the Sons of Freedom by the 'upside-down' philosophy.

Certainly all this was flimsy evidence on which to build a fantasy in which the terrorists became merely the tools of the leaders and the elders in a great conspiracy intended to blackmail the Canadian government. Yet it was precisely a fantasy of this kind that the police and the law officers of British Columbia created, and that led them to the ludicrous fiasco of the trial of the Fraternal Council of the Sons of Freedom.

On 24 March 1962 a hundred and fifty RCMP officers converged in the early morning on Krestova and arrested fifty-seven members of the council. Ten others were already in prison. Warrants were issued for the remaining three of the seventy-man council and for Stefan Sorokin, who was safe from extradition in Uruguay. Once again, thanks to government blundering, the Doukhobors became the centre of a major civil rights controversy. The arrested men were charged with conspiracy to intimidate the parliament of Canada and the legislature of British Columbia. The thought that the governing bodies of a large country could be intimidated by the activities of a small group of fanatics in a backwoods area is of course laughable, but the consequences of such a charge's being sustained might have been far more comic, since a precedent would have been created for limiting the rights of dissident groups in general. A civil liberties committee was formed in Vancouver, including several former members of the Doukhobor Research Committee, as well as representatives of the Society of Friends, the John Howard Society, the Fellowship of Reconciliation, and other groups. This committee raised money for the defence and held a watching brief over the case.

The preliminary hearing began on 11 June. Feeling was running high in the Kootenays. On 6 March terrorists had brought down with dynamite a massive pylon supporting the power lines crossing Kootenay Lake; as a result a thousand miners had been thrown out of work and had threatened to take vigilante action, so that a hundred extra Mounted Police were brought from the prairies to watch the vigilantes as well as the terrorists. In consequence, the venue of the trial was changed from Nelson to New Westminster three hundred miles away, but it was the

Nelson magistrate, William Evans, impervious to the waves of popular emotion, who presided.

The trial went on for thirty-eight days. Nearly five hundred documents seized from the Fraternal Council were presented as evidence, and ninety-eight witnesses spoke enough to fill 3,370 pages of court transcript. Most of this evidence related to statements that had been made publicly and that, though they attacked the Canadian government, could hardly be termed conspiratorial. The case for the Crown in fact rested on the evidence of two convicted terrorists who had made confessions implicating the members of the Fraternal Council. In court these witnesses withdrew their confessions, which they claimed had been made under duress, and the prosecution's fantasy of a grand conspiracy fell to the ground. On 7 August Magistrate Evans found that in all the documents presented, and in all the thousands of pages recording witnesses' testimonies, there was no evidence at all that pointed to a conspiracy. He therefore dismissed the case on which the government of British Columbia had spent an estimated $100,000 of public money.

While the trial of the Fraternal Council had been dragging through its long course in New Westminster, other events outside the courtroom were building up to make 1962 the most dramatic year in the annals of the Sons of Freedom. On 8 June the people of Krestova had been seized with one of their periodic migration frenzies and had started to burn their homes, declaring that they would not need them because the final departure would soon begin. The burnings continued until almost three hundred shacks were charred ruins.

Then on 27 July the federal government opened for the 104 Sons of Freedom still in jail a new segregated institution, the Mountain Prison, on the outskirts of Agassiz in the Fraser Valley—a compound with high barbed-wire fences and rows of fireproof hutments whose outward appearance reminds those who visit it of photographs of Nazi prison camps. To the people of Krestova, camping homeless in the ruins of their destroyed village, this institution, dedicated to Sons of Freedom only, became an irresistible magnet. During the months while the Fraternal Council waited on remand, a power shift had taken place in Krestova. Almost two hundred of the most active men were in prison, either serving sentences or awaiting trial; as in the early days on the prairies, the women had become the most important group, and one of them, Florence Storgeoff, a 250-pound giantess known for obvious reasons as Big Fanny, became a latter-day Luker'ia Kalmykova, obsessed with the idea of finding some means to release the inhabitants of the Mountain Prison. Returning from their acquittal in August, the members of the Fraternal Council found themselves overshadowed by the regiment of women, who set up their own council of thirteen and, led by Big Fanny and her principal lieutenant, Marie Schlakoff, planned the next move, an even greater pilgrimage than that which had streamed across the prairies in 1902. The Sons of Freedom would abandon their ghettos of Krestova and Gilpin. They would march through the ranges of mountains to the coast; there they would keep vigil outside the prison where their brethren were incarcerated. In this way they would draw world attention to that nebulous phenomenon they called the 'Doukhobor problem'.

The Fraternal Council banned the march, but their loss of authority became evident on 2 September when Big Fanny led nearly six hundred followers down from the plateau of Krestova and over the wooden bridge across the Slocan River to the highway for Vancouver. Others joined the march on its way down the Kootenay Valley. At Castlegar they took to cars and trucks for the journey over the mountains to Gilpin and Grand Forks, which they left on 14 September, again on wheels, and not, as their ancestors had gone, on foot. Not only did the demonstrators rely on modern means of transport; their march had also an unwonted orderliness: the Sons of Freedom were resolved to appear at their best before the people on the coast. At Bromley, in the Similkameen Valley, they were halted for sixteen days by the police, but, since they showed no inclination to return home, they were allowed to cross the Coast Range to Hope in the Fraser Valley, where they stayed for four months—twelve hundred strong—in a Seventh Day Adventist Summer Camp. Here they lived in tents and in makeshift shelters of planks with plastic roofs, but the crowded camp, which one of the writers visited just after New Year's Day 1963, was impeccably clean, the children were attending local schools, and the Sons of Freedom had behaved so peacefully that the local people had surprisingly few complaints. The pilgrims left Hope on 16 January 1963 and travelled to Vancouver, where they rented disused houses, set up small living communities, and gathered every day in Victory Square to hold their services. On 20 August, at the height of a hunger strike within the Mountain Prison, they finally travelled from Vancouver to Agassiz and squatted on a tract of waste land near the jail, building makeshift huts and intending to keep their vigil until their brethren were released. The last time we visited Agassiz, in March 1967, more than four hundred of them were still there. The men had found work locally, and they intended to stay as long as the government chose to keep the remaining thirty prisoners incarcerated. Big Fanny was no longer among them. The last of the Sons of Freedom leaders, she had died of cancer in September 1964, and lay buried in the cemetery on the mountainside that looks out over the pilgrim's encampment.

The Great March was the end of an era for the Sons of Freedom. Since then there have been no mass nude parades, no house burnings, no dynamitings. Undoubtedly the experience profoundly changed the outlook of its participants. They left the Kootenays, with their atmosphere of accumulated hostility between Doukhobors and non-Doukhobors, and found in Hope and in Vancouver people who were willing to accept them as they were and who took pains to make them feel at home. They realized that hospitality was not only a Doukhobor virtue. Many of them were attracted to the life of the city, or to the softer climate of the Fraser Valley. A considerable number of the younger people settled in Vancouver and, over the past four years, have merged into its cosmopolitan population. Some have gone back to the Kootenays, to the old settlements of Gilpin and Krestova, but even these have a different view on life.

Krestova, so long a place of violence, has now become one of the most peaceful villages in western Canada. There is no strife, because there are no longer any competing gangs of terrorists. The men who live there have found year-long employment on the various construction works in connection with the Columbia River hydro-electric project, and the traditional Krestova pattern of summer work and winter idleness is a thing of the past. Contrary to all expectations, the Sons of Freedom have recently decided to buy back the land at Krestova, and among the charred, grassgrown ruins on the plateau, new houses are being built, solid structures with none of the air of deliberate impermanence of the old tarpaper shacks. The children at Krestova now have a record of school attendance better than that of the non-Doukhobor children in the neighbourhood. Assimilation started late with the Sons of Freedom, but once begun it has been extraordinarily rapid. It is perhaps too early to prophesy that there will be no regressions into violence, but at the time of writing they seem unlikely.

Some of the Doukhobors, the first Independents, accepted assimilation soon after their arrival in Canada. Others, the Community Doukhobors, maintained their economic separateness to the end of the 1930s; but by the end of the 1950s they had recognized through a long and gradual process of adjustment the inevitability of assimilation. The Sons of Freedom kept up a determined and dramatic opposition until 1962, and then, when they were exposed to the world outside their mountain valleys and deprived of leadership, they too appear to have seen the pointlessness of resistance. Where decades of police and bureaucratic action failed, a few years of exposure to the affluent society have succeeded. It now seems likely that the Doukhobors will maintain their separateness merely as one of the many small and picturesque religious groups of Canada : their dietary rules less complex than those of the Orthodox Jews; their theological concepts no more unorthodox than those of the Mormons; their economic organization far less radical than that of the still communitarian Hutterites; their pacifism no more rigorous than that of the Quakers. Only the strange chants of the Living Book, like an unsevered umbilical cord, will unite them with their increasingly remote past in the steppes and mountains of Russia.

In the Russia of today the Doukhobors have endured even more painful and rigorous processes of assimilation than their brethren in Canada. As we have seen, by the early 1930s collectivization had already begun to affect their economic and social life, destroying the old structures of village government and replacing the surviving communal institutions by state-planned kolkhozes. The process of collectivization was a long one, beginning early in the Ukraine, Milky Waters, and Sal'sk, and coming late to parts of the Caucasus; collectivization in the Bogdanovka region was not completed until 1938.

This process was accompanied by the growing ruthlessness that marked every aspect of the Stalinist régime. Not only were the Doukhobors persecuted; those who might have been their friends were killed in the cellars of the GPU or disappeared into concentration camps. Thus their sufferings were mitigated neither by the interest of influential bureaucrats, as under Alexander I, nor by the sympathy of intellectuals whose views commanded public attention, as under Nicholas II. In general, they appear to have endured during the 1930s at least as much as the Large Party did before its emigration to Canada. This was partly because many of them were prosperous farmers and came under the category of 'kulaks', automatically suspected of being anti-Soviet. They therefore suffered as all the more enterprising peasants did, but their peculiar religious beliefs appear to have added to their troubles.

How many were actually deported is not known with any exactitude. There were certainly no mass transfers like the forced migration from Milky Waters to the Caucasus in the reign of Nicholas I, but many individuals and groups went to labour camps in Siberia and to various parts of Central Asia. Anna Markova, the mother of John J. Verigin, was sent to Novosibirsk in 1935. Her second husband, Peter Markov, died in detention, as did many other Doukhobors, including, of course, their leader, the third Peter Verigin. Peter Iastrebov, born at Slavyanka in 1904, was a quiet, diligent man, respected for his efforts to live a Christian life, avoiding enmities and loving his neighbours. Since he was already in prison years before Peter Chistiakov died in Canada, he had no opportunity of practising his leadership, but he still suffered for his name and his views. His last letter was written from a labour camp in Astrakhan in February 1942; he complained that his strength was rapidly dwindling. On 13 August, according to official Communist sources, he died, like thousands of others in the Soviet concentration camps at that period, of the malnutritional condition known as pellagra.

At this time Soviet Russia was fighting hard for its very survival, and the Doukhobors in Canada were raising money to help the victims of war in their former homeland. Like other peasants, the Doukhobors in the U.S.S.R. were deeply affected by the prevailing conditions. Their villages in the Ukraine were destroyed during the fighting with the Germans; evidence regarding the Sal'sk region is more conflicting, but there are reports that villages there also suffered. Young Doukhobors were called up for the Red Army, and though some of them were allowed to enter noncombatant battalions, others served in armed units. Many were killed, including John J. Verigin's half-brother, Peter Markov, who died in the capture of Berlin.

Since the death of Stalin in 1953, information on the Doukhobors in Russia has become somewhat more copious, though it is still scattered and unevenly reliable. It comes almost entirely through Doukhobor channels. Some Russian Doukhobors correspond once again with their brethren in Canada, and occasionally their letters are published in *Iskra*, the Russian-language paper of the Union of Spiritual Communities of Christ. Some of these letters appear to be little more than inspired Communist propaganda; others contain information that gives one some idea of the social life of modern Doukhobors.

In addition, a number of Doukhobors have visited Russia since 1953 on delegations to Soviet commemorations or World Youth Festivals, or as individuals wishing to visit the land where they or their fathers were born. Up to the present such visits appear to have been carefully controlled through Intourist; unsupervised contact between Canadian and Russian Doukhobors is not favoured by the Soviet authorities. Nevertheless, there has been a progressive easing of restrictions on actual travel in the Soviet Union. When the Canadian Doukhobor historian V. A. Sukhorev visited Russia in 1954 he was not allowed to go beyond Moscow, and two completely assimilated Doukhobors—a government official and a graduate student—were brought from the Caucasus to inform him about the situation among their brethren. In 1958 the Sons of Freedom delegates travelled into Siberia, and in 1966 a delegation from the USCC, led by John J. Verigin, was allowed to visit the Sal'sk region and was even given a special permit to enter the military zone in which the Caucasian Doukhobor villages are now situated. Direct information from Doukhobors who have lived in Russia in recent years is, of course, the scantiest of all. In fact, it is limited to one instance, that of Anna Markova, who in 1960 was allowed to leave Russia as a result of representations made to Nikita Khrushchev by Canadian Doukhobors during his visit to the Unted States in 1959. She is the only Doukhobor who has legally left the U.S.S.R. for Canada since the late 1920s.

Yet, despite the scarcity of information and the unsatisfactory nature of much that is available, it is possible to envisage in a general way the life that the Doukhobors in Russia now live. Like everyone else in Russia, they are better off than they were under the Stalinist régime. Many of the survivors of the concentration camps are known to have been released and rehabilitated. Those who remained in their villages and passed through the trauma of collectivization and wartime austerities are living, in Russian terms, comparatively comfortably. There is little information about the Sal'sk region and none about the Doukhobors in Siberia, but it seems evident that in the Caucasus, where many Doukhobors live in their own villages, conditions have improved greatly in recent years. Each village has its primary school and in Bogdanovka and Goreloye there are secondary schools. Bogdanovka has a hospital and a House of Culture. There are village clubs, libraries, medical centres, and travelling cinemas, while in some at least of the villages there are now electricity, piped water, and paved roads (none of which, incidentally, had reached Krestova in Canada by late 1966).

Probably more Doukhobors remain on the land in Russia than in Canada, and these work in kolkhozes bearing the names of non-Doukhobor celebrities like Lenin, Kirov, Engels, and Pushkin. In the Caucasus these collectives are fairly small; that in Bogdanovka consists of seventy families and that in Tambovka of forty families. But they maintain the high standards that characterized Doukhobor farming in the tsarist days. They still win prizes for their horse-breeding and for dairying, while cheese-making has remained the most important secondary industry. The days when an iron plough denoted peasant prosperity are past; the kolkhozes to which the Doukhobors belong use machinery, just as the Doukhobor farmers do on the Canadian prairies. As happens elsewhere in

Russia, the members of the Doukhobor collectives are allowed to cultivate their own gardens and to keep cows, sheep, and poultry on their
own account. Nevertheless, it is doubtful if the average Doukhobor
peasant in Soviet Russia is as well off as the average Doukhobor wheat
farmer in Canada.

In Russia as in Canada the process of assimilation has been proceeding
rapidly. Given the growing complexity of modern society, this was perhaps inevitable under any circumstances, though it has undoubtedly been
encouraged even more deliberately by the Soviet than by the Canadian
authorities. The process has been hastened by the dispersal of the Doukhobors through deportation and war, and, as in Canada, by the
imposition of universal education. It is a process that has not gone without resistance, even in recent years. Some Russian Doukhobors have
shown opposition or at least indifference to education, using arguments
very similar to those of their Canadian brethren—that what is needed is
practical training in farming techniques, and that if all men were scientists
no one would be left to till the soil.

Such people are obviously in a minority, comprised mostly of the
older generation. Education, in fact, emphasizes the generation gap, as it
does in Canada. Many younger Doukhobors leave the kolkhozes for the
factories or for white-collar occupations in the cities. Others have received university education and have become doctors, engineers, teachers,
veterinarians, agronomists, journalists, and government officials. They
form a growing Doukhobor intelligentsia that is inevitably attracted away
from the traditional Doukhobor heritage; its members absorb the values of
the wider Soviet society, and their occupations often take them to distant
regions where they mingle with strangers and frequently marry non-
Doukhobors. Many of this younger and more educated generation are
now Communists and even hold positions in the Party and in the civil service, which means that they cannot openly profess the faith of their
fathers.

It is in fact among the elderly that the vestiges of Doukhobor religion
are most alive. It is no longer the all-embracing religion whose organization dominated the community. The Doukhobor leaders are fading
memories; the councils of elders have long been dispersed; and the Orphan's Home no longer stands as a symbolic centre. Unlike the Russian
Orthodox Church and sects like the Baptists, the Doukhobors do not even
have meeting-halls; according to Anna Markova, this is because their one
consistent form of non-co-operation was a refusal to register themselves
as a religious sect. Meetings for prayer and singing are held in private

homes, and religious instruction, where it exists, is carried on by the parents. Traditional Doukhobor funerals are still occasionally held, and in the Caucasian villages the older people try to preserve their traditional costume and some of their customs. But the young dress like other Russians and, increasingly, think like them.

It is evident that, in different ways, the process of assimilating a peculiar minority has proceeded in Russia just as rapidly as in Canada. Resistance has been less determined, not only because of the harsher nature of the Soviet régime, but also because the Doukhobors who stayed behind in Russia during the 1890s were the less militant members of the sect.

Canadian Doukhobors enjoy many advantages over their Russian brethren. Even if at times unwillingly, they have benefited from living in a more prosperous society, a society that has not been directly touched by war since 1812. Whatever the blunders of Canada's governments and the prejudices of its people, the Doukhobors here have not suffered as bitterly as they would have done if they had practised their various forms of resistance under the implacable rule of a Stalin or even a Khrushchev. In Canada, during two wars, the government has kept honourably to its promise that no Doukhobor would be conscripted. In Russia conscription exists for all; this is evident from reports that have come from there, and also from the categorical statement made to a Doukhobor delegation in 1958 by the Soviet embassy in Ottawa that every young man must serve two years with or without arms. In other words, Doukhobors in Russia have enjoyed under Soviet rule no greater liberties than under the most ruthless of the tsars, while those who came to Canada, despite their many difficulties, have been at least able to sustain their objection to military service and to preserve their religion in its organized form.

Yet among Canadian Doukhobors there remains an abiding nostalgia for Russia. They still talk of some possible future return : one of the aims of the visit paid by John J. Verigin and his party in 1966 was to test how favourable the political climate might be to such a migration. Criticism of Soviet policies among Doukhobors is noticeably mild. While they make forthright denunciations of militarism among the Western powers, the u.s.s.r. is much more rarely called to order. This is not because Doukhobors are crypto-Communists. Only a tiny minority are or ever have been. It is rather because they still like to think of themselves as Russian, in culture if not in citizenship. The single advantage enjoyed by the Doukhobors who did not migrate was that they were never isolated among a people who did not speak their own language. Doubtless to them this would seem a slender compensation for all they have endured.

To the Canadian Doukhobors, on the other hand, their language and the sense of identification with their Russian past are—except for their religious observances—almost all that any longer distinguishes them perceptibly from their Canadian neighbours. Those who lose the language and the feeling of identification with Russia become mere Canadians. Those who wish to be Doukhobors remain of necessity Russophiles, and though they may never depart from Canada, the fading vision of the great return will continue to haunt them.

NOTES

PREFACE

[1] *Vancouver Daily Province*, 28 May 1945.
[2] Alexander Herzen, *My Past and Thoughts*, Vol. VI, London, 1927, p. 224.
[3] See Bibliography, p. 373.

CHAPTER I

[1] Aurelio Palmieri, 'The Russian Doukhobors and their Religious Teachings', *Harvard Theological Review* (Cambridge, Mass.), Vol. 8, January 1915, p. 62.
[2] Harry B. Hawthorn, ed., *The Doukhobors of British Columbia*, p. 168.
[3] V. D. Bonch-Bruevich, *Materialy k istorii i izucheniiu russkago sektanstva i raskola*, Vol. 2.
[4] O. M. Novitskii, *Dukhobortsy* (2nd ed., Kiev, 1882).
[5] V. A. Sukhorev, *Istoriia dukhobortsev*, p. 10.
[6] Sergei Stepniak (S. M. Kravchinskii), *The Russian Peasantry* (London, 1890), Vol. 2, p. 554.
[7] Aylmer Maude, *A Peculiar People*, p. 99.
[8] Eli Popoff, *Historical Exposition on Doukhobor Beliefs*, p. 30.
[9] Ibid., pp. 34–5.
[10] *Russkii Arkhiv* (Moscow), Vol. XLV, 1914, p. 73.
[11] Sukhorev, op. cit., p. 10.
[12] Novitskii, *Dukhobortsy*, pp. 51–3.
[13] Ibid., p. 54.
[14] Personal notes, GW.

CHAPTER 2
[1] *Zhurnaly Komiteta Ministrov*, Vol. 2 (St Petersburg, 1891), p. 409.
[2] Maude, op. cit., p. 18.
[3] V. G. Chertkov, *Christian Martyrdom in Russia*, pp. 9 ff.
[4] Popoff, op. cit., p. 12.
[5] V. D. Bonch-Bruevich, *Izbrannye sochineniia*, Vol. 1 (Moscow, 1959), p. 291.
[6] Maude, op. cit., p. 135.
[7] Ibid.
[8] Ibid., p. 134.
[9] Society of Friends Library Mss, Robert Pinkerton to Richard Phillips, St Petersburg, 13 October 1815.
[10] Maude, op. cit., p. 141.
[11] Ibid., p. 142.
[12] Ibid., p. 143.
[13] Ibid., p. 137.
[14] Ibid.
[15] Ibid., p. 138.
[16] Novitskii, op. cit., pp. 143–4.
[17] Baron A. von Haxthausen, *The Russian Empire*, Vol. 1, p. 293.
[18] Haxthausen, *Études sur la situation, la vie nationale et les institutions rurales de la Russie*, Vol. 1, Hanover, 1847, p. 376.
[19] Maude, op. cit., p. 149.
[20] Haxthausen, *Études sur la situation . . .*, pp. 377–8 (Tr. GW).
[21] Maude, op. cit., p. 149.
[22] Koozma Tarasoff, *In Search of Brotherhood*, p. 86.
[23] N. M. Nikol'skii, *Istoriia russkoi tserkvy*, p. 269.

CHAPTER 3
[1] P. N. Maloff, *Dukhobortsy, ikh istoriia, zhizn i bor'ba*, p. 25.
[2] Sukhorev, op. cit., p. 59.
[3] Maude, op. cit., pp. 23–4.
[4] Peter Brock, 'Vasya Pozdnyakov's Dukhobor Narrative', *Slavonic and East European Review*, Vol. XLIII, Nos 100 and 101, p. 161.
[5] Ibid., p. 162.
[6] Personal notes, GW.
[7] Nikol'skii, op. cit., p. 317.
[8] Brock, op. cit., p. 161.
[9] Maude, op. cit., p. 152.
[10] Ibid., pp. 153–4.
[11] Brock, op. cit., p. 163.
[12] Ibid., p. 164.
[13] Maude, op. cit., p. 155.
[14] Ibid., p. 153.
[15] Sukhorev, op. cit., p. 61.

CHAPTER 4
[1] Popoff, op. cit., p. 40 (adapted by GW).
[2] Maude, op. cit., p. 173.
[3] Brock, op. cit., p. 168.
[4] Maude, op. cit., p. 164.
[5] J. F. C. Wright, *Slava Bohu*, p. 75.

6 Maude, op. cit., pp. 162–3.
7 Ibid., p. 163.
8 Brock, op. cit., pp. 168–9.
9 Ibid., p. 170.
10 *The Friend*, 1 May 1896, p. 277.
11 Maude, op. cit., p. 34.

CHAPTER 5
1 *The Friend*, 1 May 1896, pp. 277 ff.
2 Leo Tolstoy, *Polnoe sobranie sochinenii*, Vol. 69 (1954), pp. 190–1.
3 Chertkov, op. cit., p. 1.
4 Ibid., p. 5.
5 Ibid., p. 61.
6 Ibid., p. 63.
7 Ibid.
8 *Materialy k istorii i izucheniiu russkago sektanstva*, Vol. 1 (1901), pp. 89–90.
9 *The Friend*, 6 May 1898, p. 277.
10 Ibid., 15 July 1898, p. 456.
11 Tolstoy, op. cit., Vol. 71 (1954), p. 326.
12 Ibid., p. 488.
13 Ibid., pp. 478–9.
14 Colonial Office records 67/112, Edmund W. Brookes to Chief Secretary to the Government of Cyprus, n.d.
15 Ibid., Arthur St John to Chief Secretary, Government of Cyprus, 1 June 1898.
16 Ibid., V. G. Chertkov to Arthur St John, 17 May 1898.
17 Foreign Office records, 65/1564, British Consul in Batum to the Foreign Office in London, 27 May 1898.
18 C.O. 67/112, High Commissioner of Cyprus to Joseph Chamberlain, Colonial Secretary, 5 June 1898.
19 *News of the Doukhobortsi*, No. 2, July 1898, pp. 1–2.
20 Society of Friends Mss, John Bellows to Joseph Chamberlain, 15 July 1898.
21 C.O. 67/112, John Bellows to Joseph Chamberlain, 18 July 1898.
22 Ibid., High Commissioner of Cyprus to Colonial Office, London, 20 July 1898.
23 Society of Friends Mss, H. Bartram Cox, Under-Secretary, Colonial Office, London, to John Bellows, 29 July 1898.
24 Ibid.
25 F.O. 65/1564, British Consul at Batum to Foreign Office in London, 19 August 1898.
26 *News of the Dukhobortsi*, No. 6, 20 September 1898, p. 4.
27 John Bellows, *Letters and Memoir* (London, 1904), pp. 325–6.
28 *News of the Dukhobortsi*, No. 7, November 1898, p. 7.
29 C.O. 67/116, John Bellows to an unnamed Colonial Office official, 28 December 1898.
30 Alexander M. Evalenko, *The Message of the Doukhobors* (New York, 1913), pp. 128–9.

CHAPTER 6
1 Tolstoy, op. cit., Vol. 71, p. 415.
2 Maude, op cit., p. 47.
3 Ibid.
4 *News of the Dukhobortsi*, No. 7, November 1898, p. 2.
5 Maude, op. cit., p. 61.

[6] Ibid., p. 62.

[7] Ibid., p. 49.

[8] Tolstoy, op. cit., Vol. 72, pp. 63–4.

[9] Maude, op. cit., pp. 48–9.

[10] Ibid., p. 50.

[11] F.O. 65/1564, telegram from British Consul in Batum to Foreign Office, London, 2 October 1898.

[12] Ibid., telegram from Foreign Office to British Consul in Batum, 3 October 1898.

[13] Society of Friends Mss, Minutes of Meeting of Doukhobor Committee, 5 December 1901.

[14] Brock, op. cit., p. 173.

[15] Ibid.

[16] Chertkov, op. cit., p. 76.

[17] Sukhorev, op. cit., p. 111.

[18] Brock, op. cit., pp. 175–6.

[19] Ibid., p. 175.

[20] Ibid., p. 176.

CHAPTER 7

[1] James Mavor, *My Window on the Street of the World*, Vol. 2, p. 7.

[2] Maude, op. cit., p. 184.

[3] V. D. Bonch-Bruevich, *Dukhobortsy v kanadskikh preriiakh*, p. 136.

[4] Maude, op. cit., p. 185.

[5] Bonch-Bruevich, *Dukhobortsy v kanadskikh preriiakh*, p. 190.

[6] Maude, op cit., pp. 196–7.

[7] *Regina Leader*, 21 June 1900, p. 4.

[8] Society of Friends Mss, W. F. McCreary, Commissioner of Immigration, to James A. Smart, Deputy Minister of the Interior, 4 November 1899.

[9] Ibid., W. F. McCreary, Commissioner of Immigration, to John Bellows, 14 November 1899.

[10] Maude, op. cit., p. 63.

[11] Joseph Elkinton, *The Doukhobors, their history in Russia, their migration to Canada*, p. 211.

[12] Maude, op cit., pp. 270–7.

[13] *Svobodnaia Mysl*, No. 15, September 1900. Cited in Tarasoff, op. cit.

[14] Maude, op. cit., p. 232.

[15] Ibid., p. 205.

[16] Tarasoff, op. cit., p. 262.

[17] *Svobodnoe Slovo*, No. 1, December 1901.

[18] Society of Friends Mss, Minutes of Doukhobor Committee, 1 November 1900.

[19] Tolstoy, *Polnoe sobranie sochinenii*, Vol. 72, p. 194: A. N. Konshin to Leo Tolstoy, 7 November 1899.

[20] Ibid., p. 209: V. M. Velichkina to Leo Tolstoy, 9 September 1899.

[21] Maude, op. cit., p. 240.

[22] Ibid., pp. 226–7.

[23] Ibid., p. 225.

[24] Society of Friends Mss, Helen Morland, Devil's Lake, N.T.W., to Mr Meynell, 26 October 1902.

[25] Maude, op. cit., p. 234.

[26] *Manitoba Free Press* (Winnipeg), 31 October 1902.

[27] Maude, op. cit., p. 240.

CHAPTER 8

[1] P. Biriukov, *Biografiia L'va Nikolaevicha Tolstogo*, Vol. 4, Moscow, 1923, p. 72.

[2] Alexandra Tolstoy, *Tolstoy: A Life of My Father*, New York, 1953, p. 427.

[3] *Manitoba Free Press*, 23 December 1902.

[4] Maude, op. cit., pp. 258–60; Tarasoff, op. cit., pp. 293–6.

[5] Society of Friends Mss, Commissioner of Immigration, Winnipeg, to John Ash-worth, 15 November 1905.

[6] *The Friend*, 8 September 1905, pp. 586–7.

[7] Maude, op. cit., p. 241.

[8] Simma Holt, *Terror in the Name of God*, p. 43.

[9] Maude, op. cit., p. 225.

[10] Ibid., pp. 243–4.

[11] Public Archives of Canada. Report of the Doukhobor Commissioner, John McDougall, to the Minister of the Interior, 26 November 1906.

[12] Maude, op. cit., pp. 256–7.

[13] *The Friend*, 23 March 1906, p. 183.

[14] Tarasoff, op. cit., pp. 308–12; J. F. C. Wright, *Slava Bohu*, p. 228.

[15] *Manitoba Free Press*, 5 March 1906.

[16] Sukhorev, op. cit., p. 131.

[17] *Daily News*, 21 August 1905.

CHAPTER 9

[1] Wright, op. cit., p. 204.

[2] *Manitoba Free Press*, 28 January 1903.

[3] Tarasoff, op. cit., p. 311.

[4] *The Friend*, 31 August 1900, p. 571.

[5] Ibid., 14 November 1902, p. 747.

[6] Ibid., 8 September 1905, pp. 586–7.

[7] Maude, op. cit., pp. 315–16.

[8] Ibid., pp. 314–15.

[9] *Yorkton Enterprise*, 11 April 1906.

[10] Report of the Doukhobor Commissioner, John McDougall, to the Minister of the Interior, 26 November 1906.

[11] Tarasoff, op cit., pp. 349–51.

CHAPTER 10

[1] William Blakemore, *Report of the Royal Commission on matters relating to the Sect of Doukhobors in the Province of British Columbia, 1912*, p. 29.

[2] Ibid., p. 31.

[3] Compiled from figures presented by V. A. Sukhorev to Sullivan Commission, 1947, and cited by Tarasoff, op. cit.

[4] Blakemore, op. cit., p. 35.

[5] Ibid., p. 31.

[6] Ibid., p. 40.

[7] Tarasoff, op. cit., p. 381.

[8] Typewritten statement of the Christian Community of Universal Brotherhood, 8 September 1917. Sukhorev archives.

[9] Personal notes, GW.

[10] Sukhorev, op. cit., p. 137.

[11] Statement of the Christian Community of Universal Brotherhood, 8 September 1917. Sukhorev archives.

[12] Personal notes, GW.

[13] Hawthorn, op. cit., pp. 233–9.

[14] Personal notes, GW.

[15] Blakemore, op. cit., p. 55.

[16] Maloff, op. cit., p. 143.

[17] *Regina Post*, 12 October 1917.

[18] Personal notes, GW.

[19] Blakemore, op. cit., p. 61.

[20] Ibid.

[21] Ibid., p. 64.

[22] Ibid., p. 52.

[23] Society of Friends Mss, Mitford Abraham to Isaak Sharp, 29 October 1913.

[24] *Grand Forks Gazette*, 14 March 1914. Letter signed by K. Reibin, T. Salikin, and S. Vereshchagin.

[25] Tarasoff, op. cit., pp. 266–7.

[26] *Nelson Daily News*, 19 May 1917.

[27] Ibid., 17 November 1919.

[28] *Grand Forks Gazette*, 18 July 1919.

[29] *Manitoba Free Press*, 1919 (undated cutting in Sukhorev archives).

[30] *Vancouver Daily Province*, 2 March 1925.

[31] Holt, op. cit., p. 55; Tarasoff, op. cit., p. 519.

[32] Popoff, op. cit., p. 48.

CHAPTER 11

[1] Maude, op. cit., pp. 220–1.

[2] See Bibliography, p. 372.

[3] Tarasoff, op. cit., p. 453.

[4] S. F. Reibin, *Trud i mirnaia zhizn. Istoriia dukhobortsev bez maski*, pp. 114–15.

[5] Bonch-Bruevich, *Iz mira sektantov*, pp. 43–56.

[6] A. I. Klibanov, *Istoriia religioznogo sektantstva v Rossii 60-e gody XIX v.—1917 g.*, pp. 115–21.

[7] F. M. Putintsev, *Politicheskaia rol i taktika sekt*, Moscow, 1935, p. 405.

[8] Sukhorev, op. cit., p. 244.

[9] Putintsev, *Dukhobor'e*, p. 19.

[10] Ibid., p. 29.

[11] Maloff, op. cit., p. 140.

[12] Wright, op. cit., p. 289.

[13] Bonch-Bruevich, *Izbrannye sochineniia*, Vol. 1, p. 257. Letter dated 16 November 1927 to V. I. Treglazov.

CHAPTER 12

[1] Sukhorev, op. cit., p. 177.

[2] *Vancouver Daily Province*, 28 March 1925.

[3] Tarasoff, op. cit., p. 555, citing information obtained from V. A. Sukhorev.

[4] Sukhorev, op. cit., p. 160.

[5] Tarasoff, op. cit., pp. 562–3, citing information obtained from V. A. Sukhorev.

[6] Sukhorev, op. cit., p. 178.

[7] Tarasoff, see note 5.

[8] F. M. Putintsev, *Politicheskaia rol i taktika sekt*, p. 405.

[9] Tarasoff, op. cit., p. 572.

[10] Sukhorev, op. cit., p. 177; Tarasoff, op. cit., p. 555.
[11] Popoff, op. cit., pp. 51–2.
[12] Hawthorn, op. cit., p. 54.
[13] Compiled from figures given by Tarasoff, op. cit., p. 555.
[14] Hawthorn, op. cit., p. 54.
[15] Ibid., p. 53.
[16] Ibid., p. 57.

CHAPTER 13
[1] Hawthorn, op. cit., p. 10.
[2] *Vancouver Daily Province*, 25 February 1943.
[3] Ibid., 3 May 1928.
[4] Hawthorn, op. cit., pp. 261–3.
[5] *Nelson Daily News*, 11 February 1929.
[6] Maude, *Life of Tolstoy*, Vol. 2 (Toronto, 1953), pp. 389–90.
[7] Tarasoff, op. cit., p. 605.
[8] *Vancouver Daily Province*, 15 December 1943.
[9] Personal notes, GW.
[10] *Vancouver Daily Province*, 17 October 1947.

CHAPTER 14
[1] Personal notes, GW.
[2] *Vancouver Daily Province*, 19 December 1949.
[3] Hawthorn, op. cit., p. 3.
[4] Ibid., p. 246.
[5] Ibid., p. 251.
[6] *Vancouver Sun*, 30 January 1947.
[7] J. P. Stoochnoff, *Doukhobors as they are*, p. 12.
[8] Ibid.
[9] Personal notes, GW.

A NOTE
ON TRANSLITERATION
AND DATES

In the spelling of Russian names and geographic terms, we have adhered, by and large, to the transliteration system of the Library of Congress and of the United States Board on Geographic Names. Exceptions have been made when other spellings have become more or less conventional (e.g. Leo Tolstoy) and in cases where the persons involved spent most or all of their lives in Canada and themselves used a different spelling in the Latin script (e.g. Popoff or even Papove instead of Popov). We have followed the general Anglo-Saxon custom of using the form 'Doukhobors' instead of the literal Russian transliteration of 'Dukhobortsy' or 'Dukhobory'; this custom appears to have originated with Aylmer Maude, who found the form more convenient in dealing with the Canadian authorities when he negotiated the immigration of the sect into Canada in 1898.

For dates in Russia up to 1917 we have used the Old Style or Julian Calendar.

BIBLIOGRAPHY

Archival Material

Material on the Doukhobors in Russia and their stay in Cyprus is available in the Tolstoy Museum, particularly in the P. Biriukov files.

Official British correspondence relating to the emigration of Doukhobors from Russia, their arrival in Cyprus, and their later departure to Canada is found in the Colonial Office and Foreign Office records at the Public Record Office, London.

The Library of the Society of Friends in London has a useful collection of letters, diaries, minutes, etc. dealing with the relief work organized by the Quakers among the Doukhobors at the end of the last century.

The University of British Columbia Library has a great deal of material on the Doukhobors in British Columbia, including newspaper clippings and handwritten extracts from British Columbia newspapers going back to the first years of Doukhobor settlement in the province. The Provincial Archives in Victoria has a large collection of similar material and of photographs relating to Doukhobor life in British Columbia and the Prairies, most of the latter assembled by Koozma Tarasoff.

We have also been able to make use of a considerable collection of newspaper material and some typewritten and handwritten documents relating to the Christian Community of Universal Brotherhood in the possession of V. A. Sukhorev, and of the collection of notes and transcripts of interviews relating to the Doukhobors assembled by George Woodcock during his visits to them from 1949 onwards.

Printed Sources
Most of the printed material on the Doukhobors in the eighteenth and early nineteenth centuries is widely scattered in monographs by Russian scholars devoted to sectarians in general. One of the richest sources (and also the most sensational) is F. V. Livanov's discursive *Raskol'niki i Ostrozhniki* (St Petersburg, 1872). Additional material may be found in Russian periodicals in the second half of the nineteenth century, some of whose editors were also teachers in theological seminaries of the Russian Orthodox Church.

The first scholarly study of the Doukhobors is Orest Novitskii's *Dukhobortsy* (Kiev, 1st ed., 1832; 2nd ed., 1882). Like Livanov's work, Novitskii's is based on archival sources. It has been used by a number of scholars, including Baron A. von Haxthausen, who, in his *The Russian Empire: its people, institutions and resources* (London, 1856), devotes a considerable passage to his visit to the Doukhobor settlements at Milky Waters. Earlier Western visitors, predating Novitskii, who made observations of the Doukhobors at Milky Waters, were the agent of the Bible Society, Robert Pinkerton, who notes his impressions in letters preserved by the Society of Friends and also in *Russia: or miscellaneous observations on the past and present state of that country* (London, 1833), and the Quakers William Allen and Stephen Grellet, whose diaries of the time were later incorporated in memoirs (*Life of William Allen*, London 1846–7, and *Memoirs of the Life and Gospel Labours of Stephen Grellet*, Philadelphia, 1864).

The years of persecution and emigration at the end of the nineteenth century are, of course, the best-documented period of Doukhobor history in Russia. Tolstoy's interest in and interventions on behalf of the Doukhobors can best be followed in J. Bienstock, *Tolstoi et les Doukhobors: faits historiques réunis et traduits du russe* (Paris, 1902), and in his correspondence for the years 1896–1903 published in volumes 69–74 of his *Polnoe sobranie sochinenii* (Moscow, 1933, 1954).

Tolstoy's followers kept Russian and foreign public opinion informed about the Doukhobors in Russia, Cyprus, and Canada through V. G. Chertkov's pamphlet (*Christian Martyrdom in Russia*, London, 1897; 2nd ed., 1900) and periodical publications, *Svobodnoe Slovo* (Purleigh, Essex, and Christchurch, Hants) and the shortlived *News of the Doukhobortsi*

(Purleigh), and P. Biriukov's *Svobodnaia Mysl* (Geneva). Chertkov and Biriukov worked in close co-operation with the English Quakers whose organ *The Friend* (London) is an important source for the same period.

Another friend of Tolstoy, L. A. Sulerzhitskii, wrote an account of the Doukhobors' journey to Canada and their early settlement there in *V Ameriku s Dukhoborami* (Moscow, 1905), while A. M. Bodianskii dealt with them in *Dukhobortsy* (Kharkov, 1908) and P. I. Biriukov in *Dukhobortsy* (Moscow, 1908). A. K. Borozdin's *Ocherki russkago religioz-nago raznomysliia* (St Petersburg, 1905) has some useful data on the struggle between the Large Party and the authorities in the Caucasus. V. G. Bogoraz-Tan's shorter *Dukhobory v Kanade* (Moscow, rev. ed. 1906) is the work of a well-known Russian anthropologist and traveller.

Tolstoy's aide V. G. Chertkov was closely associated for a time with the Russian Marxist V. D. Bonch-Bruevich, who over a period of several decades wrote a great deal about the Doukhobors. Bonch-Bruevich's first major work on the subject was a list of Doukhobor psalms, letters, etc. (*Spisok psalmov, pisem, razskazov i drugikh rukopisei po izsledovaniiu ucheniia zhizni i pereselniia v Kanadu zakavkazskikh dukhobortsev*, Geneva, 1900), some of which Eli Popoff published in an English translation in his *Historical Exposition on Doukhobor Beliefs* (Grand Forks, B.C., 1966).

Equally important is the four-volume collection of documents dealing with the persecution of Doukhobors in Russia that V. D. Bonch-Bruevich edited under the general title *Materialy k istorii i izucheniiu russkago sektanstva* (Christchurch, 1901–2). This includes the famous letters of Peter Verigin that caused so much excitement among the Doukhobors in Canada in 1902, and also Vasilii Pozdniakov's first narrative of the persecutions in Russia, *Razskaz dukhobortsa Vasi Pozdniakova*; a completely separate narrative, existing only in an English translation, was edited and published by Professor Peter Brock as 'Vasya Pozdnyakov's Dukhobor Narrative' in *The Slavonic and East European Review* (London), Vol. XLIII, Nos 100 and 101, December 1964 and June 1965.

On his return to Russia after the 1905 Revolution, Bonch-Bruevich broadened his studies to include, as well as Doukhoborism, other aspects of sectarianism in *Materialy k istorii i izucheniiu russkogo sektanstva i raskola* (St Petersburg, 1908–16). The Living Book is published in the second volume of this collection. His *Dukhobortsy v kanadskikh preriiakh* (Petrograd, 1918) deals with the first years of Doukhobor settlement in the Prairies, while his account of a visit to the Doukhobors in the Caucasus was republished in *Iz mira sektantov. Sbornik statei* (Moscow, 1922).

Material on the Doukhobors may also be found in the three-volume *Izbrannye sochineniia* (Moscow, 1959–61).

Interest in the sectarians in general and the Doukhobors in particular declined after the Bolshevik seizure of power. Apart from M. V. Muratov's short account of small Doukhobor communities in Eastern Siberia in the first half of the nineteenth century (*Dukhobortsy v vostochnoi Sibiri v pervoi polovine XIX veka*, Irkutsk, 1923), little of great value appeared for several decades. During that period the Doukhobors were mentioned in passing in N. M. Nikol'skii's *Istoriia russkoi tserkvy* (Moscow, 2nd ed., 1931), in atheistic publications like *Bezbozhnik* in the 1920s and 1930s and *Voprosy istorii religii i ateizma* in the 1950s and 1960s, and were criticized in some detail in F. M. Putintsev, *Dukhobor'e. Ocherk iz sovremennoi zhizni sektantov dukhoborov* (Moscow, 1928). The chapter on the Doukhobors in A. I. Klibanov's *Istoriia religioznogo sektanstva v Rossii 60-e gody XIX v.—1917 g.* (Moscow, 1965) is a good example of a somewhat more sophisticated approach to modern Russian history that one associates with post-Stalinist scholarship. The author uses a fairly wide range of sources, including the works by Doukhobor historians published in Canada.

Among these one of the most important is *Istoriia dukhobortsev* (Winnipeg, 1944) by V. A. Sukhorev, who concentrates on the Community Doukhobors under Peter the Lordly and Peter the Purger. P. N. Maloff's *Dukhobortsy, ikh istoriia, zhizn i bor'ba* (Winnipeg, 1948) is longer, more diffuse, and brings the story of the Doukhobors up to the mid-1920s. More controversial are the memoirs of S. F. Reibin, *Trud i mirnaia zhizn. Istoriia dukhobortsev bez maski* (San Francisco, 1952). He was close to Peter the Lordly for two decades and does not restrain himself in presenting his version of the antics of some Doukhobor leaders.

Like the works of Sukhorev and Maloff, Koozma Tarasoff's three-volume mineographed work, *In Search of Brotherhood* (Vancouver, 1963), is a sympathetic though not wholly uncritical account of the Doukhobors. The sections dealing with the Doukhobors in Canada are well documented. They are based on data largely culled from the National and Provincial Archives, on manuscripts in Tarasoff's possession, and on interviews with Doukhobors of many views. An extensive descriptive bibliography is included. Tarasoff edited the *Doukhobor Inquirer* (Saskatoon) in the 1950s and has been connected with his co-religionists who publish *Iskra* (Grand Forks, B.C.), a useful source of material on the Doukhobors who remain faithful to the memory of the three Peter Verigins. John Philip Stoochnoff's *Doukhobors As They Are* (Toronto, 1961) is mainly a compilation, but it contains many important documents relating to Doukhobor history from the 1890s to the death of Peter Iastrebov.

The ephemeral literature of the Sons of Freedom, mainly mimeographed and very copious, is polemical in character and largely devoted to denouncing the corruption of the world around them and to refuting some of the charges made against them by fellow Doukhobors as well as by non-Doukhobor Canadians.

Among non-Doukhobor students of the Spirit Wrestlers a wide range of attitudes has prevailed. Aylmer Maude's *A Peculiar People: the Doukhobors* (New York, 1904) is the work of a disillusioned sympathizer; Joseph Elkinton's *The Doukhobors, their history in Russia, their migration to Canada* (Philadelphia, 1903) is a sympathetic account by an American Quaker; J. P. Zubek and P. A. Solberg, authors of *Doukhobors at War* (Toronto, 1952), are trained psychologists writing for the general public. Simma Holt's *Terror in the Name of God* (Toronto, 1964) is in the tradition of controversial journalism; it concentrates on the Sons of Freedom minority. *Slava Bohu* by J. F. C. Wright (New York, 1940) was for many years the only reasonably complete account of Doukhobor history up to the collapse of the Christian Community. The genuine scholarship with which Wright collected his material was obscured by a popularized presentation, but his work helped to shape the attitudes of whole generations of those Canadians who have tried to view the Doukhobor problem constructively. James Mavor's *My Window on the Street of the World* (London and Toronto, 1932) gives valuable insights into the migration of the Doukhobors to Canada and their early years on the prairies. *A Doukhobor Bibliography*, edited by M. Horvath (Vancouver, 1968), gives a useful annotated account of material available in the University of British Columbia Library.

There have been many articles of very uneven quality in scholarly and other periodicals, but we will content ourselves with citing one good one, of a very specialized nature. This is 'The Music of the Doukhobors' by Kenneth Peacock, published in the December 1965 number of *Alphabet* London, Ont.). By the time this volume appears Dr Peacock's book, *Songs of the Doukhobors*, of which we have been privileged to see the typscript, will have been published by the National Museum of Canada.

The record of the Doukhobors in Canada would be incomplete without reference to the valuable studies sponsored by the Government of British Columbia and the University of British Columbia in an attempt to come to grips with what seemed for several decades an insoluble problem. William Blakemore's *Report of the Royal Commission on matters relating*

to the Sect of Doukhobors in the Province of British Columbia, 1912
(Victoria, 1913) gives an invaluable picture of the Christian Community
at the height of its vigour. An even more elaborate picture, this time of
Doukhobor society in disintegration, is given in the findings of the Doukhobor Research Committee of 1950–2—the Report issued by the University of British Columbia in 1952 and the amended version later published
for the general public (The Doukhobors of British Columbia, Vancouver
and Toronto, 1955); both were edited by the chairman of the committee,
Harry B. Hawthorn.

INDEX